Also in the Variorum Collected Studies Series

ALFREDO MORDECHAI RABELLO
The Jews in the Roman Empire: Legal problems, from Herod to Justinian

H.E.J. COWDREY
Popes and Church Reform in the 11th Century

DENYS PRINGLE
Fortification and Settlement in Crusader Palestine

H.S. OFFLER
Church and Crown in the Fourteenth Century: Studies in European History and Political Thought

MARJORIE CHIBNALL
Piety, Power and History in Medieval England and Normandy

NORMAN HOUSLEY
Crusading and Warfare in Medieval and Renaissance Europe

BERNARD S. BACHRACH
Warfare and Military Organization in Pre-Crusade Europe

GARY DICKSON
Religious Enthusiasm in the Medieval West: Revivals, crusades, saints

THOMAS F. MAYER
Cardinal Pole in European Context: A *Via Media* in the Reformation

MILTON McC. GATCH
Eschatology and Christian Nurture: Themes in Anglo-Saxon and Medieval Religious Life

CHRISTOPHER STEAD
Doctrine and Philosophy in Early Christianity: Arius, Athanasius, Augustine

JOHN GUY
Politics, Law and Counsel in Tudor and Early Stuart England

DAVID ABULAFIA
Mediterranean Encounters, Economic, Religious, Political, 1100–1550

VARIORUM COLLECTED STUDIES SERIES

History, Religion,
and Violence

Clifford Davidson

Clifford Davidson

History, Religion, and Violence

Cultural Contexts for
Medieval and Renaissance
English Drama

Ashgate
VARIORUM

This edition copyright © 2002 by Clifford Davidson.

Published in the Variorum Collected Studies Series by

Ashgate Publishing Limited
Gower House, Croft Road,
Aldershot, Hampshire GU11 3HR
Great Britain

Ashgate Publishing Company
131 Main Street,
Burlington, Vermont 05401–5600
USA

Ashgate website: http://www.ashgate.com

ISBN 0–86078–882–2

British Library Cataloguing-in-Publication Data
Davidson, Clifford
   History, Religion, and Violence : Cultural Contexts for Medieval and Renaissance English Drama. – (Variorum Collected Studies Series)
   1. English Drama – To 1500 – History and Criticism 2. English Drama – Early Modern and Elizabethan, 1500–1600 – History and Criticism 3. Religion and Drama 4. Violence in Literature
   I. Title
   822.1

US Library of Congress Cataloging-in-Publication Data
Davidson, Clifford.
  History, Religion, and Violence: Cultural Contexts for Medieval and Renaissance English Drama/Clifford Davidson.
     p. cm – (Variorum Collected Studies Series: CS744)
  Includes Bibliographical References and Index.
  ISBN 0-86078-882-2 (alk. paper)
     1. English Drama–to 1500–History and Criticism. 2. English Drama–Early Modern and Elizabethan, 1500–1600–History and Criticism. 3. Religion and Literature–England History–16th Century. 4. Religion and Literature–England–History–To 1500. 5. Literature and History– England–History–16th Century. 6. Literature and History–England–History–To 1500. 7. Violence in Literature. 8. Renaissance–England. I. Title.
  II. Collected Studies: CS744

PR641.D38 2002
822'.209382–dc21   2002018201

The paper used in this publication meets the minimum requirements of the
   American National Standard for Information Sciences – Permanence of
   Paper for Printed Library Materials, ANSI Z39.48–1984. ∞ ™

Printed by St Edmundsbury Press Limited, Bury St Edmunds, Suffolk

VARIORUM COLLECTED STUDIES SERIES CS744

Contents

Illustrations	vi
Preface	vii
Acknowledgments	x
Part I: Religion and Historical Crosscurrents in Renaissance Drama	
Marlowe, the Papacy, and *Doctor Faustus*	3
The History of King Lear and the Problem of Belief	24
The Anxiety of Power and Shakespeare's *Macbeth*	42
Antony and Cleopatra: Circe, Venus, and the Whore of Babylon	64
Part II: Sacred Violence and the Mysteries	
Cain in the Mysteries: The Iconography of Violence	97
The Sacrifice of Isaac in Medieval English Drama	124
Nudity, the Body, and Early English Drama	149
Sacred Blood and the Late Medieval Stage	180
Part III: Cultural Contexts for Early Drama	
Carnival, Lent, and Early English Drama	207
The Medieval Stage and the Antitheatrical Prejudice	226
Idol and Image in Late Medieval Art and Drama	240
Saints in Play: English Theater and Saints' Lives	251
Signs of Doomsday in Drama and Art	267
Index	293

Illustrations

1. The New Religion vs. the Old; Apocalypse scene. Title page, John Foxe, *Actes and Monuments* (1576). 5
2. Pope Alexander stepping on the neck of Emperor Frederick. John Foxe, *Actes and Monuments* (1576). 19
3. The Change in Religion: desecrating churches. John Foxe, *Actes and Monuments* (1576). 30
4. Fortune shakes down rewards for those who grasp for them. Cesare Ripa, *Iconologia* (1669). 46
5. An exposed tree is more susceptible to wind. Henry Peacham, *Minerva Britanna* (1612). 48
6. *Sic transit gloria mundi*. George Wither, *A Collection of Emblemes* (1635). 60
7. The transi tomb of Archbishop Henry Chichele (d. 1424). 61
8. Forza d'Amore. Cesare Ripa, *Iconologia* (1669). 69
9. Star falling as illustration of Revelation 8:10. Bishops' Bible (1569). 75
10. Face as the sun and feet as pillars of fire; illustration of Revelation 10. Bishops' Bible (1569). 93
11. Scenes from the story of Cain and Abel. Bohun Psalter. Bodleian Library MS. Auc. D.4.4. 107
12. Sacrifice of Isaac. Misericord, Worcester Cathedral. 143
13. The Creation of Adam and Eve and the warning against the Tree of Life, followed by the Fall. Wall painting, Easby, Yorkshire. 153
14. Adoration of the Shepherds. Painted glass, East Harling, Norfolk. 160
15. Crucifixion. Michael de Massa, *On the Passion of Our Lord*, Bodleian Library MS. 758. 183
16. Beheading of St. Catherine. Alabaster, Victoria and Albert Museum. 253
17. Fifteen Signs of Doomsday. Painted glass, All Saints, North Street, York. 274

Preface

The present collection of articles has as its focus the drama of the late Middle Ages and Renaissance but should be of interest to a broader range of scholars and students in history, iconography, and cultural studies. I have not attempted to be "trendy," but rather to the best of my ability to be faithful to the standards of scholarship that were promoted by my teachers many years ago. Nevertheless, I am grateful to those who, however much I disagree with them on individual points and concerning their methodology, have raised issues which have stimulated my thinking. This has very often led me back again and again to the original sources, to the images and texts and actions that were present on the early stage—and that had manifold connections with the world existing outside the theater.

Perhaps arbitrarily, I have placed the four articles on the Renaissance in Part I ("Religion and Historical Crosscurrents in Renaissance Drama"), beginning with "Marlowe, the Papacy, and *Doctor Faustus*," which has not been previously published. This essay returns to the subject matter of my article on the topic of "Faustus at Rome," published in *Studies in English Literature* as long ago as 1969 but serving more or less as a footnote to my first published scholarly article of seven years earlier. I have benefited from going back to the original editions of John Foxe and from wider reading in both primary and secondary works on the English Reformation, particularly among the latter those which are currently labeled "revisionist." This reading has also informed the next two articles, "*The History of King Lear* and the Problem of Belief" and "The Anxiety of Power and Shakespeare's *Macbeth*."

The History of King Lear is the title retained by the editors of the *Oxford Shakespeare* for the version of the play that was first published. The text of this early quarto differs from the usual edited version that appears in textbooks but is well worth studying in its own right for its perspective on English history and the violent period following the reign of the legendary King Lear. Shakespeare's own background, apparently from a family with strong connections to the "Old Religion," comes into play here as also in *Macbeth*, written after the discovery of the Gunpowder Plot.

In "*Antony and Cleopatra*: Circe, Venus, and the Whore of Babylon" my approach is iconographic—a different methodology but still one which illuminates an important aspect of the intellectual history of the time. This essay, written a quarter of a century ago, has undergone considerable rewriting here, but still retains the principal argument that Shakespeare was very alert to the action depicted in this play as preparatory to the central event of history—that is, the Incarnation.

The remaining essays deal with drama categorized as "medieval" but which actually continued until well into the reign of Queen Elizabeth I. These plays and pageants too are a window on the culture and religion of the time, both in their production and in their suppression under Protestant regimes. Part II ("Sacred Violence and the Mysteries") follows the inception of violence in history as it was understood in the fifteenth and early sixteenth centuries—that is, from the first murder, of Abel by Cain, through the implications of the sacrifice of Isaac and the Crucifixion with its display of holy blood. The latter event also calls to mind English cultural attitudes toward nudity since the Passion demanded the body of Christ to be shown as if without clothing in certain stages of torture. These attitudes also necessarily affected other plays, including the Creation and Fall and Doomsday, which provide documentation concerning the manner in which simulated nudity was displayed.

The interconnections between evil and violence as these were understood historically require more fully to be explored, and there is much that I have not attempted to analyze in these essays. The anti-Semitism inherent in various episodes, including the Crucifixion pageants, will be obvious and has been studied by other scholars, but it is important, for example, to see the executioners of the Crucifixion as not so different from ordinary local workmen who approach their job without questioning the larger implications of what they are doing. The result will be a necessary historical act which must be done if salvation is to be brought to humankind, and the great symbols of this action—the cross, the crucified Christ, the holy blood which was associated with the Eucharist—appeared not only on the early stage but everywhere in pre-Reformation England.

Further connections with English culture are explored in Part III ("Cultural Contexts for Early Drama"). However, "Carnival, Lent, and Early English Drama" explores the *lack* of connections in England between plays and the season of Carnival. The great dramatic cycles were done for a very different time of year, mainly at Corpus Christi and as a way of showing devotion to God, of displaying the city in a favorable way, and of attracting people to fairs held at the same time as the pageants. Civic control of these plays did not allow for inappropriate acting or display of the carnival spirit.

Preface

When the pageants were suppressed, however, they were put down not because they were like carnival games but because they dramatized biblical and religious material in the manner of the "Old Religion." In "The Medieval Stage and the Antitheatrical Prejudice" I attempt to show how arguments which had been present earlier found their way to the fore in post-Reformation England with immense cultural aftermath in cities such as Chester, Coventry, and York where a significant proportion of the disposable local civic wealth had gone toward the plays. The discussion is continued in "Idol and Image in Late Medieval Drama and Art," where the visual deprivation demanded by Protestantism is a focus. An interesting aspect here is the rejection of this harsh stance by Shakespeare and others affected by the nostalgia for the "Old Religion," its monuments in churches, and its ritual. But for many hard-line Protestants there was no distinction between idols and religious images such as statues of saints, and this had wide-ranging consequences for drama, art, religious practices, and culture in general.

In such an atmosphere, the saint play, which had been at one time perhaps the most common form of medieval drama, could not very well flourish, but in its heyday the sufferings and death of saints apparently were highly popular with audiences. The role of these plays is discussed in "Saints in Play: English Theater and Saints' Lives," which calls attention especially to plays about the Virgin Mary of which a segment of the N-Town collection is an example. Finally, "The Signs of Doomsday in Drama and Art" considers the end of history as it was understood prior to the Reformation and in the period immediately thereafter. The Signs of Doomsday as depicted in painted glass in a window in All Saints, North Street, York, provide a view of an arcane interpretation of the Last Days that continued to be described in the Chester plays until those pageants were abandoned. The Signs of Doomsday and Doomsday itself give us perhaps the best entry points for understanding the role of the Last Judgment in shaping English religion both before and after the Reformation.

Acknowledgments

I am grateful to the following for allowing me to reprint the articles included in the present volume: *Christianity and Literature*, for "The History of King Lear and the Problem of Belief" (1996); The University of Szeged Institute of English and American Studies, for "The Anxiety of Power and Shakespeare's *Macbeth*," from *The Iconography of Power*, ed. György Szőnyi (2000); *The Bucknell Review*, for "*Antony and Cleopatra*: Circe, Venus, and the Whore of Babylon" (1981); *Papers on Language and Literature*, for "The Sacrifice of Isaac in Medieval English Drama" (1999); Boydell and Brewer and *Fifteenth-Century Studies*, for "Cain in the Mysteries: The Iconography of Violence" (2000); The University of Illinois Press and the *Journal of English and Germanic Philology*, for "Nudity, the Body, and Early English Drama" (1999); Medieval Institute Publications and the Board of the Medieval Institute, for "Sacred Blood and the Late Medieval Stage," from *Comparative Drama* (1997), and "Idol and Image in Late Medieval Art and Drama," from *The Early Drama, Art, and Music Review* (1995); David Bergeron and *Research Opportunities in Renaissance Drama*, for "Carnival, Lent, and Early English Drama" (1997); *Parergon*, for "The Medieval Stage and the Antitheatrical Prejudice" (1997); Arizona Board of Regents for Arizona State University, for "Saints in Play: English Theater and Saints' Lives," which appeared in *Saints: Studies in Medieval Hagiography*, ed. Sandro Sticca, MRTS vol. 141 (Binghamton, N.Y., 1996), 145–60; *Historical Reflections/Réflexions Historiques*, for "Signs of Doomsday in Drama and Art" (2000).

In general, no attempt has been made to bring these articles up to date by systematically taking into account more recent scholarship, but some changes have been made as noted and citations have been transferred to more recent editions when appropriate. Minor alterations for matters of style and accuracy have been incorporated throughout, and documentation has been revised to follow a consistent form.

I owe a debt to many colleagues who read my work prior to publication, and these include the editors and the anonymous reviewers for the various journals. In particular, however, I wish to thank David Bevington for his kindness in reading and helpfully commenting on "Marlowe, the Papacy, and *Doctor Faustus*." Support was given on a number of occasions by Faculty Research Fellowships and grants from Western

Acknowledgments

Michigan University, and its Medieval Institute provided assistance without which these essays could not have been written or prepared for publication. I am also grateful to librarians and archivists who have assisted in so many ways and whose collections I have used. These include, among others, the Western Michigan University Libraries; the University of Michigan Libraries; the Warburg Institute Library; the British Library; the Bodleian Library, Oxford University; the University of Minnesota Libraries; Michigan State University Libraries; and the National Monuments Record.

Part I

Religion and Historical Crosscurrents in Renaissance Drama

Marlowe, the Papacy, and *Doctor Faustus*

Whether or not one believes Christopher Marlowe's *Doctor Faustus* to have an esoteric meaning that is subversive of Christianity as it was practiced either in England or on the Continent, the play nevertheless retains the Lutheran emphasis on the human *will* that was established in the *Faustbuch* published at Frankfurt am Main by Johann Spies (1587) and retained in the English translation by a man identified only as P. F. Gent. (1592).[1] Spies, publisher of the *Formula of Concord* (1577) and a staunch defender of Lutheran orthodoxy against Calvinism,[2] established a despairing anti-hero who, in his translator's words, ultimately blamed his "stiffe necked and rebellious will, with [his own] filthy infernall thoughts" (*EFB*, 81) for his damnation. This version of the Faust story accepts the world-view of Luther, who saw the demonic as ever-present and energetic, particularly on account of the hostile forces of the papacy that Lutheran iconography visualized as in league with the forces of darkness.[3] At the end of his *Faustbuch* Spies had appended a quotation from 1 Peter 5:8–9 in Luther's Bible; in the Geneva translation of 1560 this passage reads: "Be sober and watch: for your aduersarie the deuil as a roaring lyon walketh about, seking whome he may deuoure: Whome resist stedfast in the faith."

Marlowe might have agreed with Reginald Scot's rationalist belief as expressed in *The Discoverie of Witchcraft* that neither the devil nor a

---

[1] *Historia von D. Johann Fausten* (Frankfurt am Main: Johann Spies, 1587; reprinted 1588); *The Historie of the Damnable Life and Deserved Death of Doctor John Faustus*, trans. P. F., Gent. (London, 1592); subsequent references to specific pages in the translation are identified in my text following the abbreviation *EFB*. I initially argued for the retention of the Lutheran context in my "Doctor Faustus of Wittenberg," *Studies in Philology* 59 (1962): 514–23.

[2] See Gerald Strauss, "How to read a *Volksbuch*: The *Faust Book* of 1587," in *Faust Through the Centuries*, ed. Peter Boerner and Sidney Johnson (Tübingen: Max Niemeyer, 1989), 32–33.

[3] See, for example, R. W. Scribner, *For the Sake of Simple Folk: Popular Propaganda for the German Reformation* (1981; reprint Oxford: Clarendon Press, 1994).

3

human could have power "outside the normal field of human experience,"[4] or he may, like the scholarly John Dee, the charlatan Edward Kelly, and the flamboyant Giordano Bruno, have been fascinated with the occult or with Hermeticism.[5] In the A-text of *Faustus* (1604) which has come to be accepted as closer to what Marlowe and his collaborator wrote than the B-text of 1616, their attitude remains ambiguous with regard to the actual power of the devil and his angels. Nevertheless, the plot which the English Faustbook had offered was both sensational and topical—and hence attractive as the basis for a play to be performed in the London theaters. *Doctor Faustus* was initially staged before audiences that were on the whole accepting of the paranormal and of the idea that radical evil attached itself to the physical embodiment of the devil. The Puritan extremist and antitheatrical zealot William Prynne, writing more than a generation after the initial performances of *Faustus*, seems to have accepted without question the account he said he had heard from more than one source of an instance during a performance of the play at the Belsavage playhouse when "the *visible apparition of the* Devill" joined the players on stage "*to the great amazement both of the Actors and Spectators . . . there being some distracted with that fearefull sight.*"[6] This statement may provide verification of the earliest performances of *Doctor Faustus* in 1589 when the Belsavage Theater was still in use, but more to the point here is the likelihood that these productions of the play may have coincided with the prosecution in that year of alleged witches at Chelmsford, where four women were condemned to hang for having relationships with imps or devils.[7] The case of Joan Cunny is of particular

---

[4] Sydney Anglo, "Reginald Scot's *Discoverie of Witchcraft*: Scepticism and Sadduceeism," in *The Damned Art: Essays in the Literature of Witchcraft* (London: Routledge and Kegan Paul, 1977), 109; see also Reginald Scot, *The Discoverie of Witchcraft*, introd. Hugh Ross Williamson (Carbondale: Southern Illinois University Press, 1965), 19 and *passim*.

[5] See Frances A. Yates, *The Occult Philosophy in the Elizabethan Age* (London: Routledge and Kegan Paul, 1979), and the same author's *Giordano Bruno and the Hermetic Tradition* (Chicago: University of Chicago Press, 1964).

[6] William Prynne, *Histrio-Mastix* (London, 1633), fol. 556ʳ.

[7] *The Apprehension and Confession of Three Notorious Witches, Arreigned and by Iustice Condemned and Executed at Chelmes-forde, in the Countye of Essex, the 5. Day of Iulye, last past* (1589). The execution of one of the women was delayed until she had given birth.

1. The New Religion (left) vs. the Old (right); Apocalypse scene. Title page, John Foxe, *Acts and Monuments* (London, 1576). By permission of the Henry E. Huntington Library, San Marino, California.

interest, since she is said to have gone out into a field,

> and there making a Circle . . . and kneeling on her knees, said the praier . . . and inuocating vpon Sathan: Two Sprites did appeere vnto her within the said Circle, in the similitude and likenes of two black frogges, and there demaunded of her what she would haue, beeing readye to doo for her what she would desire, so that she would promise to giue them her soule for their trauaile, for otherwise: they would doo nothing for her.[8]

This example is intellectually very far removed from the learned Faustus's magic, influenced in its conception by Cornelius Agrippa's *De Occulta Philosophia* (including the spurious fourth book),[9] but to Elizabethan theater patrons the connections would have seemed to be present.

Keith Thomas has suggested that, though the public had not given up its belief in demonic power—for example, that which was feared from the witches who were tried at Chelmsford or from the devils with whom they had commerce—the official Elizabethan Church "had abandoned the ecclesiastical counter-magic which made such a notion tolerable."[10] In Marlowe's drama, the pope's ritual of exorcism with bell, book, and candle is ineffective and ends in the beating of the friars who are conducting it—surely, in this context, a scene also intended to involve comic anti-fraternal satire. But the handling of events here is indicative of radical weakness in personal and collective defenses against the devil and his agents. It is certain that people were made to feel particularly vulnerable to the forces of evil. The Visitation Articles disseminated in 1559 shortly after Queen Elizabeth I came to the throne had forbidden "charmes, sorcerie, enchauntmentes, inuocations, circles, witchcraftes, soothsaying, or any lyke craftes or imaginations inuented by the deuyll"[11]—prohibitions that clearly would have included not only the

---

[8] Ibid., sig. A3.

[9] Gareth Roberts, "Necromantic Books: Christopher Marlowe, *Doctor Faustus* and Agrippa of Nettesheim," in *Christopher Marlowe and English Renaissance Culture*, ed. Darryll Grantley and Peter Roberts (Aldershot: Scolar Press, 1996),148–71.

[10] Keith Thomas, *Religion and the Decline of Magic* (New York: Charles Scribner's Sons, 1971), 265.

[11] *Articles to be Enquired in the Visitation* (1559), art. 37.

conjuring done by Faustus at the beginning of the play but also other acts that were presented in the course of its staging. Ironically, exorcisms too were held to be fraudulent, while devils were believed to have extensive power in the world.

Yet further, many members of the play's earliest audiences—perhaps the majority among them—had probably swallowed the official Tudor line as graphically illustrated on the title pages of the various editions of John Foxe's *Actes and Monuments* that placed Protestant England, which offered salvation, over against the deceptions of an apocalyptically evil Roman Church (fig. 1). The designs of the woodcuts used in the 1563, 1570, and 1576 editions were based on depictions of the Last Judgment as presented in medieval wall paintings, painted glass, and manuscript illuminations, but adapted to the concept of St. Augustine's City of God and the City of Babylon which was thus given a particularly unusual and self-congratulatory twist in the depiction of the Protestant Reformation. The point at which this peculiar development of the Augustinian view finds its way most clearly into the structure of *Faustus* is in the scene in the pope's court at Rome. So too, following his initial appearance to Faustus in true demonic form, Mephostophilis had appeared in the form and costume of a friar. Even if Marlowe and his collaborator did not designate English Protestantism as representing the most pure form of Christianity, its antagonist, the Church of Rome with its allegedly corrupt monastic orders, was painted with all the attributes of its wicked opposite.

The scene at Rome was definitely no mere commercial strategy to flatter the audience's anti-Catholicism. The problems associated with the scene are related to the play's dating and authorship, the latter in current scholarly opinion involving not only collaboration at its creation initially but also the additions included in the 1616 text—probably the "adicyones in docter fostes" for which Henslowe paid £4 to William Birde and Samuel Rowley in November 1602.[12] Whatever hand Marlowe himself

---

[12] *Henslowe's Diary*, ed. R. A. Foakes and R. T. Rickert (Cambridge: Cambridge University Press, 1961), 206. For discussion of the B-text, see Eric Rasmussen, *A Textual Companion to* Doctor Faustus (Manchester: Manchester University Press, 1993), 40–61. Opinion has shifted since W. W. Greg declared his preference for the integrity of the B-text in his edition of Marlowe's *Doctor Faustus, 1604–1616: Parallel Texts* (Oxford: Clarendon Press, 1950), 21–23; quotations in my article are from this edition. I have also particularly benefitted from the Revels Plays edition of *Doctor Faustus: A- and B-Texts (1604, 1616)*, ed. David Bevington and Eric Rasmussen (Manchester: Manchester University Press, 1993).

had in the scene as it stands in the 1604 text and is retained in the expanded text in the 1616 quarto, we cannot assume his point of view simply to be a personally skeptical view of Roman Catholicism. Indeed, his stance is made all the more problematic by the suspicion that he had himself once been a Roman Catholic, by his seeming preference of Rome over the New Religion of the Church of England, and, ironically, by his role as an anti-Catholic agent of Walsingham—a role he had perhaps assumed as early as his student days at Corpus Christi College, Cambridge.[13] He was charged with being a scoffer, an atheist, a lover of tobacco, or a pederast often enough for at least some of these claims to have credibility.[14] He was a member of the Ralegh circle—Muriel Bradbrook notes the Jesuit Robert Persons's allegation that this was a "school of Atheisme"[15]—and hence suspect at a time when Dee, who had also been associated with this circle and was reputed to be a great conjurer, was in disrepute upon his return to England from the Continent in 1589.[16] Faustus and his familiar "Spirit" (the term is a translation of *Geist* in the Spies *Faustbuch*), arriving at Rome, seem in the 1604 quarto of the play to prove themselves no better than the pope and his retinue, however much the audience might have enjoyed seeing the two travelers play tricks on them. The English Faustbook had characterized the people in the papal court to be "like to himselfe [i.e., Faustus], proud, stout, wilfull, gluttons, drunkards, whoremongers, breakers of wedlocke, and followers of all manner of vngodly exercise" (*EFB*, 35). This, in spite of moments of anti-

---

[13] See especially Charles Nicholl, *The Reckoning: The Murder of Christopher Marlowe* (1992; reprint Chicago: University of Chicago Press, 1995), *passim*. Marlowe's alleged preference for Rome was reported by Richard Baines: ". . . if there be any god or any good Religion, then it is in the Papistes because the service of god is performed with more Cerimonies, as Elevation of the Mass, organs singing men, Shaven Crownes, & cta. That all protestantes are Hypcritical asses" (quoted by John Bakeless, *The Tragicall History of Christopher Marlowe*, 2 vols. [1942; reprint Hamden, Conn.: Archon Books, 1964], 1:111).

[14] Such statements as those of Richard Baines and Thomas Kyd are not, however, to be seen as the unvarnished truth. These and other allegations critical of Marlowe have received frequent mention; see especially the chapter "Marlowe's Monstrous Opinions," in Bakeless, *The Tragicall History of Christopher Marlowe*, 1:107–40.

[15] M. C. Bradbrook, *The School of Night* (Cambridge: Cambridge University Press, 1936), 12, citing the English translation of Robert Persons, *Responsio ad Elizabethae Edictum* (1592).

[16] Yates, *The Occult Philosophy*, 89–93; Peter J. French, *John Dee: The World of an Elizabethan Magus* (London: Routledge and Kegan Paul, 1972), 8–10.

papal enthusiasm, does seem to describe all the characters who take part in the scene at Rome in the 1604 version of *Faustus*.

Another point of ambiguity derives from Faustus's connection in the Spies *Faustbuch* (and in the English translation) with Lutheran Wittenberg, the university of Luther. This is a location which it would be erroneous to see as a sign of approval in the play on account of its Protestantism, for in the late sixteenth century there was a strong and widespread prejudice in England against Lutheranism. The aversion to Lutheranism was especially strong following the failure of the Colloquy at Montbéliard in 1586.[17] The historical Faustus had been known to Luther and Melanchthon, both of whom were already regarded with qualified disapproval by theologians at Cambridge at the time when Marlowe was a student at Corpus Christi College and in the following decades. Though Luther had affirmed the principles of grace alone and faith alone, late sixteenth-century Lutheran Orthodoxy as defined by the *Formula of Concord* was seen to be sharply different, especially in its conception of the deity and in the matter of the role of the will in salvation, from the English Calvinism ascendant at Cambridge.[18] The differences also involved many other aspects, including the Lutheran retention of images, vestments, and the real presence in the Eucharist, which suggested the taint of Romanism.[19]

However, while the play of *Doctor Faustus* was imbued to a considerable extent by the Lutheran theology which it derived from its ultimate source in the Spies *Faustbuch* and Marlowe's apparent willingness to maintain Wittenberg as its intellectual center,[20] its manner of

---

[17] Nicholas Tyacke, "The Rise of Arminianism Reconsidered," *Past and Present* 115 (May 1987): 205–06. The Calvinists were represented at the Colloquy by Beza, who believed that liberty of conscience was "thoroughly diabolical" (Philip Benedict, "*Un roi, une loi, deux fois*: Parameters for the History of Catholic-Reformed Co-Existence in France, 1555–1685," in *Intolerance in the European Reformation*, ed. Ole Peter Grell and Bob Scribner [Cambridge: Cambridge University Press, 1996], 68).

[18] H. C. Porter, *Reformation and Reaction in Tudor Cambridge* (1958; reprint Hamden, Conn.: 1972), 282–83.

[19] Anthony Milton, *Catholic and Reformed: The Roman and Protestant Churches in English Protestant Thought, 1600–1640* (Cambridge: Cambridge University Press, 1995), 384–95.

[20] I accept the "Wertenberg" of the 1604 quarto ("Wirtenberg" in the reprint of 1609) to be a printer's error, which was corrected in the 1611 reprint to "Wittenberg." Leah S. Marcus argues strenuously for the acceptance of Würtemberg ("Textual Indeterminacy and

presenting a protagonist afflicted with despair[21] would seem to suggest that this playwright was influenced by the bold assertion of double predestination in the teaching of some of the men at Cambridge such as William Perkins. Perkins, who had gone up to the university in 1577, would write concerning "reprobation" (a term that is applicable to Faustus) that this "decree . . . is that part of predestination, whereby God, according to the most free and iust purpose of his will, hath determined to reiect certaine men vnto eternall destruction, and miserie, and that to the praise of his iustice."[22] So too the Lambeth articles, approved in 1595 but never disseminated, would assert that "Saving grace is not granted, is not made common, is not ceded to all men, by which they might be saved, if they wish," for salvation is not to be found in the human will but "only in the will of the good pleasure of God."[23] The cruelty of such a God had already been exposed as monstrous in 1584 in a Paul's Cross sermon on Ezekiel 33:11 by Samuel Harsnett: "Now if God had cast away man before he had sinned; . . . the malicious would have cried, the Kingdome of *God* is worse then the kingdome of *Satan*. . . ."[24] God would thus be responsible for evil in the world—an objection later confirmed by the Arminians in the seventeenth century. Marlowe likewise, it would appear, agreed that such a theology involved the monstrosity of a God who would offer salvation to those from whom he had "before the foundations of the

---

to be a printer's error, which was corrected in the 1611 reprint to "Wittenberg." Leah S. Marcus argues strenuously for the acceptance of Würtemberg ("Textual Indeterminacy and Ideological Difference: The Case of *Doctor Faustus*," *Renaissance Drama* 20 [1989]: 1–29), but on grounds that seem to me to be unconvincing.

[21] Despair is an overwhelmingly important theme in *Doctor Faustus*; for historical context, see Susan Snyder, "The Left Hand of God: Despair in Medieval and Renaissance Tradition," *Studies in the Renaissance* 12 (1965): 18–59.

[22] William Perkins, *A Golden Chaine*, trans. Robert Hill, 2nd ed. [enlarged] (Cambridge, 1597), 193–94. The original Latin text of this work was published in 1590.

[23] John Strype, *The Life and Acts of John Whitgift*, 3 vols. (Oxford, 1822), 2:280, as quoted in translation in Porter, *Reformation and Reaction*, 371. See also the discussion in Peter White, *Predestination, Policy and Polemic: Conflict and Consensus in the English Church from the Reformation to the Civil Wars* (Cambridge: Cambridge University Press, 1992), 101–10.

[24] Samuel Harsnett, *A Sermon preached at Pauls Cross*; appendix to Richard Steward, *Three Sermons*, 2nd ed. (London, 1658), 149. For a summary of Harsnett's objections to double predestination, see ibid., 148–49.

world were laid" decided to deny it.[25] Thus, though his play retained the emphasis of Lutheran Orthodoxy on the will and grace, Marlowe seems also to have had a hidden agenda in his presentation of Faustus's failure to achieve repentance. As a reprobate, the character of Faustus could demonstrate the working of the reprehensible doctrine of double predestination being taught by the radical Calvinist divines at Cambridge and widely accepted in the Church of England at this time.[26] This of course does not imply that the play should be seen as a tract in defense of the Lutheran Orthodoxy that had been espoused by the author of the German *Faustbuch*, for the play's purpose was obviously far more complicated than that.

The date of the play as originally produced has been debated. The English translation of the *Faustbuch*, published in 1592, may have been previously available to Marlowe in manuscript, or there may have been an earlier printing. That this version of the Faustus story was his source there is no doubt, but earlier access seems likely in view of the apparent reference to Marlowe's play in Gabriel Harvey's *Aduertisement for Paphatchet*, attributed to 1589 but only published in 1593 in *Pierces Superogation*: "As for that new-created Spirite, whome double V. [i.e., John Lyly] like an other Doctour Faustus, threateneth to coniure-vpp at leysure, . . . were that Spirite disposed to appear in his former likenesse, and to put the Necromancer to his purgation, he could peradventure make the coniuring wisard forsake the center of his Circle, and betake him to the circumference of his heeles."[27] Prynne's location of early productions at the Belsavage playhouse also would have dated the play no later than

---

[25] See D. P. Walker, *The Decline of Hell* (London: Routledge and Kegan Paul, 1964), 48–53, esp. 49.

[26] The Bishops Bible, for example, contained a gloss on Romans 9:11 that claimed "[t]he will and purpose of God" to be "the Cause of the election and reprobation. For his mercy and calling through Christ are the meanes of salvation and the withdrawing of his mercy in the cause of damnation" (folio edition of 1585, as quoted by Maurice S. Betteridge, "The Bitter Notes: The Geneva Bible and Its Annotations," *Sixteenth Century Journal* 14 [1983], 54).

[27] Gabriel Harvey, *Pierces Superogation* (London, 1593), 131. The importance of *An Aduertisement for Pap-hatchet*, dated 5 November 1589, is stressed by John Henry Jones, ed., *The English Faust Book* (Cambridge: Cambridge University Press, 1994), 53. On questions of dating, see also the discussion in Bevington and Rasmussen, eds., *Doctor Faustus: A- and B-texts*, 1–3.

1589.[28] The establishment of an early date in 1589 or even in 1588 would be significant, since this would place *Doctor Faustus* not long after Marlowe's success with *Tamburlaine* (1587–88). Further, the late 1580s were a time of the most intense anti-Roman Catholic feeling in London in the wake of the Babington Plot, the execution of Mary Queen of Scots, and the attempted invasion by the Spanish Armada. Roman Catholics were being persecuted, and spy activity, including the work of agents provocateur, was high.[29] For a priest ordained abroad or a friar to be caught in the country would mean almost certain torture and, if he persevered in his faith, execution. It is often forgotten that persecution under Elizabeth I brought a great many to their death, some of them like the poet Robert Southwell suffering at the hands of the psychopath Richard Topcliff who reported directly to the queen.[30] Even an attractive layperson such as Margaret Clitheroe of York could be executed—she was pressed to death for allegedly harboring Roman Catholic priests and possessing Mass vestments a little more than three months before Mary Queen of Scots was brought to the block.[31]

The religious turmoil, much of it hidden away from the surface of Elizabethan political life since voicing controversial ideas could be remarkably dangerous, only encouraged outward conformity and widespread alienation of mind and spirit. Such repression, allied with official controls on publication, not surprisingly meant that comparatively few expressions of overt unorthodoxy found their way into print, even if they were combined with elements of the conventional theology of the time or with royalist political philosophy. The title page of the English Faustbook of 1592 contained the words "Seene and allowed"—a sign of the sensitivity of its contents.[32] In contrast to his *Tamburlaine* of which both parts were in print by 1590, Marlowe's *Faustus* was not published until a

---

[28] Prynne, *Histrio-mastix*, fol. 556^r. For further argument for an early date, see Scott McMillin and Sally-Beth MacLean, *The Queen's Men and Their Plays* (Cambridge: Cambridge University Press, 1998), 157–58.

[29] See, for example, John Bossy, *Giordano Bruno and the Embassy Affair* (New Haven: Yale University Press, 1991).

[30] Christopher Devlin, *The Life of Robert Southwell, Poet and Martyr* (1956; reprint London: Sidgwick and Jackson, 1967), 283–84.

[31] John Morris, *The Troubles of Our Catholic Forefathers*, 3 vols. (London: Burns and Oates, 1872–77), 3:333–40.

[32] Jones, ed., *The English Faust Book*, 186.

considerably long time after its initial composition, and we may wonder if concern about censorship may have been a factor in this delay. Entered in the Stationers' Register in January 1601, *Doctor Faustus* would only be published in 1604, early in the reign of the next monarch, James I, who to be sure had himself been the author of a commentary on witchcraft, *Dæmonologie* (1597), which had asserted that magicians and necromancers in their activities draw "nerer to the sin against the holy Ghost" than ignorant witches.[33]

In the opening scene of *Doctor Faustus*, the protagonist presents a catalogue of subject matters, including theology, as grounds for expressing his belief in the vanity of human knowledge. If at times he seems to echo Agrippa's *Of the Vanitie and Vncertaintie of Artes and Sciences* which asserted that knowledge "is the very pestilence, that putteth al mankinde to ruine,"[34] the playwright's purpose initially differs from Agrippa's in that he fails to include magic, astronomy, and alchemy with the other arts leading to destruction. On the other hand, the gist of this scene does ultimately lead nevertheless to the conclusion that knowledge for the protagonist is that which, in Agrippa's words, "hath extinguished the light of Faith, casting our Soules into blinde darknesse: which condemning the truth, hath placed errours in the hiest throne."[35] Such thinking might seem to have been characteristic of the fashion for the skepticism which was unleashed by the rediscovery of Sextus Empiricus and his predecessor Pyrrho, whose philosophical striving was said to have been characterized by "continuall inspection and never finding"[36]—and ultimately propelled him to a position of absolute doubt. The emergence of this strain of philosophical skepticism in England was described many years ago by Louis Bredvold, whose principal interest to be sure was in the later seventeenth century.[37] Giordano Bruno, during his stay in England, had espoused a skepticism that led him to a philosophical religion of aspiration not based on Christianity. In Marlowe's *Doctor*

---

[33] King James I, *Dæmonologie*, and [Anon.], *Newes from Scotland*, ed. G. B. Harrison (London: John Lane, 1924), 26.
[34] Henry Cornelius Agrippa, *Of the Vanitie and Vncertaintie of Artes and Sciences* (London: Henry Bynneman, 1575), fol. 4.
[35] Ibid.
[36] Thomas Stanley, *The History of Philosophy*, 3 vols. (London, 1660), 3:1.
[37] Louis I. Bredvold, *The Intellectual Milieu of John Dryden: Studies in Some Aspects of Seventeenth-Century Thought* (Ann Arbor: University of Michigan Press, 1934).

Faustus, skepticism is turned to use as a structural device whereby there is a rejection of orthodoxy, replaced by striving based on forbidden rituals and ideas. But the career of Faustus, albeit describing aspiration, is ultimately an intellectual fall downward like the abortive flight of Icarus, cited already in the play's prologue (A21–23, B20–22) as an antecedent for Marlowe's protagonist. Faustus, questioning conventional knowledge, is catapulted into traffic with the spirit Mephostophilis and ultimately into adventures which include seemingly miraculous travel and sensual experiences as well as trickery worthy of Till Eulenspiegel's merry pranks. Frances Yates saw *Doctor Faustus* as reflecting "the reaction against Renaissance magic, particularly as formulated by Agrippa" in his *De Occulta Philosophia*, rather than part of the enthusiasm for such thought in the work of such men as the Abbot Trithemius, Marsilio Ficino, or John Dee.[38]

Faustus's journey to Rome where he will "see the Pope, and manner of his court, / And take some part of holy *Peters* feast" (A819–20) probably is intended to refer to an actual feast day of St. Peter, not impossibly the feast of St. Peter in Chains on 1 August, but these lines are also indicative of the reputation of the pope in Protestant polemic for indulging in rich food and wine. In his *Actes and Monuments*, John Foxe typically jeered at a pope who gluttonized on peacock pie and pork.[39] In the English Faustbook as in its German source, the service at the "feast" was "unmeasurable and sumptuous," with the elaborate food served up to "these hogs of Rome" (*EFB*, 36). The A-text has Faustus wishing for a view of the "troupe of bald-pate Friers" attending at the feast "Whose *summum bonum* is in belly-cheare" (A870–71). Faustus, with Mephostophilis's aid, will become "inuisible," perhaps wearing the "robe for to goo invisibell" mentioned in Henslowe's diary,[40] and will observe a "*banket*" prepared for the Cardinal of Lorraine (a change from the Faustbook, which specifies the Cardinal of Pavia) at which he will be disruptive. The suggestion is made that this is "some ghost / newly crept out of Purgatory come to begge a pardon" of the pope (A895–97). In the Faustbook,

---

[38] Yates, *The Occult Philosophy*, 116.

[39] John Foxe, *Actes and Monuments* (London: John Day, 1576), 147; I have generally used this edition of Foxe, for which subsequent references in my text are designated *A&M 1576*.

[40] *Henslowe's Diary*, ed. Foakes and Rickert, 325.

Faustus is particularly annoyed at the pontiff's frequent "blessing and crossing ouer his mouth" (*EFB*, 36), a gesture which seems to be the one specified in the A-text and which is occasion for the "unseen" protagonist to comment: "What, are you crossing of your selfe? Well vse that tricke no more, I would aduise you" (A900–01). The sign of the cross, except during baptism and even then a point of controversy with extremist Puritans, had been proscribed in the Anglican liturgy and was considered to be a superstitious gesture until rehabilitated in the time of King Charles I.[41] At the third crossing by the pope, "*Faustus hits him a boxe of the eare*" (A903), a stage direction that modifies the English Faustbook's statement that he "vp with his fist and smote the Pope on the face" (*EFB*, 36)—a mistranslation of the Spies *Faustbuch*, which had called for Faustus to blow in the pontiff's face. We can assume that in the play Faustus's single blow was in appearance violent, since the stage direction indicates that the pope and his retinue "*alle runne away*" (A906), and in the B-text an even more elaborate episode is indicated with the pope claiming to be "slaine" and requiring to be carried off stage as he curses "for euer" the invisible offender, still perceived by him as a soul out of Purgatory, "for this deed" (B1103–05). The indicators are that the scene involved playing to an audience in the main extremely hostile to the papacy and willing to have a laugh at such a portrayal of this institution. It is of a piece with Protestant propaganda both in England and in Protestant Northern Europe. The latter was to be sure where the Faust story had originated—and where the pope was depicted as an ass or a fool, as submitting to the Devil, or even worse.[42] Quite typical is the crowning of the ass-pope by two other asses, who hold the papal tiara over his head.[43] Another typical illustration depicts a monk calf.[44] As the

---

[41] For Foxe's identification of the cross and the image of the Crucifixion with the Roman Church, see Margaret Aston and Elizabeth Ingram, "The Iconography of the *Acts and Monuments*," in *John Foxe and the English Reformation*, ed. David Loades (Aldershot: Scolar Press, 1997), 82–83.

[42] Scribner, *For the Sake of Simple Folk*, passim; Everard Schuttenium, *Het Nieuwe Roomsche Symbolum* (1630), photo of the pope submitting to the devil in Warburg Institute archives.

[43] Hartmann Grisar and Franz Heege, *Luthers Kampfbilder*, 4 vols. (Freiburg: Herder, 1921–23), 3:43, fig. 10. The depictions could be scatological; for an example, see the depiction in Luther's *Depiction of the Papacy* (1545) of a soldier defecating in an upturned tiara over the papal shield with the papal keys replaced by jemmies used by thieves to pick locks (Scribner, *For the Sake of Simple Folk*, 81, fig. 59).

[44] Philip Melanchthon, *Deuttung der czwo grewlichen Figuren* (1523); reproduced in Scribner, *For the Sake of Simple Folk*, 127–33, fig. 97.

friars are preparing to come on stage with bell, book, and candle to curse Faustus, he exclaims in the A-text: "Anon you shal heare a hogge grunt, a calfe bleate, and an asse braye, because it is S. *Peters* holy day" (A912–13).

As Bevington and Rasmussen indicate in their edition of *Doctor Faustus*, the "*Dirge*" which follows involves the confusion of "the office of excommunication . . . with that of exorcism."[45] The parodying of a religious ritual, which is interrupted by Faustus and Mephistophilis, is intended to play on the rejection of both procession and exorcism itself in Protestant England, where, for example, the *Book of Common Prayer* presented even a baptismal rite that had been shorn of the traditional exorcisms. Further, cursing with "booke, bell, and candell," said by Foxe to have been introduced in 1144 at the Council of London under Pope Celestinus, is given unfavorable mention in his *Actes and Monuments* (*A&M 1576*, 203). Quite clearly the scene in the play was designed to be staged as satire directed at Roman Catholic ceremony, and it ends with fireworks being flung among the participants in the "*Dirge*." The fireworks seem to have been quite a spectacular effect, which is thereafter parodied in a scene in which Mephostophilis terrorizes Robin and the Vintner by setting "*squibs at their backes*" (A1012). The use of squibs in later performances at the Fortune Theater, along with lightning and drumming in the tiring house to represent thunder, is affirmed by John Melton in 1620.[46] Squibs would have involved pyrotechnic devices thrown among the friars that would follow erratic trajectories, produce showers of sparks, and end with small explosions.[47]

---

[45] Bevington and Rasmussen, eds., *Doctor Faustus*, 166. The term 'dirge' is also misused in the text.

[46] John Melton, *Astrologaster, or the Figure-Caster* (London, 1620), 31. Melton mentions squibs as being in the mouths of devils running about the stage. There is no reason why devils could not have been added to this scene, though we have no evidence that they were. However, the thunder and lightning surely were not appropriate in this scene as they would be, for example, in the latter part of the play.

[47] See Philip Butterworth, *Theatre of Fire: Special Effects in Early English and Scottish Theatre* (London: Society for Theatre Research, 1998), 1, 24, 46.

In the B-text of 1616, the episode at Rome is considerably expanded with historical matter drawn from the text and illustrations of John Foxe's *Actes and Monuments* but with a few further echoes nevertheless of the English Faustbook.[48] The use of the latter probably demonstrates that this text was based on a somewhat more complete playtext than the one that is presented in the 1604 quarto or in the 1609 and 1611 quartos which preserve variants of the A-text, but it is no longer possible to claim, with W. W. Greg and Leo Kirschbaum, that the 1616 text is closer to the play which Marlowe originally created and that the A-text is a bad quarto.[49] The additions to the scene at Rome, probably the work of Samuel Rowley,[50] involve an adventurous escapade in which Faustus rescues "Saxon *Bruno*" from "Pope *Adrian*." Frederick S. Boas found the scene to involve a "reckless disregard for historical truth."[51] Bruno's historical antecedents are Frederick Barbarossa, Victor IV (an anti-pope), and perhaps Protestant reformers,[52] while Pope Adrian IV (1154–59) is deliberately confused with Adrian VI (1522–23), who served as pontiff when the historical Faustus was alive. It was Alexander III (1159–81), however, who was responsible for the event that inspired the action with which he is introduced in the play. "Cast downe our Foot-stoole," the pope demands (B895), and Bruno is made to become a stepping stool for him to ascend to his papal throne, specified as "Saint *Peters* Chaire and State Pontificall" (B898). This Bruno is apparently initially intended still to be wearing the triple crown to show his status as a rival pope, though shortly thereafter Adrian will order it sent to his treasury as confiscated goods since in his view it was worn illegally.

The most relevant illustrations in Foxe's *Actes and Monuments* are the Proud Primacy of the Popes woodcuts, which are indebted to Lucas

---

[48] For parallels between the English Faustbook and the texts of *Faustus*, see Jones, ed., *The English Faust Book*, 254, and, for the principal source of the additions, Leslie M. Oliver, "Rowley, Foxe, and the Faustus Additions," *Modern Language Notes* 60 (1945): 391–94.

[49] Greg, ed., *Doctor Faustus*, 21–23; Leo Kirschbaum, "The Good and Bad Quartos of 'Doctor Faustus'," *The Library*, 4th ser. 26 (1946): 272–94; followed in my "Doctor Faustus at Rome," *Studies in English Literature* 9 (1969): 231–39.

[50] See Greg, ed., *Doctor Faustus*, 351–52; Rasmussen, *A Textual Companion*, 90.

[51] Frederick S. Boas, ed., *The Tragical History of Doctor Faustus*, 2nd ed. (London: Methuen, 1949), 29.

[52] Since "Saxon *Bruno*" is seen as an antagonist of the pope at Rome and because he shares a given name with Giordano Bruno, the latter must also be seen as a possible figure behind this anti-pope.

Cranach the Younger.[53] The one that is echoed explicitly in Pope Adrian's stepping on Bruno's body as a footstool is labeled "Pope Alexander treading on the necke of Fredericke the Emperor" (fig. 2). This derives from Cranach's woodcut published in Robert Barnes's *Papsttrew Hadriani IV* at Wittenberg in 1545,[54] and then copied for the 1563 edition of the *Actes and Monuments*.[55] The original accompanying text proclaimed: "Auf den Ottern und Löwen wirt du gehen und treten auf den jungen Löwen und Drachen"—a text given by Foxe in Latin (*A&M 1576*, 207) and echoed in the pope's lines in *Doctor Faustus*:

> And as Pope *Alexander* our Progenitour,
> Trode on the neck of *Germane Fredericke*,
> Adding this golden sentence to our praise;
> That *Peters* heires should tread on Emperours,
> And walke vpon the dreadfull Adders backe,
> Treading the Lyon, and the Dragon downe.
> (B945–50)

Following Foxe in the *Actes and Monuments*, this glance at the Investiture Contest is, however, a dramatization of the great political conflict of sixteenth-century British history between the papacy and the crown.

This conflict, discussed at some length in terms of English royal iconography by John N. King in a chapter entitled "The Crown versus the Tiara,"[56] derives from King Henry VIII's Act of Supremacy, the Tudor program of independence from Rome (with the exception of Queen Mary Tudor), and the suppression of many aspects of traditional worship, including the cults of the saints.[57] In the 1570 and 1576 editions of the *Actes and Monuments*, the illustration showing the humiliation of

---

[53] For a listing of Foxe's woodcuts in the various editions of *Actes and Monuments* and bibliographic discussion, see Ruth Samson Luborsky and Elizabeth Morley Ingram, *A Guide to English Illustrated Books, 1536–1603*, 2 vols. (Tempe, Arizona: Medieval and Renaissance Texts and Studies, 1998), 1:365–83; and see also Aston and Ingram, "The Iconography of the *Acts and Monuments*," 66–142, as well as John N. King, *Tudor Royal Iconography* (Princeton: Princeton University Press, 1989), 127–81.

[54] Grisar and Heege, *Luthers Kampfbilder*, 3:66, 4:66.

[55] See King, *Tudor Royal Iconography*, figs. 36–37.

[56] See ibid.

[57] See Eamon Duffy, *The Stripping of the Altars: Traditional Religion in England, 1400–1580* (New Haven: Yale University Press, 1992).

Marlowe, the Papacy, and Doctor Faustus

2. Pope Alexander stepping on the neck of Emperor Frederick. John Foxe, *Actes and Monuments* (1576), p. 207. By permission of the Henry E. Huntington Library.

Frederick Barbarossa is placed next to the story of Archbishop Thomas Becket,[58] whose defense of the Church against King Henry II in the twelfth century would inspire the wrath of King Henry VIII. In 1538 this king ordered that the saint be de-canonized and his presence in texts and images obliterated throughout the realm as if he had never existed.[59] Inventing historical precedent, Bruno in the play is made to tell the pope that Emperor Sigismund had been promised by Pope Julius, binding also "the succeeding Popes of *Rome*, / To hold the Emperours their lawfull Lords" (B955–57).[60] The play's Pope Adrian's response is an ironic

---

[58] Foxe, *Actes and Monuments* (1570), 1:263ff; (1576), 207ff.

[59] See Tancred Borenius, *St. Thomas Becket in Art* (1932; reprint Port Washington, N.Y.: Kennikat Press, 1970), 11, 109–10 and *passim*.

[60] In the conflict over investiture in the eleventh and twelfth centuries, secular authority and the papacy each claimed to have primary power over the other; see the summary in *The Dictionary of the Christian Church*, 3rd ed., ed. F. L. Cross and E. A. Livingstone (Oxford:

affirmation of England's right to be free of papal authority:

> Pope *Iulius* did abuse the Churches Rites,
> And therefore none of his Decrees can stand.
> Is not all power on earth bestowed on vs?
> And therefore tho we would we cannot erre.
> (B958–61)

Aside from the comic line affirming papal infallibility, the claims here concerning the pope's power also underlie not only many of the arguments of Foxe's book but also a great deal of anti-papal rhetoric generally at the end of the sixteenth century and beginning of the seventeenth as well. As King notes, it was Foxe's view that "the church of Rome came to occupy the role of persecutor once played by tyrannical emperors" in late antiquity.[61] The apparent adoption of this point of view in the scene meant that its anti-Roman Catholicism is much less complicated than in the version retained in the A-text. The pope who claims all power on earth is to be deceived almost immediately by Faustus and his familiar spirit, Mephostophilis, in a matter of international politics.[62]

The crux of the pope's claim is the delivery of the keys to Peter in Matthew 16:19. These traditionally were considered to be the keys to the kingdom of heaven and included the power to bind and loose sin, but in the play are shifted into "Seuen golden seales" (B963)— that is, the seven sacraments—which Pope Adrian regards as providing the authority ultimately to do his own will and to indulge his own pleasure. The power of the keys and the control of the seven sacraments had been major points of Luther's attack on Rome.[63] Faustus, echoing the pope's own view of things, suggests that Bruno and the emperor should both "be held as Lollords, and bold Schismatiques, / And proud disturbers of the Churches

---

Oxford University Press, 1997), 842–43; Tudor political theology under Henry VIII, Edward VI, and Elizabeth I rejected papal authority and did so with earlier anti-papal conflicts in mind.

[61] King, *Tudor Royal Iconography*, 133.

[62] While the B-text is arguably more "internationalist," it is hard to reconcile the more strident polemic here with Marcus's view of the 1616 version as more "Anglican, or Anglo-Catholic" than the A-text ("Textual Indeterminacy," 5).

[63] See Martin Luther, *The Keys*, trans. Earl Beyer and Conrad Bergendorff, in *Luther's Works*, 55 vols. (Philadelphia, 1958–67), 40:353.

peace" (B986–87); and they should ultimately be condemned to death as decreed by the decretals. Their fate should be to be "on a pile of Fagots burnt to death" (B994). This line vividly brings to mind the woodcuts in Foxe's *Actes and Monuments* that show prominent churchmen, even the Archbishop of Canterbury with two fellow bishops being set aflame in the streets of Oxford, and others being executed by burning in Queen Mary Tudor's time. These were powerful and well-known images which would have reinforced the language of the pope's speech. To an English audience in 1603 (if indeed this addition in the B-text dates from November of the previous year) the play would have reinforced the common view among English Protestants that the papacy is the institution in charge of the City of Babylon, which had been described by St. Augustine in his *City of God* and which, as noted above, was depicted as an entity set off against the purity of true religion represented by the reformed Church of England. The clarity and lack of ambiguity in this depiction provide contrast with the version in the A-text, which was less clearly in tune with the politics of the *Actes and Monuments* and, in Frances Yates's description, Foxe's use of "a wealth of miscellaneous documentation always with a single-eyed determination to weave all the strands into patterns which suit his argument."[64] The illustration which Foxe and his publisher, John Day, intended as a precise refutation of the pope stepping on the neck of the emperor is the woodcut showing King Henry VIII suppressing the Pope Clement VII by placing his foot on the pontiff's neck.[65]

The antagonism toward Roman Catholicism that had pertained in the 1580s still survived in force to 1602 and early 1603. In 1602 the Geneva Bible, for example, was reissued with Francis Junius's virulently antipapal notes to the book of Revelation,[66] but the original 1560 Geneva gloss of Revelation 9:3 had just as shrilly proclaimed that the "Locusts" named in this passage "are false teachers, heretikes, and worldlie suttil Prelades, with Monkes, Freres, Cardinals, Patriarkes, Archebishops, Bishops, Doctors, Bachelers, and masters which forsake Christ to

---

[64] Francis Yates, "Foxe as Propagandist," *Encounter* 27 (1966): 79.
[65] Aston and Ingram, "The Iconography of the *Acts and Monuments*," 128, fig. 4.37.
[66] See Maurice S. Betteridge, "The Bitter Notes: The Geneva Bible and Its Annotations," *Sixteenth Century Journal* 14 (1983): 41–62.

mainteine false doctrine."⁶⁷ However, a substantial portion of the population hoped that the next monarch might achieve a more peaceful settlement of religion and of the political hostilities that were dragging on in Europe— and a new reign seemed imminent on account of the queen's health and age. However, between the accession to the throne of James I, followed by the publication of the first quarto of *Doctor Faustus* in 1604, and the printing of the B-text in 1616, the Gunpowder Plot, which planned to destroy Parliament as the king was addressing it, was uncovered. This plot effectively confirmed Protestant fears that Roman Catholicism was diabolical and subversive. The additions to *Faustus* probably, as we have seen, were written in 1602, but they nevertheless would have helped thereafter to keep the topic of the play current even if, in the more skeptical atmosphere of the Jacobean period, its audiences tended to be the less educated, perhaps enjoying the pyrotechnics described by John Melton more than anything else in the drama. The association of Roman Catholics with fireworks would likely have become part and parcel of the play's anti-Catholicism—and, one might speculate, this could have made the play a perennial favorite for the commemoration of Guy Fawkes Day up to the closing of the theaters in 1642.⁶⁸

When the theaters reopened at the Restoration, the great "noise" of "Devils and suchlike Tragicall sport"⁶⁹ seems to have again been a source of the play's attraction. Samuel Pepys saw *Doctor Faustus* in 1662 at the Red Bull and complained that the production was "so wretchedly and poorly done, that we were sick of it."⁷⁰ In the next year the play was re-issued in a text based on the 1616 version but with new material,⁷¹ including the substitution of a visit to the court of the Sultan instead of

---

⁶⁷ *The Geneva Bible: A Facsimile of the 1560 Edition*, introd. Lloyd E. Berry (Madison: University of Wisconsin Press, 1969).

⁶⁸ An interesting analogue to the Faust story was published in this year by Lawrence Southerne (*Feareful Newes from Coventry* [London, 1642], 3–6); the analogue includes a covetous minstrel who signed a pact with the devil, and ultimately was slaughtered by him. For a summary and the social context, see Darren Oldridge, "Protestant Conceptions of the Devil in Early Stuart England," *History* 85 (2000): 232–46, esp. 243.

⁶⁹ Edward Phillips, *Theatrum Poetarum, or a Compleat Collection of the Poets, Especially the Most Eminent, of All Ages*, 2 vols. (London, 1675), 2:25.

⁷⁰ Samuel Pepys, *The Diary*, ed. Robert Latham and William Matthews, 11 vols. (Berkeley and Los Angeles: University of California Press, 1979–83), 3:93.

⁷¹ *The Tragicall History of the Life and Death of Doctor Faustus* (London: W. Gilbertson, 1663).

the scene at the Vatican. Mention of Rome in the introduction to the scene is retained, and in the Sultan's court scene there is considerable retention of dialogue from the 1616 episode at the papal court along with some matter imported from *The Jew of Malta*. The handling lacks sensitivity, and the ending of the scene differs dramatically, for the Sultan's conjurer stands in his circle and requests to know whether the one who disturbs the peace is "a Devil, or a Ghost from hell." Mephostophilis identifies himself as "A devil," and turns flames on him.[72] In spite of the retention of pyrotechnics, the principal anti-papal scene had been suppressed, perhaps because in Charles II England now had a monarch who was secretly a Roman Catholic.[73] In spite of the subsequent hysteria of the Popish Plot, the historical circumstances which had pertained in the late sixteenth century no longer held sufficient sway to produce of the play a convincing production on stage. For audiences which no longer necessarily believed in the possibility of conjuring, the presence of demonic forces that might be called up by a Faustian ritual, or eternal punishment in hell for the predestined reprobate, the Faustus drama was destined to be debased in such productions as William Mountfort's *The Life and Death of Doctor Faustus, Made into a Farce* (1697), which again omitted the visit of Faustus and "Mephostopholis" (*sic*) to the papal court.

---

[72] Ibid., sigs. D4^r–D4^v.

[73] For another suggestion, see William Empson, *Faustus and the Censor: The English Faust-Book and Marlowe's* Doctor Faustus, ed. John Henry Jones (Oxford: Basil Blackwell, 1987), 147–48.

The History of King Lear and the Problem of Belief

Since the presuppositions of currently fashionable Marxist criticism would deny the expression of the transcendental in Shakespeare's dramas, interpretations of this school tend to see the events of the plays from the limited perspective of materialist ideology.[1] For example, Terry Eagleton makes the claim that in *Macbeth* the "witches are the heroines of the piece" since they release "ambitious thoughts in Macbeth, [and] expose a reverence for hierarchical social order for what it is, as the pious self-deception of a society based on routine oppression and incessant warfare."[2] According to this view, therefore, the witches become only a mechanical device for a secular revelation that questions hierarchy in the political order rather than the ambiguous and troubling creatures which they are in Shakespeare's play. Nevertheless, we ought not to assume that the restrictive perspective of materialist criticism can never be illuminating or useful in understanding Shakespeare's plays in their social and historical context.

Jonathan Dollimore, in a discussion of Shakespeare's *King Lear*, specifically argues against both the Christian understanding, which he feels has been "discredited" by William R. Elton among others, and what

---

[1] The present article, which is dedicated to the memory of Roy Battenhouse, is not intended as a full-scale analysis of materialist criticism, but rather is an attempt to demonstrate the usefulness of some critical insights when freed from Marxist ideology and provided with a more thorough grounding in the historical and religious milieu of the work. While it is axiomatic for Marx and materialist critics generally that "things are never quite what they seem" (see Nicholas Lash, *A Matter of Hope: A Theologian's Reflections on the Thought of Marx* [Notre Dame, Ind.: Notre Dame University Press, 1982], 63), I will argue that things also are not necessarily the way that materialist criticism conceives them to be. At the same time I will argue for giving close attention to such criticism for insights that may be expanded and modified in what has come to be labeled "essentialist" scholarship.

[2] Terry Eagleton, *William Shakespeare* (Oxford: Blackwell, 1986), 2. See also the insistence on the "centrality of the weird sisters" in James L. O'Rourke, "The Subversive Metaphysics of *Macbeth*," *Shakespeare Studies* 21 (1993): 215.

he has designated as the "humanist view." The latter, he feels, is as fully as "misguided" as the Christian interpretation because "it mystifies suffering and invests man with a quasi-transcendental identity whereas the play does neither of these things."[3] These words, to be sure, may appear to verify the long-held opinion that readers and directors/producers see in Shakespeare a reflection of their own mindset, but in the present article I wish to invite closer examination of two comments by Dollimore which in my view have serious implications beyond his materialist bias. First: "In *Lear*, as in *Troilus*, man is decentred not through misanthropy but in order to make visible social process and its forms of ideological misrecognition."[4] Here, in spite of Dollimore's prejudice against transcendence and his assumptions about authorial intent, such descriptive terms as "decentring," "social process," and "ideological misrecognition" may nevertheless prove suggestive and may open some important issues with regard to *King Lear* even though the terms themselves require qualification.

Second, calling attention to an observation in a lecture by Camus, Dollimore has acknowledged the importance of innovation and change for the development of tragedy during the Tudor and early Stuart periods:

> According to Albert Camus, tragedy is generated by a particular kind of historical transition: "Tragedy is born in the west each time that the pendulum of civilisation is halfway between a sacred society and a society built around man" (*Selected Essays and Notebooks*, p. 199). The operative word here is "halfway"—man "frees himself from an older form of civilisation and finds that he has broken away from it without having found a new form which satisfied him" (p. 194). To modify Camus' argument somewhat, certain Jacobean tragedies disclose the very process of historical transition which brings them into being.[5]

This is a statement that, applied to *King Lear*, is pregnant with interpretative possibilities, many of them quite different from the materialist assumptions in Dollimore's own analysis.

---

[3] Jonathan Dollimore, *Radical Tragedy: Religion, Ideology, and Power in the Drama of Shakespeare and His Contemporaries*, 2nd ed. (Durham: Duke University Press, 1993), 191. For an assessment of attacks on the "humanist view," see Laurence Lerner, "Against Historicism," *New Literary History* 24 (1993): 273–92.

[4] Dollimore, *Radical Tragedy*, 191.

[5] Ibid., 8.

Shakespeare's *King Lear*, particularly in the quarto text of 1608 (Q1) upon which I will focus in this paper,[6] may indeed be seen as having a direct connection to the political and social condition of England in the earliest years of King James' reign. Significantly, this quarto advertised on its title page that a performance of the play, by the King's Men, had been staged before their patron, King James, at Whitehall on the Feast of St. Stephen in 1606; the Q1 text appears to represent the play as it existed at this time.[7] Bad political judgment, for which this ruling monarch was already famous, was feared because of its capacity to jeopardize social stability in the entire national community.[8] Moreover, nervousness about the quality of rule was nothing new and was an inheritance from the Tudor period. Fears concerning the political and social order arose from an inherent distrust of what Dollimore has called "political process—a distrust gained from experience over the past century when so many venerable institutions had in fact been overthrown. This same nervousness seems to be very deeply embedded in *King Lear*, on which Shakespeare had apparently been at work in the months immediately prior to the discovery of the Gunpowder Plot in November 1605, though the play probably was not completed until after this historically memorable event—an event that seemed to underline the inherent shakiness of the English political system and that is remembered annually to this day in England as Guy Fawkes Day.

We learned in the course of the twentieth century that there are times of transition when the political ground indeed feels insecure under our

---

[6] Quotations from the First Quarto version of *King Lear* are from William Shakespeare, *The Complete Works*, ed. Stanley Wells and Gary Taylor (Oxford: Clarendon Press, 1988); references to scene and line numbers (following the abbreviation *HKL*) appear in my text.

[7] The play is registered in the Stationers' Register under the date 26 November 1607 with the information that the play had been presented "before the kinges maiestie at Whitehall" on 26 December 1606, and the First Quarto, entitled *True Chronicle Historie of the life and death of King Lear and his three Daughters*, gives the publication date of 1608. On the play's date, see the New Arden edition of *King Lear*, ed. Kenneth Muir (London: Methuen, 1952), xx–xxvi. Questions of the relationship between the First Quarto and First Folio texts are explored in Gary Taylor and Roger Warren, eds., *The Division of the Kingdoms: Shakespeare's Two Versions of* King Lear (Oxford: Clarendon Press, 1983).

[8] Stuart M. Kurland, "'The care . . . of subjects' good': *Pericles*, James I, and the Neglect of Government," *Comparative Drama* 30 (1996): 223–27.

very feet—an insecurity usually tied directly to the attitudes, beliefs, faith or lack of it, and actions of those appointed (or self-appointed) to govern. It was against such a moment in history that William Butler Yeats wrote, in his last poems, of the "tragic joy" of a time conceived by him to be the end of an age,[9] and in those years leading up to World War II there was certainly widespread apprehension. Further, the period between the World Wars saw Western European society drifting more and more in the direction of a historical transition as the tide of faith began receding and the present secularism was established. For Yeats it was a period when great poetry could be written, but it also meant the approach of historical calamity in World War II. I would place another moment of transition in the 1980s in Central and Eastern Europe as the Socialist order was about to collapse in those states. Prior to the actual collapse there could be no way of foretelling the outcome of the imminent swing of the "pendulum of civilisation," which one felt in one's bones might be calamitous—or so it appeared to perceptive visitors from the West.

Similarly, though in ways more closely approximating the historical condition observed by Camus and selected for notice by Dollimore, the England of King Henry VIII, Edward VI, Queen Mary, Queen Elizabeth, and King James found itself faced with transition—transition which resonated in Q1 of *King Lear* and which therefore deserves to be examined with considerable care in order to establish the context in which the play was introduced initially to its public.

When the political and social context in Tudor and early Stuart England is examined, then, a perception of shakiness emerges that viewed the cohesion of the family and community dissolving in a crisis—a crisis that was felt by many to be related to the erosion of belief following the Act of Supremacy proclaimed under Henry VIII. The popular religion that was practiced on the eve of the Reformation may seem to many to have fully merited the scorn of the skeptical Erasmus, who viewed such practices as pilgrimages and veneration of relics and images of saints as mere superstition,[10] but the revolution that set out to destroy the "Old Religion" had

---

[9] "The Gyres," in William Butler Yeats, *The Collected Poems* (London: Macmillan, 1955).

[10] See "A Pilgrimage for Religion's Sake," in Desiderius Erasmus, *The Colloquies*, trans. Craig R. Thompson (Chicago: University of Chicago Press, 1965), 287–311.

a broader effect, which was to shake the confidence of the people in the ordained clergy (however much they had fallen short of the ideal previously) and in the efficacy of Christianity itself. The dissolution of the monasteries, begun in 1536 with the smaller houses and the promise that only corrupt institutions would be dissolved, soon spread to the larger and more affluent abbeys, and by early in 1540 all would be confiscated by the crown to its great material benefit. Under the rubric of reform, the destruction of monastic institutions, the healthy as well as the corrupt, the thriving as well as the declining, meant the striking down within England of an entire tradition almost as old as Christianity itself—a tradition of contemplative prayer and worship which also performed important social functions. Resistance in the 1530s, especially the Pilgrimage of Grace in the North, was surprisingly weak not because only a few were disheartened about the changes in religion but because, lacking adequate communication and facing an unwillingness to challenge royal authority, the crown's critics were simply outmaneuvered.[11] Like Edmund in *King Lear*, Henry VIII, guided by the rapacious Thomas Cromwell, felt that he must have possession of land not given to him by inheritance or law. And, like Gonoril, the Crown had mistakenly understood law to be nothing more than an extension of the royal will—a view rejected by Gonoril's husband as "Most monstrous" (*HKL* 24.154–55).

The events of the Protestant revolution in England indeed destabilized much of English society in the sixteenth century, and *King Lear* does in fact reveal aspects of the social processes that were involved in this painful change from a country characterized by Catholic piety to a much more skeptical Protestant nation. One important factor was the cynicism with which the Crown approached the dissolution of the monasteries—a cynicism that may be gauged by Henry VIII's advice to the Scottish government. Secrecy is advised at the beginning to prevent the clergy from forming an opposition, then reliable commissioners ought to be sent to the abbeys "as it were to put a good order in the same" but in fact to collect information—and, we might add, to spread rumor, presumably about such things as the "unspeakable sin," sodomy—that could

---

[11] C. S. L. Davies, "Popular Religion and the Pilgrimage of Grace," in *Order and Disorder in Early Modern England*, ed. Anthony Fletcher and John Stevenson (Cambridge: Cambridge University Press, 1985), 58–91.

be used to destroy them. Thereafter, an agreement should be forged between the crown and "the chief of the noble men" who are to share the monastic lands "to their great profit and honor," while the bishops are to be bribed by offering "some augmentation of their resources." Others who were to be dispossessed should also be given financial incentives—further bribes—for leaving their monasteries.[12] It will be important to examine the entire milieu of Protestantization with view to a better understanding of the context of Q1 of *King Lear*.

The destruction of the monasteries, with their rich collections of religious art and their extensive libraries of illuminated manuscripts (so highly valued in modern times), was only a first step. The veneration of the saints, those whose relics were the precious possessions of so many churches from the time when Christianity had come to England, was denounced, and their images and candles came under attack. The desecration of holy images, wall paintings, sculptures, and even the altars of churches themselves had begun.[13] At Ely, for example, the magnificent relief sculptures of the Life of the Virgin in the Chapter House were vandalized at this time.[14] By 1547, chantries and religious guilds were outlawed and their properties confiscated, ostensibly as part of a reform program against the concept of Purgatory but certainly to the great financial benefit of the Crown. At Stratford-upon-Avon, the Guild of the Holy Cross, the Blessed Virgin Mary, and St. John the Baptist was dissolved, and the town was only allowed to retain its Guild Chapel,

---

[12] *Letters and Papers, Foreign and Domestic, of the Reign of Henry VIII*, 15:136, pt. 1, 364, as quoted by J. J. Scarisbrick, *The Reformation and the English People* (Oxford: Blackwell, 1984), 79.

[13] See Margaret Aston, *England's Iconoclasts, I: Laws Against Images* (Oxford: Clarendon Press, 1988); Eamon Duffy, *The Stripping of the Altars: Traditional Religion in England 1400–1580* (New Haven: Yale University Press, 1992); Clifford Davidson and Ann Eljenholm Nichols, eds., *Iconoclasm vs. Art and Drama*, Early Drama, Art, and Music Monograph Series 11 (Kalamazoo: Medieval Institute Publications, 1989); John Phillips, *The Reformation of Images* (Berkeley and Los Angeles: University of California Press, 1973); and Susan Brigden, *London and the Reformation* (Oxford: Clarendon Press, 1989).

[14] Clifford Davidson, "'The Devil's Guts': Allegations of Superstition and Fraud in Religious Drama and Art during the Reformation," in Davidson and Nichols, eds., *Iconoclasm vs. Art and Drama*, 122–27, figs. 18–22.

3. The Change in Religion: desecrating churches. John Foxe, *Actes and Monuments* (London, 1576), p. 1267. By permission of the Henry E. Huntington Library, San Marino, California.

across the street from the site of New Place, after the people of Stratford petitioned in February 1553 that they might be allowed to buy back the building that had been confiscated by the Crown.[15]

But worse was to come (see fig. 3). The reign of Edward VI not only witnessed the suppression of the familiar Latin service and the imposition of the new English rite, fortunately utilizing the glorious phrasing of

---

[15] *Minutes and Accounts of the Corporation of Stratford-upon-Avon*, ed. Richard Savage, 2 vols. (Dugdale Society, 1921), 1:1–22; *Victoria County History of the County of Warwick*, ed. Philip Styles, 8 vols. (London: Oxford University Press, 1945), 3:247.

Cranmer's *Book of Common Prayer*, but also saw commissioners going out to every church in the land ostensibly to inventory church goods. The extant inventories tell us much about the riches of the medieval churches and their colorful fabric, and they demonstrate how much was carted away to the Tower of London ostensibly for safe keeping—but never to be seen again. Each church was supposed to be allowed to keep only one chalice—not even a paten, apparently—of its own plate. Bells, plate, censers, and everything else of value were liable to be taken if they had not already been hidden away or sold by the churchwardens, who often were threatened because they had illegally disposed of Crown property. Churches were required to remove their roods with their supporting figures, usually Mary and John, since these were labeled idolatrous, along with other images.[16] The effect was to confuse people, who at this time became increasingly alienated from their churches.

Previously, the parish church had been at the very center of community life. Now, with the imposition of Protestantism, several signs are present to indicate that there would be a shift to a new center that may be regarded as much further from the sacred—the alehouse.[17] Likewise, the parish priest, who previously had so often been involved with the parishioner at the end of his or her life, not only being present to administer last rites but also to serve as a witness for the dying person's will, would no longer be so closely associated with his flock.[18] Mervyn James, in his study of the Durham region, has observed how the Protestant elite had only contempt for the local population.[19] Everywhere the religion of the people, loyal to their parish church which they had built and adorned with their generosity, was to be abandoned in favor of a more clergy-dominated religion with which they tended much less to identify themselves. Gifts and bequests to churches nearly disappeared, and the building of

---

[16] See Aston, *England's Iconoclasts*, 1:255–77; Duffy, *The Stripping of the Altars*, 480–503.

[17] Peter Clark, *The English Alehouse: A Social History 1200–1830* (London: Longman, 1983), 151–56.

[18] Duffy, *The Stripping of the Altars*, 523.

[19] Mervyn James, *Family, Lineage, and Civil Society: A Study of Society, Politics, and Mentality in the Durham Region 1500–1640* (Oxford: Clarendon Press, 1974), 59; see also Rosemary O'Day, *The English Clergy: The Emergence and Consolidation of a Profession 1558–1642* (Leicester: Leicester University Press, 1979), 190.

churches, which had gone on at a frenetic pace between the coming of the Black Death in 1349 and the Act of Supremacy, came to a virtual stop.

For the overwhelming majority of Englishmen the accession of Queen Mary came as a relief from the unpopular Protestantizing, but again there was failure—failure marked by her bloody repression of dissent. After her death, the Catholic cause was dissipated, though among many, especially in remotes areas like Lancaster and western Warwickshire, resistance was kept alive. Shakespeare may well have been raised in a family with Catholic sympathies,[20] even though it is recorded that his father as town chamberlain had been involved at the late date of 1563–64 in the "defasyng" of the wall paintings in the Guild Chapel at Stratford;[21] it is more certain that he died a papist,[22] and a strong argument has been entered for the retention of Catholic sympathies by the playwright himself. But what is important for our present inquiry is the sense of instability, the feeling of diminished belief, the perception of declining morals and behavior in the late sixteenth century and in the very early years of the next century. Such conditions are mirrored in Gloucester's complaint: "Love cools, friendship falls off, brothers divide; in cities mutinies, in countries discords, palaces treason, the bond cracked between son and father" (*HKL* 2.106–09). In late Elizabethan and early Jacobean England such factors might be blamed on the change in religion[23] (though, to be sure, others, especially in the Puritan camp, attributed the crisis to insufficient change and to the residue of superstition left over from medieval popular religion). The erosion of belief and morals—perceived, however correctly, across the entire spectrum of

---

[20] See H. Mutchmann and K. Wentersdorf, *Shakespeare and Catholicism* (1952; reprint New York: AMS Press, 1969), 35–50; Peter Milward, *Shakespeare's Religious Background* (Bloomington: Indiana University Press, 1973), 15–42.

[21] *Minutes and Accounts*, ed. Savage, 1:128. For extended discussion, see Clifford Davidson, *The Guild Chapel Wall Paintings at Stratford-upon-Avon* (New York: AMS Press, 1988).

[22] See Mutchmann and Wentersdorf, *Shakespeare and Catholicism*, 54–62, 369–97.

[23] See Robert Persons, *A Christian Directory*, rev. ed. (n.p., 1585), 862, for the argument that "deuision schisme and heresie, in matters of our faith," were causes of atheism: these, "by raising many doubtes and questions, and by contentious quarreling which it maintaineth, wearieth out a mans wit, and in the end bringeth him to care for no part, but rather to contemne all."

society[24]—verifiably concerned Shakespeare from the time when he wrote *Hamlet*, and his concern continues to be reflected in the great tragedies written by him in the following years. *Macbeth*, like *King Lear* completed in 1606 and with a hero who becomes a traitor and a cold-blooded killer even of children, is clearly informed by the horror of the abortive Gunpowder Plot,[25] a conspiracy that surely must have affected the playwright deeply since he was distantly related on his mother's side to actors in that drama—men who had met at Clopton House less than two miles outside of Stratford. This part of Warwickshire was central to the plot, and because they were his kinsmen some of the conspirators must have been known to the playwright.[26]

The vicissitudes of the reign of Queen Elizabeth, including the rebellion in 1569 and the queen's excommunication in the next year by the Pope, meant that the government would steer a cautious course, attempting to avoid both the extremes of religion, either open Romanism or contentious Puritanism, with the result that parishes were tended all too often by time-servers,[27] cautious men who could inspire few with their words—and, we recall, English Protestantism had so far as possible removed the visual dimension, the "books for the unlearned," as St. Gregory had designated religious images.[28] Both Roman Catholics and Puritans, though from vastly different perspectives, saw the rise of popular indifference as a great threat to morals and the practice of religion. The social conditions may indeed have been right for people to begin to free themselves from the older religious culture, to be sure, and there were those who were optimistic enough not only to desire a better future for England but also to hope for a more "enlightened" kingdom. The

---

[24] On the question of morality and behavior, see Keith Wrightson, *English Society 1580–1680* (New Brunswick: Rutgers University Press, 1982), 144–46, and Lawrence Stone, *The Crisis of the Aristocracy 1558–1680* (Oxford: Oxford University Press, 1965), 664–65.

[25] See Davidson, *The Primrose Way*, 59–61.

[26] Mutschmann and Wentersdorf, *Shakespeare and Catholicism*, 67–69 and Genealogical Charts C and D; and Williamson, *The Gunpowder Plot*, 124–79, esp. 149 for map.

[27] O'Day remarks that the first concern of Queen Elizabeth was not Protestantism in the clergy but their loyalty (*The English Clergy*, 26). For a slightly different view of the Anglican clergy, see Wrightson, *English Society*, 207.

[28] Ann Eljenholm Nichols, "Books for Laymen: The Demise of a Commonplace," *Church History* 56 (1987): 457–73.

Puritan wing of the English Church had a program for improving the religious condition of England and of its society as a whole.[29] But a pessimistic assessment of the possibilities for national improvement was also widespread. If the world, made up of fallible sons and daughters of Adam and Eve, is merely a "great stage of fools" (*HKL* 20.172), and if the England of antique times was as lacking in fixity as the present,[30] *King Lear* may then be seen as a dramatization that portrayed a nation where the "decentring" noted by Dollimore was a natural condition of communal life. If this is true, the presentation of life at the margins in the play would perhaps seem to be terribly revealing—e.g., the blinding and flight of Gloucester across the kingdom, the pretended madness of the fleeing Edgar, the clinically defined hysteria of the King himself. The prime example of "decentring" would, however, appear to be the mock trial, which was later to be eliminated in the Folio text of the play.[31]

But in a sense the term "decentring" is ultimately an inappropriate one, for *King Lear* is not in fact a play which lacks all aspects of traditional orientation. The fragmentation in the play does not in the final analysis lead to a presentation by the playwright of multi-faceted kinds of action inspired by a multiplicity of opinions. The impression of instability is instead mainly built upon a *binary* structure and, as the political and social order of the play disintegrates, is well described in terms of the *topos* of "the world upside down."[32] This "handy-dandy" world is a place where justice and crime are inverted (*HKL* 20.146–48) and where advancement is at least for a time dependent on duplicity and raw ambition.[33] If in this context fate is a factor, it is significant only in the sense of men's (and women's) weakness condemning them to an anti-

---

[29] See Wrightson, *English Society*, 204–05.

[30] Stephen Booth, *King Lear, Macbeth, Indefinition and Tragedy* (New Haven: Yale University Press, 1983), 1–11; cited by R. A. Foakes, *Hamlet* vs. *Lear: Cultural Politics and Shakespeare's Art* (Cambridge: Cambridge University Press, 1993), 64.

[31] For discussion of this scene, see Roger Warren, "The Folio Omission of the Mock Trial: Motives and Consequences," in Taylor and Warren, *The Division of the Kingdoms*, 45–57.

[32] See Clifford Davidson, "The Iconography of Wisdom and Folly," in *Shakespeare and the Emblem: Studies in Renaissance Iconography and Iconology*, ed. Tibor Fabiny (Szeged: Attila József University, 1984), 196–98; and Clifford Davidson *On Tradition: Essays on the Use and Valuation of the Past* (New York: AMS Press, 1992), 80–82, fig. 8.

[33] Cf. *HKL* 1:153–54: "kill thy physician, / And the fee bestow upon the foul disease."

utopia where the natural greed of selfish individuals will establish conditions from which rescue is required by transcendence, expressed in the acceptance of grace and the performance of good works even at the greatest risk imaginable to one's self. Such profound pessimism, paradoxically joined to an ultimate but qualified optimism concerning the power of grace, may be central to *King Lear*. "Time" does in fact "unfold what pleated cunning hides" (*HKL* 1.271) in the course of the play, and at the end the action verifies the validity of the *topos* "Truth is the daughter of Time" (*Veritas temporis filia*), a commonplace adopted first by Queen Mary and then as her own motto by Queen Elizabeth I.[34] The end of the play, which in the course of its action had displayed *inverted* values—a world *upside down*—thus, though not without tragedy of a most painful kind, achieves a kind of stasis, balance, even healing. And these values, Christian though allowing for a historical context of pre-Christian paganism in British antiquity, are a sign that Shakespeare in fact was not affirming the value of subversion, of skepticism linked to self-interest, of materialist analysis of forces whether cosmic or national or personal.

The most visible skeptic and materialist in the play is the libertine Edmund, the opportunist whose illegitimate ambition is represented as disruptive and cruel in the extreme. His skepticism is not that of Montaigne, who, we are to believe, harnessed his lack of certainty to the star of orthodox Catholicism in his *Apology for Raymond Sebond*, a work that was apparently known to Shakespeare in John Florio's translation.[35] On the contrary, Edmund represents the unscrupulousness of a Thomas Cromwell joined to the "atheism" reputed (inaccurately) to have found its way into English thought following the visit of Giordano Bruno in the 1580s.[36] Handsome and youthful, Edmund shows no sign of anxiety over

---

[34] John N. King, *Tudor Royal Iconography* (Princeton: Princeton University Press, 1989), 228–29.

[35] For Shakespeare's knowledge of Montaigne, see Muir's New Arden edition of *King Lear*, 249–53. For a survey of Renaissance skepticism, see Richard H. Popkin, *The History of Scepticism from Erasmus to Spinoza* (Berkeley and Los Angeles: University of California Press, 1979), *passim*, and Louis Bredvold, *The Intellectual Milieu of John Dryden* (Ann Arbor: University of Michigan Press, 1934), 16–46.

[36] Milward, *Shakespeare's Religious Background*, 195–214; cf. William R. Elton, *King Lear and the Gods* (San Marino: Huntington Library, 1966), 115–46.

God's silence in relation to him, and his death ultimately cannot be tragic after so wicked a life. His lack of belief in astrology or cosmic order—a belief which, however, he feigns in order to entrap Edgar—is not meant to demonstrate a new consciousness freed from the superstitions of the past, but rather to illustrate how his innovative behavior strikes at the very heart of community through its denial of the "bond" which links families and larger social units together. He is the primal individualist, philosophically the bedfellow not only of Pyrrho and Sextus Empiricus but also of Machiavelli as he was understood in the English Renaissance. As such he is a sign of the unstable times when ideals have collapsed upon themselves in a land where enforced beliefs have not necessarily brought forth the ideal social order or even the achievement of the quiet and peaceable life which the Pauline Epistles (1 Timothy 2:2) and the *Book of Common Prayer* represented as the ideal.

The skepticism inherent in the character of Edmund, however, is also more generally distributed in the play, which always presents it as a negative force. Rosalie Colie has observed that the gods worshipped in pagan antiquity in England are frequently the objects of derision in the play.[37] Edmund's statement that the "gods are just" (*HKL* 24.166) therefore is ultimately ironic, since Providence, especially in the terrible final act, seems, for example, to have abandoned the hero and heroine, Lear and Cordelia, whose deaths are nevertheless reminiscent of the martyrdom of the saints in the medieval saint plays. Suffering in Lear's case had already involved pain comparable to the depiction of the punishment of the proud in the woodcut in the various editions of the popular *Calendar of Shepherds*[38]—with the addition of flame to transform the punishing wheel into "a wheel of fire" causing him to weep tears that "scald like molten lead" (*HKL* 20.45–46). Gloucester's response to the seeming indifference of Providence is the famous line "As flies to wanton boys, are we to th' gods; / They kill us for their sport" (*HKL* 15.35– 36). It is a statement akin to Bosola's lament in *The Duchess of Malfi* (5.4.63–64) that "We are

---

[37] Rosalie L. Colie, "The Energies of Endurance: Biblical Echo in King Lear," in *Some Facets of* King Lear*: Essays in Prismatic Criticism*, ed. Rosalie Colie and F. T. Flahiff (Toronto: University of Toronto Press, 1974), 135.

[38] These editions, based on Guyot Marchant's *Calendrier de bergers* (1492), date from the period between the early sixteenth century and 1631; see Pollard and Redgrave, *Short Title Catalogue . . . 1475–1640*, nos. 22,407–23.

meerely the Starres tennys-balls (strooke, and banded / Which way please them)," which is in turn a Renaissance commonplace that reflects the fatalism inherent in the most rigid forms of Protestantism.[39] Calvin's denial of free will—a denial reflected in Article XVII of the Thirty-Nine Articles which insists on man's responsibility for sinful acts and on God's grace as responsible for all good works—was not guaranteed to inspire piety in all souls, but rather, as in Marlowe's *Doctor Faustus*, it was interpreted to encourage a literal turning away in despair at the seeming hopelessness of personal faith.[40] The instability of the social order when confronted with evil of the type represented by Gonoril and Regan—and by Edmund—is thus concurrent with the personal anxiety of the individual as reflected in characters with whom we can identify. The context is indicative of the crisis of belief in things transcendent, of trust in a world from which all coherence has departed. In the antique age of the Britain of Gonoril and Regan, atheism seemed to be threatening to become the national religion.

Skepticism and atheism are the inverse of faith and dutiful worship just as Protestant iconoclasm directed at holy images in the sixteenth century was the inverse of the respect and veneration of them in previous times. In a world that is properly oriented toward the heavenly city, such unacceptable world-views need to be identified as turning the truth inside out (see *HKL* 16.9, where Oswald reports that he has been accused of turning "the wrong side out") or achieving the condition of a "world upside down" reflected in the Fool's "we'll go to supper i'th'morning" (*HKL* 13.78) or in the commonplace of the "cart draw[ing] the horse" (*HKL* 4.218). Such an inversion of values involves a dramatic working out of an idea that has its modern correlative in Dostoyevski's probing of religionless and valueless man which may be rephrased thus: If there is no God, then I can do what I wish, even if I desire to do the most outrageous or perverse things imaginable. Gonoril and Regan are creatures of will, volition, uncontained by reason or conscience. As Elton indicates, it is remarkable "that Goneril never mentions the gods at all, an indication that her Renaissance garb has completely covered her natural condition; totally self-preoccupied with her lusts and the expansion of her will, she

---

[39] See Elton, *King Lear and the Gods*, 165–67.
[40] See the discussion of double predestination above, in "Marlowe, the Papacy, and *Doctor Faustus*."

is deaf to such counsels as Edgar's to Gloucester, 'do but look up' (IV.vi.59), and Edgar's to Lear, 'Look up, my Lord' (V.iii.312)."[41] Neither Gonoril nor Regan appears even remotely interested in religion as a means of controlling her subjects; these sisters consequently point only in the direction of pure nihilism. Embedded in their ambition are the seeds of the dissolution of their political power. Anti-values are corrosive, destructive, harmful to all those who would live in harmony with each other and with the natural order of things—a natural order that surely differs from the proto-Darwinian ("red in tooth and claw," to use Tennyson's words in *In Memoriam* [LVI.15]) (dis)order of Edmund, whose illegitimacy is more than simply a personal trait.[42] Subversion is subversive even to its own subversiveness.

Elizabethan audiences responded to stage violence—as previously medieval audiences had responded to violence in the mystery and saint plays[43]—but in the closure of the action of the play Shakespeare preferred to give some reassurance that the world is not an absurdist realm without coherence or redeeming values. It is no use reading *King Lear* as a play about a society alienated from God and waiting for a reasonably satisfactory close that does not in fact materialize. Yet the ending of this play is much less reassuring than we would like, and its crisis of belief is never quite healed. In his adaptation of scenic form derived ultimately from the medieval drama,[44] Shakespeare drew on public expectations for his depictions of suffering and martyrdom. These aspects are indebted to the stage works of the previous age with their representations of the martyrdom of saints and the Passion of Christ, though the structure of transgression and resolution in his plays marks a considerable departure from medieval practice.

Further, while Shakespeare sought to probe the weaknesses in the society of the early reign of his patron, King James I, he also attempted to reach back to make the past accessible, at least on the level of the

---

[41] Elton, *King Lear and the Gods*, 117.

[42] On the significance of Edmund's bastardy, see ibid., 132–33.

[43] See Davidson, *On Tradition*, 70–86.

[44] See Cherrell Guilfoyle, *Shakespeare's Play Within Play*, Early Drama, Art, and Music Monograph Series 12 (Kalamazoo: Medieval Institute Publications, 1990), 97–126. The term 'scenic form' was devised by Emrys Jones; see his *Scenic Form in Shakespeare* (Oxford: Clarendon Press, 1971).

imagination, and to make it available to those who sat or stood watching the play. In *King Lear* the ultimate critical questions remain difficult to answer. Is this play, which treats the problems of belief and of consequent questions of morality, in any way able to present an aesthetic experience that breaks through the historical veil and brings the reader or viewer into a relationship that overcomes the limitations of temporality? In spite of Dollimore's denial of transcendental values in the play, the cosmic perspective provides such an orientation and requires attitudes alert to permanent values even in the midst of the sea of uncertainty which is life.[45] Ultimately such a point of view must lead to understanding the play in terms of an aesthetic structure that lifts the audience up and in fact (to borrow Heidegger's terminology in his essay "The Origin of the Work of Art") deconceals Being,[46] for by placing the contemporary problem of belief within dramatic form Shakespeare has provided reference points by which human beings may come to terms with their own anxiety concerning earthly imperfection—the reality of evil in this world—and the possibility of transcendence and the redemptive power of grace.

The ancient story of King Lear as Shakespeare molded it was thus not simply a sensational tale designed to amuse a bored London theater audience, nor was it designed only to reveal the "social process" involved in a malignant patriarchy. It was instead a play that was directed to an audience still very aware of the insecurity by which the monarchy and indeed the whole government of England was supported, and it also affirmed the necessity of respect for hierarchy and custom—the latter a more valued matter for the playwright than for Francis Bacon, for example, who spoke in his essay "Of Custom and Education" about "the tyranny of custom" and who advised education to remold it into new and more acceptable forms.[47] *King Lear* was not intended to be egalitarian in spirit, but then it does not fail to remind us that some actions are more approved than others even when Providence does not come to the rescue to protect the good and punish the wicked.

---

[45] See Clifford Davidson, "Renaissance Dramatic Forms, Cosmic Perspective, and Alienation," *Cahiers Élisabethains* 27 (April 1985): 7–10.

[46] Martin Heidegger, *Poetry, Language, Thought*, trans. Albert Hofstadler (New York: Harper and Row, 1971), 15–87.

[47] Francis Bacon, *Works*, ed. James Spedding, Robert Leslie Ellis, and Douglas Denon Heath, 14 vols. (London: Longman, 1861), 6:470–72, esp. 471.

A final point may be made about the choice of Shakespeare's topic in writing *King Lear*. In the late sixteenth century and in the early years of the next century, the sense of loss for so many past traditions produced a feeling of nostalgia even among those who tended to be hostile to the old ways, especially in matters of religion and belief. Intense curiosity about the lost past could be joined to strident denunciation, as in the case of the only description of the pageant wagons used in the medieval civic drama of England; this account, from the early seventeenth century, appears in David Rogers's *Breviary*, which, drawn from his father's notes, is severely critical of the practice of presenting the religious dramas that had staged the history of the world from Creation to Doom at Chester prior to their suppression after 1575.[48] Such nostalgia spurred the "cult of antiquity" which encouraged looking back at England's past, including the long-ago period prior to the coming of the Romans to the island. Mervyn James notes correctly that the "sense of transience, nourished by religious, political, and social change, stimulated the sense of history," but he is only partly right when he continues by describing "the past [as] seeming the more poignant by contrast with the 'decay' of traditional values, which some could perceive around them, and the supposed stable permanence which antiquity had achieved."[49] *King Lear*, however, was among those plays by Shakespeare that undermined the idea of an ideal stability in past history; instead his point is the remarkably Christian conclusion that in this world there is no continuing city, but instead we are "strangers and sojourners" (see Lev. 25:23) without expectation of the cessation of intrigue or warfare in the here and now (and here I adopt a phrase designating certain bequests in pre-Reformation wills) "as long as the world shall stand." The process may destroy the good as well as the wicked, but the good will be honored, sometimes as saints, while the wicked will be held odious in memory.

---

[48] Lawrence M. Clopper, *Records of Early English Drama: Chester* (Toronto: University of Toronto Press, 1979), 238–39, 325, 355, 436. For Rogers's harsh indictment of the plays as "beinge nothinge profitable to anye vse excepte it be to show the Ignorance of oure forefathers," see ibid., 248. Shakespeare's opinion of the medieval civic drama differed significantly in being directed not against "superstition" but to its alleged lack of sophistication; see Davidson, *On Tradition*, 56–69.

[49] James, *Family, Lineage, and Civil Society*, 110.

Yet even here the situation is complex, for Edmund, the prime skeptic and libertine in *King Lear*, is in the end contrite and, as Elton suggests in words from Sonnet 124, becomes "one of Shakespeare's 'fools of time, / Which die for goodness, who have lived for crime'."[50] "The wheel is come full circled [*sic*]" (*HKL* 24.170), and Fortune, or Luck, has deposited him at the bottom. At this unhappy location where rising ambition has been followed by a fall from political power, some depictions in medieval iconography include an abyss into which the aspiring person is tumbling.[51] Certainly such a terrible end is to be understood for Gonoril and Regan, who are depicted as the unrepentant victims of their own misplaced aspirations. The justice of their deaths, as Albany says, "Touches us not with pity" (*HKL* 24.226–27). Their demise, however, establishes a distinct contrast to the deaths of Cordelia off-stage and King Lear before the audience's eyes. But these latter deaths can only be understood as tragic if the values of decency and goodness—values rooted in the transcendental—are affirmed. Here I can agree with Dollimore that the fissure opened up by the crisis of belief brought into being the conditions for tragedy,[52] but further I would assert that these same conditions enabled Shakespeare to assume a place as a major playwright within the Christian tradition as it had been handed over from generation to generation since the time of the Apostles and the Church Fathers.

---

[50] Elton, *King Lear and the Gods*, 146.

[51] Herrad of Hohenbourg, *Hortus Deliciarum*, ed. Rosalie Green *et al.*, 2 vols. (London: Warburg Institute, 1979), 2:351.

[52] Dollimore, *Radical Tragedy*, 8.

The Anxiety of Power and Shakespeare's *Macbeth*

In May 1603 the sharers in the Lord Chamberlain's Men, identified as "Lawrence Fletcher, William Shakespeare, Richard Burbage, Augustyne Phillippes, John Heninges, Henrie Condell, William Sly, Robert Armyn, Richard Cowly, and the rest of their associats," were licensed under a Royal Patent as the King's Players.[1] From henceforth they were designated as Grooms of the Chamber, associated with the household of the newly installed King James I, the son of Mary Queen of Scots who was himself a recent arrival from Scotland. James came to England with considerable Protestant and monarchist intellectual baggage, and within a little more than a year dissidents within his new kingdom would begin planning a spectacular challenge not only to their king's authority but also to the entire national government, both civil and ecclesiastical. The Gunpowder plotters, who by November 1605 were prepared to strike a blow that would destroy Parliament as the king addressed it, thus conspired to lop off the topmost branches of the British nation. Instead, the failed *coup d'etat* only succeeded in solidifying support for the monarchy and for the official ideology that was designed to support it. Catholics as well as Protestants roundly condemned the Plot as criminal and sacrilegious.[2]

---

[1] (London: Constable, 1910), 1:146; E. K. Chambers, *The Elizabethan Stage*, 4 vols. (Oxford: Oxford University Press, 1923): 1:311; Samuel Schoenbaum, *William Shakespeare: A Compact Documentary Life* (New York: Oxford University Press, 1977), 249.

[2] I recognize that the terms 'Protestant' and 'Catholic' are ambiguous in the context of Elizabethan and Jacobean England. A great many people were at heart Catholic and yet attended the services of the Church of England without objection; others did so because they were coerced to do so only. Recusancy, although encouraged by the Jesuit mission, was difficult, dangerous, and expensive. See Alexandra Walsham, *Catholicism, Conformity and Confessional Polemic in Early Modern England* (Woodbridge: Boydell Press, 1993), *passim*. There was also criticism by the more extreme Reformed element usually identified by the term 'Puritan' who tended to reject all forms of Catholic worship as well as the Church polity retained by the English Church. The Elizabethan settlement was in fact evolving, and with the philosophical base developed by Richard Hooker would develop into

The Protestant reaction to the Gunpowder Plot was immediate and hysterical, and its tenor may be gauged from the popular engravings which celebrated both the English victory over the Spanish Armada in 1588 and the discovery of the Plot on 5 November 1605 in side-by-side representations as signs that God was England's protector on each occasion.[3] In his speech before Parliament following the discovery of the Plot, James is reported to have compared the projected destruction of the entire national government to "*Domes-dayes*," like Noah's Flood and the coming day of the Last Judgment, "wherewith GOD threatned to destroy mee and all of you of this little world that haue interest in me."[4] That this also resonated in the theater among the King's Men we cannot doubt, for in the play that their principal playwright had under construction in the coming months we find the story of the killing of a king whose murder is reported in terms which identify the act as eliciting the very image of Doomsday. "Up, up, and see / The great doom's image," Macduff cries upon his discovery of King Duncan's bleeding body, and Lady Macbeth makes reference to the alarm bell as a "hideous trumpet [that] calls to parley / The sleepers of the house" (*Macbeth* 2.3.77– 78, 82–83).[5] The play was apparently completed in the summer of 1606 or at least not earlier than May of that year—that is, following the execution of the plotters and also the Jesuit Father Henry Garnet, who had prior knowledge of the plot. Garnet, as is well known, was the center of the controversy over equivocation that swirled about the sensational Gunpowder conspiracy—a controversy that is noticed in the drunken Porter's speech in which he imagines that he is porter of Hell Gate (2.3.9–12).

---

a more Catholic form of Anglicanism in the seventeenth century before the Civil Wars of the 1640s. I am here using the term 'Protestant' as shorthand for the Calvinistically and nationalistically inclined authorities and their wholehearted supporters.

[3] See, for example, the engraving designed by Samuel Ward, as illustrated in Oswald Tesimond, alias Greenway, *The Gunpowder Plot*, trans. Francis Edwards (London: Folio Society, 1973), pl. facing 48; and the title page of *A Thankfull Remembrance of Gods Mercie*, illustrated in Hugh Ross Williamson, *The Gunpowder Plot* (London: Faber and Faber, 1951), pl. facing 156.

[4] James I, *The Political Works*, introd. Charles Howard McIlwain (Cambridge: Harvard University Press, 1918), 282.

[5] Quotations are from *The Riverside Shakespeare*, gen. ed. G. Blakemore Evans, 2nd ed. (Boston: Houghton Mifflin, 1997), and are identified in my text by act, scene, and line numbers.

Henry Paul believed, on evidence that seems more slender today than half a century ago, that the drama was written and produced with the royal audience in mind and that the play's premier was a special production on 7 August 1606, during the visit of the King of Denmark, the brother of Queen Anne.[6] More recently Peter Thomson would still write that "*Macbeth* represents Shakespeare's most strenuous attempt to flatter James I."[7]

But if the play was intended *primarily* as a compliment to King James, one would hardly expect it to have focused on a regicide, the killing of a king of Scotland, especially since James was still king of that country in addition to his English crown. There is, to be sure, the patently flattering parade of the line of Banquo in act 4, scene 1, but even here it is a show put on by the witches, ambiguous creatures with powers derived from their devilish familiars—creatures who had been unequivocally condemned by the the king in his *Daemonologie*. While according to the prophecy the line of Banquo's descendants will "stretch out to th' crack of doom" (4.1.117) and thus will suggest a long rule for the house of Stuart, this "Horrible sight" (4.1.122) is credibly held to be demonic even by Macbeth, who pronounces the witches and their apparitions unreliable. When the "sisters" have vanished into thin air and Lenox has arrived on the scene, Macbeth curses even "the air whereon they ride" as well as those who, like himself, would attend to the witches' prophecies: "damned [be] all those that trust them" (4.1.138–39). Even the hour when the apparitions were set forth for him is to be "accursed in the calendar" (4.1.133–34).

The play, far from presenting the monarch as the rock upon which the realm might safely rest for generations hereafter,[8] reinforces a fear that the king's leadership would place him in a peculiar position of great danger in the realm—and that the danger to the king meant very real danger to the state which he represented. If James arrogated to himself the title of a "god" in little, set above his nation in the natural chain of Being

---

[6] Henry N. Paul, *The Royal Play of Macbeth* (New York: Macmillan, 1950), 329–30.
[7] Peter Thomson, *Shakespeare's Professional Career* (Cambridge: Cambridge University Press, 1992), 177.
[8] The rock was traditionally a symbol of stability and strength, as in Geffrey Whitney, *A Choice of Emblemes* (Leiden: C. Plantin, 1586), 96.

by the authority of the great God,[9] the Gunpowder conspiracy demonstrated that it was possible to challenge this order of things.[10] Indeed, the kingship might by itself prove to be an irresistible magnet to draw forth conspirators against the crown. Macbeth's irrational urge to overthrow the king, abetted by the prophecies of the witches and perhaps inspired by their gift of the evil eye,[11] may thus be seen as a sign of the lack of stability inherent in kingly power. Previously Queen Elizabeth I had been threatened by conspiracies and rebellions, and now James too would be the target of assassination by English hands. The murder of Duncan, who at the beginning of the play already has required the help of the loyal Scottish aristocracy to put down rebellion and foreign invasion, may therefore appear to mirror a contemporary threat to good order and to stable government by a king.

King James, who wanted very much to present himself as a wise monarch, also wished to be seen as the perfect embodiment of divine right. His sagacity was allegedly demonstrated, for example, in his decoding of the Monteagle letter that revealed the secret of the Gunpowder plotters. As a way of fashioning himself as an exemplary monarch he had himself represented on coins on horseback or seated on a throne, positioned between the pillars of Hercules,[12] the latter originally borrowed from an *impresa* designed for Charles V and adapted by Queen Elizabeth after the defeat of the Spanish Armada.[13] It would seem that thereby

---

[9] James I, *The Political Works*, 281.

[10] I am assuming that the Gunpowder Plot was not a conspiracy organized by the government of James as a propaganda ploy against English Catholics, but cf. Williamson, *The Gunpowder Plot, passim*. In any case, there is no likelihood that Shakespeare or most of his contemporaries, Catholic or Protestant, would have immediately suspected a government conspiracy except in the sense that the government conspired to allow the Plot to go forward after its discovery until a convenient time at which it might be "discovered" by the wise king himself.

[11] See Clifford Davidson, *The Primrose Way: A Study of Shakespeare's* Macbeth (Conesville, Iowa: John Westburg and Associates, 1970), 45.

[12] Jonathan Goldberg, *James I and the Politics of Literature* (Baltimore: Johns Hopkins University Press, 1983), fig. 10.

[13] Francis Yates, *Astraea: The Imperial Theme in the Sixteenth Century* (1975; reprint Harmondsworth: Penguin, 1977), 54–58; Roy Strong, *The Cult of Elizabeth* (Berkeley and Los Angeles: University of California Press, 1977), 154.

4. Fortune shakes down rewards for those who grasp for them. Cesare Ripa, *Iconologia* (Venice, 1669), page 227.

James wished to claim imperial power and, as a Protestant rather than a Catholic prince, wanted to position himself in relation not only to his people but also to the world beyond. Significantly, the king expected to be depicted as one raised up, either on a dais or throne, or on the back of a horse in an imperial pose. In the edition of his *Basilicon Doron* published in 1603 he had asserted that the role of the king involved being "*set (as it was said of old) vpon a publike stage, in the sight of all the people,*" and in the main text of his treatise he had written that "It is a trew old saying, That a King is as one set on a stage, whose smallest actions and gestures, all the people gazingly doe behold."[14] The king's outward appearance and stature are the basis of the people's judgment and hence are seen to be of very great importance for the reality of royal power. But to be placed on a stage logically also exposes the king more surely to dangers—dangers that would not be shared by persons among the lower orders of people in the commonwealth, where safety lies in their humble station in life. Kingly power presupposes anxiety about its role and maintenance.

The great, particularly the king who is the greatest of them all, among the people of a nation conventionally were regarded as most subject to fortune and chance. The iconography of Fortune's wheel is very well known and hardly needs comment here. Commonly Fortune, blind or blindfolded, stands turning her wheel, on which the rising figure at the left is being lifted up as Macbeth was in the early part of the play; then the next stage is to rule, but only temporarily, whereupon comes the fall of the one who has reigned, represented by the man tumbling from the right side of the wheel. Deep-seated suspicion of ambition was implied in such iconography, as articulated, for example, in Herrad of Hohenbourg's *Hortus Deliciarum* in which the final stage of man's fall shows a figure plunging into an abyss below.[15] In Cesare Ripa's *Iconologia* Fortune may be presented in a different way, as a nude figure, bald behind and with a flowing forelock like the traditional depiction of Occasion. A later woodcut (fig. 4), not present in the 1603 edition, shows Fortune aloft and shaking down crowns, scepters, miters, helmets, and other symbols of authority from a tree to those who greedily grasp for them below.[16] In the Hertel edition of the *Iconologia*, the artist interprets Ripa's text in another way: Fortune is standing precariously on a ball, which is a common sign of instability.[17] The association of height and of trees with the winds of chance was likewise commonplace, and informs an emblem (fig. 5) in Henry Peacham's *Minerva Britanna* of 1612; here the "loftie Pines" which "support the state / Of common wealthes, and mightie govern-

---

[14] James I, *The Political Works*, 5, 43.

[15] Herrad of Hohenbourg, *Hortus Deliciarum*, ed. Rosalie Green *et al.*, 2 vols. (London: Warburg Institute, 1979), 2:351.

[16] Cesare Ripa, *Iconologia* (Venice: Niccolò Pezzana, 1669), 227.

[17] Cesare Ripa, *Baroque and Rococo Pictorial Imagery: The 1758–60 Hertel Edition of Ripa's Iconologia*, ed. Edward A. Maser (New York: Dover, 1971), 152.

5. An exposed tree is more susceptible to wind. Henry Peacham, *Minerva Britanna* (1612), p. 68. By permission of the Glasgow University Library, Department of Special Collections.

ment" are said to "stoope . . . soon'st, vnto the blast of fate."[18] This emblem is closely related to James's statement to Parliament in 1605 that "all mankinde, so chiefly Kings, as being in the higher places like the high Trees, or stayest Mountaines, and steepest Rockes, are most subiect to the dayly tempest of innumerable dangers; and I amongst all other Kings haue euer bene subiect vnto them...."[19]

James, like the Tudors before him, was deeply concerned about the dangers against which the monarch lacked immunity. As the king explained to Parliament after the discovery of the Gunpowder Plot, he had first been exposed to mortal danger while he "was yet in my mothers belly," and as a young king in Scotland he was in constant danger.[20] Following the Gowrie conspiracy in 1600 he had even more reason to

---

[18] Henry Peacham, *Minerva Britanna (1612)* (Leeds: Scolar Press, 1966), 60.
[19] James I, *The Political Works*, 282.
[20] Ibid.

remain continually fearful—a natural consequence of such a traumatic experience. Nor was he safe from treason upon his arrival in England. Further, he also had observed the fortunes of his mother, who was eventually executed by her cousin Elizabeth's counselors in 1587. When he became king of England, he made use of the system of informers which had been developed under the Tudors and had served in lieu of a police force to ferret out not only subversion but also, more significantly, religious nonconformity. The bad reputation of James's spies—and of Elizabeth's before him—seems reflected in Macbeth's tyrannical use of such agents in Scottish households: "There's not a one of them, but in his house / I keep a servant fee'd" (3.4.130–31). Scotland has become a land of fear: "where nothing, / But who knows nothing, is once seen to smile" (4.3.166–67). These lines seem to echo the state of things in many Catholic households, where priests said Mass and hid in special priest holes such as the ones still to be seen in the Throckmortons' Warwickshire house, Coughton Court.[21] And when captured these members of the Roman clergy were subjected to terrible torture and bloody execution.

Leslie Hotson has linked Shakespeare to the network of Catholic families in the Midlands that suffered under the religious persecution of the reigns of Elizabeth and James I,[22] and recent scholarship has tended to corroborate the connection.[23] His mother's family was apparently solidly Roman Catholic, his father had literally pledged himself to the Old Religion in a document that was discovered in the eighteenth century, and one daughter, Susanna, was cited in 1606 as "popishly affected,"[24] while another, Judith, married into a family that was distantly related to the Gunpowder plotters.[25] Indeed, Warwickshire was a center for Catholic missionary activity in the period when Shakespeare was growing up, and it has been speculated that the future playwright was possibly swept up

---

[21] See Nikolaus Pevsner and Alexandra Wedgwood, *Warwickshire* (Harmondsworth: Penguin, 1966), 246.

[22] Leslie Hotson, *I, William Shakespeare* (London: Jonathan Cape, 1937), 172–202.

[23] Gary Taylor, "Forms of Opposition: Shakespeare and Middleton," *English Literary Renaissance* 24 (1994): 290–314; Richard Wilson, "Shakespeare and the Jesuits: New connections supporting the theory of the lost Catholic years in Lancashire," *Times Literary Supplement*, no. 4942 (19 Dec. 1997): 11–13.

[24] E. A. J. Honigmann, *Shakespeare: The "Lost Years"* (Manchester: Manchester University Press, 1985), 116. Susanna was later to marry Dr. John Hall, regarded as a Puritan.

[25] Hotson, *I, William Shakespeare*, genealogical chart facing 144.

in enthusiasm for the faith. In his childhood his schoolmasters, Simon Hunt and John Cottom, at the Stratford school were Catholic not only in sympathy but in fact.[26] His father's absences from church services at Stratford's parish church were, he claimed, due to his fear of attainment for debt. Adherence to the Old Religion was the most likely factor, since to have been openly a recusant would have cost ruinous fines that would quickly have destroyed him financially. John Shakespeare's wealth was, however, substantial before the mid-1570s, when he apparently went into a period of decline.[27] In c.1580 he had signed a Spiritual Testament, written by St. Charles Borromeo, by which he made a profession of loyalty to the Roman Church.[28] He seems to have died a Catholic, and it is not absolutely certain beyond all doubt that his son William also did not die "a papist," as Richard Davies, former chaplain of Corpus Christi College, Oxford, claimed.[29] Recent discoveries have given some support to the hypothesis of E. A. J. Honigmann[30] and others that Shakespeare's "lost years" were spent in Lancashire in Catholic households. In London thereafter he associated with such men as Ben Jonson, who was for many years a Catholic and who supped with the Gunpowder plotters at William Patrick's house in the Strand in October 1605.[31] Yet, as a playwright and player in the King's Men, it would seem that Shakespeare never, at least as a mature adult, would have had sympathy for the radicalism of the plotters or with their agenda. In this regard he was much like the English Catholics, the majority of whom prayed for toleration though they had lost hope that the "Old Religion" would be actually restored as the religion of all England at any time in the near future. Still, the Catholic

---

[26] Honigmann *Shakespeare*, 40–49; Wilson, "Shakespeare and the Jesuits," 11–13.

[27] D. L. Thomas and N. E. Evans, "John Shakespeare in the Exchequer," *Shakespeare Quarterly* 45 (1984): 315–18.

[28] Peter Milward, *Shakespeare's Religious Background* (Bloomington: Indiana University Press, 1973), 20–21, 44.

[29] Chambers, *The Elizabethan Stage*, 2:257. Honigmann, on the basis of Shakespeare's will, believes that he died a Protestant (*Shakespeare: The "Lost Years,"* 9). It would probably be safer to say that he died an Anglican, submitting to the broader Church of England as it was evolving—a Church which had found room, if not particularly comfortable room, for people who would have preferred much of what the "Old Religion" represented. The matter is not fully settled.

[30] Honigmann, *Shakespeare: The "Lost Years,"* 18–39. Again, the matter is definitely not settled.

[31] Hotson, *I, William Shakespeare*, 187.

connection, tentative though we must be about defining many of the specifics, would seem to explain the uniqueness of the playwright's intellectual stance and his writing of plays that represent kingship as problematic in relation to matters of power and control even in dramas designed for staging in the royal presence.

Shakespeare, as a playwright working in the theater in late Elizabethan London, had frequently emphasized the precarious and ambiguous power of the throne in his history plays, including *Richard II* with its deposition scene that remained censored and unpublished while Elizabeth was alive.[32] On a well-known occasion in 1601 his *Richard II*, including its deposition scene, was revived in order to support the conspiracy of Essex and his co-conspirators, though Shakespeare's company, which had mounted the play at their request, insisted later that they had no knowledge of the abortive real-life coup.[33] By the time the composition of *Macbeth* was underway, however, the playwright was in the midst of writing his greatest tragedies, which would analyze the problem of royal power in even greater detail than in the histories. In *Hamlet* the reigning monarch is the corrupt and slippery Claudius, who has murdered his way to the throne and whose authority therefore lacks legitimacy, and in *King Lear* the story focuses on a king who gives away his symbols of rule and his royal authority to his two evil daughters, who represent an egregious abuse of power thereafter. The themes of insecurity, legitimacy, and abuse, set off against a pattern of civil disorder and anarchy, had, of course, been already honed in the histories. The uneasy crown on Henry IV's head only is taken from him at his death, and then by his son Hal, but the king's ambition and Machiavellian rise are shown early in his reign to serve to draw forth rebellion to challenge the Lancastrian king. And the rebellion is no small matter. One rebel, the prominent Archbishop of York, Richard Scrope, who was regarded locally after his death in 1405 as a saint and whose image still appears in stained glass in the choir

---

[32] Chambers, *The Elizabethan Stage*, 1:353–55.

[33] Essex and his fellow conspirators apparently, like many "post-modern" theorists, woefully overestimated the power of the stage. As Peter W. M. Blayney has conclusively demonstrated, playbooks were not a particularly impressive part of the market for books ("The Publication of Playbooks," in *A New History of Early English Drama*, ed. John D. Cox and David Scott Kastan [New York: Columbia University Press, 1997], 383–422, esp. 416)—a sign of a more modest role for the stage generally in the sixteenth and early seventeenth centuries.

clerestory at York Minster,[34] would be part of the conspiracy against King Henry. The subsequent internal history of England in the fifteenth century was likewise unstable and, for the monarchs, a slippery arena for the display of power. The chaos of the times was to culminate in the reign of Richard III, depicted by Shakespeare in one of his early plays as the villain unfit for rule of the Tudor history books, which had already transformed his reputation for piety into hypocrisy.[35] As a bloody-handed killer of children who have claims to royalty, Shakespeare's Richard is presented as a villain who seems to be a more slick cousin of Herod, a type which had in fact appeared in the splendid amateur theater of Coventry in the pageant of the Shearmen and Taylors—a pageant that the boy Shakespeare from nearby Stratford would almost certainly have witnessed before the suppression of Coventry's Corpus Christi cycle in 1579. His description of theatrical ranting, "it out-Herods Herod" (in *Hamlet* 3.2.14), seems to be a remembrance of the Coventry Herod who, according to the stage directions of the Shearmen and Taylors' text, "ragis in þe pagond [wagon] and in the strete also" (l. 729 *s.d.*).[36] Shakespeare's handling of kingship is, of course, more subtle than this since Herod's anxiety is of the broadest and crudest sort.

The focus of much earlier scholarship, including some of my own, was on the handling of rebellion as studied against the theory of an ideal monarchical political order, but it also called attention to the providential British history of the period leading up to Queen Elizabeth. There is no doubt that the official royalist doctrines were reflected in *Macbeth*, written at a time—perhaps the only time after his initial arrival in the country—when King James achieved genuine popularity. The killing of Duncan, for example, is presented in imagery that embeds references to

---

[34] Clifford Davidson and David E. O'Connor, *York Art*, Early Drama, Art, and Music Reference Series 1 (Kalamazoo: Medieval Institute Publications, 1978), 172. Archbishop Scrope also had been represented in the painted glass in St. Mary's Hall, Coventry; see Clifford Davidson and Jennifer Alexander, *The Early Art of Coventry, Stratford-upon-Avon, Warwick, and Lesser Sites in Warwickshire*, Early Drama Art, and Music Reference Series 4 (Kalamazoo: Medieval Institute Publications, 1985), 50.

[35] See Anne F. Sutton and Livia Visser-Fuchs, *The Hours of Richard III* (Phoenix Mill, Gloucestershire: Alan Sutton, 1990).

[36] I quote from *The Coventry Corpus Christi Plays*, ed. Pamela M. King and Clifford Davidson, Early Drama, Art, and Music Monograph Series 27 (Kalamazoo: Medieval Institute Publications, 2000).

the betrayal and crucifixion of Christ, as Roy Walker suggested long ago,[37] and the crime is unsuccessful in establishing civic order, as the Elizabethan *Homilies* said would be the case following the violent overthrow of a monarch. The orthodox Tudor and Jacobean political doctrines are part of the intellectual milieu of Shakespeare's plays. Nevertheless, it is absolutely true that there is much more than a mere display of the official party line to be seen in a play such as *Macbeth* or in Shakespeare's history plays, for the playwright's inherent interest in the consequences of the urge to power displays the futility of ambitious acts and the anxiety with which power will be accompanied. At the same time there is hope in his work for the achievement of a stable order in which religion and civil society can flourish. To be sure, then, Richmond's return to England, his marriage to Elizabeth of York, and his achievement of the throne are depicted as fortuitous in ultimately achieving peace and prosperity, which should endure in spite of vicissitudes throughout the reign of the granddaughter of Henry VII. Yet Shakespeare also confirmed his deep sympathy for St. Thomas More, martyred by Henry VIII, since his contribution to the play of *Sir Thomas More* revealed considerable feeling in favor of the legendary Londoner. Ambition in kings could be brutal and tyrannical, but nevertheless the playwright recognized that the lack of power, as in the case of Lear, only created a gap into which a more wicked person or persons could step. The dilemma is that royal power is necessary, while at the same time it is always capable of being abused to a lesser or greater degree.

Shakespeare's ambiguous attitude toward power, then, is part of the great attractiveness of his work, and more than anything this may be the reason that he was for so long celebrated for his "greatness of mind" and his essential humanity. He was one who could simultaneously give sympathetic treatment to Catherine of Aragon in his *Henry VIII* and celebrate, through Cranmer's words, the birth of Princess Elizabeth as a "royal infant" who "yet now promises / Upon this land a thousand thousand blessings, / Which time shall bring to ripeness" (5.4.17–20). While it is also clear that he accepted a large portion of the Elizabethan ideal of kingship with its emphasis on the identification of the monarch with the people, he also saw the glaring ways in which the administration

---

[37] Roy Walker, *The Time Is Free* (London: Andrew Dakers, 1949), 53–55.

of Elizabeth acted when it regarded its authority to be threatened—ways that today would be classified as violations of basic human rights, anachronistic though it may seem to apply this Enlightenment concept here. In *Macbeth* the playwright would take the negative side of kingship as he knew it, and he would dwell upon the consequences of a truly bad king who in the course of the play must therefore totally lose the sympathy of his people. Macbeth is a king who represents the violation of his office from the very beginning of his reign, since his accession to the throne is tainted by an offense against the legitimate succession and by the criminal act through which he has placed himself on the throne. In the view of Rossaeus (William Reynolds) in the exposition of J. N. Figgis, the king's "power is given *in aedificationem*, it must not be used *in destructionem*."[38] The king rightly is to serve the commonwealth, but Macbeth represents an extreme disjuncture between monarch and people which may legitimately result in his deposition, as Catholic political theory taught.[39] This ruler therefore through his illegitimate acts makes himself particularly vulnerable and insecure, but the solution to the situation is hardly the one argued in the *Homily Against Disobedience and Wilful Rebellion*, which was written in response to the Northern Rebellion in 1569[40] and countered the bull *Regnans in excelsis* by Pope Pius V in 1570.[41] The *Homily* proclaimed essentially that "the first founder of rebellion and graund captayne of all rebels" was Satan.[42] Since rebellion never has right on its side, the wrongs committed by a ruler must be endured in submission with prayers for the ruler's amendment. In its most rigid form, this political doctrine claimed that even disloyal thoughts are not to be permitted. As Sir Edward Coke argued at the trial of the Gunpowder plotters, "It is treason to imagine or intend the death of the King, Queen, or Prince."[43]

---

[38] J. N. Figgis, *Political Thought from Gerson to Grotius, 1414–1625*, 2nd ed. (1916; reprint New York: Harper, 1960), 183.

[39] Ibid., 184–85; and John Bossy, "The Character of Elizabethan Catholicism," in *Crisis in Europe 1560–1660*, ed. Trevor Aston (New York: Basic Books, 1965), 237.

[40] *Certain Sermons or Homilies (1547) and A Homily Against Disobedience and Wilful Rebellion*, ed. Ronald B. Bond (Toronto: University of Toronto Press, 1987), 40–45.

[41] *The Tudor Constitution: Documents and Commentary*, ed. G. R. Elton (Cambridge: Cambridge University Press, 1960), 414–18.

[42] *Certain Sermons*, ed. Bond, 235.

[43] David Jardine, *Criminal Trials*, 2 vols. (London, 1832–35), 2:123.

In his depiction of Macbeth as a thoroughly bad rebel-king, Shakespeare likewise depicted his character as similar to Lucifer, whose attempt at revolution in heaven led to his downfall and whose ambition was thereafter held to be the model for all earthly pride and rebellion.[44] Also Macbeth's entrance into criminality further replicates in part the fall of Adam, especially in the matter of the role of Eve as temptress.[45] There are, in other words, human factors grounded in the post-lapsarian condition that serve to make life dangerous and precarious for even the most sainted kings—and in Duncan Shakespeare apparently wanted to create a monarch whose stature would differ significantly from the feeble king of Holinshed's *Chronicles*. Macbeth, in contrast to Duncan, is darkened in the course of the play's action to the point where he will also become linked with the archetypal figure of despair, the betrayer Judas, whose suicide and consignment to hell were the result of his total lack of hope, his belief in himself as one who was beyond the possibility of forgiveness. But the sickness unto death which Macbeth represents has also become the source of general disease in the body of the state, and health can only return from outside Scotland's boundaries—that is, from England, the country over which the sainted King Edward the Confessor reigns. If King James had been so bad a king as this, we would expect the dramatist to have approved the actions of the Gunpowder plotters. But Shakespeare was neither sympathetic to the lunatic fringe of Catholic society nor insensitive to the human cost of the success of such an endeavor. Further, as a member of the king's household at the time following the discovery of the plot when James's reputation was at a high peak, he apparently joined the overwhelming majority of people, Protestant and Catholic, in seeing the Gunpowder Plot as heinous. Revealing nervousness about the succession in the case of a *coup d'etat*, Shakespeare posits in his play the worst possible case, and he makes the bad ruler credible since he has opened the action with a character who represents a man of ideals whom we thereafter see corrupted by stages until in the end he is only a hollow shell of a human being.

The comparison between Herod and Macbeth is also useful but only up to a point. Macbeth, like Herod, attempts to cut off a young royal

---

[44] See Irving Ribner, *Patterns in Shakespearian Tragedy* (London: Methuen, 1962), 155–57.

[45] L. A. Cormican, "Medieval Idiom in Shakespeare," *Scrutiny* 17 (1950–51): 312–13.

claimant, in this case Fleance, and furthermore at the crisis of the play he goes on a child-killing spree. In the Coventry Shearmen and Taylors' pageant, Herod's soldiers were sent by the irascible king on a mock-chivalric mission to kill all possible candidates so that "thatt kerne of Bedlem . . . schal be ded" and the event foretold in prophecy prevented (ll. 729–30). The killing of Macduff's children in *Macbeth* likewise follows upon a prophecy, in this case one derived from a demonic rather than divine source. The episode seems specifically designed to awaken the audience to the king's tyranny. Unlike the dolls apparently used in the Coventry play to represent the Innocents, actual child players are required in *Macbeth*, and their murder signals the point where the audience is to abandon the king to his fate.[46] The scene is a powerful one, and it gives emphasis to Macbeth's extreme malevolence and, indirectly, to his sterility (see 4.2.216: "he has no children"). From this scene until he is "ripe for shaking" (4.3.238) the time will not be long, and thereafter the day is "near at hand, / That chambers will be safe" once more (5.4.1–2). The comparison of the tyrant to a tree now to be shaken is consistent with the imagery of instability both in the play and in proverbial lore. Authority over a nation may be achieved by a tyrant like Macbeth, but its exercise as unalloyed power, unscrupulous and self-directed, can only lead to catastrophe. If power even in the most ideal of circumstances is synonymous with anxiety and insecurity, the mad "butcher" of Scotland, who has used every technique of tyranny, is all the more proof that political control is hopeless as a substitute for the willing obedience and loyalty of a people.

The predicament in Scotland under Macbeth is far more extreme than it was in Protestant England, where to be sure pursuivants were always available to betray lay Catholics and priests ordained abroad, the latter being subjected to terrible torture and brutal execution, as in the cases of Edmund Campion, whose direct contact with Shakespeare and his family has been argued, and of the playwright's schoolfellow Robert Debdale.[47] Macbeth's Scotland is a land "[w]here sighs, and groans, and shrieks that rent the air / Are made, not mark'd; where violent sorrow seems / A modern ecstasy" (4.3.168–70). The cure for this extreme illness, depicted as like a most terrible visitation of the plague, will come from outside, as

---

[46] Davidson, *The Primrose Way*, 77–78.
[47] Wilson, "Shakespeare and the Jesuits," 11–12.

noted above, from England where the Catholic king, Edward the Confessor, reigns. A scene in the play is devoted to Edward's touching for the King's Evil as a sign of his ability to bring health, and indeed he is represented as the ideal English king about whose throne "sundry blessings hang" (4.3.157). Shakespeare and his contemporaries would have been aware of St. Edward's shrine, which after its desecration had been restored though not to its former thirteenth-century glory by the last abbot of Westminster Abbey, John Feckenham. As a memorial to an English king, Elizabeth had allowed the shrine to remain, and it is still in its place in the abbey in the present day. Elizabeth and James had also both claimed the right to touch for the King's Evil,[48] and it was an element in their claims to legitimacy as English monarchs—claims which Shakespeare does not deny. Yet the defense of revolutionary action against the evil king in *Macbeth* very much does run strongly counter to the Tudor and Jacobean doctrine of kingship which was designed in the first instance to counteract the bull *Regnans in excelsis* and also to proclaim as if by fiat a stable monarchy.

The inability of Macbeth and his wife to sleep in the play provides almost a parodying of the famous Rainbow Portrait of Queen Elizabeth at Hatfield House with its portrayal of her cloak emblazoned with myriad eyes and ears that represent her awareness of all that is occurring in the realm. In the portrait the queen appears as Astraea, who is the personification of Justice returned to the earth; she is the sun which is the source of the rainbow that she holds and that is a conventional symbol of hope.[49] Light is implied in her chosen motto, *Veritas temporis filia*, which is connected with a popular emblem showing Time bringing Truth out of a dark cave.[50] In contrast, the paranoia ascribed to Macbeth, whose reign is spoken of in terms of darkness, causes him to remain always wakeful and fearful, always threatened by the fear that the truth will be revealed and his power taken away. Yet he has a perceived need to know his fate. Fearing "the worst," he will choose to seek "[b]y the worst means" to

---

[48] Paul, *The Royal Play*, 368–77.

[49] Strong, *The Cult of Elizabeth*, 50–53 and frontispiece; cf. Yates, *Astraea*, 216–19.

[50] Fritz Saxl, "Veritas filia temporis," in *Philosophy and History: Essays Presented to Ernst Cassirer*, ed. Raymond Klibansky and H. J. Paton (New York: Harper and Row, 1963), 197–222; see also John N. King, *Tudor Royal Iconography* (Princeton: Princeton University Press, 1989), 229.

know what lies ahead (3.4.133–34). Yet it will need to be remembered that the Rainbow Portrait, painted for the Cecil family near the end of Elizabeth's reign, provides a sanitized and flattering representation of the aged queen's role during her reign in authorizing the ferreting out of information through the use of professional spies and of officially sanctioned torture. It is the dark side of the Tudor and Jacobean monarchy that finds its way into the distillation of evil in *Macbeth*, where the alertness of officialdom is transformed into paranoia far more extreme than James's, and the pursuivants and administrators of English justice into criminal death squads and total repression of a people.

Upon the establishment of a new regime by Malcolm at the end of the play, the exiles who "fled the snares of watchful tyranny" will be called home to Scotland (5.9.32–33), and those things are promised which are needful to be done to create a free society. As Macduff holds up the "usurper's cursed head," he proclaims: "the time is free" (5.9.21). While Time has indeed brought into the open the crimes of the criminal (that is, what Macbeth's cunning has hidden) just as, according to Coke, it had revealed the perfidy of the Gunpowder plotters,[51] there is nevertheless an element of uncertainty implied in the play's conclusion. It may be assumed that at the end the playwright intended the despairing Macbeth to be regarded as damned, his soul "[g]iven to the common enemy of man," a fate predicted by the usurper himself earlier in the play (3.1.68). His head, severed from his body, would presumably have been destined for the usual exposure (after boiling to preserve it). Thus the heads of the Gunpowder plotters Robert Catesby and Thomas Percy had been placed over the House of Lords as a deterrent to others' ambitions.[52] But as the playwright knew from his reading of Holinshed and other sources, the death and deposition of Macbeth was not the end of the story, for Malcolm, whose reign did much to encourage Christianity in Scotland, was to be followed by his brother Donalbain, who initially had fled "[t]o Ireland" (2.3.138) and who upon his return was revealed to be, like Macbeth, an unsatisfactory ruler. When we look back at Donalbain's speech upon their flight in act 1, the irony becomes all the more evident: "our separated fortune / Shall keep us both the safer" (2.3.138–39).

Like most of Shakespeare's other tragedies, *Macbeth* has a plot which

---

[51] See Antonia Fraser, *Faith and Treason* (Garden City, N.Y.: Doubleday, 1996), 225.
[52] Hotson, *I, William Shakespeare*, 199.

leads the audience (or readers) through a demonstration of the fragility of rulership and the instability of power to a resolution that more or less patches things over with the appearance of benign stasis. Here and elsewhere in Shakespeare's work the temptations of ambition and innovation are shown to be snares, while the will to power is an exercise in illusion in spite of the need for authority to help to regulate civic society. It is, then, in the nature of Shakespearian tragedy to "untune the string" of individual and/or civic harmony and to observe the dislocation that follows when the regular order of the society is fractured: "hark what discord follows" (*Troilus and Cressida* 1.3.109–10). The Great Chain of Being, an idea described at great length by Arthur O. Lovejoy,[53] is one of the components of Shakespeare's plays, as we might expect from an author who was the son of the sometime chamberlain of Stratford-upon-Avon. Oligarchies that controlled towns in the fifteenth and sixteenth centuries were very conscious of status at the same time that they regularly participated in rituals affirming the unity of the civic organization.[54] Merchants and craftsmen alike took their position in the social hierarchy seriously, both in market towns like Stratford and in larger cities. At Coventry the guilds participating in the Corpus Christi procession through the city were given their specific places according to their prestige, which might differ considerably from their level of wealth.[55] But it was the rule in such processions that "the last shall be first," according to the biblical command in Matthew 19:30, a passage asserting the principle that humility is the greatest among the virtues and the way to peace of conscience. This is a precept that, in reverse, is demonstrated in the case of Macbeth and of Lady Macbeth, the latter seen rubbing her hands as if washing them and fearing even in her hallucinatory state that they shall "ne'er be clean" (5.1.43). Not all the pomp and wealth of royalty can cure her "disease," which would require not physical medication but confession and absolution. So too her husband reveals the

---

[53] See Arthur O. Lovejoy, *The Great Chain of Being: A Study of the History of an Idea* (Cambridge: Harvard University Press, 1936).

[54] See Charles Phythian-Adams, "Ceremony and the Citizen: The Communal Year at Coventry, 1450–1550," in *Crisis and Order in English Towns 1500–1700*, ed. Peter Clark and Paul Slack (Toronto: University of Toronto Press, 1972), 57–85.

[55] R. W. Ingram, *Records of Early English Drama: Coventry* (Toronto: University of Toronto Press, 1981), 16–17.

> Even as the Smoke doth passe away;
> So, shall all Worldly-pompe decay.

SIC TRANSIT GLORIA MUNDI

6. *Sic transit gloria mundi*. George Wither, *A Collection of Emblemes* (1635), p. 98. By permission of the Glasgow University Library, Department of Special Collections.

profitlessness of ambition as he remarks on the futility of the days that merely creep onward "in this petty pace . . . / To the last syllable of recorded time" (5.5.20–22)— that is, to the final moment of history when the day of God's judgment has come. His remark again affirms his despair, his representation of his own life as desiccated, a waste land, and his actions but those of "a poor player . . . upon the stage" (5.5.24–25), terminology which strangely resonates with King James's words describing the elevated position of kingship in his *Basilicon Doron*.

An emblem by Crispyn de Passe from Gabriel Rollenhagen's *Nucleus emblematum selectissimorum* (c.1611), reprinted in George Wither's *A Collection of Emblemes* (1635), has the motto *Sic transit gloria mundi* and illustrates a great bonfire burning crowns, a tiara, a cardinal's hat, and various other symbols of power (fig. 6).[56] Wither's verse comments on such things as "*Scepters, Miters, Crownes*" and on "*Riches*"—all

---

[56] George Wither, *A Collection of Emblemes*, introd. Rosemary Freeman (Columbia: University of South Carolina Press, 1975), 98.

The Anxiety of Power and Shakespeare's Macbeth

7. The transi tomb of Archbishop Henry Chichele. ©Crown Copyright. National Monuments Record.

"poore *Vanities*" which ultimately are seen to be "fruitlesse," mere "*Bubbles*" or "*Smoke.*" Wither's English motto explains: "*Even as the* Smoke *doth passe away; / So, shall all* Worldly-pompe *decay.*" The deprecation of worldly power and of its symbols acquires significance when it is realized that Wither's book was dedicated to King James I's son and successor, Charles I, who was to be identified as a martyr in the *Book of Common Prayer* from 1662 to 1859. Not even a king could expect to live forever, even though he might be exemplary in every way. Only someone as foolish as the proud king who brags "I schal lyue evermo" in the fragmentary fourteenth-century morality *The Pride of Life*[57] could expect to defeat death. And in the face of Death, the great leveler, the earthly symbols of power and power itself are but transitory things. So Prince Hamlet, standing with Horatio in the churchyard as the grave-diggers prepare Ophelia's grave, is made to meditate on the skull of the jester Yorick (5.1.173–217). All, from the greatest to the lowliest, return

---

[57] *Non-Cycle Plays and Fragments*, ed. Norman Davis, EETS, s.s. 1 (London: Oxford University Press, 1970), 95.

to dust in the end of this earthly life, as the Ash Wednesday liturgy asserts. The greatest monarch in the world thus must play his final scene on the world's stage and come to this. The graveyard scene in *Hamlet* may seem to lack high seriousness, but it ultimately makes one of the play's most serious statements, its iconography only a short distance away from that of the transi tomb. An early example of this type of double-decker tomb was prepared for Archbishop Henry Chichele (fig. 7), who was buried in Canterbury Cathedral in 1424: above he appears in all his earthly splendor in his vestments with angels supporting his head and kneeling monks praying for him at his feet, while below he is depicted nude, as his body was when laid in earth, emaciated and lying on his shroud, no more handsome or grand than the lowliest beggar.[58] The lower level has an inscription which comments on Chichele's lowly origins, his elevation to the see of Canterbury, and, in Kathleen Cohen's translation, "Now I am cut down and ready to be food for worms / Behold my grave. / Whoever you may be who passes by, I ask you to remember, / You will be like me after you die; / All horrible, dust, worms, vile flesh."[59]

Sometimes things which one has seen in childhood press themselves most securely on the mind and are vividly retained in the memory for one's entire life. Though it is not possible to prove that Shakespeare retained such a remembrance of the wall painting of the Dance of Death on the north wall of the nave in the Stratford Guild Chapel, one may at least speculate as much. It is known that Shakespeare's father, acting to comply with iconoclastic legislation of the time, was responsible as Stratford's chamberlain in 1563–64 for whitewashing over and partitioning off the Guild Chapel wall paintings that were regarded as "papist.[60] Less well known is that all the wall paintings were not at this

---

[58] Kathleen Cohen, *Metamorphosis of a Death Symbol: The Transi Tomb in the Late Middle Ages and the Renaissance* (Berkeley and Los Angeles: University of California Press, 1973), 15–16.

[59] Ibid., 16n.

[60] *Minutes and Accounts of the Corporation of Stratford-upon-Avon*, 1, ed. Richard Savage, Dugdale Society 1 (1921), 128. The royal injunctions that demanded the defacing of "superstitious" images "so that remain no memory of them" (*Visitation Articles and Injunctions of the Period of the Reformation*, ed. W. H. Frere, 3 vols. [London: Longmans, Green, 1910], 3:16) had been promulgated more than four years before, and it would seem that John Shakespeare and the Stratford corporation were slow about complying. That Wil-

time thus removed from view, for in 1576 John Stow made an addition to Leland's *Itinerary* that reported the survival of the scenes in a Dance of Death series.[61] Fragments of this series were discovered in 1955 and described by Wilfrid Puddephat,[62] who also provided a drawing documenting Death coming to the king with the words of John Lydgate's dialogue below the picture. Puddephat's drawing of the king is a reconstruction, but it nevertheless purports to be a reasonably faithful reproduction of the original illustration and a careful restoration of the text, which reports the king's reaction to being asked by Death to join the dance. Pride is of no value at this point, and "Grete and small" are alike summoned, with the meek having the "most avauntage, / For we shall all to dede ashes tourne."[63] And there was more at the end of the Dance of Death series: a painting of a "Dead King eaten by worms."[64] The emphasis in all of this was on the insubstantial nature of the power and glory of kingship and on the kinship of all human beings up to the point of death. One may wonder, therefore, if this wall painting, along with the playwright's contact in his youth with intense Catholic religiosity in Warwickshire, might not together have served to provide a dimension crucial to the almost metaphysical linking of ideas and the thoughtful presentation of the instability and fragility of power in his dramatization of the history of "high plac'd Macbeth" (4.1.98).

---

liam Shakespeare probably felt strong revulsion at such iconoclastic acts, including his father's, may be gauged by Edward IV's words: ". . . and defac'd / The precious image of our dear Redeemer" (*Richard III* 2.1.123–24).

[61] Bodleian Library MS. 464, vol. 5, fol. 60ᵛ; see John Leland, *The Itinerary*, ed. Lucy Toulmin Smith (1908; Carbondale: Southern Illinois University Press, 1964), 2:49.

[62] Wilfrid Puddephat, "The Mural Paintings of the Dance of Death in the Guild Chapel of Stratford-upon-Avon," *Transactions of the Birmingham Archaeological Society* 76 (1960): 29–35.

[63] Clifford Davidson, *The Guild Chapel Wall Paintings at Stratford-upon-Avon* (New York: AMS Press, 1988), 52.

[64] Ibid.

Antony and Cleopatra:
Circe, Venus, and the Whore of Babylon

Antony and Cleopatra, Shakespeare's play of c.1607 about a crucial era in Roman history, seems to turn on contraries: stern, moralistic thinking is balanced against its opposite, the consummation of very human fantasies and desires. This opposition is not new to Shakespeare, for he had often previously chosen situations for dramatization that emphasize the conflict between desire and a stern, forbidding morality. Thus in *Macbeth* the doomed protagonist is poised on the wave of his illegitimate desire to ravish the crown, but ultimately becomes such a specter of a king that the playwright seems justified in coming down on the side of orthodox morality and in approving Macbeth's deposition, though the staging of the latter act required presentation in a way that did not offend his company's patron, James I.[1] The finality with which Shakespeare speaks in *Macbeth* may have been due in part to the national mood immediately following the Gunpowder Plot. When the hysteria subsided,

---

[1] See "The Anxiety of Power and Shakespeare's *Macbeth,*" above. I have made changes in this paragraph and throughout the present article so as not to conflict with my more recent thinking concerning the political and religious context of Shakespeare's tragedies. While this has slightly modified my argument, it has not substantially changed its major thrust in consideration of *Antony and Cleopatra* as a humanist drama conceived by the playwright with the shape of sacred history in mind—a factor perhaps conditioned by his early education and training. This does not mean that the playwright was not responding also to the current situation at the English court which may have made the topic of the play particularly appropriate. However, I have not added treatment of topical matters of rule involving King James I, famous for shirking his royal responsibilities and, especially during the visit of King Christian of Denmark in 1606, for drunken court revels, though it is clear to me now that these are of direct importance for the play and its relevance as a historical document. See especially the discussion in H. Neville Davies, "Jacobean *Antony and Cleopatra,*" *Shakespeare Studies* 17 (1985): 125–58. Quotations from Shakespeare's plays are from *The Riverside Shakespeare,* gen. ed. G. Blakemore Evans, 2nd ed. (Boston: Houghton Mifflin, 1997).

Antony and Cleopatra: *Circe, Venus, and the Whore of Babylon* 65

Shakespeare turned again to consideration of even more ambiguous aspects of human action. In any case, *Antony and Cleopatra* is a sophisticated product of Renaissance humanism which allows a penetrating analysis of the natural tension that exists between desire and morality—and between private indulgence and public responsibility.

The focal character in the play is Mark Antony, the triumvir whose stature grandly overshadows both Lepidus and Octavius Caesar. Balanced between honor and love, profit and loss, wonder and woe, he is a "Herculean" hero[2] and, like Tasso's Rinaldo and Spenser's Sir Verdant,[3] is captured by the fair witchcraft of a lovely enchantress. Orthodox moralism—the "tragicall face" or "grimme looke" of the Stoically inclined Romans[4]—is certainly present in the strongest terms possible, but Shakespeare works to qualify it dramatically by also presenting the contrary attitude, stressing the immense attractiveness of the soft beds in the East. He is not blind to the historical implications of the story of Antony and Cleopatra, for he does not fail to illustrate the danger of those soft beds to those who would lie in them: wrapped up in idleness and sensuous comfort, they will relax their wills and ultimately make themselves prey to those who would pursue more single-mindedly the goal of ambition and worldly power. Such an ambitious man is Octavius Caesar, who is presented as one who is much less attractive than the pleasure-loving Antony.

S. L. Bethell identified the major conflict as between two sets of values—the strict emphasis on duty of Stoic Rome *vs.* the "spontaneous affections" of the Egyptian court.[5] One's obligations to the state and moral code are set up against "love" or "pleasure"; in the end, Bethell believed, the audience must not choose the first of these, for "the Egyptian

---

[2] See Eugene M. Waith, *The Herculean Hero in Marlowe, Shakespeare, and Dryden* (New York: Columbia University Press, 1962), 113–21.

[3] Torquato Tasso, *Jerusalem Delivered*, trans. Edward Fairfax, introd. Roberto Weiss (Carbondale: Southern Illinois University Press, 1962), book 14; Edmund Spenser, *The Faerie Queene*, ed. J. C. Smith, 2 vols. (Oxford: Clarendon Press, 1909), 1:2:339 (book 2, canto 12.79–80).

[4] Geoffrey Bullough, ed., *Narrative and Dramatic Sources of Shakespeare*, 8 vols. (London: Routledge and Kegan Paul, 1957–75), 5:276.

[5] S. L. Bethel, *Shakespeare and the Popular Dramatic Tradition* (1944; reprint London: Staples, 1948), 122–23.

values are affirmative; the Roman, negative or restrictive: the good life may be built upon the Egyptian, but not upon the Roman."[6] There are serious problems with this simple dichotomizing into two value systems, however. Caesar's "sins" may indeed impress *us* as "deeper-seated and more deliberate than the sins of Antony and Cleopatra";[7] we cannot, however, be certain that a Jacobean audience would have reacted similarly. Nevertheless, there is no question about the fact that the play is in a sense like a structure built over the very deep contraries that function to polarize Rome and Alexandria as well as to complicate the presentation of the major characters themselves.

Caesar, who is relatively simplistic as a character, represents the man of ambitious striving, a successful ladder-climber like Bullingbrook in *Richard II*. History is also on his side, and hence Shakespeare shows him as one propped up by Fortune and Providence, who will ultimately bless his empire with a "universal peace" (4.6.5). Plutarch had asserted that "it was predestined that the government of all the world should fall into Octavius Caesars handes."[8] To fulfill this role, he must be efficient, businesslike, somewhat grim—and decidedly treacherous to deal with.

Because Antony and Cleopatra are much more complicated as characters, they have been the subjects of a great deal more debate and discussion. Cleopatra, the more complex of the two, has been regarded as utterly unconvincing, especially because of the apparent inconsistency between her character in the early portion of the play and her role in the last act. Schücking, for example, saw "but little in common" between "the harlot of the first part" and the thoroughly queenly woman who dies at the end.[9] I will argue that we should not submit to the temptation to gloss over the complexities and surface inconsistencies in her character,[10] though in truth Shakespeare has given us a woman who defies most conventional attempts to understand her intricacies and to flatten out her

---

[6] Ibid., 129.

[7] Ibid., 130.

[8] Bullough, *Narrative and Dramatic Sources*, 5:292.

[9] L. L. Schücking, *Character Problems in Shakespeare's Plays* (London: Harrap, 1922), 132.

[10] See, for example, Leo Kirschbaum "Shakspere's Cleopatra," *South Atlantic Bulletin* 19 (1944): 161–71; Dolora G. Cunningham, "The Characterization of Shakespeare's Cleopatra," *Shakespeare Quarterly* 6 (1955): 9–17.

"infinite variety." Historical attention to the intellectual context in which Shakespeare shared will be of assistance here. We will need to remember that he was a successful product of the grammar school at Stratford-upon-Avon though not a university graduate, and that he worked as a playwright in a particular climate of word and image.

I

A study of the play's iconography and structure will reveal the presence of traditional modes of thought that were widely shared at the time—traditional modes that inform Shakespeare's major figures, their conflicts, and the action of the drama. To be sure, *Antony and Cleopatra* is probably less "original" than any tragedy he had ever written, for in a sense it is merely a working up for the stage of Plutarch's story. Whole passages, even some of the famous purple passages, appear borrowed almost verbatim from his principal source.[11] Nevertheless, what emerges from our study is extremely illuminating, for we see that Shakespeare utilized his materials in ways that are decidedly foreign to most of the critical approaches that were applied to the drama in the past century. Shakespeare, utilizing elements of plot and even at times the exact language of his source, tends to think in terms of character types, based on archetypal patterns that appear to have their basis in the literature, thought, and tradition of his time. In *Antony and Cleopatra*, major use is made of patterns that involve contrariety. The play in this case thus became for him a humanistic project designed to explore these dimensions in his art.

Philosophically, as the above discussion will have suggested, the play rather seems to argue the case of Stoicism versus Epicureanism, though it perhaps does this superficially. Shakespeare's contemporaries, particularly those inclined toward Puritanism, preferred Stoicism, for many of its tenets were seen as resembling the teachings of St. Paul. Nevertheless, certain elements of both philosophical systems were commonly condemned. The passions should never dominate a person, nor should one make war against the passions as against an enemy.

---

[11] Concerning some significant alterations in Shakespeare's version of the story, see Julian Markels, *The Pillar of the World* (Columbus: Ohio State University Press, 1968), 6–7.

The conventional wisdom of the time held that the passions must be controlled by reason, not allowed to go out of control as when Mark Antony relaxes his will, bathes himself in Alexandrian pleasures, and consequently transforms his great person "[i]nto a strumpet's fool" (1.1.13). "And in the ende," Plutarch says, "the horse of the minde as Plato termeth it, that is so hard of rayne (I meane the unreyned lust of concupiscence) did put out of Antonius heade, all honest and commendable thoughts."[12] Antony does not control himself when tempted to indulge in "pleasure." The usual moralistic definition of the word 'pleasure' as it is used in *Antony and Cleopatra* is, according to J. Leeds Barroll, indicative of a "complex of fleshly vices."[13] Barroll calls attention to an emblem in George Wither's *Collection of Emblemes* that shows a woman representing Temperance who holds a bridle ("*Discipline*") and a carpenter's square ("*Law*"); the poet comments, "hee that can by these, his *Passions* bound, / This *Emblems* meaning, usefully, hath found."[14] We are hence reminded of Mark Antony's promise to Octavia: "I have not kept my square, but that to come / Shall all be done by th' rule" (2.3.6–7). But, since "I' th' East [his] pleasure lies" (2.3.41), Antony will allow himself to be overcome by his appetite and will return "to his Egyptian dish again" (2.6.126). By his lack of control, he will gain mirth and another chance "[t]o reel the streets at noon" (1.4.20). On one level of meaning, his choice is shown to involve the following of a terrifying illusion that is judged by the temporal impermanence of his way of pleasure and that will bring him at last to a death that cannot be canceled "with kissing" (4.15.39). Antony's epicurean ways provide a path to glory as well as to the grave. Because of his acts, he ironically will become the immortal object of wonder and the subject of art, including drama presented by "quick comedians" on the stage (5.2.216–21). Shakespeare by contraries presents for us both the positive and negative sides of Antony's character, and, paradoxically, his faults are included among his virtues.

---

[12] Bullough, *Narrative and Dramatic Sources*, 5:283.

[13] J. Leeds Barroll, "Antony and Pleasure," *Journal of English and Germanic Philology* 57 (1958): 719.

[14] George Wither, *A Collection of Emblemes* (London, 1635), 169; cited by Barroll, "Antony and Pleasure," 719.

Antony and Cleopatra: *Circe, Venus, and the Whore of Babylon* 69

8. Forza d'Amore. Cesare Ripa, *Iconologia* (Venice, 1669), page 228.

In Shakespeare's redaction of Antony's story, his incontinence and affair with Cleopatra have their roots in Idleness, a species of Sloth.[15] As

---

[15] See Barroll, "Antony and Pleasure," 714. According to Boccaccio's *De casibus vivorum illustrium*, Antony "laid down his arms as if all the prestige of Roman honor rested with [Cleopatra's] charms and gave himself over to indolence and sloth. He wasted his time in never-ending sensuality and gluttony, and allowed himself to be captured by stupidity" (*The Fates of Illustrious Men*, trans. Louis B. Hall [New York: Frederick Unger, 1965], 172). For a review of contradictory views of Antony and Cleopatra by Boccaccio and other writers before the Elizabethan period, see Marilyn Williamson, "Antony and Cleopatra in the Late Middle Ages and Early Renaissance," *Michigan Academician* 5 (1972), 145–51.

a queen, she would be taken to be the personification of "idleness itself" if she had not held "idleness [her] subject" (1.3.92– 93). The identification of Mark Antony with Idleness is made very clear in the first act of the play; it is the state that not only hatches "Ten thousand harms" (1.2.129) but also changes the valiant captain into "the bellows and the fan / To cool a gipsy's lust" (1.1.9–10). The prime characteristic of this state is its ability to sap a person's strength and to make him weak. Thus Antony's sword is "made weak by [his] affection" (3.11.67). Cesare Ripa represents Idleness or Sloth as an aged feminine figure, inert and poor. She is holding a fish: "Fish, it was believed, when touched by a net or by hands become so stupified that they cannot escape. Idleness affects the idle in the same way; they cannot do anything."[16] The hands belong to Cleopatra, who in fantasy lets her mind run upon fishing while Antony is away in Rome:

> I will betray
> Tawny-finn'd fishes; my bended hook shall pierce
> Their slimy jaws; and as I draw them up,
> I'll think them every one an Antony,
> And say, "Ah, ha! y' are caught."
> (2.5.11–15)

If we turn to Ripa's illustration of "Forza d'amore" in his *Iconologia* (fig. 8), we will see an engraving of a Cupid who holds a fish; presumably it has been caught by his "hook"[17]—a commonplace item in the writer's vocabulary in the sixteenth and early seventeenth centuries.[18] Antony indeed is the fish who is caught in this play.

II

The Cleopatra who holds Mark Antony in her toils is at once a whore, a great queen, a Circean enchantress, a gipsy, a goddess. At one point she

---

[16] Cesare Ripa, *Iconologia* (Rome, 1603), 3; translation in *Baroque and Rococo Pictorial Imagery: The 1758–60 Hertel Edition of Ripa's Iconologia*, ed. Edward A. Maser (New York: Dover, 1971), no. 39.

[17] In the 1603 edition (p. 173), Cupid is holding the fish by a line.

[18] George Whetstone speaks of "delight" as "[t]he hooke of love" that the lover of a wicked Italian countess "swallowed with the baite" (*The Rocke of Regard* [London, 1576], 6).

is said to have appeared wearing "th' abiliments of the goddess Isis" (3.6.17),[19] and Enobarbus glowingly describes her as "O'er-picturing that Venus where we see / The fancy outwork nature" (2.2.200–01) in her pavilion on the barge on the River Cydnus. Yet she herself admits elsewhere that she is one of those whose profession is to "trade in love" (2.5.2). Unlike Octavia, whose "conversation" is "holy, cold, and still" (2.6.122–23), the sanguine Cleopatra is active and hot—so hot that the seeming Cupids on her barge with their fans only make her "delicate cheeks" glow with their sensual warmth (2.2.203–04). Properly, woman ought to be passive and constant in her love, Renaissance commentators believed. For example, Julian (the Magnifico Giuliano) in Hoby's translation of *The Book of the Courtier* is indicative of the climate of opinion when he speaks of womanhood as essentially stable and quiet, with a "steadie waightinesse, and more earnest imprintings [i.e., more permanent impressions]"—traits that are attributed to a disposition more cool than the male's.[20] Another character in *The Courtier* hears the names of Cleopatra and Semiramis pronounced and attacks them both as perverse models who ought not to be followed, for they had set out primarily to take their "pleasure" and to satisfy all their "lustes" or appetites.[21] To set up incontinence as a goal is to turn nature on its head. Nevertheless, Shakespeare's paradoxical presentation of Cleopatra deliberately brings together contraries: "for vilest things / Become themselves in her, that the holy priests / Bless her, when she is riggish" (2.2.237–39). She is at once whorish and holy.

The paradoxical character of Cleopatra does not make her less immediately dangerous to Mark Antony. Dante had deliberately placed the "wanton" ("lussurïosa") queen in the second circle of Hell, along with Dido, Semiramis, Helen, and others noted for their incontinence.[22] "[F]or I am sure," shouts Shakespeare's angry Antony, "Though you can guess what temperance should be, / You know not what it is" (3.13.120–22). As Mario Praz has suggested in connection with later literature, Cleopatra is

---

[19] See Michael Lloyd, "Cleopatra as Isis," *Shakespeare Survey* 12 (1959): 88–94.

[20] *The Courtyer of Count Baldessar Castilio*, trans. Thomas Hoby (London, 1577), sig. O4ʳ.

[21] Ibid., sig. P5ᵛ.

[22] *Inferno*, canto 5:63; see Dante Alighieri, *The Divine Comedy*, Italian text with translation by Allen Mandelbaum, 3 vols. (Berkeley and Los Angeles: University of California Press, 1981), 1:40–41.

one of the incarnations of the Fatal Woman whose desires are satisfied at the expense of the male, whom she sets out to destroy.[23] She is like Spenser's Acrasia, the witch whose long parade of lovers is reduced to subjection and then transformed to beasts.[24] Cleopatra's witchcraft has brought Mark Antony to subject himself totally to her voluptuousness, but he finds that this subjection can only lead to catastrophe, for in battle she only leads him to defeat and disaster. Through her instrumentality, he loses his manhood and gives himself over to blind and irrational Fortune, who then flings him from her wheel.

In a sense, Shakespeare is here reflecting something very close to the stereotype condemned in feminist criticism—the archetypal woman who is a betrayer—and who was so in the figure of Eve even at the beginning of time in the Garden of Eden. Eve is man's temptress, deceived by the serpent but nevertheless effective in causing him to fall from any semblance of uprightness. She is the paradigm upon which all later fatal women in literature in myth or literature would, from the Renaissance (and male) perspective, seem to be based. It is a pattern to which Lady Macbeth conforms, for at a crucial point she will gain power over her husband's will and thus cause him to bend all his energies to the terrible deed of regicide in order that he might consummate his desire to be a king—which, according to the official Stuart royal theology, was to be like a god.[25] However, while Macbeth is stirred to do an act that is illegitimate, Antony is successfully tempted to relax his will in idleness. He who, according to the patriarchal customs of the time, should be Cleopatra's master because of his sex and because of his superior status in the empire, has in his negligence given up "his potent regiment to a trull" (3.6.95). As a result of his submission, he loses his potency. Hence there appears to be justified male bitterness when Canidius exclaims that his "leader's led, / And we are women's men" (3.7.68– 69).

---

[23] Mario Praz, *The Romantic Agony*, 2nd ed. (Oxford: Oxford University Press, 1951), 204.

[24] See John E. Hankins, "Acrasia," in *The Spenser Encyclopedia*, gen. ed. A. C. Hamilton (Toronto: University of Toronto Press, 1990), 6.

[25] See James VI [James I of England], *The Basilicon Doron*, ed. James Craigie, Scottish Text Society, 3rd series 16 (Edinburgh, 1944), 25, and, for discussion in relation to *Macbeth*, Clifford Davidson, *The Primrose Way* (Coneville, Iowa: John Westburg and Associates, 1970), 8–10.

Antony and Cleopatra: *Circe, Venus, and the Whore of Babylon* 73

Egypt is, like the Garden of Eden or the classical paradise as interpreted in the Renaissance, a very fertile place—though it is inhabited by snakes. Because of her function as a temptress, Antony calls Cleopatra his "serpent of the old Nile" (1.5.25). Thus, Shakespeare suggests, she usurps the phallic role; of course, such usurpation is an attempt to achieve a reversal of the natural order—a reversal that was, after all, the object of the serpent in Eden. While she is thinking amorously about her lover during his absence, Cleopatra therefore feeds herself "[w]ith most delicious poison" (1.5.27). She lives in a world that is reminiscent of Spenser's Bower of Bliss and that is fully as poisonous, especially to male visitors from Rome. Antony, once he has drawn himself away from the pleasures of Alexandria, admits to Caesar that he had "[n]eglected" his duty "when poisoned hours had bound me up / From mine own knowledge" (2.2.89–91). This poison is obviously to be identified with the great Satanic enemy of life who in the guise of a serpent conveyed death into the fertile Garden of Eden and hence into the whole world of human beings. Not inappropriately, therefore, the asp, the poisonous "worm" which "kills and pains not" (5.2.243–44), helps Cleopatra cross to her own death.

If Cleopatra indeed is playing the role of Eve against Mark Antony's Adam, the extensive food imagery in the play surely underlines a basic element—the forbidden fruit—in the Eden story. As medieval and Renaissance writers commonly insisted, the deadly sin of Gluttony also may lead to the deadly sin of Lechery.[26] Excess food and alcohol unnaturally produce excessive heat and cause an increase in amorousness and potentially a fall into promiscuity. The Elizabethan *Homilies* indicate that overeating and drunkenness cause a "gnawing in the stomach" and stimulate lewd behavior in a manner that is dangerous to body and soul, for thus "men are bereaved and robbed of their senses, and are altogether without power of themselves."[27] Such, for example, was in part the Renaissance understanding of Falstaff, whose mind is obsessed with good sherry and bawdy houses. Mark Antony and Cleopatra thus too gluttonize in Alexandria and tumble on soft beds, and she describes herself as a

---

[26] See Barroll, "Antony and Pleasure," 709–12.
[27] *Homilies Appointed to be Read in Churches in the Time of Queen Elizabeth*, 4th ed. (Oxford, 1816), 254.

"morsel" for monarchs (1.5.31). Not suprisingly, it was the first time Antony went to the "feast" as her guest that he paid with his "heart." Unfortunately, however, the meal is an "ordinary"—that is, a public dinner—for Cleopatra is not at this point an untasted "morsel." Later, in his anger in the third act, he reminds her that he found her "as a morsel, cold upon / Dead Caesar's trencher; nay, you were a fragment / Of Gnaeus Pompey's" (3.13.116–18). She stands for excess, since she will not pause at the limits set by nature. As Cleopatra is identified with the serpent whose temptation Eve relays to Adam, so now she is also identified with food, the objective sign of the temptation of Adam. It ought not to be forgotten that Gluttony had been influentially proposed as the prime cause of the Fall of Adam and Eve,[28] who thereupon were plunged into amorous desire as a result of their transgression.

Cleopatra therefore seems to sum up the destructive and negative side of Eve, for indeed our first mother had her positive side as well which made possible Christ's rescuing of her from the jaws of the underworld at the time of the Harrowing of Hell. Furthermore, it was a commonplace belief of Christian theology during the Renaissance that, as Eve brought sin into the world, so a second Eve would bring redemption into the world. The second Eve is the Blessed Virgin Mary, whose miraculous pregnancy is scheduled by Providence not long after the historical events recounted in *Antony and Cleopatra*. Cleopatra in one sense appears to be a figure ironically foreshadowing the Blessed Virgin, as, for example, the false king Herod, who also is mentioned in Shakespeare's play, foreshadows the true King of Kings. Sacred story is not overtly the subject matter of Shakespeare's drama, but he nevertheless is very much aware of the significance for sacred history of the events that he presents on stage and of their proximity to time at the center of history itself. "The time of universal peace is near," Caesar prophetically remarks in the fourth act (4.6.4). While M. R. Ridley's New Arden edition of the play did not even have a footnote on "the time of universal peace," the *Riverside Shakespeare* merely explains that this refers "to the 'Augustan peace' that attended the reign of the speaker." Yet the line is perhaps the most significant one in the play. This will be the "universal peace through Sea

---

[28] See Morton Bloomfield, *The Seven Deadly Sins* (East Lansing: Michigan State College Press, 1952), 382.

9. Star falling as illustration of Revelation 8:10. Bishops' Bible (1569), p. cxlvii^v. By permission of the Henry E. Huntington Library, San Marino, California.

and Land" that, according to Milton's "On the Morning of Christ's Nativity," prepared the scene for "the Prince of Light" to begin "His reign of peace upon the earth."[29] Within a generation after the death of Cleopatra and the establishment of peace throughout the whole world, the Virgin Mary would bring forth a Child, the Prince of Peace.

In describing the historic period immediately preceding the first coming of Christ, therefore, it is only appropriate that Shakespeare should draw on apocalyptic imagery. The old order is coming to a close, and the effect will be to reorient men who believe in the Christian message to the "new heaven" and "new earth" that will be ushered in after the Second Coming. What could be more proper than describing the final conflict of the old order, of the pre-Christian ages, through the visually rich iconography of the Apocalypse itself? Ethel Seaton has demonstrated that Shakespeare's imagery in this play provides many references to the book

---

[29] "On the Morning of Christ's Nativity," ll. 52, 63; in John Milton, *Complete Poems and Major Prose*, ed. Merritt Y. Hughes (New York: Odyssey Press, 1957), 44.

of Revelation; also, as Helen Morris shows, he was apparently influenced by those passages illustrated by woodcuts imitated from Albrecht Dürer in certain sixteenth-century Bibles, including the Great Bible of 1562 and various printings of the Bishops' Bible.[30] When the guards discover the wounded Antony, one of them exclaims: "The star is fallen," while the other adds, "And time is at his period" (4.14.106–07). In the Apocalypse, we read, "And there fell a great starre from heaven" (Rev. 8:10; see fig. 9); and "time shulde be no more" (Rev. 10:6).[31] These and other correspondences with the Apocalypse in *Antony and Cleopatra* can hardly have been a matter of accident[32] but rather must be seen as central to Shakespeare's conception of the story's meaning.

One of the most vivid passages depicted in the Apocalypse by John the Divine evokes the great Whore of Babylon, who brings together in one figure all the negative feminine qualities mentioned above. The biblical writer describes her as having "committed fornication [with] the Kings of the earth" (Rev. 17:2) in a passage that is echoed by Caesar in *Antony and Cleopatra* 3.6.66–68: "He hath given his empire / Up to a whore, who now are levying / The kings o' th' earth for war." Traditionally, as in Dürer's woodcut, the great Whore of Babylon holds out a cup to the kings before her: it is a cup of sensual pleasure intended to seduce them into bondage to her. Cleopatra has apparently held out the symbolic cup of temptation, if we may speak figuratively, to every king and potentate who has visited the Egyptian court, and she has "committed fornication" at least with Julius Caesar, Pompey the Great, and Antony, though the two earlier recorded affairs were in her "salad days." Furthermore, once Antony's fortunes seem hopelessly falling, we see her attempting to recover her own position in the world by making advances to Caesar through his messenger Thidias. The stoical Caesar, however, refuses to be tempted.

---

[30] Ethel Seaton, "*Antony and Cleopatra* and the Book of Revelation," *Review of English Studies* 22 (1946): 219–24; Helen Morris, "Shakespeare and Dürer's Apocalypse," *Shakespeare Studies* 4 (1968): 252–62.

[31] Quotations from the Bible are from *The Geneva Bible: A Facsimile of the 1560 Edition*, introd. Lloyd E. Berry (Madison: University of Wisconsin Press, 1969).

[32] See Naseeb Shaheen, *Biblical References in Shakespeare's Plays* (Newark: University of Delaware Press, 1999), 643–56, esp. 656.

III

The negative side of Cleopatra's syncretistic character not only draws on the great Whore of Babylon but also on another partially similar mythological goddess derived from the *Odyssey* as filtered through the allegorizing commentators on Homer from the early Christian centuries. The Queen of Egypt bears resemblance to the enchantress Circe, who also holds out a cup to visiting kings and other strangers—men thereby made to lose their rational human qualities as they are transformed into beasts. For the Renaissance, Circe is the classical pattern that gives life to a whole host of fatal females in epic and in other literature.[33] Her power over men has been identified as the fatal woman's wish to emasculate the man who attaches himself to her. The goddess is associated with Arachne, apparently because in the *Odyssey* Circe "is first seen weaving."[34] Chapman's translation describes her singing with "voice divine, as at her web she wrought, / Subtle and glorious, and past earthly thought."[35] As in the imagery associated with Iago, the spider, with its *web*, is regarded as a creature of death; it is normally contrasted to the bee that symbolizes life and order. Not surprisingly, Chapman's translation describes Circe disguising her venomous potions with honey as well as with other nourishing food and drink. Hence, in the seventh book of *Orlando Furioso*, Ariosto's dangerously beautiful Alcina, modeled upon Circe, cunningly entices Rogero (Ruggiero) with the drug of pleasure that causes him to forget his duty and ultimately enslaves him in its chains.[36] Cleopatra likewise holds Mark Antony in "strong Egyptian fetters" (1.2.116); her witchcraft's power, which lies in her cunning feminine attractiveness, keeps him in subjection. Sitting at dinner in Alexandria and drinking deeply of the "poisoned hours" that Cleopatra offers to his appetite, Mark Antony no longer thinks of his country or of his duty.

---

[33] See A. Bartlett Giamatti, *The Earthly Paradise and the Renaissance Epic* (Princeton: Princeton University Press, 1966), 144 and *passim*.

[34] Stephanie Ann Fisher, "Circe as the Fatal Woman in Milton's Poetry: Milton's Concept of the Renaissance Woman," Ph.D. diss. (University of Minnesota, 1971), 5.

[35] *Chapman's Homer*, ed. Allardyce Nicoll, 2 vols., Bollingen Series 41 (New York: Pantheon Books, 1956), 2:176 (*Odyssey* 10.295–96), italics mine.

[36] Ludovico Ariosto, *Orlando Furioso*, trans. John Harington, ed. Robert McNulty (Oxford: Clarendon Press, 1972).

Unlike Ulysses, Antony allows himself to be altered by the transforming pharmacological powers of a Circean enchantress. He is changed from a fierce soldier who once, in retreat after the battle of Modena, did not hesitate to "drink / The stale of horses, and the gilded puddle / Which beasts would cough at" (1.4.61–63). He is, if we may use Chapman's word, "softn'd" (*Odyssey*, trans. Chapman, 10.453). His sword is thus made "weak" (3.10.67), while his honor in the end is incapable of being raised for his country. Mark Antony's predicament at the beginning of the play is similar to Rinaldo's, caught by the webs of Armida's Circean beauty in Tasso's *Jerusalem Delivered*. Rinaldo's escape, however, is successful, for he is destined once again to devote himself to honor and Herculean tasks. But once Mark Antony has escaped from the snares of his enchantress and has returned to Rome, he will fail to make a permanent division between himself and his "pleasure." This is the kind of return to the sensual life to which Whitney's moralizing emblem on the topic of Circe directs us:

> See here ULISSES men, transformed straunge to heare:
> Some had the shape of Goates, and Hogges, some Apes, and Asses weare.
> Who, when they might have had their former shape againe,
> They did refuse, and rather wish'd, still brutishe to remaine.
> Which showes those foolishe sorte, whome wicked love dothe thrall,
> Like brutishe beastes do passe theire time, and have no sence at all.
> And thoughe that wisedome woulde, they shoulde againe retire,
> Yet they had rather CIRCES serve, and burne in theire desire.
> Then, love the onelie crosse, that clogges the worlde with care,
> Oh stoppe your eares, and shutte your eies, of CIRCES cuppes beware.[37]

Antony will not "CIRCES cuppes beware," but will instead make "division" between himself and pious Octavia in order to return to his "lust."

Cleopatra, to be sure, appeals powerfully to *all the senses*, though Shakespeare is constantly reminding us that her dusky beauty is now slightly aging and that her freshness is gone. She is compared to food,

---

[37] Geffrey Whitney, *A Choice of Emblemes* (Leyden, 1586), 82. For other representations of Circe in emblem books of the period, see Arthur Henkel and Albrecht Schöne, *Emblemata: Handbuch zur Sinnbildkunst des XVI. und XVII. Jahrhunderts* (1967; reprint Stuttgart: J. B. Metzler, 1996), 1694–95.

somewhat stale, and she possesses a wonderful, though undoubtedly unnatural feminine warmth. As she is envisioned on her barge on the Cydnus, "A strange invisible perfume hits the sense / Of the adjacent wharfs" (2.2.212–13), but in the third act she compares herself to a "blown rose" against which people stop their noses, though they "kneel'd unto the buds" (3.13.39–40). The rose is, of course, traditionally associated with the sexually alluring woman, and hence appears as the emblem of a desirable enchantress in both Tasso's *Jerusalem Delivered* (16.14–15) and Spenser's *Faerie Queene* (2.12.75–77). Spenser, whose Circean Acrasia is introduced by a song borrowed from Tasso which ironically celebrates "the Virgin Rose" that ought to be gathered "whilest yet is time," finally reveals his enchantress reclining on a fragrant "bed of Roses." But Cleopatra's femininity, attractive as it must be to any mature man, nevertheless is a bit overripe, no longer bathed in the freshness of youth or innocence.

Paradoxically, it is at precisely this point that the Circe paradigm points Shakespeare away from the negative qualities suggested by strict analogy to the moral allegory which the Renaissance saw in the *Odyssey*. Fatal female though she is in Homer's epic, she nevertheless gives valuable advice about his journey to Odysseus once he has mastered her and rendered her benign, and partly for this reason Renaissance mythographers came to believe that she also has a positive side. While on the one hand she is linked with the ultimately destructive libido that pulls rational man downward toward his sensual animal nature, on the other she came to represent a principle of physical nature that "drives the elements through the eternal process of birth and decay."[38] Thus it becomes evident that Shakespeare's Cleopatra, who is associated with decaying food, with the fertile mud of the Nile, and with her child-bearing, is not the sterile and reductive figure of feminine wiles, Spenser's Acrasia, who is totally divorced from this positive side of Circe.

According to Abraham Fraunce, Circe on the level of physical allegory is to be explained thus: "She was called *Circe, a miscendo*, of mingling and tempring: for in the generation of bodies, these foure elements, as we call them, must needs bee tempered: which commixtion and

---

[38] Merritt Y. Hughes, "Spenser's Acrasia and the Circe of the Renaissance," *Journal of the History of Ideas* 4 (1943): 397.

composition is done by the influence and operation of the Sunne: and therefore *Circe* was borne of the Sunne and *Perseis*, the daughter of *Oceanus*."[39] She hence "mingles heat and moisture from which everything is generated."[40] The "oily" or moist palm of Charmian is surely shared by Cleopatra, and, as the sensual lady in waiting quips, it indeed may be a sign of "a fruitful prognostication" (1.2.52–53), for moisture, like heat, points in a direction quite different in Shakespeare's play from the sterility stressed in Spenser's Bower of Bliss, the imitation (one might almost say *plastic*) garden where the infertile witch Acrasia stretches out her tempting limbs. Cleopatra's issue may be "unlawful," as Caesar insists, for her children, including Julius Caesar's son Caesarion, are the consequence of desire that does not respect the boundaries and bonds of marriage (3.6.6–7). Morally, of course, the acts of Cleopatra hardly seemed acceptable in the Renaissance, though through a parallel but contrary emphasis upon physical decay, moisture, and fertility Shakespeare could on the level of art redeem her and her lover Antony.

In an important sense, therefore, the legendary fertility of Egypt and the sensuousness of its women ought almost to remind us more of Spenser's Garden of Adonis than of his sterile Bower of Bliss. The Garden of Adonis is the moving symbol of the principle of generation in the third book of *The Faerie Queene*: "there is the first seminarie / Of all things, that are borne to live and die, / . . . It sited was in fruitfull soyle of old" (3.6.30–31). The roots of the plants in this remarkable place are naturally supplied with "eternall moisture" (3.6.34). Introducing the Garden of Adonis in canto 6 is the story of Chrysogonee's remarkable pregnancy, in the course of which Spenser comments:

> Miraculous may seeme to him, that reades
> So straunge ensample of conception;
> But reason teacheth that the fruitfull seades
> Of all things living, through impression
> Of the sunbeames in moyst complexion,

---

[39] Abraham Fraunce, *The Third Part of the Countesse of Pembrokes Yvychurch* (London, 1592), fol. 47ᵛ. See also George Sandys, *Ovid's Metamorphosis Englished, Mythologized, and Represented in Figures*, ed. Karl K. Hulley and Stanley T. Vandersall (Lincoln: University of Nebraska Press, 1970), 654.

[40] Don Cameron Allen, *Mysteriously Meant* (Baltimore: Johns Hopkins Press, 1970), 226.

Antony and Cleopatra: *Circe, Venus, and the Whore of Babylon*

> Doe life conceive and quickned are by kind:
> So after *Nilus* inundation.
> Infinite shapes of creatures men do fynd,
> Informed in the mud, on which the Sunne hath shynd.
> (3.6.8)

The process of impregnation is itself clearly regarded as an ecstatic act, necessarily pleasurable for the woman as well as for the man if conception is to take place. For Spenser, legitimate pleasure, fertility within a natural sphere emblematically represented by a garden, and the most basic generative principle of the universe are linked. Shakespeare would agree wholeheartedly with these positive values, though once again we encounter the contrarieties that inform his Cleopatra. One side of her character must not be overemphasized at the expense of the other.

From Antony's perspective, therefore, Cleopatra is at once the ultimately desirable woman and the Circean enchantress who changes him into "a strumpet's fool" (1.1.13). Even Enobarbus can understand her appeal as he comments: "Other women cloy / The appetites they feed, but she makes hungry / Where most she satisfies" (2.2.235–37). At the beginning of the play, Antony knows that she holds him by her fatal witchcraft. Later, he insists upon tying his heart to her rudder even in battle, and she tows him away to disaster, for he has given up his heart's "supremacy" to her (3.11.58–61). When he succeeds better on the battlefield, Antony commends his officer Scarus's acts "[t]o this great fairy" (4.8.11)—i.e., to the enchantress Cleopatra—and then goes off to march triumphantly into Alexandria to sup and carouse with the queen. Unfortunately, in the ensuing action at sea Antony is utterly betrayed once again:

> O this false soul of Egypt! this grave charm,
> Whose eye beck'd forth my wars and call'd them home,
> Whose bosom was my crownet, my chief end,
> Like a right gypsy, hath at fast and loose
> Beguil'd me to the very heart of loss.
> (4.12.25–29)

Like Hercules destroyed by the shirt of Nessus, the tortured Antony blames Cleopatra, who, he believes, has betrayed him to the "boy" Caesar. Still, in the woeful scene that gives us Antony's death, they are reconciled. And perhaps we may say that their liaison is at last legitimatized, for in dying they in a sense unite in marriage. "Husband, I come," Cleopatra says in one of her last speeches (5.2.287).

IV

The paradoxical nature of Cleopatra's character is also strongly informed by further references to another classical figure, the goddess Venus, who is set off against the mighty god of war, Mars. In this context both these mythological figures have contrary characteristics, which are deliberately present in *Antony and Cleopatra*. In the myth, Venus is dominant, and hence it may be observed that upon the aggressive woman Cleopatra hangs the whole pattern of Shakespeare's play. Again negative qualities of Venus seem to be in the fore, as we also see in the masque of spirits in Shakespeare's *The Tempest* where Venus is described as "Mars's hot minion," a creature of intrigue who would subvert the chaste vows of Ferdinand and Miranda, the betrothed couple for whom the masque is being staged. The "contract of true love" is instead celebrated by Ceres, a fertility goddess who has "forsworn" Venus "and her blind boy's scandall'd company" since the day they plotted with Pluto to ravish her daughter Proserpine (*Tempest* 4.1.84–100). A single example, however, does not provide proof that Shakespeare would always attribute only negative qualities to Venus.

Men in the Renaissance seemingly made what they would of Venus; her positive or negative qualities might be emphasized according to the writer's pleasure or purpose. Their flexibility in this instance was made all the more easy by their separation of Venus into two distinct goddesses, the earthly Venus and the heavenly Venus.[41] The earthly Venus simply leads to pleasure and is a voluptuary without a higher conscious aim; the heavenly Venus places the goal of life beyond the snare of this world and teaches men to love the permanent, eternal realities instead of immediate objects of affection. Earthly love is, as Antony and Cleopatra themselves realize in act 1, a splendid lie. The lovers "stand up peerless" in the "[e]xcellent falsehood" of their illusory love (1.1.40), while neither of

---

[41] See Marsilio Ficino, *Commentary on the "Symposium" of Plato*, trans. Sears Jayne, University of Missouri Studies 19, no. 1 (Columbia: University of Missouri Press, 1944), 141–42.

them at this point assumes any true permanence or higher value to their infatuation. Their relationship surely seems to involve a lack of candor and truth and hence is reminiscent of the falsehood of the affair with the Dark Lady in Shakespeare's *Sonnets*.

In medieval and Renaissance iconography, Venus in her earthly function is often identified with *Luxuria*, the sin of lechery which appeared among the deadly sins of Prudentius's *Psychomachia*. An illumination reproduced by Jean Seznec from a manuscript of *Ymagines secundum diversos doctores* shows nude Venus in the guise of naked desire, holding a mirror in which she admires herself.[42] The mirror likewise is held by Luxuria in the rose window in the cathedral of Notre Dame, Paris—a window that also pictures the unkissed virgin Chastity (Luxuria's opposite and nemesis in the medieval allegories of virtues and vices as they are represented in painted glass and sculpture) holding the phoenix in its flames of death and rebirth.[43] As the phoenix is emblematic of immortality, so the mirror is evidence of pride and selfishness. Because of her association with Luxuria, therefore, the proud goddess Venus in her earthly guise is at times even referred to as the mother of the vices[44] or as a planetary prostitute who trades in love.[45] She seems to be linked to the allegorical Ease (Oiseuse) of *The Romance of the Rose*[46] and hence to the Idleness that holds Antony in Alexandria.

As Enobarbus describes the first meeting of Antony with the Egyptian queen, the tableau on Cleopatra's barge shows that she is here *consciously* associating herself with Venus, just as later she will take on the role of Isis, another goddess linked with generation as well as on occasion with the Greek goddess of love.[47] With boys "like smiling Cupids" on each side, Cleopatra reclines sensuously and temptingly in her

---

[42] Vatican MS. Palat. lat. 1726, fol. 43ʳ; Jean Seznec, *The Survival of the Pagan Gods*, trans. Barbara Sessions, Bollingen Series 38 (New York: Pantheon Books, 1953), 107, figs. 85, 87.

[43] Émile Mâle, *Religious Art in France: The Thirteenth Century*, trans. Marthiel Mathews, Bollingen Series 90, no. 2 (Princeton: Princeton University Press, 1984), 119–20, figs. 76–77.

[44] Seznec, *The Survival of the Pagan Gods*, 109.

[45] Bloomfield, *The Seven Deadly Sins*, 347.

[46] Seznec, *The Survival of the Pagan Gods*, 107.

[47] See Lloyd, "Cleopatra as Isis," 91.

pavilion. The posture that she takes thus would appear to be similar to that taken by Botticelli's Venus in his *Venus and Mars* in the National Gallery, London. Indeed, Shakespeare makes us feel that, faced with such a temptress, Antony should surprise us only in the event that he might have failed to fall into the snare. Fatal woman though she is, Cleopatra is like the goddess of love and beauty herself calling the powerful Antony to rest. The rest that she offers to him is not, of course, immediately substantial, for it is based on his subservience to her and to his passions that serve her. And even in her capricious bearing toward him she takes a stance which reminds us that she views love as more of a challenge than an opportunity for real tenderness. Matthew N. Proser notes, "love for her is always a battleground—sensual and enthralling—where, ironically, she is herself the prize and booty."[48] From one perspective, Venus may be seen in terms of discord, for her affection is characterized by a contrariness that is represented in iconography by the apple of discord that she holds in many Renaissance paintings (e.g., in Angelo Bronzino's *Allegory of Time and Love*). Cleopatra likewise is viewed by Shakespeare as a major source of discord within the ancient Roman world. It is a discord that she promotes in her private relationship with Antony as well as in her less conscious public policy.

But if the temptress Cleopatra on her barge is like Venus, aping even the posture of the goddess as she commonly appears pictured, Mark Antony is the mighty Mars. He is thus identified at the opening of the first act of Shakespeare's play when Philo pours out his outrage at the way his leader has betrayed his honor:

> those his goodly eyes,
> That o'er the files and musters of the war
> Have glow'd like plated Mars, now bend, now turn
> The office and devotion of their view
> Upon a tawny front. (1.1.2–6)

According to Abraham Fraunce, Mars is "that *hote and furious* disposition, fit for wars"; thus "he is figured grim, fierce, and sterne, *all*

---

[48] Matthew N. Proser, *The Heroic Image in Five Shakespearean Tragedies* (Princeton: Princeton University Press, 1965), 194.

Antony and Cleopatra: *Circe, Venus, and the Whore of Babylon* 85

armed."⁴⁹ Antony, grand in his armor, has been the "triple pillar of the world" (1.1.12), an incarnation of military and political power. But the Circean enchantress, using the powers traditionally associated with Venus, has in Shakespeare's play effected his metamorphosis into a foolish reveler.

The story of the affair of Venus and Mars is briefly told in Ovid's *Metamorphoses*, book 4, which emphasizes the manner in which Phoebus informs on the lovers and how Vulcan "forg'd a chaine, / With nets of brasse, that might the eye deceave." This snare, which is compared to the spider's web, the outraged husband threw over the lovers Mars and Venus and caught them in his "strangely forged net": "Who, struggling, in compeld imbracements lay."⁵⁰ The story is taken up and allegorized by the Renaissance mythographers. Fraunce comments:

> *Venus*, that is to say, Wantonnes, joyned with *Mars*, which noteth hote and furious rage, giving themselves over to excessive and inordinate pleasure; are by *Phoebus*, figuring the light of reason, accused to *Vulcan*, who representeth naturall heate; which is weakned by this inordinate lust. *Vulcan*, by *Phoebus* his counsaile, linketh them together to their shame: for, when naturall heate is quailed, then the rage of lust is abated, yrkesome repentance and languishing debilitie ensuing thereupon.⁵¹

Such an interpretation of the myth would seem to have been an important element in Shakespeare's depiction of Antony and Cleopatra. Cleopatra on her barge is certainly "Wantonnes"; joined with the martial Antony, she together with him partakes of pleasure to an excessive degree. "There's not a minute of our lives should stretch / Without some pleasure now," Mark Antony says (1.1.46–47). The greatness of this love can only be measured in terms of the degree to which Antony will neglect his duty. He will "[l]et Rome in Tiber melt, and the wide arch / Of the rang'd empire fall" (1.1.33–34). Looking over the evidence of the play, Leo Kirschbaum was convinced that the playwright "never for a moment

---

⁴⁹ Fraunce, *The Third Part of the Countesse of Pembrokes Yvychurch*, fol. 39ʳ [misnumbered 32].

⁵⁰ Sandys, *Ovid's Metamorphosis*, 176.

⁵¹ Fraunce, *The Third Part of the Countesse of Pembrokes Yvychurch*, fol. 39ʳ [misnumbered 32].

ceases to picture Antony and Cleopatra as voluptuaries."[52] However, despite his flattery of the Egyptian queen in the first act, Antony's reason does tell him privately that he must break away from her debilitating witchcraft and from the "fetters" by which her love has enslaved him. He knows that his love and his consequent idleness are leading him only into "dotage," which is a state of weakness following the exercise of his lust with Cleopatra. In North's Plutarch, he rouses himself from this state "as if he had bene wakened out of a deepe sleepe, and as a man may say, comming out of a great dronkennes."[53] Like Aeneas, he leaves his mistress; his tragedy comes after he returns to the debilitating queen—the fatal woman—who in the end will sap all his warlike heat and power, and thus will lead him to utter defeat at the end of a mismanaged war.

The effects of Venus's love are set forth in Botticelli's painting to which reference has been made above. Mars, like Mark Antony, has put aside his plated armor; nude and debilitated, he sleeps as if nothing could ever wake him while Venus in a dressing gown looks dreamily past him and off into the distance.[54] Botticelli's goddess, like Shakespeare's Cleopatra, has been the seducer. As Adrien Bonjour has pointed out, the eunuch Mardian's "Yet have I fierce affections, and think / What Venus did with Mars" (1.5.17–18) tells us something about the relationship of Antony and Cleopatra: "Notice that he does not say 'what Mars did with Venus'. Apart from making some lascivious innuendoes, Mardian, it is clear, insinuates that Venus was the active agent: in other words, what Venus did with Mars was to render him her slave."[55] In his astrological discussion of these divinities, Ficino asserts that "Mars never masters Venus": "Rich men and exalted kings bow their necks to the rule of Love, but Love is subject to none of these."[56] Botticelli's painting shows that Mars's armor and weapons have become playthings for *satyrini*. Above all else, his torpor has made him very vulnerable as he has relaxed his will and enjoyed the delights of love. In this respect, he is like Spenser's Red Cross Knight, who, having put off his armor with the purpose of making

---

[52] Kirschbaum, "Shakspere's Cleopatra," 169.

[53] Bullough, *Narrative and Dramatic Sources*, 5:277.

[54] The contrast between the posture of Mars and of Venus in Botticelli's painting is discussed by E. H. Gombrich, "Botticelli's Mythologies: A Study in the Neoplatonic Symbolism of His Circle," *Journal of the Warburg and Courtauld Institutes* 8 (1945): 47–48.

[55] Adrien Bonjour, "From Shakespeare's Venus to Cleopatra's Cupids," *Shakespeare Survey* 15 (1962): 77.

[56] Ficino, *Commentary*, 177; see also Sandys, *Ovid's Metamorphosis*, 203.

love to the witch Duessa whom he believes to be "Fidessa," drinks of the waters of a spring that begin to cause "his manly forces . . . to faile, / And mightie strong was turnd to feeble fraile" (*Faerie Queene* 1.7.6). Thus when danger comes, he is caught in a state of lassitude and without his armor: he does not have a chance to succeed in the hopeless fight against the giant Orgolio (i.e., Pride).

When Antony is bound up in Cleopatra's charms, Octavius jeers that his "competitor" is not "now more manlike / Than Cleopatra"; his reveling and lovemaking have made him "womanly" (1.4.5–7). He has pawned his "experience" in order to pay for "present pleasure," which is "to tumble on the bed of Ptolomy" and "[t]o give a kingdom for a mirth" (1.4.17–18, 32). The mention of Cleopatra's bed may remind us that the beautiful woman and her bed are standard Renaissance emblems of *Impudicitia* (Lewdness). The Hertel edition of Ripa's *Iconologia*, while dating from the eighteenth century, nevertheless gives graphic illustration to this idea in connection with Sardanapalus, who appears nude on his bed with lovely women in attendance but with his symbols of rule—his crown, his scepter, his sword—cast onto the floor. In the foreground is Venus, reclining, holding some colewort that was believed to be an aphrodisiac, and fondling Cupid.[57] To give oneself over to Venus is indeed to threaten one's masculinity and power. In the second act, Cleopatra tells of the occasion when she "drunk [Antony] to his bed; / Then put my tires and mantles on him, whilst / I wore his sword Philippan" (2.5.21–23). The visual effect is reminiscent of *Venus armata*, a figure that appears in art with weapons and helmet to symbolize "the warfare of love."[58] Love functions to defeat the great soldier and to make him effeminate through the effects of drunkenness, lovemaking, and sleep. Indeed, for Antony to follow Love will mean with certainty that his own martial affairs will come to ruin, and hence, as noted above, when we see him in battle at sea he becomes a victim of female predominance. The

---

[57] Ripa, *Baroque and Rococo Pictorial Imagery*, no. 70.

[58] V. Cartari, *Imagini delli dei de gl'antichi* (Venice, 1647), 280; Edgar Wind, *Pagan Mysteries in the Renaissance*, rev. ed. (New York: W. W. Norton, 1968), 91, pl. 73. Maurice Charney also points to a passage in North's Plutarch following the story of Mark Antony in which Omphale's disarming of Hercules is explicitly compared to the manner in which "Cleopatra oftentimes unarmed Antonius, and intised him to her, making him lose matters of great importance" (*Shakespeare's Roman Plays* [Cambridge: Harvard University Press, 1961], 130, quoting *North's Plutarch: The Tudor Translation*, ed. W. E. Henley [London, 1896], 6:91).

maxim "Mars follows Venus, Venus does not follow Mars" pertains here, for it is indicative not only of Antony's willingness to be nodded back to Egypt but also of his behavior in battle. As long as he allows Cleopatra to be "[t]he armorer of his heart" (4.4.7) he will find himself hopelessly weakened through feminine predominance. Perhaps all of this also hints in another way at a reason for Antony's lack of success at sea, for according to many medieval and Renaissance writers, the sea is symbolic of the flux of the human emotions. Hence Spenser's Guyon must go by sea past numerous representations of dangers to which the emotions are subject before he can capture and enchain the witch Acrasia. Thus are men in love described as sailors; according to Fulgentius, Venus is depicted "swimming in the sea, because lust suffers shipwreck of its affairs, whence also Porfyrius in his *Epigrams* declares: 'The shipwrecked sailor of Venus [is] in the deep, naked and destitute'."[59] Behind such a vision of Venus, it is not hard to detect the Siren beckoning.

Yet for all her contrariness, Venus cannot be simply written off as evil. In the case of Cleopatra, the woman indeed does destroy Mark Antony, yet nevertheless their love points in positive as well as negative directions. It was not forgotten in the Renaissance that the love of Venus and Mars was a *discordia concors* which led to the birth of a daughter, Harmony.[60] The value of Venus's dominance over Mars will thus be found in the mitigation of the god of war's ferocity, for only through such dominance can conflict and war be reduced to harmonious peace. The Orphic hymn dedicated to Mars, for example, strongly urges the furious warrior to yield himself "[t]o lovely Venus and to Bacchus," for in that direction lies "peace" with its "gentle works."

> For arms exchange the labours of the field;
> Encourage peace, to gentle works inclin'd,
> And give abundance, with benignant mind.[61]

In the end, the love of the martial Antony and wanton Cleopatra will lead

---

[59] *Fulgentius the Mythographer*, trans. Leslie George Whitbread (Columbus: Ohio State University Press, 1971), 67.

[60] Raymond B. Waddington, "Antony and Cleopatra: 'What Venus did with Mars'," *Shakespeare Studies* 2 (1966): 221–22; see also Wind, *Pagan Mysteries in the Renaissance*, 86. Sandys comments: "*Mars* is malignant, but approaching *Venus* subdues his malignity" (*Ovid's Metamorphosis*, 202–03).

[61] *The Mystical Hymns of Orpheus*, trans. Thomas Taylor (London: Dobell, 1896), 129.

historically to the resolution of the conflict between the triumvirs and to the harmony of "universal peace" into which will be born the Prince of Peace.

There is also another important sense in which Cleopatra ought not to be viewed entirely in negative terms. Although Cleopatra, like Venus and her protégé Helen, contributed to the fall of a city and empire because of a passionate attachment, nevertheless she may not be seen only as a symbol of a passion that ought at all costs to be resisted. For, had not Antony yielded to passion, his life would hardly have appeared as appealing or as suitable for being mirrored in art. The aesthetic redemption that is effected in the last two acts of the play thus marks a departure from any rigidly orthodox moral conclusion, for Shakespeare as an artist in the final analysis has decided to conclude the play by giving his blessing to the lovers. Even Caesar, the stern victor and angered brother of Octavia who at the end of the play stands over the body of the Egyptian queen, is so softened that he feels woe at the loss of this royal pair; he promises that Antony shall lie in death by the side of his exotic queen: "No grave upon the earth shall clip in it / A pair so famous" (5.2.359–60). Caesar's attitude reflects quite clearly the sympathy and wonder with which the audience is encouraged to look upon the tragic events at the end of the lives of Antony and Cleopatra.

It may thus be suggested plausibly that the audience's sympathy is intended to rest upon the Renaissance habit of seeing Venus as double, as earthly and as heavenly. The idea of the two Venuses has its source in Pausanius's speech in the *Symposium*, where he speaks of the motherless "heavenly Aphrodite," Uranus's daughter, and "the younger daughter of Zeus and Dione," who is earthly. Of the heavenly love associated with the former, Pausanius claims that it is "innocent of any hint of lewdness" since "her attributes have nothing of the female."[62] Cleopatra as she approaches her suicide thus says, "My resolution's plac'd, and I have nothing / Of woman in me: now from head to foot / I am marble-constant" (5.2.238–40). As her eye turns now to the realm that holds her lover Antony in death, she appears paradoxically not only sensuous but also chaste. She longs no longer for any earthly man, but strongly desires immortality. She shall never again taste the earthly wine from Egypt's grapes, nor may she participate again in any earthly revels. She imagines

---

[62] *Symposium* 180–82, in Plato, *The Collected Dialogues*, ed. Edith Hamilton and Huntington Cairns, Bollingen Series 71 (Princeton: Princeton University Press, 1961).

that Antony calls to her, and she will nobly go to him as to her husband. Her baser elements are purged away so that her love may pull her up to where her desire rests upon the spirit of Mark Antony in bliss.

Earlier critics inevitably remarked that the "[i]mmortal longings" of Cleopatra (5.2.281) partake only of illusion. Dolora Cunningham, for example, believed that here "Cleopatra ultimately fails . . . to resolve the fatal confusion between sensual and religious mystery which has characterized the lovers' actions from the beginning and consequently falls short of achieving her immortal longings," though "the sensuality is nevertheless refined by the attempt to die nobly."[63] But it may be argued that Shakespeare is not in this play concerned with the question of whether or not his characters are saved from a Christian hell; the immortality that Cleopatra achieves, under the guise of the goddess Venus, is after all the immortality that art, not religion, has to offer. It is thus the same immortality that the poet of the *Amoretti* offers to his beloved: "my verse," writes Spenser, "your vertues rare shall eternize, / and in the hevens wryte your glorious name" (Sonnet 75). Therefore, unlike the wretched Lady Macbeth and Macbeth who fully deserve to enter the smoking pit of hell when they depart from their despairing lives, our imaginations are invited by Shakespeare to save his lovers from such a conclusion. The common Venus, who stood behind the Cleopatra whose mind always had been focused on the delight associated with generation, in the end by contraries melts into the heavenly Venus who sets forth to take her last immortal journey.

Such a transformation would hardly have seemed odd to the humanists and other thinkers of the Renaissance, as we must realize when we consider, for example, the surprising implications of the Hermetic thought of Cornelius Agrippa, for whom the enthusiasm of love (i.e., of Venus) "doth . . . convert, and transmute the mind to God, and makes it altogether like to God, as it were the proper image of God." Being in this manner transformed, the soul "is so formed of God, that it doth above all intellect, know all things by a certain essential contract of Divinity. . . . [It can] sometimes work wonderfull things, and greater then the nature of the world can do, which works are called miracles."[64] Whether or not Shakespeare was familiar with Agrippa's *De occulta philosophia* is

---

[63] Cunningham, "The Characterization of Shakespeare's Cleopatra," 16.

[64] Henry Cornelius Agrippa, *Three Books of Occult Philosophy*, trans. J. F. (London, 1651), 507–08. See also Frances A. Yates, *Giordano Bruno and the Hermetic Tradition* (Chicago: University of Chicago Press, 1964), 281–82.

singularly unimportant, for what he has done has in fact been to achieve a kind of artistic gnosis in which the Herculean hero, though through love cast down utterly, at last is lifted up by its miraculous force to a new and greater heroism at his "martyrdom." At the death of "Herculean" Antony, Cleopatra laments that the gods have "stol'n our jewel" (4.15.78); but he is then set as a star in the heavens toward which Cleopatra may now steer her course. "Nature wants stuff," says the queen, "To vie strange forms with fancy, yet to imagine / An Antony were Nature's piece, 'gainst fancy, / Condemning shadows quite" (5.2.97–100). Such indeed are the works of the magus who is the dramatist—one who is able to juggle the contrarieties built into the mythological models upon which he constructs his characters as well as his situations, and to achieve at the conclusion something more splendid than we could have imagined even at the opening of the first act.

But Shakespeare does not thus come down on the side of the epicurean view of pleasure as the most desirable quality of life. Mark Antony's earthly tragedy proves that the excessive pursuit of pleasure is on one level an illusion that will lead to emasculation and destruction. To follow Cleopatra's overripe beauty would not normally be wise according to either the ways of the world or the ways of the spirit. Yet Shakespeare in his drama insists upon dealing with the existential realities of the emotional life. The passions, after all, are like horses that give motion to the chariot of the mind, and hence they are of the greatest value—if they are controlled by reason. But the demands of the passions for pleasure, within proper limits, apparently must be recognized as experience potentially higher than ever can be found in the exercise of reason alone.[65] It was a commonplace among Renaissance Neoplatonists that Love is blind because it reaches a higher plane than the mere human intellect is able to achieve.[66] With serious reservations, therefore, Shakespeare allows pleasure to be made most attractive and ultimately to be changed into a quality of high aesthetic value. Like Tasso, who attempts to convert his witch Armida after Rinaldo is rescued from her power,[67] Shakespeare insists upon transforming the destructive passion that Cleopatra represents into its seeming opposite. Thus though he recognizes that in this world pleasure is dangerous and transitory, he also by contraries draws upon those elements of the thought of his age that would vindicate its value.

---

[65] See Wind, *Pagan Mysteries of the Renaissance*, 55.
[66] Ibid., 56.
[67] See Giamatti, *The Earthly Paradise*, 209–10.

V

In the first act of *Antony and Cleopatra*, the Egyptian queen threatens wittily "to set a bourn how far to be belov'd." Antony answers, "Then must thou find out new heaven, new earth" (1.1.16–17). To be sure, Antony's demise and then Cleopatra's suicide place limits on their love on this side of the valley of death. But once Antony is dead, she will put on her crown and robes and prepare herself to reach out toward a new country where she may be reunited with her "husband." Shakespeare at both ends of his drama is echoing Apocalypse 21:1–2: "And I sawe a new heaven, and a new earth.... And I John sawe the holie citie newe Jerusalem come downe from God out of heaven, prepared as a bride trimmed for her housband." Thus Cleopatra, who has been imaged forth in the play even as the great Whore of the Apocalypse, in the final portion of the play is portrayed as analogous to the "bride" of the great bridegroom, Christ, who indeed when he returns for the second time will usher in a new heaven, a new earth, and an eternity of love that is not diminished by illusion.

A final instance of apocalyptic imagery, pointed out by Seaton,[68] draws parallels between Mark Antony and the Angel with the Book, also included among the illustrations in early Bibles (fig. 10):

> His face was as the heavens, and therein stuck
> A sun and moon, which kept their course, and lighted
> The little O, th' earth....
> His legs bestrid the ocean, his rear'd arm
> Crested the world: his voice was propertied
> As all the tuned spheres, and that to friends:
> But when he meant to quail, and shake the orb,
> He was as rattling thunder. (5.2.79–86)

And I saw another mightie Angel come downe from heaven, clothed with a cloude, and the raine bowe upon his head, and his face was as the sunne, and his feete as pillers of fyre.... [A]nd he put his right fote upon the sea, and his left on the earth, And cryed with a lowde voyce, as when a lyon roareth: and when he had cryed, seven thondres uttered

---

[68] Seaton, "*Antony and Cleopatra* and the Book of Revelation," 220–21; see also Morris, "Shakespeare and Dürer's Apocalyse," 258–61.

10. Face as the sun and feet as pillars of fire; illustration of Revelation 10. Bishops' Bible (1569), p. cxlix. By permission of the Henry E. Huntington Library, San Marino, California.

> their voyces. . . . And the Angel which I sawe stand upon the sea and upon the earth, lift up his hand to heaven. . . . (Rev. 10:1–5)

The imperial spirit of Antony, generous and great, is placed at least in imagination among the angels. Mark Antony indeed will be remembered thus, for he has been miraculously converted into angelic substance as a result of the gnosis of Shakespeare's art. Shakespeare has thus selected ideas and images out of the Apocalypse by contraries, for Mark Antony's relationship with Cleopatra is ultimately shown to be not only destructive, as we would expect from the negative evidence of an affair with the great Whore of Babylon, but also creative and aesthetically redemptive.

On the whole, therefore, Shakespeare's method in this play has been to exploit a syncretism that deliberately holds together in one drama many elements of opposition and all of them traditional. Instead of trying to locate principles of unity that bind the play together in a unified whole, we need therefore to locate the elements of tension whereby through contraries the dramatist has created the magnificent effect of Antony's world crumbling about him because of a love affair that paradoxically transforms his loss into a grand and splendid event to be reenacted on the Globe stage. The result is not philosophy, nor is it even propaganda for any particular world view. *Antony and Cleopatra* is a re-presentation of Roman history at a time of preparation for the Incarnation, and it is simply consummate and miraculous theater.

Part II

Sacred Violence and the Mysteries

Cain in the Mysteries: The Iconography of Violence

In one of the choir windows of York Minster is a panel of sixteenth-century painted glass showing the fallen Adam and Eve being expelled from the Garden of Eden and followed by the Seven Deadly Sins. The glass is not part of the original glazing of York Minster or even English (it is from Rouen),[1] but it illustrates how the Fall was regarded as the entry point for transgressive behavior in the history of humankind. In the epistle of Clement of Rome, written in c.100 A.D., the Fall is defined as the source of emulation, envy, and strife as well as sedition, persecution, disorder, and war.[2] Adam and Eve had themselves not fallen into such sins directly, but the act of eating the forbidden fruit started the slide toward crime and eventually toward murder. Hence while the origins of the lapsarian condition were understood to be found in the Fall—the succumbing of Eve and Adam to the suggestions of the serpent in the garden—the first person to be fully suffused with evil was Cain, who functions as the initial human villain in the religious drama of the Middle Ages.[3] As such, he is the figure out of primordial time who establishes a

---

[1] Peter Gibson, "The Stained and Painted Glass of York," in *The Noble City of York*, ed. Alberic Stacpoole (York: Cerialis Press, 1972), 143, pl. 39.

[2] Epistle of Clement of Rome to the Corinthians 3; in *The Apostolic Fathers*, 2 vols. (London: Griffith, Farran, Okeden, and Walsh, n.d.), 1:161.

[3] Rosemary Woolf aptly comments on the significance of the emphasis in medieval drama on Cain rather than on Abel, who is not treated in depth; she sees this emphasis as demonstrating the "dramatists' interest in showing a continuation of the Fall" (*The English Mystery Plays* [Berkeley and Los Angeles: University of California Press, 1972], 124). Citations in the present article are to the following editions: *The York Plays*, ed. Richard Beadle (London: Edward Arnold, 1982); *The Towneley Plays*, ed. Martin Stevens and A. C. Cawley, 2 vols., EETS, s.s. 13–14 (Oxford: Oxford University Press, 1995); *The Chester Mystery Cycle*, ed. R. M. Lumiansky and David Mills, 2 vols., EETS, s.s. 3, 9 (London: Oxford University Press, 1974–86); *The N-Town Play*, ed. Stephen Spector, 2 vols., EETS, s.s. 11–12 (Oxford: Oxford University Press, 1991); *The Ancient Cornish Drama*, ed. and trans. Edwin Norris, 2 vols. (Oxford: Oxford University Press, 1859); *The Creacion of the*

spiritual progeny that will join him in eternal damnation—a kinship that will continue to exist upon this earth until the last day of history. Cain was thus regarded as central to the presentation of the problem of violence and evil in history; his act of fratricide was for St. Augustine the "archetype of crime,"[4] and for the dramatists of the late medieval vernacular plays of England it was the pattern of all subsequent violence, including the strife that would lead to the torture and death of the Redeemer.[5]

The present paper will attempt to examine the late medieval understanding of the first murder in its full visual dimension as it provided the ground against which violence would be presented on the civic religious stage in England.[6] In so doing I will be implicitly asserting the validity of studying the dominant urban culture—that is, the conventional views held by citizens, their wives, parish clergy, and others. This is not to say that the popular response to all biblical characters was uniform or that there was not an element even of indifference toward their stories from some quarters—or that the comic elements were not perceived from quite different perspectives by different members of the audience.[7] But with regard to acts of violence, and to their potential for repetition through acts of revenge, the complexity of public reaction nevertheless does not erase the people's generalized concern or the earlier legal response, which in

---

World, ed. and trans. Paula Neuss (New York: Garland, 1983). Quotations are identified in parentheses in my text by line numbers, preceded, in the case of the Middle English plays, by the number of the pageant.

[4] St. Augustine, *The City of God* XV.5; trans. Marcus Dods *et al.* (New York: Random House, 1950), 482.

[5] Cf. T. W. Craik, "Violence in the English Miracle Plays," in *Medieval Drama*, ed. Neville Denny, Stratford-upon-Avon Studies, 16 (London: Edward Arnold, 1973), 173–95, esp. 187–92. For the observation that domestic dissention and violence could be included, see David C. Fowler, *The Bible in Middle English Literature* (Seattle: University of Washington Press, 1984), 260.

[6] The methodology adopted in this paper is intended to examine the larger cultural context in which the iconography of the plays may be located. I have elsewhere studied the use of local iconography to illuminate the visual aspects of the plays both in instances where a direct connection between drama and art exists and where local art provides insight indirectly into the design of the plays' spectacle.

[7] See especially the excellent analysis of Hans-Jürgen Diller, *The Middle English Mystery Play* (Cambridge: Cambridge University Press, 1992), 224–31.

Germanic countries was to substitute the concept of public justice for the idea that murder was a private matter between the families affected. In place of the Anglo-Saxon practice of *Wergild*, the *Laws of Henry I* had recognized murder as an offense against the crown. The acceptance of public responsibility for bringing the murderer to justice may, at least theoretically, be seen as an attempt to limit transgressive behavior in a time when there was intense concern about social instability. Violence was often a real presence, especially as it existed outside the walls of the city (in 1520 Coventry, for example, closed its gates between 8 in the evening and 5 in the morning "for the preseruacion of good rulee etc."[8]) but not infrequently internally. The York *Ordo Paginarum*, an official civic document, found it necessary to decree "þat no man go armed in þis Citee with swerdes ne with carlill axes ne none othir defences in distourbaunce of þe kynges pees & þe play or hynderyng of þe processioun of Corpore christi" except for "knyghtes and sqwyers of wirship þat awe haue swerdes borne eftir thame."[9] Even in the Christian era when salvation was held to be available to all, Cain's act of murder was being replicated in the society—and would continue to be replicated as long as the world would continue to stand. To understand this threat to good order was to give it a historical basis in imagining the first act of murder, which was hence an obligatory episode in the dramatic presentation of the history of the world.

I

The story of Cain and Abel, which highlighted both the failure of Cain to sacrifice satisfactorily and his homicide, cannot have been visualized in the vernacular drama—or, for that matter, in art—merely as a response to some perceived external threat to the sacrifice of the Mass. For example, some Lollards objected strenuously to the sacramental theology of the Church, denied the element of sacrifice in the Eucharist, and refused to attend Mass or take communion. While such attitudes may

---

[8] *The Coventry Leet Book*, ed. Mary Dormer Harris, EETS, o.s. 134–35, 138, 146 (London: Kegan Paul, Trench, Trübner, 1907–13), 3:669.

[9] Alexandra F. Johnston and Margaret Rogerson, *Records of Early English Drama: York*, 2 vols. (Toronto: University of Toronto Press, 1979), 1:24.

plausibly have been in the mind of the dramatist who created the Towneley Cain, the story of the murder of Abel had a much broader application,[10] and it was dramatized not only in Continental drama[11] but also in a much earlier play, possibly written in England, of the early history of the world. In no sense could the latter play bear any relationship whatever to the beliefs of Wyclif or the Lollards.

A useful perspective may nevertheless be gained from glancing back at the twelfth-century Anglo-Norman *Ordo Representationis Adae*,[12] which was written long before the earliest of the great civic drama cycles. The *Ordo*'s Cain may be seen primarily as an illustration of the consequences of the Fall for human behavior, but it has some extremely interesting features. Unusually, in this play both Cain and his brother Abel are tillers of the soil, an occupation that is reminiscent of the task to which Adam had typically been set following his expulsion from Eden. As Adam's task in this earlier play had been complicated by the devil's act of planting thistles and thorns on his land, so now Cain will himself be a physical sign of human decadence. His victimizing of his brother Abel will cause him to be in turn a victim of devils, who beat him and thrust him into hell where he will be the first permanent resident.[13] Cain's immediate demise is a surprise, since this symbolic conclusion follows a rapid dramatization of the main events up to that point of the biblical story, which emphasizes the sacrifice, Cain's envy, his murder of his brother, and the curse of God, here identified as Figura. While, as Lynette

---

[10] In this respect my argument is similar to Ann Eljenholm Nichols's assertion with regard to the Croxton *Play of the Sacrament*—that is, that finding a cause of its anti-sacramentalism in Lollardy is reductive, and instead attention needs to be turned to look to the broader aspect of Eucharistic piety in East Anglia or, in the case of the Towneley play, the West Riding of Yorkshire; see Nichols, "The Croxton *Play of the Sacrament*: A Re-Reading," *Comparative Drama* 22 (1988): 117–37.

[11] See Lynette R. Muir, *The Biblical Drama of Medieval Europe* (Cambridge: Cambridge University Press, 1995), 70–71, 207–08.

[12] See for convenience the text and translation of this play in *Medieval Drama*, ed. David Bevington (Boston: Houghton Mifflin, 1975), esp. 103, 105–13.

[13] Abel will, of course, be among those delivered from hell at the Harrowing. In the Cornish *Ordinalia*, Abel is likewise taken off to hell, but Lucifer is quite mistaken in insisting that he will be a permanent resident "Notwithstanding all thy true tithe" (555–57).

Muir points out, the tithing and sacrifice have their rationale as "love of God, and an attempt to repair the sin of the First Parents,"[14] these become the source in the play of Cain's wrath when his own sacrifice is rejected. Cain absorbs in full measure the *cupiditas* that had been the motive for the Fall of his parents initially.[15] Herein, then, lies the very origin of violence among human beings—violence which will resound through history until the Last Day.

In the later vernacular drama of England, the story of Cain is even more clearly the presentation of an archetype of violence in history. Cain serves as a point of reference throughout each of the play cycles and collections, even though all are composite works by several hands and lacking the artistic unity which a single author might introduce. Cain represents the reprobate who is at once a transgressor and a sufferer from despair because of his expectation of damnation. Thus he provides a model of alienation and violence for the subsequent villains that are presented in the course of the plays, which survey human history as it was understood from the traditional accounts in the Bible and other sources. Four of these dramatizations of Cain's story are written in Middle English, while two are in Cornish.

II

The ultimate source of the story of Cain, the narrative in Genesis 4, is to be sure a passage of considerable ambiguity, though biblical scholars agree that it is part of the earliest layer of writing attributed to one known in higher criticism as the Yahwist (J), as distinguished from the later priestly redactors.[16] In one sense the narrative is straightforward in its description of events following the sexual coupling of Adam and Eve: the birth of their sons Cain and Abel, their different occupations, their offerings, Cain's envy and murder of his brother, and God's curse of the

---

[14] Lynette R. Muir, *Liturgy and Drama in the Anglo-Norman Adam* (Oxford: Basil Blackwell, 1973), 87, citing Hugh of St. Victor (*PL* 176:344).

[15] See Muir, *Liturgy and Drama*, 85.

[16] See E. A. Speiser, trans., *Genesis*, Anchor Bible (Garden City, N.Y.: Doubleday, 1981), xxvi–xxviii.

murderer. As a story about the first human beings to be born into earthly life it has a terrifying message of violence, and at its end Cain has become both a wanderer and an exile and a founder of cities.

But what is the reason for God's rejection of Cain's sacrifice? The conventional explanation is that Abel as a shepherd represented the preferred pastoral way of life, as opposed to Cain's choice of tilling the soil, for an author who romanticized a nomadic Israelite past.[17] The Hebrew God prefers the younger son, the shepherd, rather than the farmer. Why? Was it, as the gloss in the Geneva Bible (1560) insisted, merely that Cain was a "hypocrite and offred onely for an outwarde shew without sinceritie of heart"? If so, how was it that the very first man to have been born rather than created should also have been a hypocrite who only outwardly would go through the motions of piety demanded by a still present Creator? The Genesis text itself is silent in this regard. It says only in effect that God did not like Cain's offering while Abel's offering was acceptable to him.[18] As Harold Bloom comments, "J offers us no motive for Yahweh's choice, and is equally laconic as to the provocation for Cain's gratuitous, sudden murder of Abel."[19] The author, J, tantalizes and leaves room for multiple interpretations. Was it that Cain's sacrifice was fruit of the ground that God had cursed? If so, we may regard this curse as reversed at the Flood, and certainly in the rogation rites of fifteenth- and sixteenth-century England the blessing of the fields established a very different view of the ground and its fruits.[20]

Another interpretation, which contradicts the Genesis account,[21] even suggests that Cain's father was not Adam but the devil. The idea that

---

[17] See Northrop Frye, *The Great Code: The Bible and Literature* (New York: Harcourt, Brace, Jovanovich, 1982), 142–43. But something more complex is going on here; cf. René Girard, *Violence and the Sacred*, trans. Patrick Gregory (Baltimore: Johns Hopkins University Press, 1977), 4.

[18] See also Hebrews 11:4: "By faith Abel offered to God a sacrifice exceeding that of Cain, by which he obtained a testimony that he was just, God giving testimony to his gifts; and by it he being dead yet speaketh." Biblical citations in this article are to the Douay-Rheims edition, which is chosen because it the most faithful to the Vulgate.

[19] *The Book of J*, trans. David Rosenberg, Introd. and Commentary by Harold Bloom (New York: Grove Weidenfeld, 1990), 188.

[20] See Eamon Duffy, *The Stripping of the Altars: Traditional Religion in England, 1400–1580* (New Haven: Yale University Press, 1992), 136–37.

[21] See Genesis 4:1: "And Adam knew Eve his wife: who conceived and brought forth Cain, saying: I have gotten a man through God."

Satan, under the guise of the serpent, was the first seducer of a woman was known in the Christian West.[22] Some lesser-known Jewish writers and Manichaean heretics included Cain's demonic paternity as an explanation for his thoroughly bad behavior.[23] More important was the authority of 1 John 3:12: "Not as Cain, who was of the wicked one, and killed his brother . . . because his own works were wicked: and his brother's just." The *Cursor Mundi* appears to affirm this view: "And caym was þe feindes fode, / was neuer wers of moder born."[24] The Wakefield Master's Cain, on account of his perverse and even demonic behavior throughout the Towneley play, seems not very far removed from this Cain, though so far as I know there is no proof that the author drew upon the notion that he was physically sired by the devil. This Cain, however, swears by the devil even as he attempts to light the fire under his sacrifice: "Now bren in the dwillys name" (2.280). The York play's Cain, similarly willful, likewise invokes the devil in response to Abel's urging: "Ya, daunce in þe devil way, . . . / For I wille wyrke euen as I will" (VII.52–53). Being on the side of the devil does not, of course, prove diabolical paternity except in a symbolic sense. Yet there is merit in Peter Travis's observation that the Chester Cain bears comparison with the Lucifer of the Fall of the Angels, for he too appears to be "a 'congeon,' a subtle deceiver whose evil desires, although slowly revealed, are in retrospect seen to have been operative in his first words"; further, "like Lucifer, Cain shows no signs of guilt. . . ."[25] The *Cursor Mundi* says that Cain sacrificed out of an "iuel will," and for this reason "vr louerd loked noght þar-till."[26]

---

[22] Robert E. Kelly, *The Bible in the Early Middle Ages* (Westminster, Maryland: Newman Press, 1959), 36; Richard Axton, *European Drama of the Early Middle Ages* (London: Hutchinson, 1959), 125.

[23] Oliver F. Emerson, "Legends of Cain, Especially in Old and Middle English," *PMLA* 21 (1906): 835–37.

[24] *Cursor Mundi*, ed. Richard Morris, 6 vols., EETS, o.s. 57, 62, 66, 68, 99, 101 (London: Kegan Paul, Trench, Trübner, 1874–93), 1:69 (ll. 1056–57).

[25] Peter Travis, *Dramatic Design in the Chester Cycle* (Chicago: University of Chicago Press, 1982), 93. This observation applies to the Cain of the other cycles and collections as well.

[26] *Cursor Mundi*, ed. Morris, 1:70 (ll. 1065–66).

The nature of Cain's sacrifice, which many interpreters described as defective in quality or quantity, is also important. The biblical text does not specify either defect, of course, only that God did not like the sacrifice. But commonly it was believed that Cain picked out for sacrifice the inferior fruits of the earth and saved the best for himself. So Cain in the Chester play will offer the worst of his harvest ("For cleane corne, by my faye, / of mee gettst thou nought" [II.543–44]), and the Wakefield Master's Cain also offers his poorest sheaves, mixed with "Thystyls and brerys," which when they burn "stank like the dwill in hell" (Towneley 2.204, 285). The Cain of the N-Town play specifically offers only his worst; he will, he says, "tythe þe werst," for which he searches through his fields (3.96–100). When to Abel's horror he brings forth his "werst," he announces: "Here I tythe þis vnthende sheff" (101). The Chester Cain grasps at straw instead of sheaves of wheat; "Hit weare pittye, by my panne," he says, "those fayre eares for to brenne" (II.537–38). And in the Cornish *Ordinalia* Cain insists that it is folly to consign to the fire that "which a man can live upon" (*Origo Mundi* 474–75), while in the *Creacion of the World* he adulterates his sacrifice not only with brambles and thorns but also with cow dung (Cornish: *glose*) to burn for his sacrifice (1086–90). This depiction of Cain's sacrifice is consistent with the criticism developed in the St. Ambrose's *Of Cain and Abel*,[27] a work that would prove to be most influential in subsequent centuries. In the *Stanzaic Life of Christ*, for example, Cain offers "fuylet corn," which therefore burned without "light"—that is, without open flame.[28]

Hence Cain offered not the "first fruits" of his labor but inferior produce instead, nor indeed did he give willingly.[29] Cain's hostility to God, his malice toward his brother, and his blasphemous unwillingness to sacrifice anything of value are evident in all the English and Cornish

---

[27] See Emerson, "Legends of Cain," 849; John E. Bernbrock, "Notes on the Towneley Cycle *Slaying of Abel*," *Journal of English and Germanic Philology* 62 (1963): 320; and St. Ambrose, *Of Cain and Abel* 1.10.40; *Hexameron, Paradise, and Cain and Abel*, trans. John J. Savage (New York: Fathers of the Church, 1961), 396; Latin text in *PL*, 14:315–59.

[28] *A Stanzaic Life of Christ*, ed. Frances A. Foster, EETS, o.s. 166 (London: Oxford University Press, 1926), 79 (ll. 2339–40). In the Lucerne Passion, Cain has a sheaf of wheat that had "im wasser gelegen" and hence was wet (M. Blakemore Evans, *The Passion Play of Lucerne* [New York: Modern Language Association, 1943], 194).

[29] See Ambrose, *Of Cain and Abel* 1.7.25-28; trans. Savage, 383–86.

plays, and these attitudes may be translated into delaying actions that, while enhancing the dramatic interest, subvert the very purpose of sacrifice, which is, as René Girard has suggested, designed "to restore harmony to the community, to reinforce the social fabric."[30] Such perversity also offends against the demand enunciated by Ambrose for speed in making one's sacrifice. As John E. Bernbrock notes, the Towneley Abel "reiterates this need for haste four times," while Cain very obviously demonstrates his indifference and reluctance.[31] The N-Town Cain announces that he is "loth" to go to sacrifice and would rather "gon hom, well for to dyne" (3.49, 52). In the Cornish *Ordinalia*, on the other hand, Cain's haste is a sign of his impatience with the whole process of sacrifice, for he rushes off before receiving his father's blessing and then seems to resent both the time involved in making the sacrifice and the loss of good grain.

Other writers, perhaps following Josephus, were convinced that Cain, as the establisher of weights, measures, and limits, offended by offering only a limited sacrifice—and hence not out of his whole heart.[32] The *Ordinalia* shows him holding back a portion of his tithe. The Wakefield Master, who represented the sacrifice as defective in both quality and quantity, makes much of the way in which Cain counts out sheaves and uses his arithmetic to exclude God. Such ingratitude, one might expect, would thoroughly offend the Creator of all things.[33] The play especially

---

[30] Girard, *Violence and the Sacred*, 8. For corroboration of aspects of Girard's view of the purpose of sacrifice in terms of the sacrifice of the Mass in the Middle Ages, see John Bossy, "The Mass as a Social Institution, 1200–1700," *Past and Present*, no. 100 (Aug. 1983): 29–61, and Susan Brigden, "Religion and Social Obligation in Early and Modern Sixteenth-Century London," *Past and Present*, no. 103 (May 1984): 67–112. Girard's discussion is not, of course, to be regarded as the final word on the subject of sacrifice.

[31] See Bernbrock, "Notes on the Towneley *Slaying of Abel*," 318; Towneley 2.74, 106, 132, 144.

[32] See Josephus, *Jewish Antiquities*, ed. and trans. H. St. J. Thackeray, 6 vols., Loeb Classical Library (Cambridge: Harvard University Press, 1930–65), 1:28–29 (1.2.2 [61]).

[33] This does not mean that comedy is not an important element in the contribution of the Wakefield Master to the Towneley collection; see my "Jest and Earnest: Comedy in the Work of the Wakefield Master,"*Annuale Mediaevale* 22 (1982): 65–83. Other important aspects of the Wakefield Master's work are discussed generally in J. W. Robinson, *Studies in Fifteenth-Century Stagecraft*, Early Drama, Art, and Music, Monograph Series 14 (Kalamazoo: Medieval Institute Publications, 1991).

provides corroboration of the view of Cain as a false tither. This interpretation of his character should not be surprising in the light of Ambrose's derivation of his name, Cain, from "getting [acquisitio], because he got everything for himself."[34]

Less ambiguous is Cain's reaction to his rejection, for it is explicitly established that he was both resentful and envious.[35] His envy of his brother leads directly to his fratricide, his lifting of his hand against his kin. It was this murder that defined Cain in the religious drama of the Middle Ages, and it was through this act that he was believed to have established himself as a model of self-destructive infidelity and violence. Among his numerous spiritual progeny will be the biblical Judas and the mythological Grendel, who is specifically identified as "Cāines cynne" in the Anglo-Saxon epic, *Beowulf*.[36] When he appeared in the visual arts, his failed sacrifice and, even more often, his murder of his brother were depicted. These scenes are included in the *Bohun Psalter* (Bodleian Library MS. Auct. D.4.4, fol. 40) of c.1370–80 along with the infancy of Cain and Abel, one of whom is at his mother's breast, and the imposition of the mark of Cain (fig. 11). A fifth scene depicts the death of Cain from an arrow shot by Lamech from his bow.[37]

---

[34] Ambrose, *Of Cain and Abel* 1.1.3; trans. Savage, 360. Ambrose apparently received this derivation of the name from Jewish writers. See Josephus, *Jewish Antiquities*, 1:24–25 (1.2.1 [52]), and Philo, *On the Birth of Abel and the Sacrifices Offered by Him and by His Brother Cain*, in *Philo*, Loeb Classical Library, 10 vols. (Cambridge: Harvard University Press, 1929), 2:94–97 (1:1). Cain's avarice was to be stressed by Peter Comestor (*Historia Scholastica*, Liber Genesis, 26) and others.

[35] It is perhaps to be emphasized also that Cain is usually depicted as "out of charity" with his brother Abel throughout his sacrificing; for the importance of being in charity with one's neighbors prior to Mass, see Brigden, "Religion and Social Obligation," 67–84. Brigden quotes (73) a poem in British Library Harl. MS. 2252, fol. 160ᵛ, which insists that whoso "þat charyte forsakythe dothe not well / but may be comparyd to the devyll of hell."

[36] For Judas, see below, and for Grendel see *Beowulf*, ed. F. Klaeber, 3rd ed. (Boston: Heath, 1950), 5 (l. 107), and David Williams, *Cain and Beowulf: A Study in Secular Allegory* (Toronto: University of Toronto Press, 1982), *passim*.

[37] The *Bohun Psalter* is briefly described by Otto Pächt and J. J. G. Alexander, *Illuminated Manuscripts in the Bodleian Library, Oxford*, 3: *British, Irish, and Icelandic Schools* (Oxford: Clarendon Press, 1973), no. 665. See also Ruth Mellinkoff, *The Mark of Cain* (Berkeley and Los Angeles: University of California Press, 1981), and Louis Réau, *Iconographie de l'art Chrétien*, 3 vols. (Paris: Presses Universitaires de France, 1955–59), 1:2:94–97.

Cain in the Mysteries 107

11. Scenes from the story of Cain and Abel. Bohun Psalter, Bodleian Library MS. Auc. D.4.4, fol. 40ʳ. By permission of the Bodleian Library, University of Oxford.

None of the scenes in the *Bohun Psalter* possesses the detail and elaboration that are displayed in the fourteenth-century *Holkham Bible Picture Book* (British Library MS. 47,680), which has been associated with a London workshop. There is no reason to believe, as W. O. Hassall has suggested, that there was a connection between these illuminations and the religious drama,[38] but the manner in which the biblical account was expanded cannot fail to be seen as a foreshadowing of the Cain and Abel episode in the Towneley *Mactacio Abel*, though the opening of the pictorial narrative is closer to the ordering in the N-Town collection and

---

[38] W. O. Hassall, *The Holkham Bible Picture Book* (London: Dropmore Press, 1954), 34–36. While useful for its preservation of much iconography of biblical narrative as it was commonly understood, this work, on account of its provenance and date (c.1320–30), needs to be used with considerable care as a document corroborating stage picture in drama that is dated a hundred or two hundred years later and from different regions in England.

the Cornish plays with Adam's admonition to his sons to sacrifice their first fruits.[39] On the lower half of the illumination on fol. 5ʳ in the *Holkham Bible Picture Book* Adam lectures his sons, who stand by in postures that signify their attitudes toward him and his suggestions. Cain, standing beside sheaves of grain and grasping a two-pronged pitchfork, has his back to his father but turns his head toward him. His jaw juts out, and the expression on his face is meant to convey hostility.[40] In contrast, Abel, who is positioned among his sheep, holds his shepherd's staff in his left hand and extends his right upward with his palm turned toward his father in what is clearly intended to be a gesture of acceptance. The contrast between the two brothers is continued above in the upper portion of the miniature which shows their sacrifices. Here Cain, his face turned so his eyes glare with even greater hostility at his father, is pitching another bundle onto the fire, which, unlike Abel's clean burning sacrifice with its smoke going upward toward heaven, emits a smudge that does not rise but instead goes downward and joins the smoke emitted by a hellmouth positioned below it. This example may be compared with an early fourteenth-century wall painting in the church of All Saints at East Hanningfield, Essex, in which the smoke from the sheaves of grain of Cain's sacrifice likewise descends into the mouth of hell.[41] Emerson notes that the description of the smoke from Cain's fire as going downward was a common addition to the story that appeared first in the prose *Lyff of Adam and Eue*: "Crist vnderfong wel fayre þe tiþe of Abel: for þe smoke wente euene vpward, as hit brende; and þe smoke of Caym wente dounwart, for he tiþede falsliche."[42] Often elsewhere too smoke and flames

---

[39] Hassall, *Holkham Bible Picture Book*, 66, notes the source of Adam's admonition as the *Historia Scholastica*, Liber Genesis 26 (*PL* 198:1077). At Lucerne, Abel's sacrifice was a wooden effigy of a lamb, filled with shavings so that it would burn brightly (Evans, *The Passion Play of Lucerne*, 194). However, there was apparently a live lamb for which the effigy was exchanged in the course of the scene; see also Peter Meredith and John E. Tailby, *The Staging of Religious Drama in Europe in the Later Middle Ages*, Early Drama, Art, and Music, Monograph Series 4 (Kalamazoo: Medieval Institute Publications, 1983), 118.

[40] Cain's hostile facial expressions are also noted in the prose *Lyff of Adam and Eue*, in *Sammlung altenglischer Legenden*, ed. Carl Horstmann (Heilbronn: Henninger, 1878), 224.

[41] E. W. Tristram, *English Wall Painting in the Fourteenth Century*, ed. Eileen Tristram (London: Routledge and Kegan Paul, 1955), 177.

[42] Emerson, "Legends of Cain," 848; *Lyff of Adam and Eue*, in Horstmann, *Sammlung altenglischer Legenden*, 224. The fire for the sacrifice fails to be ignited in the N-Town and

ascend from Abel's offering but drift downward from Cain's offering. So it is, for example, in the fifteenth-century blockbook *Speculum Humanae Salvationis*, printed in the Low Countries but widely distributed, and in painted glass of c.1480 at St. Neot, Cornwall.[43] The smoke and flame also come down upon Cain in a carving in the Chapter House at Salisbury.[44] In the Towneley play Cain's sacrifice does not burn cleanly but, as noted above, produces a cloud of evil-smelling smoke that almost chokes him.[45] A further aspect of the hellmouth near Cain's sacrifice in the *Holkham Bible Picture Book* illumination is that it is located exactly in the same position as the mouth of hell in conventional depictions of the Last Judgment—that is, below and at the left of those in the scene.[46] The typological connection between the first Adam and his good and bad sons on his right and left in this scene, and the second Adam, Christ, with the good and bad thieves also on his right and left, should be obvious,[47] but

---

Chester plays and the Cornish *Ordinalia*. In the *Creacion of the World* Cain apparently breaks off before completing his sacrifice, though he has promised that his bad produce will make "a huge bush of smoke" (1091). The York play is defective and lacks the folios that contained the sacrifice.

[43] Adrian Wilson and Joyce Lancaster Wilson, *A Medieval Mirror: Speculum Humanae Salvationis* (Berkeley and Los Angeles: University of California Press, 1984), 177; G. McN. Rushforth, "The Windows of the Church of St. Neot, Cornwall," *Exeter Diocesan Architectural and Archaeological Society* 15 (1937): 156, pl. 39.

[44] William Burges, "The Iconography of the Chapter-House, Salisbury," *The Ecclesiologist* 20 (1859): 149; Selby Whittingham, *Salisbury Chapter House* (1974; reprint Salisbury: Dean and Chapter of Salisbury Cathedral, 1986), fig. 13; M. D. Anderson, *Drama and Imagery* (Cambridge: Cambridge University Press, 1963), 144, 212. Anderson also reports another example of smoke from Cain's offering descending downward on the Fitzroy tomb at Framlingham, Suffolk (144).

[45] In contrast, the smoke from Abel's sacrifice is described as "sweet" in the *Creacion of the World* (1100).

[46] Further it should be noted that hell was conventionally associated with unpleasant odors; thus a closer association may exist between this one aspect of the iconography of the *Holkham Bible Picture Book* illumination and the Towneley play than previously suspected. For the odor of hell, see Thomas Seiler, "Filth and Stench as Aspects of the Iconography of Hell," in *The Iconography of Hell*, ed. Clifford Davidson and Thomas H. Seiler, Early Drama, Art, and Music, Monograph Series 17 (Kalamazoo: Medieval Institute Publications, 1992), 132–40.

[47] With regard to this typology see also Gertrud Schiller, *Iconography of Christian Art*, trans. Janet Seligman, 2 vols. (Greenwich, Conn.: New York Graphic Society, 1968), 2:124.

the scene also therefore looks forward to the separation of the good and the evil human beings at Doomsday.

On fol. 5ᵛ of the *Holkham Bible Picture Book*, Cain, having led Abel to a different place, grasps him by the shoulder with his left hand and delivers the fatal blow to his head with his right. The instrument that he uses for this irrational act of violence is the jawbone of an ass, which had become the conventional murder weapon in England from Anglo-Saxon times and also appeared in some Continental examples in the visual arts.[48] In the Caedmonian *Genesis* (Bodleian Library MS. Junius 11) the instrument had been a club (p. 49),[49] but the jawbone would appear perhaps for the first time in an eleventh-century manuscript of Aelfric's translation of the Pentateuch (British Library, Cotton MS. Claudius B.iv, fol. 8).[50] Meyer Schapiro's explanation of the adoption of the jawbone as the result of an association between the Anglo-Saxon *cinbān* and *Cāin bana* has been convincingly refuted by George Henderson, who argues that the jawbone as weapon was adapted from book illustration showing Samson's slaying of one thousand Philistines in Judges 15:15.[51] The Towneley and N-Town plays and the Cornish *Creacion of the World* call for this instrument. As the rubrics in the Cornish play indicate, Cain has a "*chawbone readye*" as he threatens Abel with a beating, whereupon he hits him with it and he dies (*s.d.* at ll. 1110, 1116).[52] In the N-Town play, Cain says, "With þis chavyl bon I xal sle þe" (3. 149), and he of course

---

[48] See Meyer Schapiro, "Cain's Jaw-Bone That Did the First Murder," in *Late Antique, Early Christian and Mediaeval Art: Selected Papers* (New York: George Braziller, 1979), 255. Schapiro was apparently not aware of Scandinavian examples; see Knud Banning, *A Catalogue of Wall-Paintings in Medieval Denmark, 1100–1600: Scania, Halland, Blekinge*, 4 vols. (Copenhagen: Akademisk Forlag, 1976), 1:42–44, figs. 45, 48, 50.

[49] Thomas Ohlgren, *Anglo-Saxon Textual Illustration* (Kalamazoo: Medieval Institute Publications, 1992), 550.

[50] George Henderson, "Cain's Jaw-Bone," *Journal of the Warburg and Courtauld Institutes* 24 (1961): pl. 16b.

[51] Ibid., 111–12. For another suggestion, see A. A. Barb, "Cain's Murder-Weapon and Samson's Jawbone of an Ass," *Journal of the Warburg and Courtauld Institutes* 35 (1972): 386–89.

[52] The term *challa*, meaning jawbone, is used in the *Origo Mundi*, but is transferred to Abel's anatomy. Norris translates: "That thou mayest never thrive, / Take this on the jawbone" (539–40). Immediately thereafter the rubric commands Cain to hit his brother on the head: "*Tunc percuciet eum in capite et morietur....*"

does as he has promised to do: "With þis strok I þe kylle" (152).⁵³ In the blockbook version of the *Speculum Humanae Salvationis* Cain holds Abel by the throat as he lies on the ground; his right arm is raised with his hand grasping the jawbone in preparation for striking another blow at his brother.⁵⁴ In the *Holkham Bible Picture Book* Cain will now try to cover over his brother's body, and in the *Cursor Mundi* his attempt to hide the corpse fails—it will not stay buried.⁵⁵ Exhibiting an unfeeling nature, the Cain of the Cornish *Creacion of the World* will simply *"Cast Abell into a dyche"* (*s.d.* at 1136). In the Towneley play Cain quakes with fear and tries to hide,⁵⁶ while in the York play he is challenged by an angel who pronounces God's curse on him.⁵⁷ The most terrifying detail is his despair, for he believes that his "synne it passis al mercie" (York VII.119).

But in the other plays and in the *Holkham Bible Picture Book* Cain will now be challenged directly by God rather than an angel. Again in the

---

⁵³ See the discussion in Cherrell Guilfoyle, "The Staging of the First Murder in the Mystery Plays in England," *Comparative Drama* 25 (1991): 42–51. The York play probably also utilized the jawbone of an ass, according to Guilfoyle; this instrument is named in works with associations with the York play (ibid., 42). For discussion of the iconography of a panel in the East Window of York Minster in relation to the missing section of the York play, see Clifford Davidson, *From Creation to Doom* (New York: AMS Press, 1984), 15. The figure of Abel in this panel was made up in the restoration of 1953, but there is no doubt about either his head or Cain with his jawbone lifted high to bring it down on his brother's head. See also Clifford Davidson and David E. O'Connor, *York Art*, Early Drama, Art, and Music, Reference Series 1 (Kalamazoo: Medieval Institute Publications, 1978), 25, fig. 6; Thomas French, *York Minster: The Great East Window*, Corpus Vitrearum Medii Aevi, Summary Catalogue 2 (Oxford: Oxford University Press, 1995), 52. Muir also notes the use of the jawbone as the murder instrument at Valenciennes (twenty-day play) (*The Biblical Drama*, 208).

⁵⁴ Wilson and Wilson, *A Medieval Mirror*, 177.

⁵⁵ *Cursor Mundi*, ed. Morris, 1:70 (ll. 1075–80).

⁵⁶ Subsequently the Towneley Cain will want to hide Abel's corpse "For som man myght com at vngayn," so he calls for Pikeharness to help bury him (2.380–87). For dramatic treatment elsewhere, see Muir, *The Biblical Drama*, 71, 208.

⁵⁷ Eleanor Prosser suggests a reason for the substitution of the angel for God: "Clearly because our author confuses dramatic 'action' with violence and wants Cain to strike back physically at the curse-giver. Since he certainly could not strike God, God thus becomes an angel..." (*Drama and Religion in the English Mystery Plays* [Stanford: Stanford University Press, 1961], 75).

manuscript illumination Cain has his back turned to the speaker with only his face turned in the direction of God. His face is even more filled with hostility than before, if that is possible. Cain, a diminutive human with his right hand still clutching the jawbone, is standing before the large figure of the God who accuses him of crime. In the Cornish *Creacion of the World* he looks down when the Father speaks to him, but he does not repent. In this play as in the *Ordinalia* the disembodied voice of Abel's blood cries out.[58] The scene is actually a key to the entire narrative, for here it becomes clear that, as Ricardo Quinones has argued, Cain's anger against his brother has in fact been "a displaced anger that is really directed against God. . . . The quarrel of envy is ultimately a quarrel with God—its arena, or façade, is a hatred of those whom God favors."[59] Violence, then, is seen as a theological problem and as the ultimate form of rebellion against both the Creator and things-as-they-are. Violent acts serve to separate persons from the community—"I haue no frende," Cain says in the N-Town play (3.177)—and precipitate them into an abyss of alienation. In the Towneley play Cain will go forth "And to the dwill be thrall, / Warld withoutten end" (2.467–68). Here the phrase "Warld withoutten end" is a direct translation of concluding words of the *Gloria Patri*. Violence without repentance and forgiveness reverses the song of praise to the Trinity and insures an ultimate place in a "stall" in hell "[w]ith Sathanas the feynd" (377, 470). For the time being, however, he will be marked by God so that the one who slays him will in turn be "punyshid sevenfold" (375).

The *Holkham Bible Picture Book* does not illustrate the imposition of a mark upon Cain by God, but in the *Bohun Psalter* this is shown as God with his finger making a sign on Cain's forehead. There is some

---

[58] Compare the painted glass at St. Neot, Cornwall, which includes the text "En sanguis fra*tr*is tui" ("Behold thy brother's blood"); see Rushforth, "The Windows of the Church of St. Neot," 157. In an early wall painting on the south wall of the parish church at West Kingsdown, Kent, a small figure representing Abel's blood is crying out for vengeance (Hassall, *Holkham Bible Picture Book*, 68, and, for verification, I am grateful to James Gibson and also the churchwarden, Neale J. Muller). For the use of a small child to represent Abel's blood crying out for vengeance at Mons, see Meredith and Tailby, *The Staging of Religious Drama*, 96–97.

[59] Ricardo Quinones, *The Changes of Cain: Violence and the Lost Brother in Cain and Abel Literature* (Princeton: Princeton University Press, 1991), 16.

confusion about what the mark of Cain meant, whether a physical mark on his body or a shaking or trembling of his head, as indicated in the *Historia Scholastica* of Peter Comestor.[60] In the *Holkham Bible Picture Book* Cain's mark is visible as a pair of horns on his forehead (fols. 6^v–7^r).[61] In the Cornish *Creacion of the World* the mark is placed on his forehead, and it is the Greek letter Omega (*s.d.* at 1180)—a sign of closure, of the closing of the book of history at the Last Day. In the Great East Window at York Minster the topmost tracery panel shows God with the Book of Creation open before him with the words "Ego sum alph*a* & *omega*,"[62] the beginning and ending letters of the Greek alphabet representing the beginning and end of the world. Yet this mark will protect Cain from the immediate death that he deserves,[63] at least until he is mistaken for a beast and killed by his descendant Lamech—a popular episode shown, for example, in the *Holkham Bible Picture Book* (fols. 6^v–7^r), in a window at St. Neot, Cornwall,[64] and on a nave roof boss at Norwich Cathedral.[65] The death of Cain appears as an extended segment in the *Creacion of the World* (1429–1725). The Cain of this play is at this time deformed and "overgrown with hair" (1664–65)—a wild man of medieval and Renaissance tradition but also a demonic figure destined for hell.[66] The mark on his forehead here is appropriately identified as a horn

---

[60] *PL* 198:1078, as cited by Mellinkoff, *The Mark of Cain*, 49, 118–19. According to the prose *Lyff of Adam and Eue*, "Crist" placed "a marke vp on him: þat he waggede alwey forþ his heued" (Horstmann, *Sammlung altenglischer Legenden*, 224). For a Continental play that follows this tradition, see Muir, *The Biblical Drama*, 71. A literal translation of the original Hebrew text designates Cain as a "totterer and wanderer" (Speiser, *Genesis*, 31).

[61] For further examples of horns as the mark of Cain, see Mellinkoff, *The Mark of Cain*, figs. 7–8 (capital at Vézelay), 15 (Pamplona Bible), 19–20 (Cambridge, St. John's College MS. K.26).

[62] Davidson and O'Connor, *York Art*, fig. 2; French, *York Minster: The Great East Window*, 17.

[63] For the mark of Cain in terms of a protective sign (*sphragis*), see Jean Daniélou, *The Bible and the Liturgy* (Notre Dame, Indiana: University of Notre Dame Press, 1956), 60–61.

[64] Rushforth, "The Windows of the Church of St. Neot," 157, pl. XXXIX.

[65] C. J. P. Cave, *Roof Bosses in Medieval Churches* (Cambridge: Cambridge University Press, 1948), fig. 148; the boss is noted by Anderson, *Drama and Imagery*, 89, 145

[66] See, for example, the wild man and woman in Walter de Milemete, *De Nobilitatibus, Sapientiis, et Prudentiis Regum* (Oxford, Christ Church MS. 92, fol. 64^v), reproduced in Clifford Davidson, *Illustrations of the Stage and Acting in England to 1580*, Early Drama,

(1616; Cornish: *corne ow thale*),[67] which of course has associations with demons since they also very often have horns in depictions in the visual arts. At the end of the scene in the Cornish play two devils come forth to carry the "outcast Cain" (Cornish: *Cayne adla*) to the place of torment "*with great noyes*" (1712–13, *s.d.* at 1721). In the Lamech episode inserted into the Noah play in the N-Town collection, Cain is mistaken for a "best" under a "grett busche" by the boy who is assisting the blind Lamech (4.166). As in the Cornish *Creacion*, the ending is violent. Lamech, attacking the boy, beats and kills him, then in his despair goes into hiding as an outlaw—a repetition of Cain's attempt to hide following his fratricidal act against Abel.

Prior to the crucial events of Cain's story—i.e., the sacrifice and murder—in the Chester cycle he is shown with a plough, a symbol which defines his role as a farmer (*s.d.* at II.517), and this is an implement which the Wakefield Master also introduced in association with Cain in the Towneley *Mactacio Abel*. The plough in the latter play is more than a simple wheeled plough that Cain can push onto the stage. It must be an actual wheeled farm implement that is pulled by a team, which has consistently been interpreted as including several draught animals (A. C. Cawley specified four horses and four oxen[68]). A recent study, however, has reduced the number to a more reasonable two, a horse and a mare named Don and Molly.[69] The different names that Cain calls out may thus be attributed to a combination of rural practice in driving teams of animals and his verbal aggressiveness, which also is displayed in the language he uses to address his servant and his brother. Hostility in language extends to physical aggression, as when Cain initially beats his boy Pikeharness (2.50); gestures, such as his invitation to Abel to kiss his

---

Art, and Music, Monograph Series 16 (Kalamazoo: Medieval Institute Publications, 1991), fig. 120. For discussion of the Lamech episode in the medieval English drama, see Edmund Reiss, "The Story of Lamech and Its Place in Medieval Drama," *Journal of Medieval and Renaissance Studies* 2 (1972): 35–48.

[67] See R. Morton Nance, *A New Cornish English Dictionary* (St. Ives: Federation of Old Cornwall Societies, 1938), s.v. 'corn.'

[68] A. C. Cawley, ed., *The Wakefield Pageants in the Towneley Cycle* (Manchester: Manchester University Press, 1958), 91, 186–87.

[69] Margaret Rogerson, "The Medieval Plough Team on Stage: Wordplay and Reality in the Towneley *Mactacio Abel*," *Comparative Drama* 28 (1994): 182–200.

posterior (61), are a preliminary to his refusal to enter into the sacrifice with a right spirit—and to his fratricide thereafter.

The plough, an implement used in Plough Monday ceremonies in rural England,[70] also appears in the *Holkham Bible Picture Book* on fol. 6^r, between the page illustrating the sacrifice and the murder of Abel and the two pages (fols. 6^v–7^r) which contain the story of Cain's death. While in Plough Day ceremonies this farm implement is associated with beneficence, Cain's plough here and in the Towneley and Chester plays is hardly symbolic of goodness. The illumination in the *Holkham Bible Picture Book* shows a mixed team of two oxen and one ass pulling the plough, which is guided by Cain, who wears a hood that covers the mark on his forehead. He is looking down as he ploughs, and the expression on his face is apparently to be interpreted as displaying anger and malice.[71] The oxen seem to show signs of stress, and a boy wearing a hat stands with a whip over them. A third man is sowing, while below are shown the wicked children of Cain. The illustrator has chosen to present a picture of alienation and hostility in an agricultural setting rather than of Cain as the founder of cities. At his death in the subsequent illuminations Cain will become himself a victim of violence. The *Holkham Bible Picture Book*, like the vernacular plays of medieval England, has attributed to him the deadly sins of Covetousness, Sloth (for not being quick about attending to sacrifice), Envy, and Wrath. To these may be added Pride, which is central to his behavior and stands in direct contrast to Abel's humility.

Cain is ultimately an exemplar of the antisocial principle. In the Towneley play Cain orders Pikeharness to take the plough away from the acting area; then his farewell to the audience is followed by a statement of his intention to find a place to hide, perhaps for the forty days mentioned previously in the text (2.342) since that would be the time allotted under the English law for sanctuary granted to outlaws.[72] Quite clearly the pardon which the Towneley Cain attempted to proclaim for himself could

---

[70] See A. R. Wright, *British Calendar Customs*, ed. T. E. Lones, 3 vols. (London: Folk-Lore Society, 1938), 2:101–03; John Brand, *Observations on Popular Antiquities* (London: Chatto and Windus, 1913), 273–75. A ceremonial plow is still retained, for example, at Selby Abbey in Yorkshire.

[71] See Hassall, *Holkham Bible Picture Book*, 68–69.

[72] See Bennett A. Brockman, "The Law of Man and the Peace of God: Judicial Process as Satiric Theme in the Wakefield *Mactacio Abel*," *Speculum* 49 (1974): 704.

not have been taken seriously even if it had not been undermined by the sarcasm of Pikeharness. Cain's felonious act of violence against his brother is not a pardonable offense, and would have merited execution immediately upon apprehension in late fifteenth-century England.[73]

While it may be difficult to reconcile the accounts of the outlaw Cain in the late medieval vernacular plays with the biblical writer's claim that he established cities, there is nevertheless a connection with St. Augustine's view of him as the founder of the earthly city, Babylon, as enunciated in his *City of God*.[74] For the earthly city is ruled by supreme selfishness, a culture antithetical to salvation. Persons who participate in this culture and do not repent will have no hope of salvation, and symbolically it represents the dominance of those who share with Cain a kinship of despair. It is a culture of "getting," of possession, and hence of violence. In contrast, those who are of the City of God have, like Abel, a different spiritual orientation, for they are motivated by a different love—not of self but "by the love of God, even to the contempt of the self."[75] St. Ambrose commented that Abel, unlike his brother, "did not . . . refer everything to himself. Devotedly and piously, he attributed everything to God, ascribing to his Creator everything that he had received from Him."[76] Thus the followers of Abel, of the City of God however imperfectly realized, are the "true wanderers and wayfarers" of this world—pilgrims in an alien land whose great wish is to reach the heavenly city that can be entered only by means of the sacraments and a "good death."

III

As Alexandra F. Johnston remarks, the Wakefield Master's Cain "sets the pattern for all the evil figures who will follow him in this sequence of plays."[77] But this view of Cain's legacy is hardly limited to

---

[73] Ibid., 704-07.

[74] Augustine's discussion of Cain and Abel appears in *The City of God*, XV.

[75] Ibid., XIV.28; trans. Dods *et al.*, 477. See also the comments by Alexandra F. Johnston, "Evil in the Towneley Cycle," in *Evil on the Medieval Stage*, ed. Meg Twycross (Lancaster: Medieval English Theatre, 1992), 97–99.

[76] Ambrose, *Of Cain and Abel* I.i.3; trans. Savage, 360.

[77] Johnston, "Evil in the Towneley Cycle," 100. See also my article "The Unity of the Wakefield 'Mactacio Abel'," *Traditio* 23 (1967): 497–99.

Cain in the Mysteries 117

the Towneley cycle alone. In historical terms, Cain was regarded as a prototype of both those among the Jews who rejected Christ—and thus subjected him to violence even unto death on the cross—and all those who lived after Christ but rejected grace. In contrast are those who have served the principle of goodness and who have taken on the role of peacemakers rather than promoters of dissension. These are the two nations, the Church and the Synagogue, described as "two classes of people" by St. Ambrose.[78] The Jews who rejected Jesus are represented in the visual arts of the Middle Ages by a common symbolism, as in an example of painted glass at in the York Minster Chapter House vestibule;[79] in contrast to the crowned figure of the Church, who holds a cross and a model of a church building, is the figure of the Synagogue, with her banner staff breaking, her eyes blindfolded, and her crown falling from her head—that is, with her authority crumbling and her intellectual and spiritual vision limited. So those who question, arrest, torture, and execute Jesus in the vernacular plays in Middle English and the Cornish *Ordinalia* are of this class of people. Significantly, their acts are, like Cain's, directed out of envy at their brother Christ—the one who has, in Anselm's terms, become incarnate in order to be our brother.[80] The identification of Abel as a type of Christ at the Betrayal that began his Passion ordeal is made clear in the blockbook *Speculum Humanae Salvationis* not only in the arrangement of the woodcuts but in the texts below each of them: "Cristus dolose traditus"; "Caym dolose interfecit fratrem suum Abel."[81] Abel's name, according to St. Augustine, signified

---

[78] Ambrose, *Of Cain and Abel* I.ii.5; trans. Savage, 361–62.

[79] Davidson and O'Connor, *York Art*, 183. Another York example of the Synagogue, in a painted ceiling in the Chapter House, was removed in 1798; see Joseph Halfpenny, *Gothic Ornaments in the Cathedral Church of York* (York, 1795), pl. 95.

[80] See Anselm, *Cur Deus Homo*, esp. II.viii–xiii. Anselm emphasizes the point that Christ's death could have saved his murderers, for their sin was done out of ignorance: "no man could ever, knowingly at least, slay the Lord; and therefore those who did it out of ignorance did not rush into that transcendental crime with which none others can be compared" (II.xv; St. Anselm, *Basic Writings*, trans. S. N. Deane [LaSalle, Illinois: Open Court, 1962], 264).

[81] Wilson and Wilson, *A Medieval Mirror*, 176–77.

"grief" ("luctus"),[82] while Christ of course will be revealed as the "Man of Sorrows."

The Middle English text of the *Speculum Humanae Salvationis* outlines a direct kinship between those who tortured and executed Christ and "the enevyous Kaym" who "slewe his innocent brothere þat neuer trespast til hym." The scene that is invoked is the Betrayal:

> With glosing wordes tillid forth his brothere this fals Cayme,
> And having forth at the large with wikkid strokes he slewe hym:
> So Judas with faire wordes Oure Lord Crist he salutyd,
> And til his enemys to slee vndere that hym presentid.
> Abel his wombes brothere be Kaym to deth done was,
> And Crist, thaire fadere and brothere, slewe the Jewes and Judas.[83]

Among the enemies of Christ, Judas is the one who is of course most like Cain, and in the Towneley *Suspencio Iude* he describes himself as of "That cursyd clott of Camys kyn" (32.17).[84] In the *Conspiracy* in the same play collection, Pilate names those who are intent on violence against Christ as "kamys kyn" (20.663). And in the Harrowing in the York cycle, Anima Christi, speaking to Satan, links "cursed Cayme þat slewe Abell" with other suicides, including Judas, "And alle of þare assente, / Als tyrantis euerilkone / Þat me and myne turmente" (XXXVII.306–12). These lines are retained with only minor changes in Harrowing as it was adapted from the York text in the Towneley collection.

The brutality of the torturers in the vernacular plays of the Passion has long been recognized. In the Towneley Resurrection play Christ is said to have been wounded 5,400 times, with wounds covering his entire

---

[82] *The City of God* XV.18; trans. Dods *et al.*, 504; *De Civitate Dei*, ed. Emmanuel Hoffmann, 2 vols. (1900; reprint New York: Johnson Reprint, 1962). The etymology is incorrect; Hebrew scholars are instead more likely to see Abel's name as meaning "puff, vanity," though this too may be fanciful. See Speiser, *Genesis*, 30.

[83] *The Mirour of Mans Saluacioune*, ed. Avril Henry (Philadelphia: University of Pennsylvania Press, 1987), 113 (ll. 2087–88, 2095–2100). This text preserves the traditional notion that Cain and Abel were twins. Cain in all accounts is the elder of the two.

[84] For physical resemblances between Cain and Judas, see Ruth Mellinkoff, *Outcasts: Signs of Otherness in Northern European Art of the Late Middle Ages*, 2 vols. (Berkeley and Los Angeles: University of California Press, 1993), 1:134.

body from the top of his head to the soles of his feet (26.292). Representations in the visual arts showing his wounded body were ubiquitous and were often, as in the illuminations illustrating the Passion in the *Holkham Bible Picture Book* (fols. 29^v, 30^v, 31^v–33^r) and in the example of East Anglian painted glass showing Our Lady of Pity at Long Melford, Suffolk, extremely detailed in the depiction of the effects of the scourging and crucifixion.[85] The wounded body was commonly set forth as a devotional image, which might be on the cross (every church had a rood with Jesus, Mary, and, usually, St. John) or in some other form such as alabaster carvings showing Christ with his torturers, many of whom had darkened faces to represent their anger.[86] One of the signs of the Passion on the roof bosses of Winchester Cathedral shows a torturer spitting in contempt[87]—a gesture that is present also in the *Holkham Bible Picture Book*, which presents the faces of the soldiers and torturers as grotesque and distorted in representation of their hostility and anger. Here, as in the case of the murder of Abel, violence and killing are directly associated with sacrifice, in this case the atonement of the innocent Christ for the sins of all. While the malevolence is here directed against the one who is to surrender his life out of unlimited love for humankind, the spiritual progeny of Cain as often turn their violence against others of their own kind. The sons of Cain are liable in their wickedness to involve both Christ and his followers as well as members of their own wicked people in all manner of rapine and murder.[88]

Doomsday will be a time when such earthly violence and dissension are put down forever. In spite of spectacular representations of the end of

---

[85] Christopher Woodforde, *The Norwich School of Glass-Painting in the Fifteenth Century* (London: Oxford University Press, 1950), pl. XXVII.

[86] See Francis Cheetham, *English Medieval Alabasters* (Oxford: Phaidon, Christie's, 1984), nos. 159, 163–64, 166, 168, 170. In alabasters of the Betrayal on which some paint remains the faces of all except Jesus and Peter were either black or dark brown; see ibid., nos. 151, 156–57. Executioners and torturers in alabasters showing the martyrdom of saints were similarly presented with darkened faces; see, for example, ibid., nos. 15, 25–26. Cain also has a dark face—and negroid features—in Cambridge, St. John's College MS. K.26, fol. 6^v; see Mellinkoff, *Outcasts*, 1:134, and vol. 2, pl. VI.50.

[87] Cave, *Roof Bosses in Medieval Churches*, fig. 245.

[88] See Josephus, *Jewish Antiquities*, 1:30–31 (1.2.2 [66]).

history according to the book of Revelation in manuscript tradition and in such examples of public art as the East Window of York Minster,[89] the usual depiction of the Last Judgment followed the account in Matthew 25.[90] This iconography was ubiquitous and very often appeared above the chancel arch of parish churches, as in the case of the famous restored wall paintings in the church of St. Thomas of Canterbury in Salisbury[91] or the church of the Holy Trinity in Coventry, the latter depiction now totally obscured by grime and in need of restoration.[92] The York play, for which a remarkable inventory of 1433 corroborates the iconography suggested by the play text,[93] culminates in a scene of good and bad souls being consigned to heaven and hell. This play, like the final play in the other Middle English cycles and collections, dramatizes the recitation of the Seven Corporal Acts of Mercy as a test by which the souls are judged.[94] The wicked know in advance that they are destined "to dwell with feendes blake" in hell (York XLVII.143) even before they are separated from the good by the archangel Michael and the Judge descends to perform the ritual that seals their fate. Jesus shows his "woundes wide" as a sign of the violence that was wrought upon him and mentions the

---

[89] See *The Apocalypse in the Middle Ages*, ed. Richard K. Emmerson and Bernard McGinn (Ithaca: Cornell University Press, 1992), esp. 105–289; French, *York Minster: The Great East Window*, 72–136, pls. 6–17.

[90] See especially Pamela Sheingorn and David Bevington, "'Alle This Was Token Domysday to Drede': Visual Signs of Last Judgment in the Corpus Christi Cycles and in Late Gothic Art," in *Homo, Memento Finis: The Iconography of Just Judgment in Medieval Art and Drama*, Early Drama, Art, and Music, Monograph Series 6 (Kalamazoo: Medieval Institute Publications, 1985), 121–45.

[91] This wall painting has been frequently reproduced; see, for example, ibid., fig. 14.

[92] Clifford Davidson and Jennifer Alexander, *The Early Art of Coventry, Stratford-upon-Avon, Warwick and Lesser Sites in Warwickshire*, Early Drama, Art, and Music, Reference Series 4 (Kalamazoo: Medieval Institute Publications, 1985), 37; George Scharf, Jr., "Observations on a Picture in Gloucester Cathedral and Some Other Representations, of the Last Judgment," *Archaeologia* 36 (1855): pl. XXXVI, fig. 1; Jennifer Alexander, "Coventry Holy Trinity Doom," *EDAM Newsletter* 11 (1988): 37.

[93] Alexandra F. Johnston and Margaret Rogerson, *Records of Early English Drama: York* (Toronto: University of Toronto Press, 1979), 1:55–56.

[94] The Cornish *Ordinalia* does not conclude with a Doomsday play.

specific acts that were committed against him (245ff).[95] These violent acts were suffered, he says, for love of humankind; he was the human sacrifice for all men and women if they would only reciprocate his love. But for the sacrifice to have been effected, of course, it was necessary for the act to be committed by those who, like Cain, were hostile to God and to the welfare of their fellow men.

Those who have performed the Corporal Acts of Mercy have comforted and aided the homeless, the hungry and thirsty, the sick, prisoners, and those lacking clothing—deeds depicted in a famous window in the church of All Saints, North Street, York.[96] Such acts are precisely opposed to the selfishness and egoism of Cain and his followers, who are specifically designated as the "cursid caytiffis of Kaymes kynne" that will for their selfishness and lack of concern for others be consigned to dwell in sorrow and "dole" through eternity (XLVII.317–20). This designation of the wicked at the Last Day appears in precisely the same terms as the "cursid catyfs of Kames kyn" in the Towneley *Iudicium* (30.648) in a section of the text of that play which is borrowed from York. For those, whether high or low in either the secular or ecclesiastical hierarchy, who have refused grace there will be no mercy. In the N-Town play, the devils specifically contrast the Corporal Acts of Mercy with the Deadly Sins, beginning with Pride, which is identified by a mark on the forehead, and

---

[95] In the Chester Last Judgment, a rubric indicates that Christ's wound in his side actually appears to be bleeding (XXIV.428 *s.d.*)

[96] The York play omits visiting prisoners here; this is added in reference to the evil souls (XLVII.355) and in the Towneley play: "In hard prison when I was sted / On my penance ye had pyté" (Towneley 30.620–21). For the Corporal Acts window, see Eric A. Gee, "The Painted Glass of All Saints' Church, North Street, York," *Archaeologia* 102 (1969): 162–64, pls. XXV–XXVII; Davidson and O'Connor, *York Art*, 116–17. A seventh Corporal Act, not pictured in the All Saints glass, is the Burial of the Dead. This Act derives from Tobit 1:17–18 rather than from the account in Matthew 25:35–36; it does not appear in the York Doomsday play, but is mentioned in the N-Town play (42.85). Further examples of the Corporal Acts in painted glass are noted in Woodforde, *The Norwich School of Glass-Painting*, 193–96, pl. XLII; Richard Marks, *The Stained Glass of the Collegiate Church of the Holy Trinity, Tattershall (Lincs.)* (New York: Garland, 1984), 204–08, pl. 28. For examples of the Corporal Acts of Mercy in wall paintings, see Tristram, *English Wall Painting of the Fourteenth Century*, 99–101; A. Caiger-Smith, *English Medieval Mural Paintings* (Oxford: Clarendon Press, 1963), 53–55, pls. XVIII, XIXb.

Covetousness: "On covetyse was all thy thought" (42.100). Reference to Wrath, Envy, Sloth, Gluttony, and Lechery follows. Augustine's Babylon, the city founded by Cain, will be handed over to the torture house of hell, where violence and indeed all manner of malevolence will prevail without ending in the isolation of that infernal kingdom.

IV

There is no doubt that in the main the citizens of cities and towns such as York, Coventry, and Chester took very seriously their obligation to perform the Corporal Acts of Mercy, support their parish churches and chantry chapels, and live amicably. While they may have violated such ideals on occasion, as when the Cordwainers were "mysbehauyng in bering of þer torches" and fighting with the Weavers in the Corpus Christi procession at York over the matter of their specific position in the Corpus Christi procession[97]—and hence over their standing in the social order within the city—their determination in these matters is well documented in civic records, generosity in building programs, and wills. Violence, especially against guild brethren and kinsmen, was strongly condemned, perhaps no more strongly than during the Wars of the Roses when violent and disorderly acts in the larger society were being committed in the course of the struggle among the aristocracy. In such an era of shifting loyalties and sporadic fighting, their belief in the historical origin and pattern of violence allowed people to categorize acts of transgression and therefore to come to terms with the evil represented by them. Herein must lie an important social role of the Cain and Abel plays, for they reinforced a collective memory that connected the present to the past—indeed, to the earliest instance of violence.

It will further be useful to note as a kind of postscript to this article that the story of Cain and Abel remained of very great significance in this regard through the early modern period. Shakespeare, whose parentage and roots were in the social order represented by craftsmen, merchants, and yeomen, would make much of social prohibitions against violence,

---

[97] Johnston and Rogerson, *REED: York*, 1:158–59. The fine for the Cordwainers' offense was a hefty £10.

especially as these involved family, kinsmen, and residual feudal obligation. Macbeth's murder of his kinsman and king is one example, but more explicit is Claudius's homicide in which he killed his brother and thereafter specifically identified himself as one who has replicated Cain's crime. His "offense" has "the primal eldest curse upon't, / A brother's murther" (*Hamlet* 3.3.36–37).[98]

---

[98] The citation is to *The Riverside Shakespeare*, gen. ed. G. Blakemore Evans, 2nd ed. (Boston: Houghton Mifflin, 1997). For a recent study which treats the first murder as a paradigm for subsequent violence in Shakespeare's time, see Naomi Conn Liebler, "Shakespeare's Medieval Husbandry: Cain and Abel, Richard II, and Brudermord," *Mediaevalia* 18 (1995 [for 1992]): 451–73.

The Sacrifice of Isaac in Medieval English Drama

The absence of staged tragedy in the Middle Ages is a commonplace of theatrical history. However, there was no lack in the late medieval period of a vernacular drama that specialized in pain, suffering, and that deeper sort of mental hurt that usually is classified under the term *Angst*. These qualities had been far less noticeable in the liturgical drama, though such twelfth-century plays as the Fleury *Lazarus* and *Ordo Rachelis* or the Beauvais *Ludus Danielis*[1] did dramatize moments of severe anxiety. In its emotional structure, the music-drama of the Church with its beautifully stylized presentation was intended for production indoors in nave and choir and hence differs greatly from the more realistic and often violent scenes in the mainly outdoor vernacular plays which were designed to capture the attention of ordinary people. These vernacular plays, whether dramatizing a saint's martyrdom or the Passion of Christ, were capable of the same kinds of sensationalism and intense audience response that can be traced in secularized form in the great Renaissance tragedies of Shakespeare and his contemporaries.[2]

There is nothing inherently bland about these early vernacular plays, which have been proven to be vibrantly stageworthy in modern production when not subverted by either excessive piety or fashionable

---

[1] See Karl Young, *The Drama of the Medieval Church*, 2 vols. (Oxford: Clarendon Press, 1933), 2:199–211, 110–17, 290–306; *The Fleury Playbook: Essays and Studies*, ed. Thomas P. Campbell and Clifford Davidson, Early Drama, Art, and Music, Monograph Series 7 (Kalamazoo: Medieval Institute Publications, 1985), figs. 45–51, 64–74 (facsimiles); Dunbar H. Ogden, ed., *The Play of Daniel: Critical Essays*, Early Drama, Art, and Music, Monograph Series 24 (Kalamazoo: Medieval Institute Publications, 1996), 91–116 (transcription), pls. 1–27 (facsimile).

[2] See, for example, "The Phenomenology of Suffering, Medieval Drama, and *King Lear*," in Clifford Davidson, *On Tradition: Essays on the Use and Valuation of the Past* (New York: AMS Press, 1992), 70–86.

antagonism to religion.³ Developing in the small cities and towns of pre-industrial and pre-Reformation England, these were in the main civic plays that were produced for both spiritual and financial gain by amateur actors of the community. Shielded from a tragic view of history by an essentially optimistic religious belief, the producers and performers were not isolated from violence, which nevertheless their communities worked diligently to overcome, sometimes, as in the application of cruelty in the punishment and execution of criminals—for example, in drawing and quartering, and in exposing their decapitated heads in public places—with methods that were themselves violent. It is in this context that the sacrifice of Isaac by his father Abraham, one of the most popular of the Old Testament stories to appear on the late medieval stage, will need to be understood.

Narratives such as the story of the sacrifice of Isaac may not at first impress us as wildly violent and disturbing on account of their familiarity. In the version told by the authors of the Genesis account, Isaac is the miraculous child of aged parents.⁴ Much loved, he nevertheless is to be given up in a sacrificial act to be performed by his father on Mount Moriah. The act of sacrifice has been commanded by God himself, and Abraham will do as he has been told. In Genesis Abraham is given the ordeal as a test of his obedience. Obedience is also at the core of medieval accounts and explains the presence of Abraham's sacrifice as the subject of the initial illustration at the beginning of the tenth- or eleventh-century manuscript containing the *Psychomachia* of Prudentius that is now British Library, MS. Cotton Cleopatra C.VIII.⁵ In the Middle English *Cursor*

---

³ For the latter I am thinking particularly of *The Mysteries* as presented a few years ago at the National Theatre in London. This production aimed at a desacralization of the text through inappropriate comedy that removed much of what was serious from the visual effect of the play. It is hard to see any real threat from Herod in the escape into Egypt of the holy family when Joseph was shown towing Mary and Child along on a toy donkey.

⁴ The authorship of the Genesis story of Abraham is divided between writers known as J, P, and E. The section on the sacrifice of Isaac bears marks of both J and E, and it is not known which should be given credit for primacy; see E. A. Speiser, trans. and ed., *The Anchor Bible: Genesis* (Garden City, N.Y.: Doubleday, 1981), esp. 166.

⁵ See Thomas Ohlgren, *Anglo-Saxon Textual Illustration* (Kalamazoo: Medieval Institute Publications, 1992), pl. 15.1. In another Anglo-Saxon *Psychomachia*

Mundi the Lord merely orders, in a single sentence, that "I will þou offer [Isaac] to me" (3130), and Abraham acquiesces with hardly any qualms: "Blythly, lauerd, þou me him gaue, / Gode skill es þat þou him haue" (3131–32). Abraham is utterly acquiescent; his will is entirely subsumed by God's inscrutable will.

"Figures and their fulfillment," V. A. Kolve has argued, establish the "formal shape" of the English play cycles that treat Old Testament material.[6] Careful attention to the iconography and the structure of individual plays will qualify this view somewhat, but unquestionably the choice of episodes following the Creation and Fall does result in the presentation of characters and the dramatization of events that look forward to their fulfillment in the life, suffering, and resurrection of Christ. The selection of the Abraham and Isaac story is a primary exhibit, for it demonstrates how what might be regarded as a difficult and even outrageous lesson in obedience had received widespread attention and eventually became rich material for the stage.[7]

The significance of the sacrifice of Isaac as foreshadowing Christ's act of immolation apparently may be traced to the New Testament itself. For example, Romans 8:32—"He . . . spared not even his own Son"—seems to echo the angel's words to Abraham in Genesis 22:12. Jean Daniélou describes how the Church Fathers developed the story as a foreshadowing of the sacrifice on the cross.[8] Their work was thus instrumental in bringing the Abraham and Isaac story into the consciousness of Christian Europe in the Middle Ages, and it will be seen

---

manuscript, Cambridge, Corpus Christi College, MS. 23, scenes from the life of Abraham are included; see Mildred Budny, *Insular, Anglo-Saxon, and Early Anglo-Norman Manuscript Art at Corpus Christi College, Cambridge*, 2 vols. (Kalamazoo: Medieval Institute Publications, 1997), pls. 224–25.

[6] V. A. Kolve, *The Play Called Corpus Christi* (Stanford: Stanford University Press, 1966), 99.

[7] See especially Rosemary Woolf, "The Effect of Typology on the English Mediaeval Plays of Abraham and Isaac," *Speculum* 32 (1957): 805–25; and Thomas Rendall, "Visual Typology in the Abraham and Isaac Plays," *Modern Philology* 81 (1984): 221–32.

[8] Jean Daniélou, *From Shadows to Reality: Studies in the Biblical Typology of the Fathers*, trans. Wulstan Hibbard (London: Burns and Oates, 1960), 115–30.

that the invoking of typology in the interpretation of the event was as much alive in the fifteenth century as it had been in the Patristic period.[9] In the Sarum liturgy for Quinquagesima Isaac is specifically identified as a type of Christ.[10] This hermeneutic method was capable of enriching a story so long as it did not become a mechanism for denying its literal meaning by resolving it into a mere abstraction.

The Middle English text of the *Speculum Humanae Salvationis* specifically draws out the typological meaning of the event: "In Ysaac, Abraham son, hadde prefiguracioune: / For Ysaac on his awen shuldres wodde mekely bare & brought / Be whilk his fadere to Godde þat tyme hym sacrifie thoght," and so Christ had carried the wood of the cross at his Crucifixion. Further, as ultimately a sheep was substituted for Isaac, so Christ has been substituted "for vs alle." Like Isaac, Christ would willingly in obedience offer himself up to be sacrificed. While earlier manuscripts of the *Speculum* such as Pierpont Morgan Library MS. M.766 show Isaac carrying the wood for his sacrifice as Christ carried his cross on the way to his Crucifixion, the illustration in a typical later block-book *Speculum* shows instead the crucial near-death scene, which is rescued from apparent tragedy by the appearance of an angel who comes down to prevent the father from beheading his son.[11] The *Biblia Pauperum* makes the correspondence even more clear: Isaac carrying the wood and following his father, who has a falchion at his side and is holding a lighted torch, foreshadows Christ with his cross on his shoulder in the adjoining panel; the angel arresting the arm of Isaac's father in turn foreshadows the Crucifixion event, which is to be understood ultimately as a rescue from death.[12] But even with the typological pattern in mind it

---

[9] See, for example, John Mirk, *Festial*, EETS, e.s. 96 (1905; reprint Millwood, N.J.: Kraus, 1987), 76–78.

[10] *Breuiarium seu horarium domesticum* (Paris: C. Chevallon, 1531), pt. 1, fol. lxxxv (*STC* 15830).

[11] *The Mirour of Mans Saluacioune: A Middle English Translation of Speculum Humanae Salvationis*, ed. Avril Henry (Philadelphia: University of Pennsylvania Press, 1987), 115–16 (ll. 2450–52, 2458); Adrian Wilson and Joyce Lancaster Wilson, *A Medieval Mirror: Speculum Humanae Salvationis, 1324–1500* (Berkeley and Los Angeles: University of California Press, 1984), 47, 184.

[12] See Avril Henry, *Biblia Pauperum* (Ithaca: Cornell University Press), 93, 95–96, 98. While the woodcut showing the carrying of the wood does not display

is hard not to imagine the scene that might have presented itself if the angel had been delayed even for one moment: the son, whom Abraham valued more than anything else in the world, would have been sacrificed in unreasoning response to a sadistic command from on high. It is a terrible thought. Further, it is a thought that underlies the dramatic presentations of the story on the English stage and is in large measure responsible for their effectiveness both in the Middle Ages and in modern revivals.

A connection between God's will, sacrifice, and the death of a family member also is implicit in another well-known account in Genesis that was taken up by the vernacular dramatists. Paradoxically, in the story of Cain and Abel the sacrifices of the two brothers are in response too to the divine command, and here the sacrificial act does in fact lead, indirectly, to the shedding of the blood of Adam's son Abel. In Genesis, the account of God's choice of Abel over Cain, attributed to the writer known as the Yahwist (J), had no basis except in his preference for the one over the other.[13] God thus was exercising his will in making his choice, and his will seems not to have been based on any principles that could be deciphered by the humans involved in the sacrifices. Medieval commentators, following the statement in 1 John 3:12 that Cain's "works were wicked: and his brother's just," would, however, interpret God's choice as consistent with reason. The Towneley *Mactacio Abel* is a demonstration of the rule that to sacrifice of one's first fruits with a willing heart is necessary if one is to retain the good will of the jealous God who has

---

it in the shape of a cross, quite possibly in some play productions it would have been thus arranged to emphasize the connection with the New Testament. For an example in which two bundles of wood are made up like a cross, see the misericord at Worcester Cathedral (M. D. Anderson, *The Imagery of British Churches* [London: John Murray, 1955], pl. 5); there was also a wall painting with this iconography at Peterborough Cathedral which is now lost (M. R. James, "On Paintings Formerly in the Choir at Peterborough," *Cambridge Antiquarian Society Proceedings* 38 [1896]: 192–93). But in some form the iconography followed in Continental as well as in English drama traditionally shows Isaac carrying the wood on his back or shoulders; see Lynette R. Muir, *The Biblical Drama of Medieval Europe* (Cambridge: Cambridge University Press, 1995), 213, n. 6.

[13] See "Cain in the Mysteries," above.

made all things of nought.[14] To sacrifice stingily or to present an inferior offering is indeed hazardous and will result in God's approbation. But what happens when God, as in the story of Abraham, demands *human* sacrifice? In the Genesis account God's will, then, seems to be arbitrary and amoral, differing from the law which he will give in the Ten Commandments delivered to Moses on another mount, Sinai. For Cain the killing of Abel leads to God's curse and a mark which will set him off from the community of men forever. On the other hand, Abraham's guilt in intending to kill his son is set aside because it is not executed. But, in line with God's apparent will, he has been willing to do the deed, and Isaac has become an accomplice since he has been willing that he should have his life surrendered to the will of an inscrutable God.[15]

It will not do to explain away the story by means of some abstraction or other that will purportedly provide a full answer to the questions which are raised. Little merit adheres to the anthropological-historical speculation that the event was "really" about the abandoning of human

---

[14] In the *Mactacio Abel*, 226, Abel thus appropriately scolds his brother: "Caym, thou tendys wrang, and of the warst" (*The Towneley Plays*, ed. Martin Stevens and A. C. Cawley, EETS, s.s. 13–14 [Oxford: Oxford University Press, 1994], 1:18). See Exodus 22:29: "Thou shalt not delay to pay thy tithes and firstfruits: thou shalt give the firstborn of thy sons to me"—a text which, incidentally, would seem to include the sacrifice of children. Child sacrifice, however, is specifically prohibited as an abomination elsewhere; see Deuteronomy 12:31.

[15] Isaac's willingness to participate in his own sacrifice appears to derive from the account in Josephus, *Jewish Antiquities* 1.232: "The son of such a father could not but be brave-hearted. . . . He exclaimed that he deserved never to have been born at all, were he to reject the decision of God and of his father and not readily resign himself to what was the will of both, seeing that, were this the resolution of his father alone, it would have been impious to disobey; and with that he rushed to the altar and his doom. And the deed would have been accomplished, had not God stood in the way . . ." (*Jewish Antiquities*, ed. and trans. H. St. J. Thackeray, 6 vols., Loeb Classical Library [Cambridge: Harvard University Press, 1930-65], 1:115). Only his young age would save Isaac from the charge of self-murder; see William Blackstone, *Commentaries on the Laws of England*, 4th ed., 4 vols. (Dublin: John Exshaw *et al.*, 1771), 4:189.

sacrifice by an antique civilization.[16] Such an explanation will hardly elucidate the popularity of the story in the Christian Middle Ages and subsequently. In this respect the commentary of the nineteenth-century Danish philosopher Søren Kierkegaard may be useful. In his examination of the sacrifice of Isaac in *Fear and Trembling* Kierkegaard saw it as demonstrating an abstract principle—the teleological suspension of the ethical—which he saw as revealing the highest stage that the religious life is capable of achieving.[17] While Kierkegaard understood the event as a lesson in faith which asserted a religiosity that was superior not only to merely conventional morality but also to ethical behavior in the purest sense, he nevertheless also recognized the predicament faced by Abraham in all of its terror. God demanded that Abraham should commit the most terrible crime and the most horrible deed that anyone could imagine. In the end God rescinded his command, but only when he saw that Abraham was poised to comply. The ethical is thus, for Kierkegaard, not abrogated but is proven to be in fact taken up (*aufgehoben*, in Hegelian terms) into a religiosity which asserts an absolute duty toward the Absolute. This, in Kierkegaard's view, does not diminish the frightening aspects of the episode when one considers it in all its aspects.

It is possible, on the other hand, for typological interpretation, especially as it has been applied to literary texts in twentieth-century criticism, to dilute the more terrible aspects—and, therefore, the more overtly theatrical aspects—of the Abraham and Isaac plays. Arnold Williams's 1968 article "Typology and the Cycle Plays: Some Criteria" argues against what he saw as the misuse of such interpretation, specifically in the case of the Abraham and Isaac plays.[18] Because the texts were not open to view except as spoken from the stage, the test of any interpretation should in his view be dramatic effectiveness. He also insisted that dramatists who overused typology produced less aesthetically satisfactory plays, as in the case of the text of the York

---

[16] On the sacrifice of Isaac and the context of human sacrifice in biblical antiquity, see the useful comments of Northrop Frye, *The Great Code: The Bible and Literature* (New York: Harcourt Brace Jovanovich, 1982), 183–85. Historically the sacrifice of firstborn sons was not unusual in ancient Palestine.

[17] Søren Kierkegaard, *Fear and Trembling [and] Repetition*, trans. Howard V. Hong and Edna H. Hong (Princeton: Princeton University Press, 1983), 5–123, esp. 54–67.

[18] Arnold Williams, "Typology and the Cycle Plays: Some Criteria," *Speculum* 43 (1968): 677–83.

Abraham and Isaac, which, following Peter Comestor and the exegetical tradition, presents an Isaac who is slightly more than thirty years of age.[19] An older Isaac such as this can hardly compete with dramatic versions of the story that utilized child actors to put forward an Isaac who is innocent and very young. To be sure, Isaac, as one of the patriarchs of ancient Israel, was seen as an object of veneration, and the child Isaac would have represented expectations that, in order to complete salvation history, especially required fulfillment. The sacrifice of Isaac as a child would at once have canceled not only the life of the son miraculously born of Sarah in her old age but also the whole plan of salvation history. A useful parallel here would seem to be the killing of the Innocents by Herod's henchmen, for this later event too would threaten the plan of salvation, and once again the threat would be averted by divine intervention.

Thus the purely *human* level may seem to be the essential ingredient in the Abraham and Isaac plays in which Isaac is presented as a child, but this level is not disconnected from other aspects of meaning, including the typological. Still, there is merit to the critical opinion that finds Isaac to be less attractive when he is presented as a young adult. Quite possibly even the York *Abraham and Isaac* play at one time accommodated a child Isaac. The play text in the York Register may not represent the drama as it always was staged by the Parchmentmakers' and Bookbinders' guilds since the *Ordo Paginarum* of 1415 in the *York Memorandum Book A/Y* summarized the play as follows: "Abraham immolans filium suum Isaac super altare garcio cum bosco & angelus."[20] If Isaac was the boy (*garcio*) with the wood, then he would seem to have been a child rather than the adult for which the extant play text calls. This would not have aborted the typology inherent in the York play, but it would have insured a far more moving theatrical experience.

---

[19] Ibid., 683. See also Minnie Wells, "The Age of Isaac at the Time of the Sacrifice," *Modern Language Notes* 54 (1939): 579–82. I have previously discussed the York *Abraham and Isaac* in my *From Creation to Doom: The York Cycle of Mystery Plays* (New York: AMS Press, 1984), 52–55.

[20] *Records of Early English Drama: York*, ed. Alexandra F. Johnston and Margaret Rogerson, 2 vols. (Toronto: University of Toronto Press, 1979), 1:18. Signs of possible corruption in the York text which may be "due to revision or to deterioration of the text in the process of transmission" are noted by Richard Beadle, ed., *The York Plays* (London: Edward Arnold, 1982), 422.

In the Abraham and Isaac play in the Brome Hall manuscript,[21] the use of a boy actor becomes the focus of the very curious epilogue spoken by the Doctor. The Doctor stresses the lesson of the "solom story to gret and smale" which is to keep "Goddys commawmentys wythowt grochyng" (436, 442), but then continues with the construction of a hypothetical predicament:

> Trowe ȝe, sorys, and God sent an angell
> And commawndyd ȝow ȝowre chyld to slayn,
> By ȝowre trowthe ys ther ony of ȝow
> That eyther wold groche or stryve therageyn? (443–46)

The Doctor's initial object seems to be to make the members of the audience call to mind the emotions implied in the threat of *Kindermord* against Isaac in the play. But thereafter his argument takes a very unusual turn, for he applies the Old Testament story to remembrance of the weeping of mothers for their children who have died. Such sorrow is consistent with nature,[22] but, he says, "Yt ys but folly . . . / To groche aȝens God or to greve ȝow" (452–53). God takes away, and he also makes amendment; his followers should, according to his view, serve the deity without questioning or deviating from his commandments. His argument favors a kind of Christian stoicism. A child who has died will, if baptized, be favored with salvation, toward which we all should strive: "Bryng vs all to heuyn-blysse!" (465). Needless to say, the logical flaw in the argument presented in the epilogue is that it fails to keep in mind an obvious but important point. Isaac's demise, unlike the deaths of the children of English parents who weep for them, would have been filicide at the hands

---

[21] *Non-Cycle Plays and Fragments*, ed. Norman Davis, EETS, s.s. 1 (London: Oxford University Press, 1970), 43–57. Citations to the Brome play and other plays are to line numbers in parentheses in my text.

[22] Quite clearly parents' attitudes toward their children were not characterized by the indifference claimed by Philippe Ariès, *Centuries of Childhood: A Social History of Family Life* (New York: Knopf, 1962). The Brome epilogue had, however, a broader purpose, which was to encourage hardships without complaint in a general way. This interpretation of the sacrifice of Isaac has been traced to Vincent of Beauvais and ultimately to the Church Fathers; see David Mills, "The Doctor's Epilogue to the Brome *Abraham ad Isaac*: A Possible Analogue," *Leeds Studies in English* n.s. 11 (1980): 105–10.

of his beloved father; a similar event, had the killing been executed, in an English town would have been punishable as murder, and, if apprehended, the guilty parent would undoubtedly have been hanged.[23]

The Brome epilogue may, however, serve to provide verification of the one of the arguments in defense of religious drama listed in *A Tretise of Miraclis Pleyinge*: the stage presents vivid and memorable pictures of the scenes of salvation history which are hence more likely to be impressed on the memory than mere static pictures.[24] The well-known dictum of Gregory the Great concerning the role of religious art as "laymen's books" identifies one of the principal functions claimed for painting and sculpture: "For what writing is to those who can read, a picture presents to the uneducated, those who observe with their eyes, because in this picture the ignorant see what they ought to do, in this picture those who do not know their letters can read. Thus a picture is for

---

[23] Harriet Frazier, J.D., has suggested to me in conversation that, since Abraham's motive was not malice, the charge might have been reduced to manslaughter. But child murder was regarded with a particular horror, as when Macbeth's henchmen kill the children of Macduff in Shakespeare's play, and Abraham's plan to kill his son was further a case of premeditation. Blackstone observes that to kill one's parents or children meant more harsh punishment than for other crimes of murder under Roman law (*Commentaries on the Laws of England*, 4:202–03). Blackstone would likely have classified this unnatural crime as one for which the punishment was, for a man, "to be drawn and hanged" (4:204). The most common type of child murder was infanticide by the mother of a new-born illegitimate infant which, even if judged to be manslaughter, was nevertheless a capital offense. When Fortescue sought to illustrate how a ruler's decrees might be the reverse of justice, he cites a case of infanticide—Herod's order for the children of Bethlehem to be killed. Of this royal decree, which he admits "hath force of law," he comments that "nothing could be more iniquitous than such a law" (*De Natura Legis Naturae* 1.28, in *The Works of Sir John Fortescue, Knight*, ed. and trans. Thomas Fortescue, 2 vols. [London, 1869], 2:220). If God had permitted the murder to take place at his command, he would have been verifiably a tyrant (see ibid., 2:220).

[24] *A Tretise of Miraclis Pleyinge*, ed. Clifford Davidson, Early Drama, Art, and Music, Monograph Series 19 (Kalamazoo: Medieval Institute Publications, 1993), 98; see also 23–27, 133–34. Further, the Wycliffite writers of the *Tretise* saw the plays as representing "signis withoute dedes" (99) and thereby denied the function of imagination in religious devotion.

reading, especially for the people."[25] But the use of pictures, like the religious plays, was considerably more complex than this might imply.[26] Pictures were hardly the best teachers of morality and were most useful when allowed to serve a mnemonic function in bringing to mind the events and personages that had been taught in sacred history. Together pictures and plays may be seen as devices to achieve the remembrance of past events—events which had taken place centuries prior to the presentation of the picture or the play itself. Materialist critics would identify their function as constructing a religious past that would exist as part of the collective memory of a people.[27] And, according to the view reported in the hostile Wycliffite *Tretise of Miraclis Pleyinge*, the art form that had the greater emotional impact was the stage:

> sithen it is leveful to han the miraclis of God peintid, why is not as wel leveful to han the miraclis of God pleyed, sithen men mowen bettere reden the wille of God and his mervelous werkis in the pleyinge of hem than in the peintinge? And betere they ben holden in mennes minde and oftere rehersid by the pleyinge of hem than by the peintinge, for this is a deed bok, the tother a quick.[28]

According to this view, a story such the sacrifice of Isaac could shock and disturb an audience much more than a mere picture when presented by living actors, who would make the past seem *as if* real in the mimetic representation involved in their acting.[29]

---

[25] Gregory the Great, Letter to Serenus, as quoted in translation by Ann Eljenholm Nichols, "Books for Laymen: The Demise of a Commonplace," *Church History* 56 (1987): 458.

[26] Further complexities with regard to Gregory's concept of religious art are discussed by Lawrence G. Duggan, "Was Art Really the 'Book of the Illiterate'?" *Word and Image* 5 (1989): 227–51.

[27] See, for example, Maurice Halbwachs, *On Collective Memory* (Chicago: University of Chicago Press, 1992).

[28] *A Tretise of Miraclis Pleyinge*, 98.

[29] The vivid appeal of the story as staged was consistent with the Franciscan emphasis on the function of imagination in spiritual experience; see, for example, Nicholas Love, *Mirror of the Blessed Life of Jesus Christ*, ed. Michael G. Sargent (New York: Garland, 1992), 161: "Bot þerfore here aȝeynus fort haue trewe ymaginacion & inwarde compassion of þe peynes & þe passion of oure lorde Jesu verrey god & man. we shole vndurstande þat as his wil was to suffre þe hardest deþ & most sorouful peynes, for þe redempcion of mankynde. . . ."

Of course, historical primacy must be given to visual representations of the sacrifice of Isaac by Abraham in the visual arts. The seven extant plays from medieval England—six in Middle English and one in Cornish —which dramatize the incident are all of them no earlier than the last quarter of the fourteenth century and some may be dated as late as the sixteenth century.[30] In contrast, representations in the visual arts date back to the third and early fourth centuries.[31] The sacrifice scene had regularly

---

[30] The earliest has conventionally been thought to be the Abraham segment in the Cornish *Ordinalia* (*The Ancient Cornish Drama*, ed. and trans. Edwin Norris, 2 vols. [Oxford: Oxford University Press, 1859], 1:97–105), which, however, has recently been plausibly dated between 1395 and 1419; see Gloria J. Betcher, "A Reassessment of the Date and Provenance of the Cornish *Ordinalia*," *Comparative Drama* 29 (1995–96): 436–39. For the extant Middle English texts, see *The York Plays*, ed. Beadle, 91–100; *The Towneley Plays*, ed. Stevens and Cawley, 1:48–57; *The Chester Mystery Cycle*, ed. R. M. Lumiansky and David Mills, EETS, s.s. 3, 9 (London: Oxford University Press, 1974–86), 1:56–79; *The N-Town Play*, ed. Stephen Spector, EETS, s.s. 11–12 (Oxford: Oxford University Press, 1991), 50–58; *Non-Cycle Plays and Fragments*, ed. Davis, 32–42 (Northampton play) and 43–57 (Brome play). For discussion see Rosemary Woolf, *The English Mystery Plays* (Berkeley and Los Angeles: University of California Press, 1972), 145–53; Janet A. Bakere, *The Cornish Ordinalia* (Cardiff: University of Wales Press, 1980), 54–55; and, for a European perspective, Muir, *The Biblical Drama of Medieval Europe*, 75–77.

Records also indicate the presence of Abraham and Isaac plays or processional tableaux at Dublin (John T. Gilbert, *Calendar of Ancient Records of Dublin*, 16 vols. [Dublin: J. Dollard, 1899–1919], 1:239, citing a Corpus Christi pageant of the Weavers guild in 1498), Canterbury (J. M. Cooper, "Accounts of the Churchwardens of St. Dunstan's, Canterbury, A.D. 1484–1580," *Archaeologia Cantiana* 17 [1887]: 80, citing "a booke of Abraam and Isaacke" belonging in 1520 to the parish guild), Dundee (Anna Jean Mill, *Mediaeval Plays in Scotland* [1924; reprint London: Benjamin Blom, 1969], 173, citing "abraamis hat" in an inventory of properties for the Corpus Christi procession in c.1520), and Oxford (John P. Driscoll, "A Miracle Play at Oxford," *Notes and Queries* 205 [1960]: 6, citing a student production presented perhaps as late as the early part of Queen Elizabeth's reign and thereafter noted in Edmund Bunny's *Briefe Answer* 1589]).

[31] See Isabel Speyart van Woerden, "The Iconography of the Sacrifice of Abraham," *Vigiliae Christianae* 15 (1961): 221–23, figs. 1–7; Alison Moore Smith, "The Iconography of the Sacrifice of Isaac in Early Christian Art," *American Journal of Archaeology*, 2nd ser. 26 (1922): 159–73.

come to be regarded as one of the great instances of the foreshadowing of the Crucifixion *ante legem* long before the heyday of the vernacular drama, though of course typological interpretation had been frequently enough set aside in favor of other aspects of the story in these illustrations. The illumination in the twelfth-century Hunterian Psalter (Glasgow University Library MS. Hunter 229), for example, shows no immediate signs of the influence of typological interpretation.[32] In the upper panel the angel comes to Abraham, whose son Isaac is seated at his feet, and carries the message indicated on his scroll to the effect that the father must sacrifice his beloved son. In the lower panel, the son, now nude and kneeling on an altar at the right, extends his hands as his father grasps him by the hair and raises his sword to behead him. An angel (upper left) grasps the sword in his high hand to prevent the deed and points with his left to a sheep with his horns caught in the bush immediately below him; on the other side the hand of God extends from a cloud in approval of Abraham's obedience. While it is difficult to read the expression on the boy's face and his gesture, comparison with the face in the upper panel suggests not only acquiescence but terror.

In the Sacrifice of Isaac in thirteenth-century painted glass in Canterbury Cathedral, the positioning of the angel, Abraham, and the ram is not so different, allowing for the shape of the panel, a half-roundel in the Redemption Window in the corona. Here Abraham has swung his sword back over his shoulder with obvious vigor in preparation for bringing it down on his son. Abraham, as Madeline Caviness has suggested, was most likely originally looking backward at the angel who is grasping the weapon.[33] But here typology does come into play in the design of the scene, for Isaac is placed on bundles of wood in the shape of a cross on the altar. The positioning of the scene is also typological, for the panel is placed in a window that also illustrates not only scenes of the Passion but also other types which foreshadow specific Passion scenes. In spite of the

---

[32] T. S. R. Boase, *The York Psalter* (London: Faber and Faber, 1962), pl. 2.

[33] Madeline Harrison Caviness, *The Early Stained Glass of Canterbury Cathedral* (Princeton: Princeton University Press, 1977), 131–32, who suggests that the head of Abraham may have been altered in the restoration of George Austin, Jr., in the nineteenth century. See also Caviness's *The Windows of Christ Church Cathedral Canterbury*, Corpus Vitrearum Medii Aevi 2 (London: Oxford University Press, 1981), 167, figs. 217, 217a.

weathering and damage to the glass, it demonstrates that the typological approach does not need to be seen as antithetical to a powerful visual rendition of the event. Typology and other levels of meaning are capable of existing side by side. Thus typology is able to enrich the other meanings of the episode.

However, as the discussion earlier in this paper has suggested, the presence of typology in drama may not be so satisfactory when it is overly heavy-handed. For example, though Peter Travis has claimed the play dramatizing the Abraham story in the Chester cycle to be "typological drama at its best" for its union of typology and "'realistic' mimetic action,"[34] the added commentary in the play that argues for a typological understanding of the event seems in this case imposed on the drama and a hindrance to its dramatic effectiveness. David Mills seems quite correct in noting that the Chester dramatist "can be seen resisting the emphatic model of naturalistic drama offered by its source."[35]

The Chester Barbers' play of *Abraham* appears to be an expansion of the Brome text and includes 192 lines of material that seems to be borrowed from the non-cycle play.[36] In the Chester pageant, the play text covers more of Abraham's history (though in rather abbreviated fashion) than the sacrifice of Isaac, and as noted above includes an affirmation of the typological significance of the story as its core meaning. Attention is thus given to Abraham's meeting with Melchysedeck which was generally regarded as a foreshadowing of the institution of the Mass.[37] As Yumi Dohi has observed, the text of this play fails to call attention to the

---

[34] Peter W. Travis, *Dramatic Design in the Chester Cycle* (Chicago: University of Chicago Press, 1982), 83.

[35] David Mills, "The Chester Cycle," in *The Cambridge Companion to Medieval English Theatre*, ed. Richard Beadle (Cambridge: Cambridge University Press, 1994), 125.

[36] J. Burke Severs, "The Relationship Between the Brome and Chester Plays of *Abraham and Isaac*," *Modern Philology* 42 (1944–45), 137–51.

[37] This episode is the one chosen for illustration in the Great East Window created for York Minster by John Thornton of Coventry in 1405–08; see Thomas French, *York Minster: The Great East Window*, Corpus Vitrearum Medii Aevi, Summary Catalogue 2 (Oxford: Oxford University Press, 1995), fig. 14e. Melchisedek holds a loaf of bread, while a man behind him holds a chalice; the latter, however, is a piece of fourteenth-century glass from elsewhere that was inserted in the restoration of 1953.

relationship between this episode and the Eucharist, but the Expositor will intrude to explain how animal sacrifice was to be replaced by the remembrance of Christ's death in the bread and the wine of the Mass.[38] This method of "signification," already visually shown by means of stage properties in the "standinge-cuppe" and the offering of "wynne and bred" (IV.65 *s.d.*, 73 *s.d.*; cf. 129–32), seems to be an attempt to supplant the literal meaning of the story in favor of the typology inherited from the Church Fathers but adapted on this occasion to assert that Abraham signifies God the Father,[39] who is set over against Melchysedeck, prefiguring a priest who celebrates the Eucharist. This is followed by Abraham's lament that he has no legitimate child to take his place after him and then by God's response, which includes the command to impose circumcision on Isaac. The Expositor in turn explains that this practice according to the "ould lawe" is abrogated by the New Testament practice of baptism (195–200). Immediately thereafter comes the scene of God's direct command to Abraham requiring him to sacrifice his son.

The stage directions in the Chester play serve as a sign that the actors had a less abstract view of the sacrifice scene than the redactor who added the lines spoken by the Expositor. The stage directions require Abraham to lift his hands upward toward heaven as he exclaims how his "harte will breake in three" (253), while Isaac is to express fear: "fearinge leste his father will slea him" (265 *s.d.*). At line 323, Abraham is seen "wringinge his handes"—a sign of despair, sometimes applied to the damned in Last Judgment iconography as at Autun.[40] As a response, one manuscript (Harley 2124) reads: "Here Isaake askinge his father blessinge one his knyes" (328 *s.d.*)—a gesture corroborated by the text. When Abraham calls his son "soe sweete" to him (357), Isaac obediently "cometh to his father, and hee taketh him and byndeth him and layeth him one the alter for to sacrifyce him" (359 *s.d.*). While the binding is part of the typological pattern, it also is an act specified in the biblical account (Genesis

---

[38] Yumi Dohi, "Melchisedek in Late Medieval Religious Drama," *Early Drama, Art, and Music Review* 16 (1993–94): 87–88.

[39] Very likely, as Rendall has suggested, the Expositor here is following a "visual clue," since Abraham is now a very old man who thus would be made to resemble God the Father in the visual arts ("Visual Typology," 225).

[40] See Moshe Barasch, *Gestures of Despair in Medieval and Early Renaissance Art* (New York: New York University Press, 1976), fig. 8.

22:9).[41] In line 389 Abraham says farewell to his "sweete sonne of grace" and then kisses him before placing the "carchaffe about his head" and kneeling before the child that he seems about to sacrifice (390 *s.d.*). A curious shift in the text after line 420—the point at which the parallel with the Brome text ceases—has Abraham once again preparing his son for the sacrifice and immediately raising his sword to behead him: "Here lett Abraham take and bynde his sonne Isaack upon the aulter, and leett him make a signe as though hee would cutt of his head with the sword. Then lett the Angell come and take the sworde by the end and staye yt. . . ." But two angels appear, and it is the second angel who announces that God has provided "a lambe" (434) for the sacrifice instead of Isaac.[42] A final stage direction has "Abraham take the lambe and kyll him" (444 *s.d.*). The substitution of a lamb for the mature ram of the biblical text is typological, for the lamb is to be interpreted as the Lamb of God who is Christ, slain for the sins of the world. Yet the Expositor, in a passage that is very near to a statement in a well-known sermon collection,[43] also identifies Isaac as foreshadowing Christ, whose Father, like Abraham, was willing to allow his Son to shed his blood in sacrifice "to breake that bonde / that the dyvell had brought us to" (470–71). The final speech by the Doctor is a prayer, spoken kneeling (476 *s.d.*), that focuses on Abraham's obedience, which ought to serve as a model for all. The Expositor thus is guilty of attempting to erase the anguish which is central to the episode.

Anguish and dread are certainly present elsewhere. In the Cornish *Ordinalia*, Abraham is heartsick as he asks Isaac to lie down on the wood on the altar, and the latter requests that his arms and legs be tied down so

---

[41] See also Woolf, who remarks that Christ's hands also had been reported to be tied in the Gospel of Nicodemus ("The Effect of Typology," 807). Rendall further notes that the connection between Isaac and Christ is specifically made in the *Glossa Ordinaria* ("Visual Typology," 227, citing *Patrologia Latina*, 113:139). Biblical paraphrases such as Nicholas Love's *Mirror of the Blessed Life of Jesus Christ* described how Christ was stripped and bound during his Passion (170–71).

[42] Probably an artificial animal was used, as at Lucerne; see *The Staging of Religious Drama in Europe in the Later Middle Ages*, ed. Peter Meredith and John E. Tailby, Early Drama, Art, and Music, Monograph Series 4 (Kalamazoo: Medieval Institute Publications, 1983), 118.

[43] Mirk, *Festial*, 77.

that he will not flee when the flames reach him, for his "pains will be cruel / Before being burnt to ashes" (1349–55). In the text of the York play, which presents, as noted above, an Isaac who is slightly more than thirty years old, Abraham is literally "wighte and wilde of thoght" (X.222) when he contemplates what he must do. He will do God's command even though he would rather himself die than see his son sacrificed. Isaac in his dread asks that his father should place "þis kyrcheffe on myn eghne" (288). The Towneley Abraham, having prepared Isaac and placed a cloth over his eyes so that he will not see the blade when he strikes, pauses and weeps profusely as he thinks about what he is to tell Sarah. The weeping must continue for some time while God speaks to an angel, who is sent to stop the killing at the very moment when Abraham has mustered the courage to slay Isaac. The joy with which Abraham speaks to his son, whom he also kisses, is mixed with terror at what might have happened: "Son, thou has skapid a full hard grace; / Thou shuld haue beyn both brent and brokyn" (4.279–80). "For ferd, syr, was I nerehand mad," Isaac explains (286).[44] In the N-Town play, Abraham is at first apprehensive when the Angel relays to him God's command that "Thy welbelouyd childe þu must now kylle" (5.81); he accepts the command as necessarily to be followed, but reveals that "ȝitt þe fadyr to scle þe sone, / Grett care it causyth in my thought" (91–92). He weeps, and tells Isaac that he has been ordered to "kylle" him, that the fire prepared for the sacrifice must be for him, and that "Þi careful fadyr must be þi fo" (138–44). The deed will be unnatural and a most terrible thing; he will cover his son's face with a "kerchere" so that when he slays him he will not be able to see his "lovely vesage" (179–81). As he prepares to spill his son's blood, the Angel calls out to him. The tone of these plays would have been quite different if Abraham had in fact been represented as utterly confident that God would send a substitute sacrifice. The conclusion in which the sacrificial animal is miraculously supplied must seem to come to him as a surprise. The plays are hence in spirit not inconsistent with the earliest iconography of the sacrifice of Isaac which developed the theme of deliverance.[45]

---

[44] At this point the Towneley play breaks off; two leaves are missing from the playbook.

[45] See van Woerden, "The Iconography of the sacrifice of Abraham," 238, 242.

The medieval dramatists thus were capable at their best of drawing selectively from the curious account of Abraham in Genesis[46] to produce plays of considerable power. The choice of incidents in these plays may be usefully compared to the episodes illustrated in fifteenth-century painted glass at Great Malvern Priory, which possesses a fairly well developed Abraham and Isaac cycle in the south clerestory windows of the nave.[47] The first scene shows God appearing out of the clouds at the left before a kneeling and hatless Abraham, to whom he promises that he will have a son who will be born to his wife Sarah though she is now beyond the normal age of child-bearing. The next scenes present Sarah's incredulity when her husband, now wearing a hat, tells her that she is to bear a child,[48] and the circumcision of Isaac. The costumes of Abraham and his wife are richly portrayed to indicate that these are persons of social consequence; Sarah wears a red garment with an ermine border, over which she has a blue mantle that is ermine-lined. Abraham has a gold girdle with a large jewel surrounded by smaller jewels suspended from it.[49]

The command to Abraham to sacrifice his son is given to him by an angel who has golden hair and wings touched with gold and who also wears an alb and cope, which is fastened at the neck with a morse. Abraham receives the message with hands raised in adoration. On the

---

[46] The authorship of Genesis 22:1–19 is uncertain, but has characteristics of both J and E, the latter identified by his use of Elohim instead of Yahweh for God. For J, who focuses on the roles of individuals in Jewish history, the purposes of the deity are inscrutable though ultimately just and consistent with reason; see Speiser, trans., *Genesis*, xxviii. E, in contrast, tends to be more oriented toward events rather than toward individuals, and the deity is more remote, usually communicating with men through angels rather than directly (ibid., xxx–xxxii). For the curious structure of the Abraham story, see *The Literary Guide to the Bible*, ed. Robert Alter and Frank Kermode (Cambridge: Harvard University Press, 1987), 47–50.

[47] Gordon McN. Rushforth, *Medieval Christian Imagery* (Oxford: Clarendon Press, 1936), 166–71, figs. 75–78, 80.

[48] A fragment of a Dutch play on this subject is reported by Mary Jo Arn, "A Little-Known Fragment of a Dutch Abraham-and-Sarah Play," *Comparative Drama* 17 (1983–84), 318–27.

[49] That such rich garments were used in drama is suggested by the costume list from Lucerne; see *The Staging of Religious Drama*, ed. Meredith and Tailby, 133.

following journey to Mount Moriah he is walking with a crutch staff, wearing a scabbard that holds a falchion, and carrying a torch in his right hand. The figure of Isaac is lost, but presumably he was carrying the wood.[50] The sacrifice of Isaac completes the Abraham cycle (the next scene is the marriage of Isaac and Rebecca). A hatless Abraham, standing with his sword raised above his head and his left hand on Isaac's head, looks back and sees the angel, who has his left hand raised in a sign of caution and his right pointing to Isaac. Isaac, who is blindfolded and kneeling on the wood, faces Abraham and has his hands joined in the late-medieval position of prayer with hands joined. In this case Isaac is not nude but wears tunic and hose.[51]

Neither these illustrations in Great Malvern painted glass—nor, for that matter, other examples in the visual arts such as woodcarvings like those on misericords at Worcester Cathedral (see fig. 12)—could have provided the emotional impact of a play performed by real-life actors. This hence brings to the fore once again the point cited by the author of the *Tretise of Miraclis Pleyinge*—that is, that the same scenes when played by living actors would be transformed into a vivid semblance of reality that more urgently would impress itself on the mind. The Great Malvern glass furthermore is placed in clerestory windows where the scenes are difficult to see with the unaided eye. Like the remarkable series of roof bosses in Norwich Cathedral to which drama scholars have called attention,[52] therefore, these scenes in Great Malvern's glass are

---

[50] In another Abraham and Isaac series in the fourteenth-century *Queen Mary's Psalter*, Isaac carries the wood on his head while Abraham holds an unsheathed "fauchion," which he seems to be shielding from his son's view. See George Warner, *Queen Mary's Psalter* (London: British Museum, 1912), 60, pls. 13–22, esp. 21.

[51] It may be illustrative to compare the iconography here with a scene in a roundel in a series of Old Testament illustrations in a genealogical roll (British Library MS. Add. 14,819) of c.1300 in which Isaac as a child is facing *away* from Abraham as he kneels on the altar. The child is clothed in a gown and holds up his hands in prayer. Abraham is holding his left hand on Isaac's head. See Lucy Freeman Sandler, *Gothic Manuscripts 1285–1385*, 2 vols., Survey of Manuscripts Illuminated in the British Isles, 5 (London: Harvey Miller; Oxford: Oxford University Press, 1986), no. 22, plate fig. 50.

[52] See especially M. D. Anderson, *Drama and Imagery in English Medieval Churches* (Cambridge: Cambridge University Press, 1963), *passim*.

12. Sacrifice of Isaac. Misericord, Worcester Cathedral. ©Crown Copyright. National Monuments Record.

perhaps less important for their visibility than simply for their inclusion in the iconographic program of the church building. The pictures translate the event from biblical antiquity into the present, and they thus help to connect the present sacred space of the church to the history of salvation. They are like a static *thing done*, a silent ritual object abstracted from time.[53] In plays, particularly those in the vernacular, the static and sometimes partially hidden scene was given life and movement, for they brought episodes from salvation history before the eyes of the spectator as they *might have* occurred. The effect may have been considerably less than full-scale realism in the modern sense, for to achieve the desired theatrical effects such aspects as anachronistic costumes and speech were

---

[53] I am thinking here of Jane Ellen Harrison's translation of the Greek term *dromenon* (*Ancient Art and Ritual*, 2nd ed. [London: Williams and Norgate, 1918], 26–27, 35–38).

utilized and the action was telescoped into a conveniently short space of time.

Along with the Brome play, the Northampton Abraham and Isaac play has generally been highly regarded.[54] This play was formerly sometimes called the "Dublin play" since its text is uniquely found in Trinity College, Dublin, MS. D.4.18. The Dublin *Chain Book* records a Corpus Christi Weavers' pageant of "Abraham Ysack, with ther auter and a lambe and ther offerance,"[55] but the Trinity College manuscript has no connection with that city and instead is determined from its other contents to be a commonplace book of 1461 from Northampton, where the play may have been written and copied.[56] There is no proof that the play was ever performed there, however, though late medieval Northampton had a town square that would seem to have been ideal for the kind of fixed-stage production required by the Abraham drama. The storage of pageants (presumably pageant wagons) in St. George's Hall in Northampton in the earlier sixteenth century[57] does not necessarily have any link with the play. The play itself is unique among British Abraham dramas, for it includes the role of Sarah and also calls for two servants, whose presence is derived from the biblical account.[58] And it uses horses for transport to the mount where the sacrifice is to be made—an indication that the staging involved at least two locations considerably separated from each other.[59]

---

[54] Williams, "Typology and the Cycle Plays," 683.

[55] Gilbert, *Calendar of Ancient Records of Dublin*, 1:239.

[56] Davis, ed., *Non-Cycle Plays and Fragments*, xlvii–lviii.

[57] J. Charles Cox, *The Records of the Borough of Northampton, 1550 to 1835* (Northampton: Birdsall, 1898), 184.

[58] For the role of Sarah, Davis (*Non-Cycle Plays and Fragments*, lii–liii) calls attention to another play in which she is introduced similarly, the French *Le Mystère du Viel Testament* (Paris, 1539).

[59] The use of a beast of burden also appears in sculpture in the Chapter House of Salisbury Cathedral where Abraham leads the ass with Isaac on its back and a burden of wood for the sacrifice; see William Burges, "The Iconography of the Chapter-House, Salisbury," *The Ecclesiologist* 17 (1859): 152. An ass was used in the Lucerne Passion play for the Abraham segment; the scene was begun in an area of the market square to the east, and then moved to a stage specially erected for the sacrifice; see M. Blakemore Evans, *The Passion Play of Lucerne* (1943; reprint Millwood, N.Y.: Kraus, 1975), 194, plan facing 141; *The Staging of Religious Drama in Europe in the Later Middle Ages*, ed. Meredith and Tailby, 117, 133.

The Sacrifice of Isaac in Medieval English Drama 145

The beginning of the play introduces Deus, who, announcing that he is the "begynnere" of "all þing" (1), expresses his dissatisfaction with the human race. But there is one "of his kynd [who] shal plese me ayeyne" (10), and this is Abraham to whom he has granted a child late in life. He announces that he will test him by commanding that he should "make sacrifise vnto me of Isaac his son ȝynge" (25). The angel whom he sends down to earth to communicate his command will come before Abraham at just the moment when he is affirming the dependence of all things on God and giving thanks for his beloved son. The message will here, as in the other plays on this topic, be a harsh one, but Abraham does not hold back or complain, "[f]or of me his wille shal neuer be withnayde / Whil I am on lyve" (62–63). The play thereafter will examine the difficulty of executing God's will, especially since it is guaranteed to be contrary to the will of his spouse Sarah as well as his own natural feeling.

Sarah, then, provides a complicating factor not present in the other British plays on the subject. Abraham would rather face her displeasure than God's, but still the opportunity is present for the actor playing the role to stress the anxiety that naturally would come of such a conflict. Interestingly, he does not at this point think about the welfare of his son; if God will grant him the determination to do the deed, he will fulfill it "[w]ithout fraude outher cauelacion" (71). It would seem that the actor is expected to illustrate his agitated state when he comes to the door of the house and demands that the "yates" be opened. When Sarah lets him in, she shows at once that she senses a grievous change in him. He will then equivocate, for he will only tell her about the command to sacrifice "vpon þat hille on hye" (96) at once and not about the child to be sacrificed. He nevertheless must overcome her reluctance to allow Isaac to accompany him, and he will deceive her by his insistence that it is time for the child to "know and se / How þat God shal plesid be" (117–18).

The servants are played by non-speaking supers but are important in that they help to transport the father and child along with the equipment for the sacrifice—"fyre and stikkes to bren" (130)—to a point near the place where it is to occur. They will not, however, be allowed to come to the place of sacrifice itself, but must hold the horses, presumably out of sight, during the rite. At this point Isaac must take off his hood so that he can carry the wood and the fire. The wood is tied, presumably in bundles and placed on his back for ease in carrying. Isaac will also now ask about the whereabouts of the live animal for sacrifice. Then Abraham, alone with his son as they arrive at the altar that has been prepared in advance, finally tells him "þe truthe certayne" (161). He relays the command that his son's body will be "brouȝt to nought" by means of the sacrifice "on this hille" (166–67). Isaac is bluntly told to put the wood on the altar and quickly to "delyuer þe and do of þi gere" (168–69).

Isaac's response is fear. He asks for an explanation ("Haue I displesid you any thing?" [171]) and begs not to be put to death. We must always do as God wills, Abraham explains, and this is what he *intends* to carry out. Has God then been offended by me, Isaac asks, "Þat I shal be martyred in þis mysse?" (185). Isaac is innocent, as Jesus later will be when he is presented as a living sacrifice on the cross, but in no way can Abraham be moved to relent. However, mention of Isaac's mother, Sarah, is another matter. It is assumed that when she hears of the sacrifice she will be unhappy in the extreme, and Abraham also is reminded that if she had her way her son would not have been allowed to accompany him on this day. Abraham, even as he grieves, is, however, determined to carry through the deed, and when he has convinced Isaac that this is the case his son will prepare for his death. Isaac, slipping off his gown, remains concerned about his mother ("Let neuer my moder se my cloþus," he says [205]), and his father falls into the despondency that will accompany his actions in preparing to execute the deed that will take away the one who is more important to him than all the other things that he possesses.

Isaac willingly takes on the role of sacrificial victim, but the horror of the impending sacrifice is invoked not only by his father's grief at what he feels he must do but also by the son's continued mentioning of his mother. Like none of the other plays on the subject of the sacrifice of Isaac, Sarah focuses the theatrical effect of the scene so that the conflict between obedience and morality is presented with forcefulness and even brilliance. Abraham seems nearly speechless, and it is now Isaac who requests that his hands and legs should be tied. Further, he objects when his father thoughtlessly causes pain in the process. Isaac also will request to be placed on the altar softly, then to be killed quickly, "For I am hampred and in dispeyre/ And almost at my lives ende" (234–35). The audience is to see Abraham as one who abhors what he is about to do. A later speech reports that he has "made fyre and smoke," taken out his knife, and prepared to "smyte of his hed and bren hym veralye" (336–39). His final speech is literally blood-chilling, for he begs Isaac to kiss him and then asks him to "ly downe, strecche out þi throte" (257).

When Abraham raises his sword to do the Lord's "plesaunce" (259), the Angel intervenes and commands that "þat wedyr there" should serve as the sacrifice on the altar instead of his son. The test is over, and Abraham gives thanks to God that his son has been spared. But the fearfulness of the event is still a presence, for in his prayer he reports: "Haddest not sent þyn aungil, Isaac had died þis day" (279). And he then says, "þis pref was riȝt sore" (280). Isaac is told to put on his clothing again and not to reveal anything to his mother about very nearly being a victim of human sacrifice. The event leaves Abraham in an unheroic posture, hardly like the heroes of tragedy. As Kierkegaard rightly insisted, Abraham is no tragic hero.[60]

Deus explains to Abraham and Isaac that now both of them will be objects of veneration as long as "þe world shal last" (293). Their descendants will be as numerous "as gravel in þe see" (298). The ordeal has been safely passed, and the victorious passage through danger has been successfully completed. The father and son will re-mount their horses and return to Isaac's mother. Sarah's response to knowledge of the aborted sacrifice is instructive: "Alas, all þen had gone to wrake" (342). The ordeal, however, is one that is said to encourage obedience and to deter disobedience, and the advice at the very end is that "What God commaundeþ say not nay, / For ye shal not lese therby" (368–69).

The Northampton play as well as the other Abraham and Isaac plays are much more, then, than didactic dramas which merely preach obedience. The intended sacrifice of Isaac posits a potential loss that would ultimately have been catastrophic for the human race since his descendants established the Israel of the later patriarchs and prophets —and of the Savior whom they foreshadowed and prophesied. Further, Isaac was identified by St. Paul as a child of promise, just as Christ's followers are "the children of promise" (Galatians 4:28). As the loss of Abraham's son is averted, so also the Christian community of future generations is made secure. The sacrifice of the Lamb of God is represented typologically in these plays by the lamb, sheep, or ram, literally

---

[60] See Kierkegaard, *Fear and Trembling*, 79 and *passim*.

the animal that serves as a substitute for Isaac and that also allows for a viable solution that will not contaminate Abraham through shedding the blood of his son or mark the beginning of a cycle of violence.[61]

Suffering and anxiety are therefore ultimately regarded as necessary in history for the achievement of stability and amity in the Christian community and of the hope of salvation for those who worship the Creator of all things and his Son. Within this scheme of things there is a need for people individually or collectively to experience *Angst* either actually or in imaginative and devotional experience. God, by ordering Abraham to transgress, may seem to us to be as terrifying as the imagined spider god seen by the character Karin, who is descending into madness in Ingmar Bergman's film *Through a Glass Darkly*.[62] But God is also the source of love as well as of terror, and ultimately he acts to affirm his plan of redemption in history. It is within this context that the Abraham and Isaac dramas need to be understood, and it is this context that suffuses the medieval plays of Abraham and Isaac with theatrical vitality.

---

[61] Cf. the discussion of sacrifice in René Girard, *Violence and the Sacred*, trans. Patrick Gregory (Baltimore: Johns Hopkins University Press, 1977), 1–67.

[62] See Ingmar Bergman, *A Film Trilogy*, trans. Paul Britten Austin (London: Calder and Boyars, 1967), 57–58. For the Swedish text of this film, see Ingmar Bergman, *En filmtrilogi* (Stockholm: Norstedt, 1963), 62–64.

Nudity, the Body, and Early English Drama

Attitudes toward the human body were an important factor affecting the production of the late medieval religious drama of England. The unclothed post-lapsarian body was regarded as a sign of shame, as opposed to the perfect human body of Christ, but nude pre-lapsarian and post-lapsarian bodies as well as an unclothed Christ all demanded representation on the stage by actors whose own bodies were understood to be shameful. A Middle English translation of the pseudo-Bonaventuran *Stimulus Amoris* establishes a significant contrast:

> 3if þou wolt al-gatis loue fleshli loue, I praie þe other flesh loue þou non þan þe flesh of ihesu criste, þat for thi loue and al man kynde was nailid on þe cros and offred to þe fadir in raunsom for oure synnes. Forbeden be from þe liikynge in any odir flesh, but only in þe swete fleshe of ihesu criste, þat is clene withouten wemme of synne. . . . For þis shal þou loue, þat holy flesh, and souke out of hit at his woundes þat aren so wyde þe swetnesse of grace þat is hid wiþinne.[1]

However, it is vital to understand that while Christ's body was regarded as the object of strong devotion because of its role in one's salvation, its stripping and exposure during his Passion were paradoxically seen in terms of the shame with which the human body was otherwise associated. Thus an important Old Testament type foreshadowing the violent mocking and stripping of Christ during his Passion was the shame of Noah.

The shame of Noah occurs very rarely in drama and never in the extant English or Cornish plays,[2] but in the visual arts it makes its

---

[1] *The Prickyng of Love*, ed. Harold Kane, 2 vols. (Salzburg: Institut für Anglistik und Amerikanistik, Universität Salzburg, 1983), 1:5–6. Attention is called to this passage by Sarah Beckwith, *Christ's Body: Identity, Culture and Society in Late Medieval Writings* (1993; reprint London: Routledge, 1996), 57. Beckwith's interpretation of the passage, however, is faulty in both conception and terminology.

[2] Lynette Muir, *The Biblical Drama of Medieval Europe* (Cambridge: Cambridge University Press, 1995), 74.

appearance, for example, in the fourteenth-century *Holkham Bible Picture Book* where one of his sons looks upon him in mockery as he lies inebriated and with his sexual member exposed.³ The typological meaning of this scene is revealed in the *Speculum Humanae Salvationis* and the *Biblia Pauperum*. The English text of the *Speculum* edited by Avril Henry comments:

> And thogh Noe of his son was scornyd vnhonestely
> 3it was Crist vnlike with bejaped more vileynsly,
> For in his tabernacle was Noe scornyd, no man seeyng,
> Bot Crist in the bisshopis hows, fulle many one on lukyng.⁴

Further, as this text explains, Noah was asleep, but Christ was wide awake at the time of his mocking (2179–80). The *Biblia Pauperum* likewise emphasizes the shame and mockery endured by Jesus during the trial which preceded the exposure of his nude body on the cross.⁵ According to the typological interpretation of the Noah episode, the two sons who entered Noah's tent backwards so as not to see his shame, and who then covered his nakedness (Gen. 9:21–23), foreshadowed the placing by the Virgin Mary of her veil around Christ so that his genitals would

---

³ W. O. Hassall, *The Holkham Bible Picture Book* (London: Dropmore Press, 1954), fol. 9ʳ; see also ibid., 78. In the illumination, the mocking son, Ham, points at his father, while the second son covers Noah's nakedness; the third son covers his own face so that he does not see his father's shame.

⁴ *The Mirour of Mans Saluacioun*, ed. Avril Henry (Philadelphia: University of Pennsylvania Press, 1987), 117 (ll. 2175–78); subsequent reference to this work will be by line number. See also Adrian Wilson and Joyce Lancaster Wilson, *A Medieval Mirror: Speculum Humanae Salvationis, 1324–1500* (Berkeley and Los Angeles: University of California Press, 1984), 179.

⁵ *Biblia Pauperum*, ed. Avril Henry (Ithaca: Cornell University Press, 1987), [93], 94. The central figure in the block book combines the Buffeting and Crowning with Thorns, but that the typological meaning is even broader is indicated by the texts from Lam. 3:14, Ps. 21:8, and Is. 1:4. The text explains that "Noe signifies Christ, whom the mocking Jews crowned and stripped—and similarly the unworthy sons [sic] jeered at him as if at a fool." The iconography appeared as early as the Caedmonian *Genesis* (Bodleian Library, MS. Junius 11, p. 78); see Thomas H. Ohlgren, *Anglo-Saxon Textual Illustration* (Kalamazoo: Medieval Institute Publications, 1992), 570.

not be seen. The stage presentation of nudity was clearly a problem in a society that found the body to be the locus of shame. The exploration of this matter would appear to be of considerable importance for the understanding of the religious stage and also to have some relevance for the interpretation of certain images involving nudity in the visual arts, which in turn provide much information that can usefully be applied to the study at hand. My purpose in the present paper will be to provide a description of the context in which nudity was presented on the early British stage.

The difficulty for the producers of the great civic cycles of English biblical drama, then, was that nudity was frequently required of characters, as for example in rubrics in the Chester Drapers' play, which specifies: "Then Adam and Eve shall stand naked and shall not bee ashamed" (II.161 *s.d.*).[6] The nude bodies of our first parents here are thus dissociated from the shame with which such exposure, including uncovered genitals, would normally have been associated, and serve as powerful reminders of how things were understood to have changed in the post-lapsarian world. The presentation of such nudity, representing innocence, was a challenge for the early stage since actual nakedness on the English stage would presumably have been out of the question, especially since Eve would normally have been played by a man. The technical solution to the problem is revealed in the rubrics in the Cornish *Creacion of the World* which specify that Adam and Eve are to be "aparlet in whytt lether" (344 *s.d.*)—that is, tawed leather, produced by the whittawers.[7] In contrast to the red tunic ("tunica rubea") worn by Adam and the white

---

[6] Citations to the English civic cycle plays from Chester, York, and Coventry are to the following editions: *The Chester Plays*, ed. R. M. Lumiansky and David Mills, EETS, s.s. 3, 9 (London: Oxford University Press, 1974–86); *The York Plays*, ed. Richard Beadle (London: Edward Arnold, 1982); *The Coventry Corpus Christi Plays*, ed. Pamela M. King and Clifford Davidson, Early Drama, Art, and Music, Monograph Series 27 (Kalamazoo: Medieval Institute Publicatons, 2000). For the N-Town and Towneley collections, see *The N-Town Play*, ed. Stephen Spector, EETS, s.s. 11–12 (Oxford: Oxford University Press, 1991); and *The Towneley Plays*, ed. Martin Stevens and A. C. Cawley, EETS, s.s. 13–14 (Oxford: Oxford University Press, 1994). For the Cornish plays, see *The Creacion of the World*, ed. and trans. Paula Neuss (New York: Garland, 1983); *The Ancient Cornish Drama*, ed. and trans. Edwin Norris (Oxford: Oxford University Press, 1859).

[7] For the technology involved, see John Cherry, "Leather," in *English Medieval Industries*, ed. John Blair and Nigel Ramsay (London: Hambledon Press, 1991), 299.

gown with silk wimple of Eve in the twelfth-century Anglo-Norman *Ordo Representationis Adae*,[8] a more realistic presentation of the pre-lapsarian condition was expected by audiences of the late medieval plays. The use of such body stockings of white leather, called "lybkleidern" at Lucerne where they are specified for Adam and Eve, appears to have been the usual way to represent nudity in adults.[9] At Norwich these garments for Adam and Eve are described as "cote[s]" and "hosen," which were "steyned."[10]

Sexuality is suppressed or muted in pre-lapsarian representations of Adam and Eve in the visual arts, as would appear in a wall painting at Easby, Yorkshire (fig. 13).[11] In the depiction of the Fall in the Great East Window by John Thornton of Coventry in York Minster, Eve has her right leg thrust forward to hide her genital area, and Adam's penis is barely showing above the lead lines designed to obscure this detail. While the light showing the creation of Adam in the same window has been unreliably restored, the man's figure nevertheless seems to be in good

---

[8] For convenient text and translation, see *Medieval Drama*, ed. David Bevington (Boston: Houghton Mifflin, 1975), 80.

[9] *The Staging of Religious Drama in Europe in the Later Middle Ages*, ed. Peter Meredith and John Tailby, Early Drama, Art, and Music, Monograph Series 4 (Kalamazoo: Medieval Institute Publications, 1983), 130. William Tydeman writes that "the total nudity of Adam and Eve before the Fall is not impossible, since we know that naked women posed in street pageants during the fifteenth and sixteenth centuries and appeared in Italian court entertainments . . . , but given that Eve was usually played by a man, some kind of basic garment to conceal the fact was no doubt needed . . ." (*The Theatre in the Middle Ages* [Cambridge: Cambridge University Press, 1978], 212–13). The street pageantry to which reference is made here was at Lille, where "three handsome girls, representing quite naked sirens," apparently with bare breasts, were part of the entry for Charles the Bold; see Johan Huizinga, *The Autumn of the Middle Ages*, trans. Rodney J. Payton and Ulrich Mammitzsch (Chicago: University of Chicago Press, 1996), 374, and also George R. Kernodle, *From Art to Theatre* (Chicago: University of Chicago Press, 1944), 66. Tydeman's skepticism is well founded, for nudity is doubtful on other grounds than cross-dressing for Eve, especially with regard to the British civic drama.

[10] *Non-Cycle Plays*, ed. Norman Davis, EETS, s.s. 1 (London: Oxford University Press, 1970), xxxv.

[11] G. Rowe, "The Frescoes in Easby Church," *Reports and Papers Read at the Meetings of the Architectural Societies . . . during the year 1875* (Lincoln: James Williamson, n.d.), 69–71; see also E. Clive Rouse, *Medieval Wall Paintings* (Princes Risborough: Shire, 1991), fig. 47.

Nudity, the Body, and Early English Drama 153

13. The Creation of Adam and Eve and the warning against the Tree of Life, followed by the Fall. Wall painting, Easby, Yorkshire. Drawing by Marianne Cappelletti after an engraving accompanying an article by the Rev. G. Rowe (1875).

condition, again with lead lines hiding the genital area.[12] The Chester play's dialogue and rubrics indicate the sequel: shame, focused on the genitals. "Adam, husbande, I reade we take / this figge-leaves for shames sake, / and to our members an hillinge make / of them for thee and mee"; "And therwith my members I will hide, / and under this tree I will abyde"; "Then Adam and Eve shall cover ther members with leaves, hydinge themselves under the trees" (II.273–78, 281 *s.d.*). But it is questionable whether the genitals were ever represented on the leather body stockings worn by the actors.

To be sure, in the visual arts Adam's member might be shown, as in the illumination showing the creation of Eve in the manuscript *Speculum Humanae Salvationis* in the Newberry Library (MS. 40, fol. 1^v), but more commonly, as in the block book version of the *Speculum*, he is shown without sex.[13] In the latter, Adam and Eve are grasping at fig leaves to place before themselves even as they are receiving and biting into the apples offered by the serpent.[14] The reason for their act of covering themselves is explained by St. Augustine in sexual terms: "there began in the movement of their bodily members a shameless novelty which made nakedness indecent."[15] An interesting late twelfth-century font at Oxhill, Warwickshire, depicts Adam and Eve, shown frontally, as very elongated figures with their hands clutching fig leaves—a graphic representation of

---

[12] Thomas French, *York Minster: The Great East Window*, Corpus Vitrearum Medii Aevi—Great Britain, Summary Catalogue 2 (Oxford: Oxford University Press, 1995), 49; Clifford Davidson and David E. O'Connor, *York Art*, Early Drama, Art, and Music, Reference Series 1 (Kalamazoo: Medieval Institute Publications, 1978), 21–22, fig. 4.

[13] Wilson and Wilson, *A Medieval Mirror*, 142. For the illumination from Newberry Library MS. 40, fol. 1^v, see ibid., pl. III-9. For other examples showing Adam's member, see Cambridge, Trinity College MS. O.4.16, fol. 113^v, and the Vernon Psalter (Huntington Library MS. EL 9.H.17, fol. 14^v), the latter a figure in the Harrowing of Hell (Lucy Freeman Sandler, *Gothic Manuscripts, 1285–1385*, 2 vols., Survey of Manuscripts Illuminated in the British Isles 5 [London: Harvey Miller; Oxford: Oxford University Press, 1986], plate figs. 34, 130). In Walters Art Gallery MS. W.102, fol. 8, Adam appears in the Harrowing with a fig leaf over his genitals (Sandler, *Gothic Manuscripts*, plate fig. 28).

[14] Lancaster and Lancaster, *A Medieval Mirror*, 144.

[15] *City of God* XIV.17; trans. Marcus Dods *et al.* (New York: Random House, 1950), 465.

their shame.[16] A woodcarving on a benchend at Osbournby, Lincolnshire, also shows them clutching fig leaves in postures that suggest severe discomforture.[17]

The shame with which the sinful human body was regarded therefore is a commonplace in particular because of the sexual nature of humans.[18] The point is illustrated in the N-Town *Woman Taken in Adultery* in which the young man, having been caught in an act of fornication, threatens the Scribes and Pharisees with a dagger as he runs away partially clothed. There is no reason to believe that the woman emerged from her "chawmere" without clothes in early productions, but she asks for mercy and attempts to bribe her accusers "[s]o þat in clennes ȝe kepe my name"; "Lete not þe pepyl know my defame," she begs, preferring even death to the open publication of her sin (24.164, 176). Jesus' response, in contrast to that of the accusers, is of course on the side of mercy, for he exposes the hypocrisy of those who would condemn her. But the scene reveals not only the shame associated with the physical body and sexuality but also

---

[16] Clifford Davidson and Jennifer Alexander, *The Early Art of Coventry, Stratford-upon-Avon, Warwick, and Lesser Sites in Warwickshire*, Early Drama, Art, and Music, Reference Series 4 (Kalamazoo: Medieval Institute Publications, 1985), 105, fig. 35.

[17] Arthur Gardner, *Minor English Wood Sculpture, 1400–1550* (London: Alec Tiranti, 1958), fig. 43.

[18] Though the Lady Godiva procession at Coventry was instituted only in the late seventeenth century and hence is not directly relevant to the present discussion, the story of Godiva as it was told in the chronicles confirms the medieval English attitude toward the display of the nude body. According to early accounts that were reported by William Dugdale, this "most beautiful and devout Lady" indeed did ride through Coventry "from the one end of the town to the other, in the sight of all the people," but her nakedness was veiled by her long hair "so that it covered all her Body but the Legs" (*Antiquities of Warwickshire* [1656], 86). She was apparently thus shown in painted glass in a window in Holy Trinity Church, Coventry; for a drawing of the remains of this glass in the early nineteenth century, see Birmingham Reference Library, Aylesford Collection: Warwickshire County Seats, Castles, etc., I, 168. Later accounts assert that she rode naked only after ordering all inhabitants to stay indoors with their windows closed, whereupon one person, called Peeping Tom, alone was guilty of illicit voyeurism. The procession, which was a favorite civic exercise from c.1678 until it was discontinued in the nineteenth century, typically included a horse bearing a young woman in a tight-fitting costume of the color of flesh. See Diane K. Bolton, "The Legend of Godiva," in *A History of the County of Warwickshire*, vol. 8, ed. W. B. Stephens (London: Oxford University Press, 1969), 42–43; F. Bliss Burbidge, *Old Coventry and Lady Godiva* (Birmingham: Cornish Brothers, n.d.), 34–63.

the potential for forgiveness to those who fail to achieve perfection. And it is expected that all shall fall short of such perfection except one, Jesus, who according to the theologians became man in every way but resisted all temptations of the flesh.

It is interesting therefore that much of the remaining nudity in the cycle plays was represented by the actors playing Jesus. There was, of course, the Harrowing, in which nudity is traditionally associated with the souls of Adam, Eve, and the patriarchs who are extracted from the mouth of hell by Christ, and there also were the "souls" of the saved and the damned rising from the grave at the Last Day of history—souls which at Coventry were dark for the wicked, white for those destined for bliss. The Coventry Last Judgment pageant was under the sponsorship of the affluent Drapers, who paid for blackening the faces of the wicked and for making the "sollys cottys," apparently of canvas.[19] The "soles" were six in number, equally divided between "blake" and "wytte."[20] Body stockings (if that is what they were) which are thus color coded would, if we are to believe the evidence of the visual arts, have avoided realism with regard to their sexual organs. The wall painting of the Last Judgment at Stratford-upon-Avon, which is still barely visible over the chancel arch of the Guild Chapel, shows an array of resurrected figures that apparently were relatively sexless, depicting few figures fully frontally and among these no males.[21] In the case of this wall painting we are aided by the colored drawings made of the wall painting by Thomas Fisher in the early nineteenth century.[22]

Nor would we expect the shapes of Adam, Eve, and all the others being extracted from Limbo in the Harrowing to appear in fully realistic

---

[19] *Records of Early English Drama: Coventry*, ed. R. W. Ingram (Toronto: University of Toronto Press, 1981), 474, 478; see also Clifford Davidson, "The Fate of the Damned," in *The Iconography of Hell*, ed. Clifford Davidson and Thomas Seiler, Early Drama, Art, and Music, Monograph Series 17 (Kalamazoo: Medieval Institute Publications, 1992), 49; and also Meg Twycross, "'With what body shall they come?' Black and White Souls in the English Mystery Plays," in *Langland, the Mystics, and the Medieval Religious Tradition*, ed. Helen Phillips (Cambridge: D. S. Brewer, 1990), 271–86, and "More Black and White Souls," *Medieval English Theatre* 13 (1992): 52–63.

[20] *REED: Coventry*, 478.

[21] Davidson and Alexander, *The Early Art*, 69–71, figs. 28–29.

[22] Clifford Davidson, *The Guild Chapel Wall Paintings at Stratford-upon-Avon* (New York: AMS Press, 1988), fig. 17.

detail. These souls of the righteous who lived before Christ are released from their dark prison and receive his blessing before they are taken up into heaven. The usual iconography depicts Jesus grasping the nude Adam by the forearm (the gesture derives from the *Gospel of Nicodemus*[23]), as in a fifteenth-century alabaster in the Victoria and Albert Museum; here the Anima Christi himself is clothed in a cape closed only at the neck and wearing a loincloth.[24] Such a cape could have been the garment designated as the "spirits cote" in the Coventry Cappers' pageant in 1576.[25] In the alabaster, the nude figures of the souls of the righteous are stepping out of the hell-mouth positioned at the right with their left legs forward to preserve their modesty. The Harrowing as shown in the fourteenth-century *Holkham Bible Picture Book* differs from the usual iconography in that Adam and Eve are shown already outside of the hellmouth and standing behind Christ, who is assisting another nude soul out of Limbo; and while Eve's genital region is barely visible, Adam again turns so that his member is not seen.[26] Clearly full nudity in the male was more of a taboo than in the woman.

In depictions of the Nativity, however, nudity is often present in the visual arts, and in the York Tilethatchers' play the iconography indeed demands a Child who is without clothing at his first appearance. The play as it appears in the Register draws on Brigittine iconography, which presents the birth as an event that takes place without the usual pain of childbirth while Mary is alone. He appears on the ground before her, in all instances of such iconography surrounded by an aureole of light, whereupon his Mother worships him before picking him up in her arms

---

[23] *The Apocryphal New Testament*, trans. M. R. James (1924; reprint Oxford: Clarendon Press, 1953), 137.

[24] Francis Cheetham, *English Medieval Alabasters* (Oxford: Phaidon, Christie's, 1984), no. 198; in this alabaster, all the souls are not, of course, nude, for John the Baptist wears a simple gown as he steps forth immediately behind Eve. Something more like frontal nudity, but without sexual designation so far as I can see, appears in two English alabasters published by W. L. Hildburgh, "English Alabaster Carvings as Records of the Medieval Religious Drama," *Archaeologia*, 93 (1949), pl. XXc, d. For discussion of the iconography of the Harrowing pageant at York, see Clifford Davidson, *From Creation to Doom: The York Cycle of Mystery Plays* (New York: AMS Press, 1984), 135–51.

[25] *REED: Coventry*, 277.

[26] *Holkham Bible Picture Book*, fol. 34.

to dress him "in þis poure wede" (XIV.67).[27] Examples of such iconography in the visual arts are frequent after c.1420, though it does not appear in extant examples that we know to have originated in the city of York.[28] In York Minster Library MS. Add. 2, a book of hours, Mary is in bed, while the Child is bound up tightly in cloth and is placed in a crib in front of an ox and an ass (fol. 36^r). But in a printed book of hours, published at Rouen for York use in 1517,[29] the Brigittine iconography is present; here the Child appears on cloth which is an extension of Mary's cloak, and Joseph too is in a posture of adoration. The Child's genitals are visible in spite of the crudity with which he is depicted by the artist.[30] The block book *Speculum Humanae Salvationis* has the Child on the ground surrounded only by a dish-shaped aureole with rays, but his genitals are not visible.[31] The Fitzwilliam Missal, which was illuminated in Yorkshire, also has the Virgin and Joseph adoring the Child (Fitzwilliam Museum, MS. 34, p. 37). A woodcarving on a chancel stall filial at Rotherham shows the Child up against his Mother in a mandorla set against her skirt, which she is grasping; the nude Child covers his genitals with his left hand.[32] In a variant design, a woodcut in an edition of the *Legenda Aurea* printed by Caxton in c.1483, the Child appears nude in an aureole in a

---

[27] Brigittine iconography also seems to be implied in the Coventry *Pageant of the Shearmen and Taylors*, ll. 268ff.

[28] Davidson and O'Connor, *York Art*, 46–48. For discussion of Brigittine iconography in relation to the York Tilethatchers' play, see my *From Creation to Doom*, 16–18, and J. W. Robinson, *Studies in Fifteenth-Century Stagecraft*, Early Drama, Art, and Music, Monograph Series 14 (Kalamazoo: Medieval Institute Publications, 1991), 60–80. For examples of Brigittine Nativity iconography in painted glass, see Gordon McN. Rushforth, *Medieval Christian Imagery* (Oxford: Clarendon Press, 1936), 278–81, fig. 136; Hilary Wayment, *The Stained Glass of the Church of St. Mary, Fairford, Gloucestershire* (London: Society of Antiquaries, 1984), pl. IV.

[29] *Hore beatissime Virginis Marie* (Rouen, 1517) (*STC* 16,104).

[30] Davidson and O'Connor, *York Art*, 48, fig. 11.

[31] Wilson and Wilson, *A Medieval Mirror*, 156. In the Presentation of the Child Jesus in the Temple, his genitals are, however, very clearly shown (ibid., 160).

[32] Barbara Palmer, *The Early Art of the West Riding of Yorkshire*, Early Drama, Art, and Music, Reference Series 6 (Kalamazoo: Medieval Institute Publications, 1990), 77–78, fig. 15.

Nudity, the Body, and Early English Drama 159

manger before the ox and the ass, with Mary kneeling below him; here the Child's sexuality is ambiguous though he has his legs spread.[33]

Further examples of Brigittine iconography are present in two alabaster carvings in the Victoria and Albert Museum. In one of these the Child, who is holding forth his right hand in blessing toward his mother, shows no signs of his sex, while the other modestly holds his left hand over his genital area.[34] In other instances, however, the Child also appears nude, most surprisingly in representations of the Adoration of the Magi. One fifteenth-century English alabaster shows the Child with legs spread wide as if to show off his sex, though with the loss of the original gesso and paint it is not possible to know the design intended by the artist.[35] In a panel of painted glass at East Harling, Norfolk, the seated Virgin holds a naked Child, who is standing on her lap before three Shepherds; however, he is turned so that he does not display his genitals to them (fig. 14).[36] But in an example to which the late J. W. Robinson called attention in his *Studies in Fifteenth-Century Stagecraft*—the East Window of St. Peter Mancroft at Norwich—a similar scene includes the nude Child with his penis visible.[37] A rare woodcarving of Mary holding her Son on her lap appears on a benchend at North Cadbury, Somerset, where he is fully nude and with genitals displayed.[38] The exhibition of the nude Child rather than a clothed Infant was a demonstration of his humanity and

---

[33] Edward Hodnett, *English Woodcuts 1480–1535* (1935; reprint Oxford: Oxford University Press, 1973), fig. 5.

[34] Cheetham, *English Medieval Alabasters*, nos. 105–06.

[35] Ibid., no. 108. For discussion of the nude Child in Magi scenes in Continental art, see Leo Steinberg, *The Sexuality of Christ in Renaissance Art and Modern Oblivion* (New York: Pantheon, 1983), 65–70.

[36] See also Christopher Woodforde, *The Norwich School of Glass-Painting in the Fifteenth Century* (London: Oxford University Press, 1950), 46–47.

[37] Robinson, *Studies in Fifteenth-Century Stagecraft*, fig. 12; see also Woodforde, *The Norwich School of Glass-Painting*, 25, frontispiece. The Virgin's breast is exposed, and she is about to begin feeding the Child.

[38] Gardner, *Minor English Wood Sculpture*, fig. 47. This image may be compared with another benchend, at Wigtoft, Lincolnshire, on which a standing figure of Mary holds her Son on her arm; here the the nude infant holds his left hand over his genital area (ibid., fig. 42). But in a roof boss at St. Helen's Hospital, Norwich, the Child is seated on the lap of the Virgin with genitals in full view while a midwife, behind, holds up a piece of cloth in which he is to be wrapped and Joseph looks on; see C. J. P. Cave, *Roof Bosses in Medieval Churches* (Cambridge: Cambridge University Press, 1948), fig. 166.

14. Adoration of the Shepherds. Painted glass, East Harling, Norfolk. ©Crown Copyright. National Monuments Record.

therefore a reminder of the prevailing popular theology that placed great stress on the Anselmian concept of Christ as a fellow human being. Additionally the presence of the genitals would have been considered evidence of Christ's complete manhood, for, as Leo the Great insisted, he was "born true God in the entire and perfect nature of true man, complete in his own properties, complete in ours."[39] So too St. Augustine had de-

---

[39] Leo the Great, Epistle 28, as excerpted in translation in *Documents of the Christian Church*, ed. Henry Bettenson (London: Oxford University Press, 1947), 70; the passage is quoted by Steinberg, *The Sexuality of Christ*, 16.

scribed Christ as perfect, whose body "is made up of all the members."[40] This does not mean, as Carolyn Walker Bynum has warned, that even when Christ's penis is visible there was a connection made with adult sexuality;[41] nevertheless, the image of the Child and the representation in drama were apparently intended to stir an emotional response through the presentation of an imitation of the perfect and stainless body of the incarnate Christ.

It is, however, unlikely that an actual boy child should have been used in the York Tilethatchers' play to represent the newborn Christ, nor would a generic doll (of the type suggested for representing the infants in the Slaying of the Innocents[42]) have served. Instead, it would seem quite possible that a religious image of Christ of the type seen in alabaster carvings represented the Child in this pageant. Whether the Child's sex was represented or not, he nevertheless was initially shown in the York play without clothing. Whether this way of showing him was continued when the York playtext was rewritten to add midwives and presumably to set aside the Brigittine imagery sometime after c.1470 cannot be ascertained.[43] In the N-Town Nativity play, Zelomy, one of the midwives, notes that Mary's breasts are full of milk (15.236). The nursing of the Christ Child in the iconography identified as *Maria lactans*, involving the baring of the breast of the Virgin, was another sign of his humanity. An example of the nursing Child appears in the west window in the north aisle of the nave of York Minster,[44] and another was once present in a roof boss in the nave of the Minster—a boss which, after a fire in the

---

[40] *City of God* XXII.18; trans. Dods *et al.*, 841.

[41] Carolyn Walker Bynum, "The Body of Christ in the Later Middle Ages: A Reply to Leo Steinberg," *Renaissance Quarterly* 39 (1986): 407.

[42] See M. D. Anderson, *Drama and Imagery in Medieval English Churches* (Cambridge: Cambridge University Press, 1963), 137.

[43] See the *Ordo paginarum,* in *Records of Early English Drama: York,* ed. Alexandra F. Johnston and Margaret Rogerson, 2 vols. (Toronto: University of Toronto Press, 1979), 1:18. Though dated 1415, the *Ordo* was updated to reflect later practice, and the entry specifying midwives appears to have been a later addition.

[44] Thomas French and David O'Connor, *York Minster: A Catalogue of Medieval Stained Glass,* I: *The West Windows of the Nave,* Corpus Vitrearum Medii Aevi—Great Britain 3 (Oxford: Oxford University Press, 1987), 72–73, pl. 15b, e. The body of the Child is heavily patched, and portions of the Virgin, including the head, are eighteenth-century replacements.

nineteenth century, was replaced with the figure of the Christ Child being nursed from a bottle.[45] But the traditional iconography was very widespread and appeared in the popular alabasters which were more or less mass-produced in workshops in Nottingham, York, and elsewhere.[46]

An episode that, like the shame of Noah, was not included in the English plays was the Circumcision, about which to be sure there appears to have been some confusion.[47] At Lucerne the act of circumcision seems to have been performed with concern for modesty but with stage blood serving as an important effect—a prefiguring of the blood that would be shed at the Crucifixion:

> Zacharias puts the Child on the altar, has it in his arms. Salmon lifts up the basin and with the other hand the can of water, also the towel on his shoulder, so that after the circumcision Raabod shall be able to wash his hands. Raabod circumcises the Child, Josaphat lifts his clothes or the shift [*hembdlin*] on one side and Amalech on the other side, then Zacharias speaks....
>
> Raabod has a sponge full of blood hidden in his hand, has a sharp stone, so that he can act as though he were cutting it off, then Urias offers him a small box in which there should be powder so that he can sprinkle it on. . . .[48]

Accounts of the Circumcision differ, and though the dramatization at Lucerne is quite different from the version in the *Meditations on the Life of Christ*, the instrument which is used is the same; in Nicholas Love's translation, "þis day he shedde his blode, when þat aftur þe rite of þe

---

[45] John Browne, *The History of the Metropolitan Church of St. Peter, York*, 2 vols. (London, 1847), pl. CI; Davidson and O'Connor, *York Art*, 47; Clifford Davidson, *On Tradition: Essays on the Use and Valuation of the Past* (New York: AMS Press, 1992), 129, fig. 11.

[46] For a defaced example at Broughton, see Palmer, *The Early Art of the West Riding*, 84, fig. 20.

[47] For discussion of Christ's circumcision, which is seen as symbolic—i.e., not "for eny nede but for signyficacion"—see *Speculum Sacerdotale*, ed. Edward H. Weatherly, EETS, o.s. 200 (London: Oxford University Press, 1936), 16–18, esp. 16; see also Steinberg, *The Sexuality of Christ*, 50–57. Theologically there was also controversy about the foreskin of Christ which was preserved as a relic at Rome; the lack of a foreskin would make Christ imperfect at his Ascension, some claimed.

[48] *The Staging of Religious Drama*, ed. Meredith and Tailby, 161.

lawe, his tendere flesh was kut, with a sharp stonen knife, so þat ʒonge child Jesus kyndly wept for þe sorow þat he felt þerþorh his flesh. For without doute he hade verrey flesh & kyndly suffrable as haue oþer children."[49] A misericord at Worcester Cathedral shows a priest, with a knife in his hand, on one side and Mary on the other side of the nude Child as he stands, with his genitals displayed, on a square altar.[50] The Child depicted in the Robert de Lisle Psalter (British Library MS. Arundel 83, fol. 124) shrinks back into his Mother's arms as the priest reaches toward his penis with his knife.[51] A seated Jewish priest holds the Child's penis in his left hand and reaches with the knife in his right to circumcise him as he is held by his Mother, who is comforting him by breast-feeding him, in a carved oak roof boss at Salle, Norfolk.[52] In the *Holkham Bible Picture Book*, Jesus is circumcised not in the Temple but by Joseph, an iconography that follows the *Gospel of Pseudo-Matthew*.[53]

At the next point in the play cycles at which the nudity of Christ might be expected—that is, the Baptism—attention is directed to his sinless body (see, for example, N-Town 22.95–96), but undressing seems not to have been demanded for the rite. This is in contrast to the usual iconography, which tended to follow the Near Eastern pattern of having Christ standing, nude except for a loincloth, in the river Jordan, the waves of which reached up to cover his genitals.[54] In the *Holkham Bible Picture*

---

[49] Nicholas Love, *Mirror of the Blessed Life of Jesus Christ*, ed. Michael G. Sargent (New York: Garland, 1992), 41; see also *Meditations on the Life of Christ*, trans. Isa Ragusa and Rosalie B. Green (Princeton: Princeton University Press, 1961), 42–45.

[50] Francis Bond, *Wood Carvings in English Churches*, I: *Misericords* (London: Oxford University Press, 1910), 142–43.

[51] Lucy Freeman Sandler, *The Psalter of Robert De Lisle* (London: Harvey Miller; Oxford: Oxford University Press, 1983), pl. 11.

[52] Cave, *Roof Bosses in Medieval Churches*, 28, fig. 191. As M. D. Anderson notes (*History and Imagery in British Churches* [London: John Murray, 1971], 113), the iconography at Salle is influenced by the *Meditations on the Life of Christ*. In Love's translation, Mary comforted her Son by "kyssyng him and puttyng þe pappe in his mouþe" (*The Mirror of the Blessed Life*, 41).

[53] *Holkham Bible Picture Book*, fol. 13ᵛ. For this iconography, see Gertrud Schiller, *Iconography of Christian Art*, trans. Janet Seligman, 2 vols. (Greenwich, Conn.: New York Graphic Society, 1971), 1:89.

[54] This conventional iconography appears in an Anglo-Saxon ivory; see John Beckwith, *Ivory Carvings in Early Medieval England* (London: Harvey Miller and Medcalf, 1972), fig.

Book, John the Baptist is first shown baptizing in the river, with the water covering the bodies of men and women to their waists but without any attempt to hide their sex; however, on the next folio when the artist depicts the baptism of Jesus the water, also rising as high as his waist, blurs his sexual organs so that nothing can be seen of them.[55] Interestingly, he uses a dish from which he pours water upon the group of four men and women, while for Jesus he pours water from a jug immediately over his head. Later iconography, shown in the *Biblia Pauperum*, dispenses with the mound of water and has Jesus, dressed only in a loincloth, merely standing in the stream while an angel holds his clothing and John the Baptist pours water from a vessel over his head.[56] In the Towneley play Jesus asks for baptism and requests: "dyp me in this flume Iordan" (19.148). This should not be taken as a stage direction invoking immersion since here too the representation of the rite clearly involved infusion instead.[57]

An early French play translated by John R. Elliott, Jr., and Graham Runnalls, however, provides a more explicit representation of the biblical event than was apparently seen on the English stage. St. John the Baptist speaks:

> Oh, precious, holy flesh,
> I would not dare to touch you.
> Naked must I see you, my Lord,
> To begin the New Law.[58]

According to the stage direction, Jesus then "disrobes" ("Expoliet"), whereupon he speaks: "Now I am naked; baptize me / Without further protest." John then will pour water over Jesus. Nakedness presumably did

---

35. For examples of the iconography at York, see Davidson and O'Connor, *York Art*, 65–67; but the water sometimes reaches partway up Christ's legs only. On the covering of the genital area in depictions of the Baptism of Christ, see Steinberg, *The Sexuality of Christ*, 135–39.

[55] *Holkham Bible Picture Book*, fols. 18ᵛ–19ʳ.

[56] Avril Henry, *Biblia Pauperum* (Ithaca: Cornell University Press, 1987), 64.

[57] On this point see Rosemary Woolf, *The English Mystery Plays* (Berkeley and Los Angeles: University of California Press, 1972), 218.

[58] *The Baptism and Temptation of Christ*, trans. John R. Elliott, Jr., and Graham Runnalls (New Haven: Yale University Press, 1978), 78–79.

not include exposure of the genitals; the most important aspect of the scene was the showing of the sacred body of Christ in a rite which superseded circumcision.[59]

Just as the shedding of Christ's blood at his Circumcision looked forward to the shedding of blood during his Passion and Crucifixion, so also the displaying of the holy body in his infancy and at his baptism foreshadowed its exposure during his final ordeal in the violent Flagellation and death on the cross as well as afterward in the course of the Deposition and Burial.[60] At the Flagellation his clothing was removed. In the York Tilemakers' play, the torturers prepare to carry out Pilate's orders to beat him, and the one identified as IV Miles says, "Late vs gete of his gere. . . ." The first soldier responds that they should quickly pull off "his trasshes" (XXXIII.348–49). In the Towneley Scourging play, Pilate himself orders:

> Syrs, looke ye take good hede
> His cloysse ye spoyll hym fro;
> Ye gar his body blede,
> And bett hym blak and bloo. (22.157–60)

The gown worn by Christ may be understood as the one over which the torturers gamble in the Play of the Dice (Play 24). In the Chester Fletchers, Bowiers, Cowpers, and Stringers' play Christ is stripped and tied to the column of the Flagellation (XVI.315 *s.d.*), and in the Ironmongers' play his clothing is also forcibly taken from him— "This coate gettes thou never agayne," Primus Judeus says (XVIA.71)—and the torturers gamble to see which one will "wyn" it (83–84). His other garments, identified as his kirtle and "pawlle"—will then be divided up.

In the N-Town plays, a stage direction indicates that *"Here þei pulle of Jesus clothis and betyn hym with whyppys"* at the Scourging (30.237 *s.d.*), and again immediately afterward Simon takes up the cross from Jesus and Veronica wipes his face: *"Þan xul þei pulle Jesu out of his*

---

[59] Ibid.

[60] On Christ's body in plays of the Passion, see also Peter W. Travis, "The Social Body of the Dramatic Christ in Medieval England," in *Early Drama to 1600*, ed. Albert H. Tricomi, Acta 13 (Binghamton: Center for Medieval and Early Renaissance Studies, State University of New York, 1987), 17–36.

clothis and leyn them togedyr; and þer þei xul pullyn hym down and leyn hym along on þe cros, and aftyr þat naylyn hym þeron" (32.49 s.d.). At the Scourging, the body of Christ is bloodied from the top of his head to the bottom of his feet. A sermon quoted by G. R. Owst describes the event in even more gruesome detail as the torturers are said to cease only when they see Christ standing "in his blode up to the anclees. Fro the top of the hed to the sole of his fote, hole skyn saved they non. His flesch they rase to the bone, and for werynesse of hemself they him leevyd almost for dede."[61] In the Coventry Smiths' pageant of the Passion, four scourges and a pillar were repaired for this scene in 1490.[62] In the Towneley Resurrection play he is said to have been wounded as many as 5,400 times (26.292). In his nudity after the Scourging and then on the cross, where the wounds were very much in evidence, his blood and flesh both are clearly designed to be objects of veneration rather than repulsion.[63] We cannot assume, however, that very many would have responded with the exaggerated emotionalism of a Richard Rolle, who concluded a lengthy meditation on Christ's body with the statement that Jesus' "body is lyk to a medow ful of swete flours and holsome herbes; so is þy body fulle of woundes, swet savorynge to a devout soule, and holsome as herbes to euch synful man."[64] Ironically, the humiliation which the torturers inflict on Jesus in the Passion plays serves instead to make of his body and blood a holy image like the images inside the churches of pre-Reformation times.

---

[61] British Library, Harley MS. 2398, fol. 186ᵛ, as quoted by G. R. Owst, *Literature and Pulpit in Medieval England*, 2nd ed. (1961; reprint Oxford: Blackwell, 1966), 508.

[62] *REED: Coventry*, 74.

[63] The wounds and the parts of the body with which they are associated—feet, hands, and heart—were frequently depicted and were the objects of special devotion; see, for example, the shield with the five wounds thus depicted on a Carthusian holy card (Eamon Duffy, *The Stripping of the Altars* [New Haven: Yale University Press, 1992], fig. 99), in painted glass in the church of St. Mary-on-the-Hill, Chester (Sally-Beth MacLean, *Chester Art*, Early Drama, Art, and Music, Reference Ser., 3 [Kalamazoo: Medieval Institute Publications,1982], 37–38, fig. 18), and on a roof boss at Broadhembury (Cave, *Roof Bosses in Medieval Churches*, fig. 59). Prayers to the five wounds were included in printed books of hours; see Duffy, *The Stripping of the Altars*, 238–48. See also Campbell Dodgson, "English Devotional Woodcuts of the Late Fifteenth Century, with Special Reference to Those in the Bodleian Libary," *Walpole Society* 12 (1928–29): 102, pl. XXXVI.

[64] Richard Rolle, *English Writings*, ed. Hope Emily Allen (Oxford: Clarendon Press, 1931), 36.

A poem on the Passion in Huntington MS. HM 142 describes the stripping as occurring immediately before Christ was nailed to the cross on the mount of Calvary:

> Thi bodyly wounde were woxe al drye,
> The purpure þer-to was cleued ful fast.
> They rent it of with a grete haste,
> And þat was, good lord, more peyne to þe
> Than al þe scourgynge þat was now past,
> And þus þi blode þou sched for me.[65]

The stripping of Jesus' clothes from him is, however, a subject that apparently was quite rare in the visual arts in England, though it does occur in the *Holkham Bible Picture Book*, where it is attached to a second scourging by two soldiers with whips.[66] Here his clothing is being pulled over his shoulders by a third man as bloody wounds begin to appear on his back. The subject of Christ being stripped is the subject of an article by Susan L. Smith, who points to this iconography in the so-called "Munich-London group" of the printed *Biblia Pauperum*.[67] In one of these books (Munich, Staatsbibliothek Clm. 28,141) and in a book of hours now in the British Library (MS. Add. 50,005, fol. 112^v), the disrobing is accomplished in the same way as in the *Holkham Bible Picture Book*.[68] Smith makes the unusual point that this scene was connected typologically with the stripping and scourging of the Bride in the Song of Songs 5:7.[69] But even without the connection with the Bride, which suggests the symbolism of Christ's body as the Church, we can posit a

---

[65] *Religious Lyrics of the XVth Century*, ed. Carleton Brown (Oxford: Clarendon Press, 1939), no. 92 (ll. 43–48). An unusual depiction of the Stripping of Christ appears in Melk, Stiftsbibliothek MS. 1903, fol. 47^v, in which Christ, wounded over his whole body, is being stripped of his gown as he steps up the ladder that will take him to the cross; see Anne Derbes, *Picturing the Passion in Late Medieval Italy* (Cambridge: Cambridge University Press, 1996), fig. 84.

[66] *Holkham Bible Picture Book*, fol. 30^v; for commentary, see ibid., 131.

[67] Susan L. Smith, "The Bride Stripped Bare: A Rare Type of the Disrobing of Christ," *Gesta* 34 (1995): 126–46.

[68] Ibid., figs. 6, 9.

[69] Ibid., 126.

potential for a quasi-erotic response. The longing of the soul for a sight of Christ and, eventually, for union with him was a medieval commonplace but was particularly significant in mystical thought.[70] In this life there were, however, some ways in which the ordinary person might come closer to Christ. One was to look with devotion at the Eucharistic Host after its transubstantiation into the true body of our Lord, a transformation which was the high point of the Mass in fifteenth-century popular practice. As the *Lay Folks Mass Book* explained, during the canon at the ringing of the sacring bell "ihesu crist awen presence" has been effected, and when the Host is seen at the elevation, one can know that this is indeed "he þat iudas salde, / and sithen was scourged and don on rode, / and for mankynde þere shad his blode. . . ."[71] Another way of coming closer might be the sight of an iconic representation of Christ's wounded and bloody body in an image, play, or pageant.[72]

The connection between Host and Christ, on the one hand, and the plays, on the other, is of particular significance for the play cycles from York and Coventry, since in those municipalities the drama was normally presented on the Feast of Corpus Christi—a feast dedicated to the veneration of the Host, which was carried through the city on this day.[73] In spite of the problems of maintaining both a sequence of pageants and a Corpus Christi procession on the same day in these cities—and we know that at York both for many years followed essentially the same route—the

---

[70] See Wolfgang Riehle, *The Middle English Mystics*, trans. Bernard Standring (London: Routledge and Kegan Paul, 1981), 34–56, and also Jeffrey Hamburger, *The Rothschild Canticles: Art and Mysticism in Flanders and the Rhineland circa 1300* (New Haven: Yale University Press, 1990), 105–17. For other aspects of Passion iconography, see James Marrow, *Passion Iconography in Northern European Art of the Late Middle Ages and Early Renaissance*, Ars Neerlandica 1 (Kortrijk: Van Ghemmert, 1979), and F. P. Pickering, *Literature and Art in the Middle Ages* (Coral Gables: University of Miami Press, 1970).

[71] *The Lay Folks Mass Book*, ed. Thomas Frederick Simmons, EETS, o.s. 71 (London: N. Trübner, 1879), 38.

[72] See Duffy, *The Stripping of the Altars*, 95–102; Ann Eljenholm Nichols, *Seeable Signs: The Iconography of the Seven Sacraments 1350–1544* (Woodbridge: Boydell Press, 1994), 241–59, figs. 58–66, and "The Bread of Heaven: Foretaste or Foresight?" in *The Iconography of Heaven*, ed. Clifford Davidson, Early Drama, Art, and Music, Monograph Series 21 (Kalamazoo: Medieval Institute Publications, 1994), 40–68.

[73] See Miri Rubin, *Corpus Christi: The Eucharist in Late Medieval Culture* (Cambridge: Cambridge University Press, 1991), *passim*.

common ground of meaning shared by the procession and the plays was an important factor that was made all the more significant by the exposition of both the holy bread and the body of Christ as shown from processional stages by the actors.[74]

The linkage between the bread and the body of Christ was, of course, a direct one which was illustrated most graphically in the iconography of the Mass of St. Gregory. The episode is not told in the *Golden Legend* and seems to be a late addition to the story of the saint.[75] After a skeptical member of the congregation had expressed doubts about the Mass, Christ appeared in the Christ of Pity iconography above the altar at which St. Gregory was saying Mass, as illustrated in painted glass of c. 1420 in York Minster.[76] Typically, as on the Kirkham monument at Paignton described by Rushforth, the full length figure of Christ is displaying the five wounds, from which blood flows directly into the chalice.[77] In this symbolism the body and blood are directly connected to the bread and wine of the Eucharist. The devotional image itself was regarded as expressing the essential meaning of the Mass, which connected the rite to the historical soteriological event in a manner which erased time and made the celebrant and congregation alike contemporaries with the sacrificed Savior.

This point is made in a somewhat different way in *The Play of the Sacrament*,[78] for here the consecrated Host stolen for a repetition of the Passion will bleed when stabbed five times in a ritual of desecration (469–84). Then the Host is placed in a boiling cauldron of oil along with the nails and the hand of his principal tormentor which has become detached and stuck to it, whereupon the "oyle waxyth redde as blood, /

---

[74] See also Peter Travis's attempt to link the Eucharist and the Chester Whitsun plays in his *Dramatic Design in the Chester Cycle* (Chicago: University of Chicago Press, 1982), chap. 1; however, Travis's remarks apply better to the York and Coventry cycles, which were directly associated with the feast day of Corpus Christi, than to the Chester plays, which were presented in Whitsun Week.

[75] See Émile Mâle, *Religious Art in France: The Late Middle Ages*, trans. Marthiel Mathews, Bollingen Series 90, pt. 3 (Princeton: Princeton University Press, 1986), 95, and also Duffy, *The Stripping of the Altars*, 238–39.

[76] Davidson and O'Connor, *York Art*, 159.

[77] G. McN. Rushforth, "The Kirkham Monument in Paignton Church," *Transactions of the Exeter Diocesan Architectural and Archaeological Society* 15 (1927): 23–25.

[78] *Non-Cycle Plays and Fragments*, 58–89.

And owt of the cawdron yt begynnyth to rin" (674–75). Finally, cast into an oven which will explode and bleed "*owt at þe cranys,*" the Host resolves into an "*image . . . with woundys bledyng*" (713 *s.d.*). The mistreatment of the Host is identified as blasphemy (731), and the malefactors' disbelief in the doctrine of transubstantiation is confounded. Christ's body and the Eucharistic bread and wine are shown to be identical, and finally, after the miracle which restores his tormentor's hand, the image changes once more "*into brede*" (826 *s.d.*). A number of stage effects were involved in this play, not the least of which was to have "A chyld apperyng with wondys blody" (804) rise above the oven in the same position as the man of sorrows above the tomb in the iconography of the Mass of St. Gregory.

In the pageants of the English drama cycles the bloodied body of Christ in the Flagellation and Crucifixion was, so far as the evidence shows, always a body-stocking of glove leather. In 1452 the Coventry Smiths paid eighteen pence "for vj skynnys of whitleder to godds garment" and ten pence "for makyng of the same garment," and in 1554 they paid three shillings "for v schepskens for gods coot & for makyng."[79] In 1565 a painter was paid "for payntyng & gylldyng the . . . pyllar, the crose & Godes cote."[80] For a Passion play at New Romney, Kent, in 1555 a payment of four shillings and eight pence was made "to burton for skynes for the ij^d godheddes Coote & for makyng" and two shillings "for di' dosyn shepeskynes for ye godheddes coote for the iiijth playe."[81]

Richard C. Trexler has quoted Johannes Molanus's statement that "Christ *was* crucified naked, but I think it is pious to *believe* that his shameful organs were [then] veiled for decency."[82] The wounded body of Christ being stretched to fit on the cross in the *Holkham Bible Picture*

---

[79] *REED: Coventry*, 25, 200.

[80] Ibid., 231.

[81] *Records of Plays and Players in Kent, 1450–1642*, ed. Giles Dawson, Malone Society Collections 7 (Oxford, 1965), 208, 210. The "fyrst godheddes Coote" cost only eight pence, suggesting that the role for this pageant did not require a leather body stocking.

[82] Quoted in translation by Richard C. Trexler, "Gendering Jesus Crucified," in *Iconography at the Crossroads*, ed. Brendan Cassidy (Princeton: Index of Christian Art, Princeton University, 1993), 114, from J.-C. Bologne, *Histoire de la Pudeur* (Paris, 1986), 281. Molanus was the Spanish censor in the Netherlands; see also David Freedberg, *The Power of Images* (Chicago: University of Chicago Press, 1989), 369.

Book is nude but without showing his genitals (only pubic hair may be seen), and when he is first depicted on the cross he is still naked, though he is turned so that the genital area is not to be seen. The next scene will show Jesus' Mother wrapping a cloth about his loins.[83] However, in a Continental stage direction from Mons, the soldiers are directed to "pretend to strip [Christ] naked and lay him on the ground," and then, following a short scene, his Mother "goes to Jesus and pretends to fasten her wimple round him, but there is one already there."[84] In the fifteenth-century Abingdon Missal (Bodleian Library MS. Digby 227, fol. 113^v), the Virgin stands beside the cross with the body of the nearly nude Jesus, whose loincloth seems transparent as if made of very light silk, though the genitals cannot be seen through it.[85] The Virgin's act in covering her Son's nudity follows the *Meditations on the Life of Christ*, which, in Love's translation, describes her act of veiling her Son's nakedness:

> Now also first his modere seeþ how he is so takene and ordeynede to þe deth. Wherefore she sorouful out of mesure, and hauyng shame to se him standyng alle nakede. For þei laft him not so miche as hese pryue cloþes'. she went in haste to hir dere sone, and clippede him and girde him aboute þe leendes with þe kerchefe of hir hede.[86]

The humiliation of Christ at the hands of his violent tormentors, then, is extreme and shameful. Though his body does not share in the lapsarian condition normally inherited from Adam, he nevertheless is reduced to nudity, which normally would be a sign of disgrace. In the N-Town play, the Virgin Mary indeed sees her Son's condemnation to the cross as "þe most shamful deth among þese thevys fere" (32.96). Yet, if Christ is not

---

[83] *Holkham Bible Picture Book*, fols. 31^v–32^v. See also the discussion of Mary's use of her veil to cover Jesus' nakedness in Gail McMurray Gibson, *The Theater of Devotion* (Chicago: University of Chicago Press, 89), 52–53.

[84] *The Staging of Religious Drama*, ed. Meredith and Tailby, 146.

[85] Margaret Rickert, *Painting in Britain: The Middle Ages*, 2nd ed. (Harmondsworth: Penguin, 1965), fig. 186; for this manuscript, see Otto Pächt and J. J. G. Alexander, *Illustrated Manuscripts in the Bodleian Library*, 3: *British, Irish, and Icelandic Schools* (Oxford: Clarendon Press, 1973), no. 1065. See also ibid., pl. XCIXa, for another illustration from this manuscript that shows Christ at his Resurrection with a similar light veil over his genital region.

[86] *The Mirror of the Blessed Life of Jesus Christ*, 176.

fully naked but is graced with a loincloth provided by his Mother, his humiliation would paradoxically seem to be lessened. Preachers were, according to some, to be careful about emphasizing Christ's nudity since this would encourage not devotion but a lack of respect.[87]

In most representations, including the alabasters carved at Nottingham and York, Christ appears on the cross in the loincloth.[88] And even though the actor in the civic drama only represented nudity by means of his leather body stocking, he was nevertheless most likely presented to audiences with a loincloth. The covering of Christ's body would have had a specific function in preserving modesty in practice, for a devotional attitude toward the scenes of the civic plays was encouraged and indulgences seem to have been offered if they were viewed in a right frame of mind.[89]

The display of the body of Christ for devotional meditation involved a deliberate effort to bring the Crucifixion into the consciousness of viewers in the case of the visual arts, where the iconic function of the image was to transport the person into the presence of the depicted event imaginatively.[90] When we see a scene such as the Our Lady of Pity in painted glass at Long Melford, Suffolk—a window in which a patron establishes its meaning by appearing with hands joined in prayer as he venerates Christ and his Mother—it becomes obvious that the display of the body has as its purpose more than a merely didactic function.[91] The depiction is designed to be a mnemonic device that also stirs the emotions, literally eliciting pity and veneration from the viewer.

In the popular alabaster carvings of the Entombment, the corpus is shown either still wearing only the loincloth and about to be covered with the burial shroud, or with body partially or fully covered with the shroud.[92] The gestures of prayer (with hands joined, according to the late

---

[87] Trexler, "Gendering Jesus Crucified," 119, citing Johannes van Palz and Jacob Wimpfeling.

[88] Cheetham, *English Medieval Alabasters*, nos. 170–85.

[89] *REED: York*, 1:43; *Records of Early English Drama: Chester*, ed. Lawrence M. Clopper (Toronto: University of Toronto Press, 1979), 28.

[90] See especially Sixten Ringbom, "Devotional Images and Imaginative Devotions," *Gazette des Beaux-Arts* 111 (1969): 159–70.

[91] Woodforde, *The Norwich School*, 117–18, pl. XXVII.

[92] Cheetham, *English Medieval Alabasters*, nos. 191–97.

medieval practice) by those in attendance provide clues to the appropriate response to the scene. In two alabasters in which the body is yet to be encased in its shroud, Jesus' left hand is placed over his genital area.[93] This gesture, which Leo Steinberg described as a "groin-searching hand,"[94] is in fact related to other gestures of modesty, even involving some of the Infancy portraits cited in Steinberg's work. That the gesture was well known is suggested in *The Hieroglyphics of Horapollo*, which asserts that a "penis pressed by a hand means temperance in a man."[95] Thus the gesture perhaps pointed not only to modesty and the shame associated with Christ's nudity but also to the control which he exerted in the course of his life, for unlike other men he had resisted all temptations of the body.

In the York Butchers' *Mortificacio Cristi*, Joseph of Arimathea and Nicodemus reverently take down the body and rather quickly wrap him in a "sudarye" (XXXVI.387). After anointing the body with "myrre and aloes" (403), Joseph kneels before it with a prayer requesting that the Savior should "belde me in blisse" (406–07). At the conclusion of the Chester Ironmongers' play, Joseph promises to bury Christ's "blessed bodye . . . / with all worshipp and honestie / and menske all that I may" (XVIA.449–50) and with the expectation that he will rise again on the third day "in flesh and blood" (453), but the act of preparing the body for the grave seems to have been even more abbreviated than in the York play. The Deposition and Burial in N-Town are also fairly short, but the taking down of Christ from the cross implies a gentle and devotional handling of the incident,[96] which culminates when Joseph places the body

---

[93] Ibid., nos. 191, 193–94. In another example, no. 197, Christ's hands are crossed above the genital area.

[94] Steinberg, *The Sexuality of Christ*, 102–03.

[95] *The Hieroglyphics of Horapollo*, trans. George Boas, Bollingen Series 23 (New York: Pantheon Books, 1950), 88; the passage is cited by John H. Astington, "Three Renaissance Prints," *Shakespeare Quarterly* 47 (1996): 184n, following a suggestion by Karl Josef Höltgen. The illustration in Valeriano's woodcut in seventeenth-century editions of Horapollo is, however, different in that "a nude man [is shown] standing with legs apart and with both hands clutching his groin" (ibid., 184n).

[96] The emotional tenor of the scene in the play may be compared to depictions such as the wall painting at Chalgrove, Oxfordshire, where the Virgin Mary is tenderly holding Christ's right arm; see E. W. Tristram, *English Wall Painting of the Fourteenth Century* (London: Routledge and Kegan Paul, 1955), fig. 33. This iconography is conventional; see,

"*in oure Ladyes lappe*" with the words "Lo, Mary, modyr good and trewe, / Here is þi son, blody and bloo" (34.122–23). He continues: "For hym myn hert ful sore doth rewe. / Kysse hym now onys eer he go" (124–25). Mary's *planctus* punctuates her gesture in taking her Son's body in her arms:

> A, mercy! Mercy, myn owyn son so dere,
> Þi blody face now I must kysse.
> Þi face is pale, withowtyn chere;
> Of meche joy now xal I mysse.
> Þer was nevyr modyr þat sey this,
> So here sone dyspoyled with so gret wo.
> And my dere chylde nevyr dede amys.
> A, mercy, Fadyr of Hefne, it xulde be so.
> (34.126–33)

Thereafter the men take the body, lay it "*in his grave*" (138 s.d.), wind it in "þis syndony" which Joseph has brought, and apply "an onyment" brought by Nicodemus (138–41).

With the Burial, however, does not come the last sight of Christ's body, for in his Resurrection he displays his wounded corpus in representations in the visual arts and, for example, in the Towneley play where he calls attention to his physical self:

> Behold my body, in ilka place
> How it was dight—
> All to-rent,
> And all to-shentt,
> Man, for thi plight. (26.250–54)

His body and blood are the focus of his speech, and it is emphasized that these are given for those who are onlookers. Further, a direct connection is made in this speech with the Mass in which the "veray brede of lyfe / Becommys my fleshe in wordys fyfe" (345–46), and it is explained by Christ that one's reception of the Host is a matter of eternal life or death.

---

for example, Cambridge, Trinity College MS. O.4.16, fol. 113ᵛ; and Bodleian Library MS. Gough liturg. 8, fol. 61ᵛ (Gough Psalter), illustrated in Sandler, *Gothic Manuscripts*, plate figs. 33, 95.

Christ's body, represented in this play partially exposed though not in full nudity, is hence proclaimed to be of crucial significance for everyone.[97]

English alabasters in the Victoria and Albert Museum show Christ in the Resurrection as a figure wearing a loincloth and with arms covered with the shroud, which in only one instance is draped over his shoulders and in front of him.[98] In each of the alabasters he steps out of the tomb onto one of the soldiers—a sign of the resurrection of his body—as also in Robert the Glazer's Great West Window in York Minster.[99] A merely spiritual body would have had no weight, while, as Primus Miles says in the Chester Skinners' play, Christ's foot on his "backe" caused "everye lythe" to begin to "cracke" (XVIII.274–75). This iconography and its significance is in general corroborated elsewhere but is subject to small variations—for example, in the *Holkham Bible Picture Book*, which shows Christ, holding the vexillum that signifies his resurrection and with the shroud draped over his shoulders and down over his hips and right leg, as he steps out of the tomb, in this case not directly onto a soldier.[100]

What is remarkable, however, is how often after the Resurrection the risen Christ is shown in the visual arts in a similarly shaped garment with chest and wound exposed—and with wounds still visible in feet and hands. In the Cornish *Ordinalia*, however, Jesus explains to his Mother

---

[97] See Meg Twycross's comments on staging the York pageant ("Playing the 'Resurrection'," *Medieval Studies for J. A. W. Bennett*, ed. P. L. Heyworth [Oxford: Clarendon Press, 1981], 273–96), though the photograph which she presents of a modern production shows a completely clothed Christ with a vexillum rising from a coffer tomb (fig. 2b). On the staging of the Resurrection, see also Anderson, *Drama and Imagery*, 148–50.

[98] Cheetham, *English Medieval Alabasters*, nos. 199–208.

[99] French and O'Connor, *York Minster: The West Windows of the Nave*, 54–55; for a roof boss with this design formerly in the nave, see Browne, *The History of the Metropolitan Church of St. Peter, York*, pl. CXI. For an example on a benchend, at Bishops Hull, Somerset, see Gardner, *Minor English Wood Sculpture*, fig. 45; and for a roof boss, at Salle, see Cave, *Roof Bosses in Medieval Churches*, fig. 193. The iconography is discussed by Hildburgh, "English Alabaster Carvings," 92, and Anderson, *Drama and Imagery*, 149–50.

[100] *Holkham Bible Picture Book*, fol. 34^v. See also Henry, *Biblia Pauperum*, 104, and a late fourteenth-century misericord at Lincoln Cathedral which is conveniently illustrated in Arthur Gardner, *English Medieval Sculpture* (1951; rpt. New York: Hacker, 1973), fig. 562. A fully clothed Christ, as in a historiated initial in a York book of hours (York Minster Library MS. XVI.K.6, fol. 83^v), is unusual, but a panel of early fourteenth-century painted glass in York Minster provides covering for almost his entire body with the exception of a portion of his torso (Davidson and O'Connor, *York Art*, fig. 26).

in the first of his Resurrection appearances that he no longer feels pain in the wounds inflicted during his Passion. As Jane Bakere notes, the notion "of wounds healed but still remaining, here introduced at a tender human level, recurs throughout the *Resurrexio* reaching its triumphant climax in the Ascension sequence, a powerful crescendo from human tenderness to cosmic grandeur."[101] The non-biblical meeting with Mary is the Resurrection appearance illustrated in the seal of the dean and chapter of Chester Cathedral from the middle of the sixteenth century; here Jesus extends his wounded left hand toward the Virgin, who is at a prayer desk, while he holds the vexillum in his right hand. His legs, arms, and chest are bare, and the cloak he has wrapped around him is fastened at the neck.[102]

In the Last Judgment as depicted in the *Holkham Bible Picture Book* Christ appears in the clouds with a cloak held together with a morse at the neck but exposing arms, torso, and feet with the five wounds prominently visible. In the final illuminations in the manuscript his cloak is folded over his knees just above where the pubic hair should be located.[103] So too in an illumination depicting the Last Judgment in an early fifteenth-century Book of Hours in the York Minster Library (MS. Add. 2, fol. 208) the garment, which is unattached at the neck, falls across Christ's abdomen below the navel as he sits on a rainbow and shows his bleeding wounds.[104] This familiar iconography formed the basis for the York Mercers' Doomsday pageant. An inventory dated 1433 provides a listing of "Array for god þat ys to say a Sirke Wounded a diademe With a veserne gilted" and also a rainbow "of tymber" as well as a lifting mechanism to lower him from heaven.[105] The presence of a gilt mask is not surprising since God's face sometimes is gold with a golden cross nimbus in the visual arts, as in the Te Deum window in York Minster.[106]

---

[101] Jane A. Bakere, *The Cornish Ordinalia: A Critical Study* (Cardiff: University of Wales Press, 1980), 138.

[102] MacLean, *Chester Art*, 44–45, fig. 23.

[103] *Holkham Bible Picture Book*, fol. 42^r–42^v.

[104] Davidson and O'Connor, *York Art*, 115–16, fig. 33. Pamela King, in an unpublished paper presented at the International Congress on Medieval Studies in 1996, argued for dating this manuscript very early in the fifteenth century, and more recently has suggested a connection with the Great East Window (1405–08) in York Minster.

[105] *REED: York*, 1:55.

[106] See Davidson and O'Connor, *York Art*, 17.

The shirt "Wounded" presumably was a body stocking of leather which would cover the body of the actor playing the Judge. Such a garment would have made the wound in Christ's side more visible than a painted-on wound, and also it is likely that this way of representing it would have been more acceptable than bare skin in a community where the civic plays were carefully controlled and were required to reflect the honor of the city and to express devotion to God.

At Doomsday, then, the wounded body of Christ—the sacrifice for the sins of humankind on the cross—requires to be seen. While setting aside the loincloth-only nudity that was a sign of his shame on the cross, he nevertheless appears not fully clothed in this scene. The body still points back to the Crucifixion, which was the central event of the biblical story that was remembered on the level of realistic detail in the rood. The rood prominently placed the crucified figure of the Savior between his Mother and (usually) St. John in every church in the country. While roods were pulled down at the Reformation and not replaced in English churches until the nineteenth and twentieth centuries, we know their design and iconography from various sources, including Continental examples. And we know that their location in churches either suspended or attached over the entrance to the chancel was ubiquitous. Above the chancel arch, as at Holy Trinity, Coventry, or the Guild Chapel at Stratford-upon-Avon, might be a wall painting of the Last Judgment, and placed centrally before or under it was an image representing the sacrificial act in which Christ, the second Adam, restored the possibility of salvation for all believing humans.[107] As Adam was naked and, following

---

[107] Davidson and Alexander, *The Early Art*, 37, 69–71, fig. 28; George Scharf, Jr., "Observations on a Picture in Gloucester Cathedral and Some Other Representations, of the Last Judgment," *Archaeologia* 36 (1855): pl. XXXVI, fig. 1; Davidson, *The Guild Chapel Wall Paintings at Stratford-upon-Avon*, fig. 17. For further examples over the chancel arch, see A. Caiger-Smith, *English Medieval Mural Paintings* (Oxford: Clarendon Press, 1963), pl. XVI (Stanningfield, Suffolk), and David Bevington et al., *Homo, Memento Finis*, Early Drama, Art, and Music, Monograph Series 6 (Kalamazoo: Medieval Institute Publications, 1985), figs. 14 (St. Thomas of Canterbury, Salisbury) and 17 (Wenshaston). An unusual example of c.1400, placed on the West wall of the nave at Trotton, Sussex, nevertheless shows the figure of Christ with the expected bare torso as well as wounded hands and feet. Such a manner of depicting Christ in the Last Judgment also was conventional in manuscript illuminations; see, for example, the Huth Psalter (British Library MS. Add. 38,116, fol. 13v), possibly illuminated at York or Lincoln (Nigel Morgan, *Early Gothic Manuscripts, 1250–*

the Fall, ashamed, so Christ, with no reason in the perfection of his nature for any shame, was brought to a violent and shameful end that paradoxically was a glorious victory over death and the grave. So too memory of the Crucifixion in the presence of Christ's bleeding body in the Last Judgment was regarded as a sign of hope for the time when at the Last Day all one's secret sins will be revealed and weighed against one's good deeds. In the *Speculum Humanae Salvationis* one further element is present in the Last Judgment: Mary, the Mother of Jesus, displaying her breast to her Son as a reminder to him not to forget his humanity.[108] For, as Anselm insisted in his *Cur Deus Homo*, Christ is our brother, and he thus shares a physical form with all other humans. For humans the physical body may still have been seen to be associated with shame, but through the encouragement of the love of God as revealed in the second person of the Trinity one's body itself is capable of being regenerated by seeing and thereby participating in the Mass in which Christ's body is made present.

Nevertheless, in popular religion the emotional expression of love toward Christ was likely, in the Midlands and North of England especially, to be carried much further than the above might suggest. Northern piety generally was not adverse to tears shed for the suffering of the Redeemer by those who looked upon images and pictures such as the ones created by the Flemish painters—tears which the great Michelangelo scorned.[109] Empathy with the suffering Christ was not infrequently taken to extremes, and, according to the evidence of the Wycliffite *Tretise of Miraclis Pleyinge*, this was carried over to the witnessing of religious plays, during the viewing of which people were also "movyd to compassion and devocion, wepinge bitere teris."[110] Devotional images

---

1285, 2 vols., Survey of Manuscripts Illuminated in the British Isles, 4 [London: Harvey Miller, 1988], pt. 2, no. 167, plate fig. 339).

[108] Wilson and Wilson, *A Medieval Mirror*, 198. In this illustration, the figure at the right is St. John the Baptist, who sometimes appears in place of the disciple John.

[109] Francesco de Hollanda, *Dialogos de Hollandia*, as quoted by Huizinga, *The Autumn of the Middle Ages*, 320. For discussion of affective piety, see also my essay "Northern Spirituality and the Late Medieval Drama and Art of York," in Clifford Davidson, *On Tradition: Essays on the Use and Valuation of the Past* (New York: AMS Press, 1992), 30–55.

[110] *A Tretise of Miraclis Pleyinge*, ed. Clifford Davidson, Early Drama, Art, and Music, Monograph Series 19 (Kalamazoo: Medieval Institute Publications, 1993), 98.

focusing on the Crucifixion such as the image showing the crucified Christ and the implements of the Passion were designed for intimate private meditation,[111] and the writings of Richard Rolle expressing a highly charged love of Jesus were widely disseminated. A poem such as an example in the famous *Carthusian Miscellany* contained in British Library Add. MS. 37,049 can ask Jesus to "mak me luf þe of al þinge best, / And wounde my hert in þi luf fre . . .";[112] these lines sound more like courtly love than religious verse. Margery Kempe's devotion to the physical body of Christ was indeed not all that unusual and points to the widespread existence of a popular spiritual eroticism that owes much to the spirituality deriving from the sermons by St. Bernard of Clairvaux on the Song of Songs. But exactly how these attitudes might have had relevance to the English wish to preserve Christ's modesty in the visual arts—and also presumably in the drama—we cannot know. The desire of the City Corporation at York and elsewhere for the proprieties and for all that would reflect well on the municipality would surely have counted for much. But, as David Freedberg has shown with regard to religious images, anxiety about sexual arousal may be regarded as a factor.[113] A truly nude man playing the role of the adult Christ would have been regarded as a scandal perhaps even bordering on blasphemy, for thus the actor—a sinful person who, like Adam and Eve, should be admonished to cover his shame—would have encountered resistance sufficient to suppress his impertinence.[114]

---

[111] See the devotional image with Christ on the cross surrounded by all the implements of the Passion in Cambridge, Trinity College MS. O.3.10, fol. 13, illustrated in John B. Friedman, *Northern Books, Owners, and Makers in the Late Middle Ages* (Syracuse: Syracuse University Press, 1995), fig. 39. Friedman's entire chapter entitled "'Hermits Painted at the Front': Images of Popular Piety" (148–202) is a valuable contribution.

[112] *Religious Lyrics of the XVth Century*, ed. Brown, no. 67.

[113] Freedberg, *The Power of Images*, 369–70. See also Trexler, "Gendering Christ Crucified," esp. 118–19.

[114] See Trexler, "Gendering Christ Crucified," 119, who quotes Jacob Wimpfeling (from G. Knod, "Jacob Wimpfeling and Daniel Zanckenried: Ein Streit über die Passion Christi," *Archiv für Literaturgeschichte* 14 [1886]: 5) to the effect that emphasis on Jesus' nakedness "doesn't move one to devotion, but rather to a certain *vilitas* or disrespect for our lord Jesus."

Sacred Blood
and the Late Medieval Stage

The Wycliffite *Tretise of Miraclis Pleyinge* alleges that the late medieval religious stage, specifically "miraclis pleyinge," is a vehicle by which audiences see "veine sightis of degyse."[1] While this allegation reflects the opinion of hostile writers, the terms that they use serve to identify precisely the *visual* nature of the late medieval religious drama. To be sure, the Wycliffite polemic does not distinguish between secular entertainment and sacred drama, and thus the *Tretise* is able to insist upon the ability of all theatrical spectacle to stir "to leccherie and debatis" and to other vices.[2] 'Degyse,' referring to costumes, masks, and other aspects of disguise taken on by actors, and 'sightis' are both terms which confirm Pamela Sheingorn's insistence on medieval drama as essentially one of the visual arts of the Middle Ages.[3] The terms also seem to be consistent with Graham Runnalls's argument, referring to the great French mystery plays, that "the medieval theatre was a place where the spectacle was considered to be more important than the text."[4]

In contrast to the early medieval rejection of verisimilitude and specific detail in the depiction of religious scenes, late medieval art and drama tended to be both very precise and realistic in the representation of the Passion and the martyrdom of saints.[5] The spectacle, because it has

---

[1] *A Tretise of Miraclis Pleyinge*, ed. Clifford Davidson, Early Drama, Art, and Music, Monograph Series 19 (Kalamazoo: Medieval Institute Publications, 1993), 96.

[2] Ibid.

[3] Pamela Sheingorn, "The Visual Language of Drama: Principles of Composition," in *Contexts for Early English Drama*, ed. Marianne Briscoe and John Coldewey (Bloomington: Indiana University Press, 1989), 173–91.

[4] Graham Runnalls, "Were They Listening or Watching? Text and Spectacle at the 1510 Châteaudun *Passion Play*," *Medieval English Theatre* 16 (1994): 25.

[5] To be sure, leaving aside fragments and plays about Mary embedded in the N-Town cycle, extant examples of Middle English saint plays are only two in number: the Digby plays of *Mary Magdalene* and the *Conversion of St. Paul*. For lost saint plays from England, see Clifford Davidson, "The Middle English Saint Play," in *The Saint Play in Medieval*

not been preserved for us except in descriptions in texts, stage directions, and theatrical records, is of primary concern for investigation at the same time that it is most elusive. One of the primary hermeneutic problems in need of exploration in this drama therefore involves how we are to *visualize* the scenes presented on the medieval stage and how we are to understand their visual dimension. While the study of fixed pictures and sculpture—e.g., wall paintings, stained glass, alabaster carvings—may illuminate this study, the late medieval stage must not be understood as static. It is clear that the effects produced by the producers and actors of the vernacular religious drama would hardly have been rigidly presented or lifeless. Indeed, all the evidence seems to point to decidedly effective theatrical presentation, designed often, as is consistent with the insistence on identification with the Passion of Christ and with the popular appeal of veneration of martyr saints, to bring the individual viewer to an emotional response to the events being depicted.[6]

The audience response to religious drama in the fifteenth and early sixteenth centuries would be difficult if not impossible to replicate today. While the encouragement of strong identification with the suffering Christ in plays of the Passion resulted in the presentation of a character who would appear to be beaten until wounded from his head to his feet, the response of a modern audience to such a realistic scene is likely to be one of revulsion rather than sympathy at the sight of blood that is represented as Christ's. An incident a few years ago in a parade in a small American town may serve to verify this point. According to an Associated Press story, a local church sponsored "a bloody Jesus wearing a bloodstained robe dragging a cross before whip-wielding Roman soldiers" in the Railroad Days parade at Durand, Michigan. Complaints were

---

Europe, ed. Clifford Davidson, Early Drama, Art, and Music, Monograph Series 8 (Kalamazoo: Medieval Institute Publications, 1986), 31–71, and the listing in "Saint Plays and Pageants of Medieval Britain," *Early Drama, Art, and Music Review* 22 (1999): 11–37.

[6] See Nicholas Love, *Mirror of the Blessed Life of Jesus Christ*, ed. Michael A. Sargent (New York: Garland, 1992), 161, and, for the best-known compendium of lives of the saints, Jacobus de Voragine, *The Golden Legend*, trans. William Granger Ryan, 2 vols. (Princeton: Princeton University Press, 1993). For use of visual depictions to stir the emotions rather than to impart knowledge, as in Gregory the Great's concept of pictures as books for the illiterate, see Rosemary Woolf, *The English Lyric in the Middle Ages* (Oxford: Clarendon Press, 1968), 183–84.

registered with the parade committee, and it was emphatically decided that "This type of parade entry will not be permitted in our future . . . parades."[7] The scene of wounded Christ carrying the cross was seen as offensive, and certainly was not viewed as conducive to devotion by the spectators who saw it and complained. The stage blood and the tormentors were apparently seen as inappropriate violence, hardly reflecting the sacrificial act of a Savior whose blood thus is to be apprehended as ritually pure.[8]

In contrast, late medieval spirituality accepted Christ's blood as pure because of his sinlessness. Joseph of Arimathea thus exclaims concerning the Crucifixion in the Bodley *Burial of Christ*:

> O innocent bloode,
> Most of vertue, most graciose and gude,
> This day stremyt owt lik a floode. . . . (24–26)[9]

In this scene the Virgin Mary is unable to touch her Son because the cross is "so high," yet "euer sho kissid the droppes of blood / That so fast ran down" (177–80). The reaction represented by the actor playing the role of Mary cannot simply be dismissed as that of a mother's feeling for her child, for there is the implication that the blood of the Crucifixion had an important role as part of a divine purpose for all humankind. Christ's blood is to be valued for his generosity in giving his life for the establishment of a sacramental process for the forgiveness of sins. He is the Lamb of God, given for the sins of the world. His wounds are "welles of mercy," and they are "fontains flowinge with water of life, / To wash away corrupcion of wondes infectyfe / By dedly syne grevose!" (364, 367–69). The slain body is "most holy" (382) and is the object of veneration in spite of—indeed, because of—its bloodied and lacerated state, even having been stretched so that his "synows and vaynes" have

---

[7] *Kalamazoo Gazette*, 24 May 1996, sec. A, p. 4. I am also indebted to the Rev. Randall Fuson for additional information about this presentation.

[8] See René Girard, *Violence and the Sacred*, trans. Patrick Gregory (Baltimore: Johns Hopkins University Press, 1977), 1–38.

[9] Citations to this play are to the text in *The Late Medieval Religious Plays of Bodleian MSS Digby 133 and E Museo 160*, ed. Donald Baker, John L. Murphy, and Louis B. Hall, Jr., EETS, 283 (Oxford: Oxford University Press, 1982).

15. Crucifixion. Michael de Massa, *On the Passion of Our Lord*. Bodleian Library, MS. 758, fol. 1ʳ. By permission of the Bodleian Library, Oxford University.

been "brokyn sonder by payns vngude," as Mary observes in the course of her lament (674–75).

Only the guilty person not in harmony with God and one's neighbor would be expected to react negatively to Christ's blood, and then, as an exemplum in a medieval sermon explains, it might still serve to bring one to a reconciled state. John Mirk tells of a woman who, ashamed to confess her sins, met the risen Christ. He took her hand and then, placing it in his side and drawing it out "all blody," said:

"Be þou no more aschamed to opyn þy hert to me, þen I am to opon my syde to þe." Then was þys woman agrysed of þe blod, and wold haue weschyn hit away; but scho myght not, be no way, tyll scho had schryuen hur of þat synne. Then, when scho was schryuen, anon þe hond was clene as þat oþyr.[10]

While this is hardly a narrative that would grace a twentieth-century sermon, its presentation of popular theology nevertheless was quite typical for its time. There are points here of direct resemblance to the pageants and plays of the Passion in the fifteenth and early sixteenth centuries. As the York pageant of the Death of Christ asserts, in a stanza reflecting the *Improperia* recited on Good Friday, the Savior sheds his blood for humankind's "goode" (XXXVI.127–28).[11] Christ's wounds and his blood thus could be regarded as a source of great comfort, not as offensive. Similarly, the blood of a saint such as St. Edmund or St. Thomas Becket was regarded as holy, and their mutilated bodies were preserved in reliquaries, in the case of these saints serving as the focus of pilgrimage at Bury St. Edmunds or Canterbury Cathedral.[12] The blood of a saint was regarded as having spiritual value as a relic, which would be carefully preserved. For example, a relic inventory of the Collegiate Church of St. Mary in Warwick lists the stone upon which St. George was believed to have shed blood when he was martyred.[13]

North European affective piety, in spite of its responsiveness to the Passion and to the martyrdom of saints, was not, however, as emotional as the religion of Italy or Spain, areas in which flagellant societies thrived.[14] In Castile, especially on Maundy Thursday, the day when the

---

[10] John Mirk, *Festial*, ed. Theodor Erbe, EETS, e.s. 96 (1905; reprint Millwood, N.Y.: Kraus, 1987), 90. While echoes are to be seen of Christ's invitation to the apostle Thomas to place his hand in his side, the purpose here is to impel one to confession and penitence rather than to belief.

[11] Citations to the York plays are to *The York Plays*, ed. Richard Beadle (London: Edward Arnold, 1982).

[12] See Jonathan Sumption, *Pilgrimage: An Image of Mediaeval Religion* (London: Faber and Faber, 1975), 122–23, 127, 152, 215, and *passim*.

[13] William Dugdale, *The Antiquities of Warwickshire* (London, 1656), 487–88.

[14] Cyrilla Barr, *The Monophonic Lauda and the Lay Religious Confraternities of Tuscany and Umbria in the Late Middle Ages*, Early Drama, Art, and Music, Monograph Series 10 (Kalamazoo: Medieval Institute Publications, 1988), 31–59; Maureen Flynn, "The

Last Supper and Christ's washing of the feet of his disciples were commemorated, processions of flagellants used whips upon themselves—whips which were designed to enable the participants to identify physically with the pain suffered by their Savior. The object of self-flagellation, according to a scholar writing about Castile in the sixteenth century, was the "performance of penance, a sense of sorrow proceeding from love of God, that was supposed to produce for them forgiveness of sins."[15] At the same time, those who as spectators looked on these processions with their display of bleeding and bodily pain were encouraged to see the ritual as "done in honor and reverence of the shedding of His precious blood, and in honor of the five thousand lashes that they gave Him in order to redeem and save us."[16] Nevertheless, holy suffering, martyrdom, and the shedding of blood were viewed without revulsion in England and other Northern countries in the late Middle Ages.

Because of the immense shift in sensibility and spirituality between the late Middle Ages and our own time, therefore, actual modern productions of medieval plays have tended to handle such visual aspects quite differently from the ways in which they must originally have been presented. The change in England may be dated in the late sixteenth and early seventeenth centuries, following the imposition of Protestantism and, eventually, its acceptance by the people. With the destruction of so much ecclesiastical art, especially that which depicted the suffering of Christ and the saints, the very idea of the sacredness of blood and of a bleeding body when associated with Christ or the saints seems to have been weakened and disappeared, at least as a physical reality. By denying the sacrificial element in the Mass, the theology of the Church of England likewise tended to minimize the physical connection between Christ's blood and the Eucharist,[17] and Calvinism, which for a time was a considerable force in the country's religious life, went further in denying

---

Spectacle of Suffering in Spanish Streets," in *City and Spectacle in Medieval Europe*, ed. Barbara A. Hanawalt and Kathryn L. Reyerson (Minneapolis: University of Minnesota Press, 1994), 153–68.

[15] Flynn, "The Spectacle of Suffering," 157.

[16] Ibid., quoting (in translation) a manuscript from Arlanzón now in the archives at Burgos Cathedral.

[17] *Articles of Religion*, XXXI.

even the idea of the Real Presence.[18] The *Lay Folks Mass Book* had depicted the elevation of the Host, signalled by the sacring bell, as indicating the moment of transubstantiation when reverence is due to Christ's presence:

> And so þo leuacioun þou be-halde,
> for þat is he þat iudas salde,
> and sithen was scourged & don on rode,
> and for mankynde þere shad his blode....[19]

In contrast, the Communion rite in the *Book of Common Prayer* of 1552 insisted upon the Crucifixion as a historical event only—"a full, perfecte and sufficiente sacrifice, oblacion, and satisfaccion, for the synnes of the whole worlde"—not as something replicated in the Eucharist each time the canon of the Mass was recited.[20] Nor was even the rood with its crucified Christ, Mary, and John to be displayed over the chancel arch of churches.[21] Under Protestantism both ritual and visual replication of the Crucifixion event were to be utterly eliminated from the consciousness of the people. Only in the nineteenth century would these Catholic aspects of religious practice be fully returned to Anglicanism. Not surprisingly, the blood of the Crucifixion tended to become a pale abstraction rather than a living form.[22]

While Father Gardiner's classic study of the suppression of the late medieval religious drama in England is now properly to be seen as

---

[18] See, for example, Richard Baxter, *A Christian Directory* (London, 1677), pt. 3:151.

[19] *The Lay Folks Mass Book*, ed. Thomas Frederick Simmons, EETS, o.s. 71 (London: N. Trübner, 1879), 38. It was this moment of transubstantiation when the Host was elevated that was normally shown in illustrations of the Mass on fonts or in painted glass; see Ann Eljenholm Nichols, *Seeable Signs: The Iconography of the Seven Sacraments, 1350–1544* (Woodbridge: Boydell Press, 1994), 251–53.

[20] *The First and Second Prayerbooks of King Edward the Sixth* (London: Dent, 1910), 389.

[21] See Margaret Aston, *England's Iconoclasts*, I: *Laws Against Images* (Oxford: Clarendon Press, 1988), 302–03, 319, 330–32

[22] There were, of course, exceptions. The blood of Christ and the martyrs was important for Recusant spirituality, and Christ's blood for a considerable length of time was an important aspect of the imagery of religious verse. In the eighteenth century, William Cowper could write a hymn on the theme of "a fountain filled with blood," for example.

dated,[23] the "New Religion," supported by the doctrine of the Word alone that may be traced to Luther and Erasmus, must still be credited with a program of iconoclasm that eventually rejected the visual representation of the religious scenes of suffering and death in both the saint plays and the Passion of Christ.[24] The change was not particularly rapid, and in the time of Queen Mary the playing of the great civic cycle at the Protestant city of Coventry still had strong support from the citizens. There is, for example, the story of John Careles, a weaver who was imprisoned in Mary's time for his Protestant sympathies but was allowed to leave the prison to act in the Coventry cycle.[25] But by 1580 the great cycles of Chester, York, and Coventry had already been suppressed. Nevertheless, one civic play cycle remained as late as the early seventeenth century, and the documents which report it are of considerable interest for the present study.

In his *Ancient Funerall Monuments* (1631), John Weever reported that a Corpus Christi play had survived at Kendall until the "beginning of the raigne of King *Iames*; for which the Townesmen were sore troubled; and vpon good reasons the play finally suppresst" as had been the case "in all other Townes of the kingdome."[26] Whether Weever was correct or not in identifying the Kendall play as typically treating sacred history "from the creation of the world" cannot be absolutely ascertained, but he speaks

---

[23] Harold C. Gardiner, *Mysteries' End* (New Haven: Yale University Press, 1946).

[24] *Iconoclasm vs. Art and Drama*, ed. Clifford Davidson and Ann Eljenholm Nichols, Early Drama, Art, and Music, Monograph Series, 11 (Kalamazoo: Medieval Institute Publications, 1989), *passim*. For the role of Erasmus, who of course did not abandon the Roman Catholic Church, see Michael O'Connell, "God's Body: Incarnation, Physical Embodiment, and the Fate of Biblical Theater in the Sixteenth Century," in *Subjects on the World's Stage*, ed. David G. Allen and Robert A. White (Newark: University of Delaware Press, 1991), 62–63. It should also be noted that all regions affected by the Reformation did not suffer from the violent iconoclasm experienced in England; Lutheran countries were largely spared, and Lutheran spirituality hence retained a more vivid impression of the blood of Christ, as in the hymn *In Christi Wunden schlaf' ich ein* (*I fall asleep in Jesus' Wounds*). Passion iconography in seventeenth-century English verse is surveyed by J. A. W. Bennett, *Poetry of the Passion* (Oxford: Clarendon Press, 1982), 157–67.

[25] John Foxe, *Actes and Monuments* (London, 1583), as quoted in *Records of Early English Drama: Coventry*, ed. R. W. Ingram (Toronto: University of Toronto Press, 1981), 207.

[26] John Weever, *Ancient Funerall Monuments* (London, 1631), 405.

with some authority since he indicates that he himself was a witness to the production "which I haue seene acted at Preston, and Lancaster, and last of all at Kendall."[27] The Kendall play was not put down until c.1605,[28] approximately twenty-five years after the suppression of the famous Coventry plays in 1579.

Not much is known about the Kendall play since its text is lost, though the dramatic records show that it was acted at one outdoor station and hence was not presented on pageant wagons.[29] But local memory of it is recorded a generation after its suppression in the diary of the Puritan clergyman John Shaw, who had gone to Cartmell to preach and teach the catechism. Shaw was utterly appalled to hear from a man of about sixty years of age that he had only learned of the way of salvation through the Kendall Corpus Christi play:

> I told him, yat the way to Salvation was by Iesus Christ God-man, who as he was man shed his blood for us on the crosse etc Oh, Sir (said he) I think I heard of that man you speake of, once in a play at *Kendall*, called *Corpus-Christi play*, where there was a man on a tree, & blood ran downe etc And after, he professed, that tho he was a good Church-man, yat is, he constantly went to Common-prayer, at their chappel, yet he could not remember thatever he heard of Salvation by Iesus + but in that play.[30]

The vividness of the stage blood had deeply impressed this man many years before, and it is hard to believe that the theatrical effect involved was not highly realistic according to the standards of the time.

In contrast, twentieth-century revivals of medieval religious plays have tended to avoid the extensive use of stage blood because it has been felt, apparently quite correctly, that audiences would not respond positively to such effects. However, the anemic presentation of effects which ought according to the text to involve bloody torture and an even bloodier execution contradicts an element that was expected by the original playwrights, as when the N-Town *Passion Play II* specifies that Christ

---

[27] Ibid.
[28] See Audrey Douglas and Peter Greenfield, *Early English Drama: Cumberland, Westmorland, Gloucestershire* (Toronto: University of Toronto Press, 1986), 18.
[29] Ibid., 168–80.
[30] Ibid., 219.

should be beaten by his torturers *"tyl he is all blody"* (30.243 *s.d.*).³¹ Peter Travis has remarked on the way in which modern productions have failed to represent the wounded body of Christ after his treatment before the high priests and Pilate, and even on the cross the effects have been distinctly bland. Such productions thus are indeed "sanitized and civil" in contrast to the cruelty and injustice represented in earlier spectacle.³² In other pageants such as the Chester Last Judgment, which also demands the display of the bleeding wounds, modern performances have drawn back from the kind of vivid representation that characterized the fifteenth-century religious stage.

In the visual arts blood appears both profusely seeping from the wounds on the body of Christ and also pouring forth from the five wounds. Some information is available about the techniques that were required in order to stage such scenes in the drama. One method of releasing stage blood is revealed in the Canterbury dramatic records where it was indicated that leather bags of blood were used in the Thomas Becket pageant.³³ Yet there is a serious problem with the use of actual blood or even of colored water or vinegar,³⁴ for these are a clear and present danger to the costumes being worn by the actors. As Leo Kirschbaum noted in his pioneering article on stage blood, focusing to be

---

³¹ Citations are to *The N-Town Play: Cotton Vespasian D.8*, ed. Stephen Spector, EETS, s.s. 11–12 (Oxford: Oxford University Press, 1991).

³² Peter Travis, "The Social Body of the Dramatic Christ in Medieval England," in *Early Drama to 1600*, ed. Albert H. Tricomi, Acta 13 (Binghamton: Center for Medieval and Early Renaissance Studies, State University of New York at Binghamton, 1987), 25–26.

³³ Canterbury City Accounts FA2, fol. 411ʳ. I am grateful to James Gibson for this reference.

³⁴ Reference to *"A little bladder of vineger prickt"* is made in Thomas Preston's *Cambyses*, written in the 1560s; this stage direction is cited by Leo Kirschbaum, "Shakespeare's Stage Blood and Its Critical Significance," *PMLA* 64 (1949): 517. Paint, probably meaning water-soluble pigments, was used in some cases on the Continent; see *The Staging of Religious Drama in the Late Middle Ages*, ed. Peter Meredith and John Tailby, Early Drama, Art, and Music, Monograph Series 4 (Kalamazoo: Medieval Institute Publications, 1983), 108–09. At Modane in 1580, the stage direction teasingly reads: "Then they shall make a dagger with which someone can be struck in the breast and die from the blow. And they will make blood issue forth in the accustomed way (*à la maniere accoutumée*)" (ibid., 105). For special effects involving the bloodied bodies of saints at Bourges, see ibid., 102–03.

sure on the Renaissance stage, "blood is both factual and messy."[35] In an age when costumes were an enormous expense, the economics of production could hardly be ignored.

Jesus' garments in the pageants representing the Passion were, however, ideal for displaying his blood, for in the most brutal sequences he was apparently usually dressed in a body stocking of soft leather in order that he would appear as if nude and yet retain his kingliness. Such garments are noted in the Coventry Smiths' records for their play of the Passion:

1452:
Item payed for vj skynnys of whitleder to godds garment   xviij d
Item payed for makyng of the same garment   x d

1499:
Item payd for mendyng a cheverel [*wig*] for god and for sowyng of gods kote of leddur and for makyng of the hands [*gloves*] to the same kote   xij d

1554:
Item payd for v schepskens for gods coot & for makyng   iii s
(*REED: Coventry*, 25, 93, 200)

Most revealing of all perhaps is a record of 1565 that reports payment of two shillings and sixpence to one Hewyt for "payntyng & gylldyng ... the pyllar [of flagellation], the crose & Godes cote."[36] Such examples of the crucified Christ as the panel of fifteenth-century painted glass at Long Melford show every part of his body afflicted with lacerations from the scourging.[37] Gail McMurray Gibson notes that verses by John Lydgate were also displayed in this church to encourage meditation on the wounds

---

[35] Kirschbaum, "Shakespeare's Stage Blood," 529.

[36] *REED: Coventry*, 231. For a record indicating that Christ wore a gold wig, see ibid., 74; this document also lists four scourges and a "piller" for the Flagellation and specifies the garments worn by the tormenters (73–74). See also Clifford Davidson, *From Creation to Doom: The York Cycle of Mystery Plays* (New York: AMS Press, 1984), 111–12. A fragment of the pillar of the flagellation was present at York Minster where it was regarded as a valuable relic (see ibid., 112).

[37] Christopher Woodforde, *The Norwich School of Glass-Painting in the Fifteenth Century* (London: Oxford University Press, 1950), 117, pl. XXVII.

of Christ and on the name of Jesus: "With near-hallucinatory intensity, Lydgate's visual imagination invites the meditator to make the word flesh, to transform the very word *Jesus* into a gaping wound that assaults all the bodily senses—and imbues that meditator with remorse for human sin."[38] In the Towneley Resurrection play (26.292),[39] Christ is reported to have 5,400 wounds on his body—a number that seems fairly conventional when compared to the number specified by other writers.[40]

The wounds are not only therefore the five wounds in hands, feet, and right side, but also the multitude of other wounds from the extensive beatings suffered after his arrest. The wounds become progressively worse through the Buffeting, Mocking, Flagellation, and carrying of the cross. The York *Mortificacio Cristi*, appropriately presented by the Butchers, who might well have used animal blood as a theatrical substitute for the blood of Christ, shows the culmination of these beatings in this cycle, for here the ultimate scene occurs in which the Savior's blood is spilled. In the previous play he had been cruelly placed on the cross by being stretched since the holes for the nails had been drilled too far apart. As in a panel of York painted glass of c.1370 formerly in St. Saviour's Church but now in All Saints, Pavement, ropes have been used to pull his body until "all his synnous go asoundre" (XXXV.131–32) before all the nails can be inserted.[41] In this glass, the nails being driven into place by

---

[38] Gail McMurray Gibson, *The Theater of Devotion: East Anglian Drama and Society in the Late Middle Ages* (Chicago: University of Chicago Press, 1989), 87.

[39] Citations to the Towneley plays are to the edition of Martin Stevens and A. C. Cawley, EETS, s.s. 13–14 (Oxford: Oxford University Press, 1994).

[40] Andrew Breeze, "The Number of Christ's Wounds," *The Bulletin of the Board of Celtic Studies* 32 (1985): 89–90; W. Sparrow Simpson, "On the Measure of the Wound in the Side of the Redeemer," *British Archaeological Journal* 30 (1874): 369. See above for the Castilian estimate of five thousand wounds. The high number of wounds may have been determined by a daily devotion to the Passion of reciting fifteen *Aves* and fifteen *Pater nosters*; see Woolf, *The English Religious Lyric*, 204.

[41] Various lines in the scene in the York play under discussion have been noted to echo the *Northern Passion*; see Frances A. Foster, *A Study of the Middle-English Poem Known as* The Northern Passion *and Its Relation to the Cycle Plays* (London and Bungay: Richard Clay, 1914), 83–84. For the painted glass at All Saints Pavement and other examples in the visual arts, see my *From Creation to Doom*, 125–26. Another useful representation of Christ being attached to the cross in this way appears in an English alabaster carving; see Francis Cheetham, *English Medieval Alabasters with a Catalogue of the Collection in the Victoria*

the executioners with their hammers are not, however, the stubs or short nails specified by the soldiers in the York *Crucifixio Christi* (102) sponsored by the Pinners and Painters, the latter another guild that would have been able to supply ample stage blood by the use of available pigments to amplify the visual effects of the scene. In the end the figure of Christ must be seen as dripping with blood from bruises and wounds that extend from the top of his head to the bottom of his feet—a reflection of Isaiah 63:1–3, which identifies a man who comes from Bosra with red "garments like theirs that tread in the winepress."[42] Fulfilling the prophecy of Isaiah 53:4, his body is also as full of sores as a leper.[43] The audience, however, is not expected to experience revulsion at this sight any more than viewers would be offended by the scene of the Flagellation in which the body of Christ, nude except for a loincloth, is being beaten in a historiated initial in the so-called *Bolton Hours*, a manuscript apparently written and illuminated at York early in the fifteenth century.[44] Even more detailed in its representation of the wounded body of Christ is the Resurrection in the same illuminated manuscript, for here Jesus steps forth out of a coffer tomb with bleeding wounds on his legs, arms, torso, and head as well as the usual wounds on hands, foot, and side.[45] He makes a sign of blessing with his right hand, and with his left holds the vexillum which signifies his victory over death. The scene is a demonstration of power at the same time that it enlists the viewer's sympathy for the human sufferings which

---

and Albert Museum (Oxford: Phaidon, Christie's, 1984), no. 170. For discussion of the tormentors and executioners at the Crucifixion, see James Marrow, "*Circumdederunt me canes multi*: Christ's Tormentors in Northern European Art of the Late Middle Ages and Early Renaissance," *Art Bulletin* 59 (1977): 167–81. F. P. Pickering discusses relevant changes in the depiction of the Crucifixion in the late Middle Ages; see his *Literature and Art in the Middle Ages* (Coral Gables: University of Florida Press, 1970), 223–307.

[42] I have used the Douay-Rheims translation here and elsewhere.

[43] For a connection between Job *in stercore* suffering from boils and the wounded Christ, see Davidson, *From Creation to Doom*, 110.

[44] York Minster Library MS. 2, fol. 57ᵛ; see Clifford Davidson and David E. O'Connor, *York Art*, Early Drama, Art, and Music, Reference Series 1 (Kalamazoo: Medieval Institute Publications, 1978), 74. In an unpublished paper read at the 31st International Congress on Medieval Studies in 1996, Pamela M. King dated the manuscript 1405–10 and more recently has connected it stylistically with the Great East Window in York Minster.

[45] York Minster Library, MS. 2, fol. 37; Davidson, *From Creation to Doom*, fig. 14.

he has endured for all men and women.[46] Likewise, in a Middle English lyric noted by Rosemary Woolf, Christ, coming to the soul very much like a courtly lover, shows his wounds and announces: "I am sore woundet, behold on my skyn, / Leve lyf, for my love, let me comen in."[47]

Positive audience reaction is strongly implied in the Towneley Resurrection play to which reference has been made above. Here Christ, having risen to the sound of angels singing *Christus resurgens*—a chant which had commonly been used in the *Elevatio* ceremonies on Easter morning[48]—will appear as the Man of Sorrows, a devotional figure asking for veneration. Here his wounds are still "weytt and all blody" (26.237) because of the blood which flowed out of his heart and side. "Behold my body" which was "All to-rent / And all to-shentt, / Man, for thi plight," Jesus says (250–54). He notes that "cordes" and "ropys" had been used to draw out his limbs unto the holes drilled in the cross—a feature also emphasized in the York plays. Then he calls attention to the crown of thorns, which presumably should be imagined as like the "original" at Sainte Chapelle,[49] and to his "shankes" and "knees" as well as his "armes" and thighs. "Behold my body," he says, "how Iues it dang / With knottys of whippys and scorges strang" (283–84): "As stremes of well the bloode out-sprang / On euery syde" (285–86). This blood is the source of healing and is necessary to salvation:

> If thou thy life in sin haue led,
> Mercy to ask, be not adred;

---

[46] In this respect Christ here represents an important aspect of Northern piety of the late Middle Ages, for which see my *On Tradition: Essays on the Use and Valuation of the Past* (New York: AMS Press, 1992), 30–55. Jesus' humanity is emphasized in the manner for which Anselm, Bernard of Clairvaux, and mystics such as Richard Rolle prepared the way.

[47] Rosemary Woolf, "The Theme of Christ the Lover-Knight in Medieval English Literature," *Review of English Studies* n.s. 13 (1962): 7; quoted by Bennett, *Poetry of the Passion*, 67, where he notes that the final line is reminiscent of the Song of Songs at the same time that Christ's "wounds and suffering touch the same springs of pity that Meditations on the Passion were at this very time releasing" (67–68).

[48] See Pamela Sheingorn, *The Easter Sepulchre in England*, Early Drama, Art, and Music, Reference Series 5 (Kalamazoo: Medieval Institute Publications, 1987), 116, 130, 134, 249, 349, 365.

[49] Ethelbert Horne, "The Crown of Thorns in Art," *Downside Review* 53 (1935): 48–51.

> The leste drope I for the bled
> Myght clens the soyn,
> All the syn
> The warld within
> If thou had done. (311–17)

His very body has also become available as the "veray brede of lyfe" which is the Eucharist, according to the final lines of Christ's speech—lines which were canceled in the manuscript after the Reformation by a Protestant sympathizer.[50] In the Towneley play, Christ's body—as in the York Tilemakers' play in which it is beaten until it is "al beflapped" and "all bloo" (XXXIII.431–32)[51]—and his blood are no more to be seen as repulsive than the transubstantiated elements of bread and wine in the Mass.

Devotion to the body of Christ with all its wounds is evidenced in an important iconographic type found in late medieval York. This is the representation of the Trinity in which the Son is shown not on the cross but as a wounded and bleeding body held by the Father. There are two examples in painted glass in York Minster, one of them now in the north transept but formerly in the church of St. John Ousebridge, York, and dated c.1498.[52] A second example in painted glass is in the choir of the Minster.[53] Though in this example the head of God the Father has been replaced with an undersize and misplaced head of a saint, the body of the Son is remarkably intact. This Corpus Christi form of the Trinity, which

---

[50] See *Towneley Plays*, 1:356, 2:607. The history and provenance of the Towneley plays are not at all clear; see Barbara D. Palmer, "Corpus Christi 'Cycles' in Yorkshire: The Surviving Records," *Comparative Drama* 27 (1993): 218–31.

[51] For the word 'bloo' or 'blae,' meaning 'livid,' see J. W. Robinson's review in *Comparative Drama* 19 (1986): 366. "Bloo" also appears as a descriptive term referring to Christ's body in the Passion text on the roof of the church at Almondbury; see Barbara D. Palmer, *The Early Art of the West Riding of Yorkshire*, Early Drama, Art, and Music, Reference Series 6 (Kalamazoo: Medieval Institute Publications, 1990), 278. Bennett points out that "'blody' and 'blo' (livid) became the characteristic epithets for the rent body on the Rood" (*Poetry of the Passion*, 39).

[52] Davidson and O'Connor, *York Art*, 85–86, fig. 24.

[53] Ibid., 85.

also appears in the Low Countries and southwestern Germany,[54] must be seen as a devotional image intended to draw out the sympathy of the worshipper. In York this type of the Trinity was apparently a popular subject, if we may judge from extant examples.[55] Very likely the Corpus Christi Trinity was connected with the Corpus Christi Guild, as suggested by glass in the church of Holy Trinity, Goodramgate, which includes the figure of a patron, John Walker, who was a member of this guild.[56] This image illustrates the offering of the Son as a sacrifice by the Father. Christ's death is the epitome of God's love for mankind, and hence the body of the Savior demands a reciprocal outpouring of love.

J. W. Robinson saw the devotion to Christ's body, blood, and wounds as central to a "Cult of Jesus" and identified some ways in which the visual arts shared motifs with the plays.[57] As we have seen, the focus tended to be on the wounds and the blood, which in its shedding provides the means of salvation. Through Christ's blood were humans redeemed from damnation. This was the reason for the popularity of relics of the Holy Blood, for example those brought from the Holy Land to Bruges, supposedly by Thierry of Alsace in 1148, and to Westminster by Henry

---

[54] See the *Mayer van den Bergh Breviary*, fol. 295, in the Mayer van den Bergh Museum, Antwerp, and also H. Rode, *Die Mittelalterlichen Glasmalereien des Kölner Domes*, Corpus Vitrearum Medii Aevi: Deutschland, 4, no. 1 (Berlin, 1974), pls. 186–87.

[55] See Davidson and O'Connor, *York Art*, 87. The assessment of the depth of spirituality among the citizens of York before Protestantism is not a simple matter. D. M. Palliser, writing about religion in York in the sixteenth century, wonders if most people were not merely conventionally religious; he quotes J. A. F. Thomson's remark in the *Journal of Ecclesiastical History* 16 (1965): 194, about piety in London which tended to take "a middle course between religious apathy and religious enthusiasm" (quoted in *Tudor York* [Oxford: Oxford University Press, 1979], 231). Yet the York plays show evidence of the emotional piety that characterized Northern Europe in the late Middle Ages; see my "Northern Spirituality and the Late Medieval Drama and Art of York," in Davidson, *On Tradition*, 30–55.

[56] Peter Gibson, "The Stained and Painted Glass," in *The Noble City of York*, ed. Alberic Stacpoole (York: Cerialis Press, 1972), colour pl. 3A; Davidson and O'Connor, *York Art*, 87; for an interesting alabaster in which the Father and Holy Spirit are holding and displaying the wounded body of Christ, see Cheetham, *English Medieval Alabasters*, no. 236.

[57] J. W. Robinson, "The Late Medieval Cult of Jesus and the Mystery Plays," *PMLA* 80 (1965): 508–14.

III in c.1247.⁵⁸ Less successful was the Blood of Hailes, which suffered from negative publicity from as early as c.1264 when it had been brought to Hailes Abbey and which was to be roundly denounced as a fraud by Protestant reformers in the sixteenth century.⁵⁹ Even a humble woodcut illustrating the Man of Sorrows in British Library Egerton MS. 1821 placed the greatest emphasis on the blood, for drops of the holy blood are dripping across the entire surface of the woodcut and hence are shown not only on the bleeding body, which is shown wearing only a loincloth and standing in the tomb between the spear and the lance.⁶⁰ Other signs of the Passion arrayed around the edges of the woodcut even include the spitting executioner and the lantern often carried and sometimes dropped by one of the soldiers at the time of Jesus' arrest. In the bottom row, flanking Judas's kiss of betrayal, are the three spice jars carried by the holy women to anoint Jesus' body and also the three nails with which his feet and hands had been attached to cross. Blood is shown dripping from the three nails.

---

⁵⁸ For the cult of Christ's blood and the Holy Blood at Bruges, still venerated on Friday of each week and the focus of an annual procession, see Émile Mâle, *Religious Art in France: The Late Middle Ages*, trans. Marthiel Mathews, Bollingen Series 90, no. 3 (Princeton: Princeton University Press, 1986), 105–06, but for a review of recent scholarship see Wim Hüsken, "The Bruges 'Ommegang'," in *Formes teatrals de la tradició medieval*, ed. Francesc Massip (Barcelona: Institut del Teatre, 1996), 77–85. Hüsken notes that the first reference to the relic was nearly a hundred years later, in 1256, though it may have been brought from the Holy Land earlier in the century during the Second Crusade.

For Matthew Paris' description of Henry III's act of bringing the relic of Christ's blood to Westminster, see M. E. Roberts, "The Relic of the Holy Blood and the Iconography of the Thirteenth-Century North Portal of Westminster Abbey," in *England in the Thirteenth Century*, ed. W. M. Ormrod (1985, reprint Woodbridge: Boydell Press, 1986), 137–39, quoting Matthew Paris, *English History*, trans. J. A. Giles (London, 1852–54), 2:239–43. See also Suzanne Lewis, *The Art of Matthew Paris in the* Chronica Majora (Berkeley and Los Angeles: University of California Press, 1987), 225–26 and (for the illustration drawn by Matthew himself in Cambridge, Corpus Christi College MS. 16, fol. 215) pl. X.

⁵⁹ John Leland, *Collectanea* (Oxford, 1715), 6:283–84; St. Clair Baddleley, "The Holy Blood of Hayles," *Transactions of the Bristol and Gloucester Archaeological Society* 23 (1900): 276–84; John Phillips, *The Reformation of Images* (Berkeley and Los Angeles: University of California Press, 1973), 76.

⁶⁰ British Library, MS. Egerton 1821, fol. 8ᵛ; reproduced by Robinson, "The Late Medieval Cult of Jesus," pl. II.

An Arma Christi shield formerly in St. Saviour's and now in All Saints, Pavement, York, is also covered with numerous small representations of Christ's wounds.[61] Otherwise the design is quite conventional, with a cross in the center displaying the crown of thorns at its top. The three nails are attached to the cross, and across its front are the spear and staff with a sponge. The column of the flagellation and rope, whips, dice, and gown appear along with hammer and pincers, the one for nailing to the cross and the other for use in removing the corpus. The Arma Christi in this case is closely related to another devotional image, a woodcut inserted at fol. 44^v of York Minster Library MS. XVI.K.6, a book of hours dated c.1420. Intended according to the caption to be looked upon devoutly by the beholder, the woodcut again has the cross with nails attached to it, crown of thorns, spear, sponge, scourges, hammer, and pincers. But at the center is the wounded heart from which blood is running forth into a chalice placed immediately below it.[62]

This iconography should not be surprising, since iconographic details such as angels holding chalices at the Crucifixion were not uncommon. For example, in mid-fifteenth-century glass from the Church of St. Denys at York described by F. Harrison, "from our Lord's left arm a stream of blood, coloured white in the window, drops into a chalice"; blood is being collected in chalices by two angels.[63] In the Charterhouse at Coventry fragments of a wall painting of the Crucifixion remain in which angels collect blood from Christ's feet into chalices.[64] A Continental Corpus

---

[61] Davidson and O'Connor, *York Art*, 77, fig. 22. On the Arma Christi, see Gertrud Schiller, *Iconography of Christian Art*, trans. Janet Seligman, 2 vols. (Greenwich, Conn.: New York Graphic Society, 1972), 2:184–95; and Rossell Hope Robbins, "The Arma Christi Rolls," *Modern Language Review* 34 (1939): 415–21. As Robbins points out, looking at such images was regarded as spiritually beneficial, and indulgences were granted for doing so.

[62] See the commentary by Douglas Gray, "The Five Wounds of Our Lord," *Notes and Queries* 208 (1963): 88–89.

[63] F. Harrison, *The Painted Glass of York* (London: SPCK, 1927), 165; Davidson and O'Connor, *York Art*, 82.

[64] Clifford Davidson and Jennifer Alexander, *The Early Art of Coventry, Stratford-upon-Avon, Warwick, and Lesser Sites in Warwickshire*, Early Drama, Art, and Music, Reference Series 4 (Kalamazoo: Medieval Institute Publications, 1985), 31; Pierre Turpin, "Ancient Wall Paintings in the Charterhouse, Coventry," *Burlington Magazine* 35 (1919): pl. facing 252. See also Nichols, *Seeable Signs*, 255–57.

Christi Trinity—a wood relief from the Altar of the Virgin, Wienhausen, published by Gertrud Schiller—is even more explicit, for in it blood is shown streaming in five streams from Christ's wounded body into a chalice held by two angels; further, immediately above the chalice is the Host.[65] The connection between the holy blood and the Eucharist is thus visibly displayed in such popular representations.

Examination of lyrics of the Passion provide further corroboration of the significance of the holy blood, as in the famous "Wofully araide," which imagines Christ speaking from the cross:

> Wofully araide,
> My blode, man, ffor thee ran,
> hit may not be naide,
> My body blo and wanne,
> Wofully araide.[66]

The following, from John of Grimstone's commonplace book, in which the speaker is a man desiring identification with Christ, is a plea for identification with the body that has shed blood for all humankind:

> I wolde ben clad in cristes skyn,
> Þat ran so longe on blode,
> & gon t'is herte & taken myn In—
> Þer is a fulsum fode.[67]

In connection with this poem, Douglas Gray calls attention in a note to a statement by Julian of Norwich, who "has a vision of the wound in the side as 'a fair delectable place, and large enough for all mankind that shall be saved to rest in peace and love'."[68] In a verse from Isaiah that was interpreted typologically, the significance of the wounds of Christ was anticipated: "But he was wounded for our iniquities, he was bruised for

---

[65] Schiller, *Iconography of Christian Art*, 2: fig. 785.

[66] *Religious Lyrics of the XVth Century*, ed Carleton Brown (Oxford: Clarendon Press, 1939), no. 103 (refrain).

[67] *Religious Lyrics of the XIVth Century*, ed. Carleton Brown, 2nd ed., rev. G. V. Smithers (Oxford: Clarendon Press, 1952), no. 71.

[68] Douglas Gray, *Themes and Images in the Medieval English Religious Lyric* (London: Routledge and Kegan Paul, 1972), 271.

our sins: the chastisement of our peace was upon him, and by his bruises we are healed" (53:5).⁶⁹ The wounds had become a primary symbol of the atonement in medieval iconography, and they were to be thus seen as the object of the most intense devotion.

The nature of Christ's offering of his heart and man's response are indicated in a poem with an accompanying illustration in a Carthusian Miscellany (British Library MS. Add. 37049, fol. 20ʳ).⁷⁰ At the right a wounded Christ stands with bruises on every part of his body. His bleeding left hand is held to his chest immediately below his wound in his right side, and his bleeding right hand is held out to indicate a large heart, upon which are four bleeding wounds resulting from the nails as well as a large wound inscribed "Þis is þe mesure of þe Woundes Four / Iesus crist sufferd for oure redempcioun." A scroll gives Jesus' words: "Þes woundes smert bere in þi hert and luf god aye. / Yf Þou do þis, Þu sal haf blys wythowten delay." Below and at the left is a small bearded man with hands extended in supplication and prayer. The accompanying poem provides Christ's speech as well as the man's reply. Christ implores the "unkynde" man to keep his pains "in mynde" and to *see* the bleeding heart; and, above all, he asks that man love him "Al thyng abofe." The man's response indicates that he has heard Christ's words and that he needs the assistance of grace so that he may lastingly perform deeds pleasing to the deity in order at the Last Day to enter into the "halle" of heaven.⁷¹ The poem recommends meditation on the wounds and blood of Christ as a means of drawing closer to him and identifying with his pain.

---

[69] As an example of the power of Christ's blood to heal physically, note Longinus, the blind centurion, who received his sight after he touched his eyes with the blood that had run down the spear which he had thrust into the side of the Savior. For an example, see the York Butchers' *Death of Christ* (XXXVI.291–312). For a useful example of this iconography in York glass, albeit earlier than the plays, see Thomas French and David O'Connor, *York Minster: A Catalogue of Medieval Stained Glass*, Fascicule 1: *The West Windows of the Nave*, Corpus Vitrearum Medii Aevi 3 (Oxford: Oxford University Press, 1987), 79–80. Located in the south aisle window in the west end of the nave, this glass dated c.1339 illustrates the Crucifixion with a "poorly preserved" Longinus, on the left. He holds a spear and is apparently "kneeling on one knee; he looks up toward Christ, his right hand raised . . ." (ibid., 79–80).

[70] For the text and illustration, see Gray, *Themes and Images*, 53–54, pl. 2. See also Woolf, *The English Religious Lyric*, 185–87.

[71] Gray, *Themes and Images*, 53–54.

Such an example suggests how the drama also would have served to draw the members of the audience into the essential action being depicted and to make them participants in the event being recalled in an act of collective memory that makes visible the events of salvation history.

Obviously actual audience response would not have been identical in all the individuals viewing a scene such as the Flagellation or the Crucifixion with Christ's wounded body displayed on the cross. Nevertheless—and this point is central to my argument in this article—it is not farfetched to believe that a great many did in fact respond emotionally and positively to the sacred image when it was given lively depiction by actors. However, the liveliness seems not to have been intended to inspire a carnivalesque atmosphere, and all the evidence points to every attempt being made to engage the audience on the side of Christ and against his executioners.[72]

Michael O'Connell notes, "What is striking about these scenes on stage . . . is that they are developed—prolonged one is tempted to say—almost beyond endurance."[73] Such violent effects were almost obligatory; as a stage direction in a fifteenth-century French play cited by John Spalding Gatton insists, "There must be blood."[74] Such violent and bloody effects were, however, seen as indicative of the gift of grace to all humankind and as reflective of the saving power of the beloved Christ; hence that which for men and women of a later time would be unendurable would potentially have precipitated a deeply spiritual experience. Scenes of this kind in drama might impress the Wycliffite writers of *A Tretise of Miraclis Pleyinge* as "veine sightis of degyse," but for many in the audience the act of seeing religious plays was perceived as enriching. The experience could be, on account of the realistic depiction in the plays of the Passion—or, for that matter, in the bloody martyrdom of a saint, whose blood was regarded by Tertullian as the seed

---

[72] See also Hans-Jürgen Diller, "The Torturers in the English Mystery Plays," in *Evil on the Medieval Stage*, ed. Meg Twycross (Lancaster: Medieval English Theatre, 1992), 37–65.

[73] O'Connell, "God's Body," 80.

[74] John Spalding Gatton, "'There must be blood': Mutilation and Martyrdom on the Medieval Stage," in *Violence in Drama*, ed. James Redmond, Themes in Drama 13 (Cambridge: Cambridge University Press, 1991), 79.

by which the Church had been planted[75]—a vivid bringing to mind of the essentials of the salvation story and an imaginative act of devotion.

A central role for stage blood also appears in the Croxton *Play of the Sacrament*, which according to the banns dramatizes "a new passyoun" in which the Host is nailed "to a pyller" and "with pynsons plukked . . . doune" (38–40).[76] The wicked Jews, of whom Jonathas is the chief, obtain a Host and torture it by giving it five wounds, whereupon the stage direction states: "*Here þe Ost must blede*" (480 s.d.). "Yt bledyth," Jonathas says, "as yt were woode, iwys" (483). In connection with this effect, Darryll Grantley has called attention to a Sacrament play at Metz in 1513: "Then by a device which had been made, a large quantity of blood sprang up high from the said Host, as if it was a pissing infant and the Jew was covered and bloodied by it and it made his person very wet."[77] The effects thereafter presented in the Croxton play become even more spectacular.

When Jonathas tries to take the Host up to throw it into a cauldron of oil, it sticks to his hand; then when they try to remove it, his hand "*shall hang styll with þe Sacrament*" (515 s.d.). His companion Jason pries the nails out of the Host and throws both it and the hand into the cauldron, which boils, "*apperyng to be as blood*" (672 s.d.), and runs forth. A hot oven is now prepared, the Host is taken out of the cauldron with a pair of pincers and is cast into the oven, and then "*the owyn must ryve asunder and blede owt at þe cranys, and an image appere owt with woundys bledyng*" (712 s.d.).

The bleeding Child that appears above the oven is reminiscent of the Man of Sorrows or the bleeding figure of Christ that materializes above the altar in the Mass of St. Gregory. The figure here, as in the Mass of St.

---

[75] Tertullian, *Apology* 50.13; cited by Gatton, "There must be blood," 89. The passage was (and still is) well known.

[76] Citations are to *Non-Cycle Plays and Fragments*, ed. Norman Davis, EETS, s.s. 1 (London: Oxford University Press, 1970).

[77] L. Petit de Julleville, *Les Mystères*, 2 vols. (Paris, 1880), 2:103, as quoted in translation by Darryll Grantley, "Producing Miracles," in *Aspects of Early English Drama*, ed. Paula Neuss (Cambridge: D. S. Brewer, 1983), 83. Modern directors have been more willing to depict stage blood in the *Play of the Sacrament*; see ibid., 84–85.

Gregory,[78] is designed to inspire faith and to put down skepticism. The bloody Child is described as a "swemfull [*distressing*] syght . . . to looke vpon" (805), but it is also a source of healing for Jonathas, whose hand is restored as an encouragement to faith. The stage blood that appears in this anti-Semitic play is more sensational than it is devotional, and indeed the drama has been described as propaganda designed to counter the Lollard attack on the theology of the Eucharist.[79] Yet as Ann Eljenholm Nichols has argued, the play involves deliberate reference to Holy Week and its liturgy—particularly, in the speech of the bleeding figure of Jesus, to the *Improperia*—and the drama is given depth of emotion through this connection.[80]

The Play of the Sacrament thus after all is an important document with regard to our understanding of stage blood in the late medieval religious plays of England. The connection with conversion, with the Eucharist, and with the Passion itself is indicative of late medieval popular theology, which valued the blood of Christ—and the blood of martyrs who likewise gave their lives as a devotional offering to God—very highly indeed.[81] One of the results of this aspect of the devotion to Christ's redeeming blood was the development of the iconography of the Fountain of Life. An example, now in the crypt of St. Bavo's Cathedral in Ghent, is a painting by an unidentified master which presents the Savior standing with his wounds in hands, feet, and side bleeding into a

---

[78] See Eamon Duffy, *The Stripping of the Altars* (New Haven: Yale University Press, 1992), 102–04.

[79] See Cecilia Cutts, "The Croxton Play: An Anti-Lollard Piece," *Modern Language Quarterly* 5 (1944): 45–60.

[80] Ann Eljenholm Nichols, "The Croxton *Play of the Sacrament*: A Re-Reading," *Comparative Drama* 22 (1988): 129. See also Duffy, *The Stripping of the Altars*, 105–07. For a different approach to the play, see Sarah Beckwith, "Ritual, Church and Theatre: Medieval Dramas of the Sacramental Body," in *Culture and History 1350–1600: Essays in English Communities, Identities and Writing*, ed. David Aers (Detroit: Wayne State University Press, 1992), 65–89.

[81] On martyrdom as the basis for theatrical spectacle, see my "Violence and the Saint Play," *Studies in Philology* 98 (2001): 292–14.

fountain, while some people below are washing their hands in the streams of blood issuing forth from the fountain and others are drinking it.[82]

A little-known poem on the Five Wounds either written or copied by William Billyng provides corroboration of the warmth of feeling rather than repulsion felt toward Christ's blood.[83] The first stanza defines the iconography of the fountain of life:

> Cometh nere ye folkes temptyd in dreynes
> Wyth the drye dust of thys erthly galle
> Resorte anone wyth alle your vysyaes
> To the V stremes flowen over alle
> With precius payment for us in generalle
> Make no delay who lyst cum nere and drynke
> And fylle all your hertys up unto the brynke. (1–7)

The wounds are identified as wells of life, which are "bored so depe for alle my neglygence" (16) and which are the source of cleansing for the soul. From the right foot is a fragrant stream that is described as a "skarlet floode" which "dystyllyth habundantly/ Most ioyouse in thought most helpyng at our nede . . ." (26–28). The blood from the wound in the side is described as "most aromattyf" and "swetyst soukate [*socket*] to us most sanatyfe" (38, 44) serving as ransom for the sinful souls of humans. The wound is a "lauatorye," a place of bathing and a source of joy (55–57). In the course of the concluding stanza the following line is most significant: "Of thys blody streme thereof take no dysdane" (106).

The same attitude toward Christ's blood infused the religious plays, and hence it is no wonder it was believed that the Chester plays, if viewed "in pecible manner with gode devocion," would release one from forty

---

[82] See Clifford Davidson, "Repentance and the Fountain: The Transformation of Symbols in English Emblem Books," in *The Art of the Emblem: Essays in Honor of Karl Josef Höltgen*, ed. Michael Bath, John Manning, and Alan R. Young (New York: AMS Press, 1993), 12–13; see also Gray, "The Five Wounds of Our Lord," 132–33.

[83] Citations are to the text of this poem in William E. A. Axon, "The Symbolism of the 'Five Wounds of Christ'," *Lancashire and Cheshire Antiquarian Society Transactions* 10 (1882): 71–74. Axon's edition is based on W. Bateman's early nineteenth-century facsimile, *The Five Wounds of Christ: A Poem from an Ancient Parchment Roll* (Manchester: R. and W. Dean, 1814). On this poem, see also Gray, "The Five Wounds of Our Lord," 50–51.

days in Purgatory.[84] These plays, like the pageants in the other Creation to Doom cycles and collections, were not merely didactic teaching devices, but rather they also served mnemonic and devotional functions. Looking upon stage blood in the context of the religious dramas was felt to bring people into touch through the sense of sight with the saving blood of Christ or the health-giving blood of the saints; this was potentially an "ocular experience" that would result in communication with a transcendent reality.[85] Nevertheless, as the introduction to the pre-Reformation banns of Chester indicated, the Creation to Doom cycle of that city served not only for "the Augmentacion & incresse of the holy and catholyk ffaith of our sauyour cryst Iesu" and for the exhorting of "the myndes of the comen peple to gud deuocion and holsom doctryne ... but Also for the comen welth and prosperitie of this Citie."[86] Spiritual and physical well-being were not separated in the minds of the patrons and producers of the plays, and the object of the civic drama in Chester and elsewhere was to enhance both.

As seen by the Wycliffite authors of the *Tretise of Miraclis Pleyinge*, however, the plays were extended exercises in vanity and, even more importantly, untruthfulness. The scenes may have called to mind with incredible vividness the sufferings of Christ and the saints, but the actors were only pretending to the actions being represented. The blood shed in the plays was only stage blood and not the actual blood shed by the Lamb of God or by martyr saints. But to devout viewers of the plays, or even to those less devout, the late medieval civic religious drama represented blood in these circumstances as sacred, not as the impure and polluted result of violence.

---

[84] *REED: Chester*, 28.

[85] See Peter Travis, *Dramatic Design in the Chester Cycle* (Chicago: University of Chicago Press, 1982), 15–19; though Travis's comments, since they focus on Corpus Christi, are problematic when applied to the Chester cycle which had been moved to Whitsun Week, his remarks about the experiencing of religious festival in the late Middle Ages are otherwise concise and very useful. The term "ocular experience" is Travis's.

[86] *REED: Chester*, 33.

Part III

Cultural Contexts for Early Drama

Carnival, Lent, and Early English Drama

Unlike the well-established practice of staging plays at Nuremberg and elsewhere on the Continent on the days immediately before Ash Wednesday,[1] no such dramatic tradition seems to have developed in any city or town in England. The Nuremberg Carnival plays are well documented and seem to represent a secular genre not extant among the existing English play texts of the late Middle Ages or the beginning of the Early Modern period. Inevitably, however, there are some records of English plays in this season, which was known in England as Shrovetide rather than Carnival. For example, Shrovetide plays are recorded at Lincoln College in Oxford, in 1513,[2] and in the household of the Earl of Northumberland, at Wressle in Yorkshire, in 1524–27.[3] A Shrovetide play was suppressed at Hatfield Broad Oak, Essex, in 1556 and an inquiry made into "who shulde be the plaiers, what theffecte of the playe is, with suche other circumstaunces as [the examiner] shall thinke mete."[4] Both plays and masques were planned and staged at court,[5] and in 1549 a play, apparently of anti-Catholic satire since it included a king, "a dragon of vij heades," priests, and hermits, was presented by the King's players.[6] In 1555 a

---

[1] For a short introductory essay, see Laurel Braswell-Means, "*Fastnachtspiele*," in *A Companion to the Medieval Theatre*, ed. Ronald W. Vince (Westport, Conn.: Greenwood Press, 1989), 119–21.

[2] Ian Lancashire, *Dramatic Texts and Records of Britain: A Chronological Topography to 1558* (Toronto: University of Toronto Press, 1984), no. 1268.

[3] *Antiquarian Repertory*, ed. Francis Grose and Thomas Astle (London, 1807–09), as cited by Lancashire, *Dramatic Texts and Records*, no. 1543.

[4] *Acts of the Privy Council*, ed. D. R. Dasent (London: HMSO, 1890–1907), 5:234. The inquiry determined that the players were merely "honest householders and quiet personnes" (ibid., 5:237–38).

[5] Lancashire, *Dramatic Texts and Records*, nos. 730, 1025, 1058, 1081, 1087, 1752, 1805.

[6] W. R. Streitberger, *Court Revels, 1485–1559* (Toronto: University of Toronto Press, 1994), 185, 287.

mock siege was mounted as an entertainment at York.[7] It should be noted that the end of Shrovetide also concluded the theatrical season, since plays were prohibited during the penitential season of Lent.[8]

Shrovetide, which began on the Saturday before Ash Wednesday and concluded on Shrove Tuesday, was, however, a period characterized by license, including the playing of rough and even cruel games, and involving the consumption of all remaining meat prior to the meatless season of Lent. A Protestant clergyman, William Kethe, called the culminating day of this season "a day of great glottonie, surfeiting, and dronkennes."[9] Football, played virtually without rules and described by Philip Stubbes as a "bloody and murthering practise,"[10] was a favorite sport for Shrove Tuesday,[11] and at Chester there was an attempt in 1539–40 to proscribe the game, sponsored by the leather crafts, as one that was continued by "euill Disposid persons" to the "grete Inconuenynce" of the citizens.[12] However, as a seasonal custom football was still being played in this city on Shrove Tuesday in the early seventeenth century.[13] Even less commendable was the tradition of cockthrowing, which involved what today would be called extreme animal cruelty: a cock, tied to a stake by its leg, would be used as target practice by the participants, who threw sticks at

---

[7] *York Civic Records*, ed. Angelo Raine, 8 vols. (York: Yorkshire Archaeological Society, 1939–53), 5:117; Lancashire, *Dramatic Texts and Records*, no. 1581.

[8] *Acts of the Privy Council*, 6:169, which cites an order "not to playe any plaies but betwene the Feast of All Saintes and Shrofetide, and then only as are seen and allowed by thordynarye."

[9] William Kethe, *A Sermon Made at Blanford Forum* (London, 1572), fol. 18ᵛ. Kethe was a Sabbatarian and a former Geneva exile; see James Cuthbert Hadden, "William Kethe," *DNB*, 11:73–74. He complained about the Christmas revels of Roman Catholic times (*A Sermon*, fol. 18ᵛ) and about the common designation of Sunday as "reuelyng day," which was "spent in bulbeatings, bearebeatings, bowlings, dicyng, cardyng, daunsynges, drunkennes, and whoredome" (sig. 8ᵛ).

[10] Philip Stubbes, *The Anatomie of Abuses* (1583; fasc. reprint New York: Johnson Reprint, 1972), sig. Pviʳ.

[11] Joseph Strutt, *The Sports and Pastimes of England*, rev. Charles Cox (London: Methuen, 1903), 93–97; A. R. Wright, *British Calendar Customs*, 2 vols. (London: Folk-Lore Society, 1936), 1:26–28.

[12] Lawrence M. Clopper, *Records of Early English Drama: Chester* (Toronto: University of Toronto Press, 1979), 40–41.

[13] Ibid., 234, 351.

it, either knocking it down or killing it.[14] Such games were widespread throughout the kingdom at Shrovetide. There is no evidence that plays were even a weak rival to sports of these kinds, and there is every reason to see the Christmas season and summertime as the primary periods of drama, including festival plays such as the great Corpus Christi or Whitsun cycles. When the Corpus Christi play was not played and the Pater Noster play was substituted at York in 1536, the date of performance was also summer, on the Sunday after Lammas Day.[15]

Considering the lack of extant Shrovetide plays and the paucity of records of such plays in England, it is very curious, therefore, that the religious drama of England has in recent years been subjected frequently to cultural criticism which has applied the Carnival-Lent paradigm to it. While this paradigm, which may be traced to the fashion for the literary criticism of Mikhail Bakhtin, represents interest in seeing this drama in broader perspective than would be possible through the study of texts alone as literary constructs, closer examination shows that it is capable of promoting deeply distorted descriptions of the medieval religious stage, at least in England. Further, since Bakhtin provides a romanticized view of the carnivalesque,[16] there is a tendency to celebrate transgressive behavior or to extend sympathy to criminal characters in a play.

The most radical presentation of the Carnival-Lent paradigm appears in Anthony Gash's article "Carnival against Lent: The Ambivalence of Medieval Drama," which appears in a collection of essays edited by David Aers.[17] Gash criticizes V. A. Kolve's conception of the plays as analogous to sermons and visual arts such as "the stained glass, the altarpieces, the wall paintings, and the sculpture of a church," all of which were visual extensions of clerical education for illiterate viewers,[18] and

---

[14] Wright, *British Calendar Customs*, 1:22–23.

[15] Alexandra F. Johnston and Margaret Rogerson, *Records of Early English Drama: York*, 2 vols. (Toronto: University of Toronto Press, 1979), 1:262. The Creed Play was presented before King Richard III even later in the season, on 7 Sept. 1483 (ibid., 1:131).

[16] Katerina Clark and Michael Holquist, *Mikhail Bakhtin* (Cambridge: Harvard University Press, 1984), 310–11.

[17] Anthony Gash, "Carnival Against Lent: The Ambivalence of Medieval Drama," in *Medieval Literature: Criticism, Ideology and History*, ed. David Aers (New York: St. Martin's Press, 1986), 74–98.

[18] See V. A. Kolve, *The Play Called Corpus Christi* (Stanford: Stanford University Press, 1966), 58; cited by Gash, *Carnival Against Lent*, 75.

to a certain extent it would be hard to argue with the rejection of a simplistic understanding of medieval drama as mere books of instruction for the unlearned in spite of medieval precedent for such a view.[19] Yet late medieval culture was deeply enriched by a wide repertoire of religious images in sculpture, wall paintings, and stained glass, and the religious drama of the great cycles in English cities dramatized these scenes as well as the events described in sermons, though of course it is true that drama demands a more complex way of presenting such material than either homilies or art. On the other hand, the fact that medieval entertainers commonly utilized improvisation on other occasions does not mean that theatrical improvising in religious plays would have been of a sort that subverted the very meaning of the religious stories.

The first example that Gash draws upon to demonstrate the ambiguity of medieval religious drama is the Towneley *Mactacio Abel*, which indeed is a play that, like the *Secunda Pastorum* also written by the dramatist known as the Wakefield Master, is rich with comedy and satire. But these plays differ at least in degree from the plays included in the York and Chester cycles and, judging from the two pageants which are extant, in the Coventry cycle. The Towneley plays appear to be a Yorkshire compilation rather than a cycle regularly presented in any known town, for they must no longer be considered to have been the Wakefield Corpus Christi play, and indeed their provenance must now be regarded as unknown.[20] So too their date is a mystery. They appear in a manuscript that seems to be very late fifteenth-century if we judge by the calligraphy, but the strapwork initials would point to an even later date, probably well into the next century. In any case, their absorption of the techniques of farce in the work of the dramatist generally called the Wakefield Master

---

[19] See Clifford Davidson, ed., *A Tretise of Miraclis Pleyinge*, Early Drama, Art, and Music, Monograph Series 19 (Kalamazoo: Medieval Institute Publications, 1993), 23–28, 104, 145–46.

[20] See A. C. Cawley, Jean Forrester, and John Goodchild, "References to the Corpus Christi Play in the Wakefield Burgess Court Rolls: The Originals Rediscovered," *Leeds Studies in English*, n.s. 19 (1988): 85–104; Barbara D. Palmer, "'Towneley Plays' or 'Wakefield Cycle' Revisited," *Comparative Drama* 21 (1987–88): 318–48, and "Corpus Christi 'Cycles' in Yorkshire: The Surviving Records," *Comparative Drama* 27 (1993): 218–31.

also argues for a late date and for seeing some of the pageants as representative of a different genre than we find in the great cycle at York. The only firm evidence that the Wakefield Master's plays were ever staged is, as the late John Robinson noted, "their eminent playability."[21]

Gash sees folk play elements, comic "festive reversal," and parody that he interprets on three levels, two of which challenge authority and theological principles, in the *Mactacio Abel*.[22] There is certainly tension here, a balancing between obedience and rebellion, between humility and pride, between the representation of faithfulness and outrageous murder. The play quite interestingly mirrors the human propensity to selfishness, anger, and self-justification, and in doing so must have had some resonance with members of the audience, each of whom would not necessarily have responded exactly like everyone else even at the same performance. But it is dangerous to make assumptions about the manner of audience response in another time and place than our own—or even in our own since different audiences respond differently. Laughter is certainly not a cultural constant, and ultimately this very human response to the absurd has a considerable repertoire of emotional meanings from sympathy to outright hostility. Delight in the play would not necessarily translate to approval outside of the framework of the drama; Cain remains the outcast, famous for being the first murderer.

The problem of audience response also becomes apparent in Gash's analysis of another play, the morality *Mankind*, which he sees as a Shrovetide play in which rebelliousness against the Church and religion are dramatized.[23] Elements of Shrovetide have been previously identified as integral to the play,[24] and there are echoes throughout the drama of the license-penitence pattern which characterizes the shift from Shrovetide

---

[21] J. W. Robinson, *Studies in Fifteenth-Century Stagecraft*, Early Drama, Art, and Music, Monograph Series 14 (Kalamazoo: Medieval Institute Publications, 1991), 207, n. 21.

[22] Gash, "Carnival Against Lent," 77–78.

[23] Ibid., 82–96.

[24] See Sister Mary Philippa Coogan, *An Interpretation of the Moral Play, Mankind* (Washington: Catholic University of America Press, 1947), 1–21. A case has also been made by Tom Pettitt, "*Mankind*: An English *Fastnachtspiel?*" in *Festive Drama*, ed. Meg Twycross (Cambridge: D. S. Brewer, 1996), 190–212, which was not available to me in print when the present article was written.

to Lent. Gash quite correctly connects Nought with the festive fool who does not know any boundaries to his actions,[25] and insists on seeing the mock "trial scene" (687–717) as a parody which involves not only "festive reversal" but also a "mood of sheer Dionysiac release," particularly in the affirmation of denial that requests the response "I wyll" of Mankind.[26] Gash believes that the audience would probably have exploded here in "wild laughter," especially if the lines were intoned in a way suggesting "solemn plainsong"—a quite unlikely interpretation since what is being parodied here is not the liturgy but a court proceeding. However, it is more likely that the audience, while earlier tricked into joining in the singing of the bawdy "Crystemes songe" (332–43) with gusto and otherwise becoming implicated in the action, would by this time have found the antics of the subversive characters quite insufferable. Modern audience response may not be a good test of the reaction of medieval people, but in my own experience I have seen two performances of the play in which the subversive element was emphasized at the expense of the character Mercy and what he represents.[27] Neither impressed its modern audience, presumably more accustomed to subversive theatrics than were medieval audiences, and indeed the reaction to both these performances of the play was decidedly cool. *Mankind* depends on a strong actor in the role of Mercy and on a careful shaping of the action so that both the fall of Mankind into sin and his eventual despair and recovery seem logical and natural. If the play were focused on the "body-denying, death-oriented doctrine of the Church" in a way which culminated in sympathy for vice and disdain for the sacraments,[28] the entire drama would

---

[25] Gash, "Carnival Against Lent," 87. Citations are to *The Macro Plays*, ed. Mark Eccles, EETS, 262 (London: Oxford University Press, 1969).

[26] Gash, "Carnival Against Lent," 88.

[27] One of these was by the Lewditores of the University of Alberta at the Eighth International Colloquium of the Société Internationale pour l'Étude du Théâtre Médiéval at Toronto in August 1995. Experiments such as this are, however, extremely useful.

[28] Gash, "Carnival Against Lent," 90. Gash seems to take a position concerning the medieval Roman Catholic Church and the "Gothic age" that is similar to Bakhtin's; see Mikhail Bakhtin, *Rabelais and His World*, trans. Helene Iswolsky (Cambridge: M.I.T. Press, 1965), 268. However, Bakhtin's view of the "Gothic age, with its one-sided seriousness based on fear and coercion," seems more applicable to the repressive Stalinist period in Soviet history than to pre-Reformation Western Europe.

seem to represent a Carnival that would give way to Lent only because of the brute authority of the ecclesiastical system. The "divisions within the audience" which are allegedly exploited "to intensify the serio-comic game" may have been present,[29] but it is simplistic to see these "divisions" as merely between social classes or between one audience member and another; the divisions are psychologically present within each person, and if along the way the play absorbs a certain amount of anti-clericalism, it also ultimately affirms that the good of both society and the individual is served best by rejecting theft, murder, and blasphemy. But it affirms not by merely making a didactic pronouncement, for the play succeeds through a *process* which is both delightful and purposeful.

Necessarily, therefore, there are also some other echoes in the play that extend it well beyond the Carnival *vs.* Lent paradigm. *Mankind* might even more appropriately be described as a rogationtide or springtime play which, presenting the conflicts to which the flesh is heir and the temptations to which it is susceptible, dramatizes the human condition in which all participate. Elements of festivity of course appear in the protagonist's relinquishing of work in favor of fun, but the play (and presumably the audience) must know that ultimately, if persevered in, that way madness lies. If corn is not planted, or if the good deeds and beneficent actions required of men and women are not done, the race will be faced with starvation and with moral anarchy.[30] Audience response to a play such as this would have been complex and would have reflected the humanity of those who looked on and listened to the actors. The intent of the play would seem to be to take its viewers into the realm of the liminal, to be sure, and then to return them in a fuller knowledge of what it means to be persons existing between birth and death, the latter an event that is inescapable and for which one will be much better prepared if one has not wasted his or her life.

---

[29] Gash, "Carnival Against Lent," 96.

[30] Mankind's tempters appear to be his social superiors; in a sense his initial attitude toward them may be seen as representing the attitude of lower status people to the privileged, who were seen as idle and decadent in their behavior. The contrast between those who work and those who are privileged is illustrated in the woodcut of *Spring* by Jerome Cock after Brueghel; see H. Arthur Klein, *Graphic Worlds of Peter Bruegel the Elder* (New York: Dover, 1963), pl. 19.

A recent attempt to see another play, the Towneley *Magnus Herodes*, in terms of the Carnival-Lent pattern appears in Martin Stevens's article "Herod as Carnival King in the Medieval Biblical Drama."[31] Deriving his understanding of Carnival from Michael D. Bristol's *Carnival and Theater: Plebian Culture and the Structure of Authority in Renaissance England*, he quotes from this book a passage which notes the lack of a specific period of Carnival immediately prior to Ash Wednesday—a passage in which Bristol, however, insists on seeing the carnivalesque in various seasons and "pervad[ing] every celebration, those of May and midsummer no less than the winter observances."[32] The plays within the great medieval vernacular Corpus Christi and Whitsun cycles were, Stevens insists, most likely "composed orally at the outset and later written out by the 'pageant masters' of individual guilds, by town clerks, by clerics in minor orders, by antiquarians or any combination of these."[33] This sketch of the presumed origins of the plays in oral tradition is intended to establish them as "clearly an expression of holiday spirit."[34] At the same time he wishes to see them as a serious attempt to juxtapose moral and spiritual values with the social order in which people actually lived. In attempting to reconcile these dimensions of the civic cycles, he focuses on the figure of Herod in the Towneley play by the Wakefield Master.

There is, of course, no evidence concerning audience response for the *Magnus Herodes* since, as noted above, we do not in fact have any record of the performance of any of the plays by the Wakefield Master, and also we may be extremely skeptical of the idea that this play was presented as part of a large cycle as at York. But, lacking evidence concerning the reception of the plays in the Towneley manuscript, Stevens calls attention to a record concerning audience behavior at York in the well-known reference in the 1426 sermon of William Melton, who urged the city Corporation sponsoring the plays to separate the plays from the regular Corpus Christi procession—something, however, that was not done until

---

[31] Martin Stevens, "Herod as Carnival King in the Medieval Biblical Drama," *Mediaevalia* 18 (1995): 43–66.

[32] Michael D. Bristol, *Carnival and Theatre* (London: Methuen, 1985), 41; quoted by Stevens, "Herod as Carnival King," 47–48.

[33] Stevens, "Herod as Carnival King," 43.

[34] Ibid., 43.

Carnival, Lent, and Early English Drama 215

many years later, when the procession, not the play cycle, was moved to another day.[35] Melton is reported to have complained about "disorder, drunkenness, singing, and wantonness" among those at the play, who thus "lose the indulgences granted to them [for attending the play] by Pope Urban IV of happy memory."[36] Exactly how widespread was the disorder Melton was describing is now impossible to determine, but, considering the Corporation's strong commitment to the control of the plays to see that they were decorously presented, it is hard to imagine widespread disruption. Much more likely, as at Lille, the city fathers were determined not to allow dramatic shows to disintegrate into audience behavior that would embarrass the city.[37] In no sense can one say that at York "the pageants, with their idiosyncratic representations of biblical history brought anachronistically into the present, celebrate the freedom and disorder of the city." Nor do "[t]hey attest to the spirit of new interpretation, to the power of strife and conflict, and to the absence of a prescribed, approved, and constant text."[38] At York the city clerk was positioned at the first station, at Holy Trinity Priory, with the Register containing the approved texts of the plays to see that nothing of this sort

---

[35] See Johnston and Rogerson, *REED: York*, 1:125–26. On Corpus Christi processions, cf. Miri Rubin, *Corpus Christi: The Eucharist in Late Mediaeval Culture* (Cambridge: Cambridge University Press, 1991), 243–71.

[36] Johnston and Rogerson, *REED: York*, 1:43, 2:728.

[37] Alan E. Knight, "Beyond Misrule: Theater and the Socialization of Youth in Lille," *Research Opportunities in Renaissance Drama* 35 (1996): 74–75. There are no illustrations of the English Corpus Christi or Whitsun plays, but, while quite late historically, Denis van Alsloot's painting showing the pageants in the Brussels Ommegang of 1616 may be relevant here. On the whole it seems to be a fairly staid affair, with citizens in their best clothes watching along the side of the square and from the windows in the adjoining buildings. But the event is clearly a festival, and the buildings are decorated with branches. Rushes are being strewn in the path of the pageant wagons (in the painting, actually behind a float carrying the Pillars of Hercules, pulled by sea elephants). The entire display is spectacular, with mounted horsemen, camels, and fabulous animals in addition to the biblical *tableaux*. The most lively happening shown in the painting is a wildman with a club (to which is attached a bladder) chasing boys who have strayed out into the path of the pageants. See Bryan Holme, *Princely Feasts and Festivals: Five Centuries of Pageantry and Spectacle* (London: Thames and Hudson, 1988), 46–49.

[38] Stevens, "Herod as Carnival King," 52; see also Clopper, *REED: Chester*, 33, for stern warnings against those who would not assemble "peceably without making any Assault Afrey or other disturbans wherby the . . . playes shalbe disturbed."

happened in the course of presentations by the various guilds.[39] These pageants were for the honor of the city and the glory of God, not celebrations of the subversive—that is, affirmations of structure, not of antistructure.

This certainly does not mean that the pageants at York were all simply pious skits that would have pleased the most prudish Victorian ladies, and it does not mean that they were viewed identically by all members of the audience—or that the principles of dialogic theater were of no significance in York. Such characters as Annas and Caiphas, "bishops" of the pre-Christian order in Jerusalem, seem to have been characterized like arrogant contemporary clerics, in some cases perhaps like the higher clergy associated with York's own cathedral. About the loyalty and generosity of the citizens to their parish churches we know, and about their tendency to give little or nothing to the cathedral we also have evidence from wills.[40] There was constant tension between the city and the Liberties of St. Peter, which were controlled by the Minster.

As at Coventry and Chester, in York holiday exuberance certainly was present. Here the streets were cleaned and prepared for the procession and plays on Corpus Christi. Hangings were hung out of windows along the pageant route, which traced its way through the most affluent sections of the city. The craft guilds, which spent enormous amounts of money for their pageants, could hardly have entered unwillingly into this community effort unless impoverished on account of changes in the economy.[41] The idea that the Corporation made them do it against their

---

[39] Johnston and Rogerson, *REED: York*, 1:278; for opposition by sponsoring craft guilds to inappropriate audience response, see ibid., 1:47–48. In 1431–32 the Masons objected to the subject matter of their play, the Funeral of the Virgin, since it did not inspire to devotion but rather led to rowdiness on the part of the audience. The play, later given to the Linenweavers, remained unpopular with its sponsors, who apparently rarely performed it, and its text was not entered in the Register.

[40] See *Testamenta Eboracum*, ed. James Raine and John W. Clay, Surtees Soc., 4, 30, 45, 53, 79, 106 (Durham, 1836–1902), *passim*.

[41] At Coventry, which suffered from severe depression in the early sixteenth century, distressed guilds spoke of their poverty in petitions to the Mayor and Corporation; for the context of Coventry's urban decline and its effect on the Corpus Christi play, see especially Charles Phythian-Adams, *Desolation of a City: Coventry and the Urban Crisis of the Late Middle Ages* (Cambridge: Cambridge University Press, 1979).

will is, quite frankly, preposterous.[42] But so is the notion that the impetus for the pageants came from below, from folk festival, from oral traditions of verse and horseplay.[43]

When he treats the Towneley Herod, Stevens envisions a Carnival king who is a parody of kingship.[44] The identification of Herod as parodying royalty is of course undeniable. But that Herod was seen as a parody of the King of England might be another matter, depending on the shifting historical loyalties prevailing at the moment at a particular location. A more secure argument may be made for seeing Herod in terms of the mock kings, both of the summer season and the winter, that have been studied by Sandra Billington,[45] who also has suggested another context for Herod: the "fool king."[46] A further dimension is added in the matter of his extreme and legendary cruelty; in glass in York Minster he is shown overseeing the carnage of the Massacre of the Innocents, perhaps by mistake ordering the death of his own son.[47] Flemish glass of c.1500 at Fairford that is probably contemporary with the Towneley play quite typically pictures this tyrant with a child impaled on his sword.[48] As a parody of kingship, Herod is representative of the anarchy which was universally feared, and as a threat to the Christ Child who is the hope of the nations he is also a threat to all future stability and all subsequent

---

[42] This idea has been revived by John C. Coldewey, "Some Economic Aspects of the Late Medieval Drama," in *Contexts for Early English Drama*, ed. Marianne Briscoe and John C. Coldewey (Bloomington: Indiana University Press, 1989), 86–87.

[43] Recent research, published subsequent to the initial appearance of the present article, seems to corroborate the view that the plays were organized by the Corporation, which then enlisted the guilds in the project of play production; see Jeremy Goldberg, "Craft Guilds, the Corpus Christi Play and Civic Government," in *The Government of Medieval York*, ed. Sarah Rees Jones, Borthwick Studies in History 3 (York: Borthwick Institute of Historical Research, 1997), 141–63.

[44] Stevens, "Herod as Carnival King," 53–54.

[45] Sandra Billington, *Mock Kings in Medieval Society and Renaissance Drama* (Oxford: Clarendon Press, 1991); see es25.

[46] Sandra Billington, *A Social History of the Fool* (New York: St. Martin's Press, 1984), 18–20.

[47] Clifford Davidson and David E. O'Connor, *York Art*, Early Drama, Art, and Music, Reference Series 1 (Kalamazoo: Medieval Institute Publications, 1978), 59–60, fig. 16.

[48] Hilary Wayment, *The Stained Glass of the Church of St. Mary, Fairford, Gloucestershire* (London: Society of Antiquaries, 1984), 79–80, pl. XXXIX.

sense of community. In his incarnation in the Coventry plays Herod will apparently serve Shakespeare, who almost certainly had seen these pageants when he was a boy, as a model of outrageous behavior; "it out-Herods Herod" was for the Renaissance playwright an expression of scorn, aimed at the ranting actor who would effectively parody kingship. All of this is of course not to deny that the parody in the case of Herod would not have elicited festive laughter from spectators watching the Corpus Christi or Whitsun plays in the streets of Coventry, York, or Chester.

A yet more serious problem with Stevens's analysis comes with his assertion that Herod as Carnival king is supplanted by Christ, who is said to be the Lenten king. This pattern Stevens also extends to the N-Town play of the Death of Herod, which he analyzes against the iconography of Brueghel's *Battle of Carnival and Lent*. In the play Herod the Great is at banquet—emblematic of excess and regarded as typical of Herod by transference from the story of Herod Antipas, who at banquet would have the head of John the Baptist brought before him—when Mors comes to him and the Devil receives his soul. The N-Town Herod may be a lord of misrule of sorts, but in no sense is this Brueghel painting directly relevant to the N-town or Towneley plays. The painting shows excess in various forms but in particular in the allegorical figure of Carnival, who is fat, drunk, and riding on a barrel in a mock chivalric pose.[49] A pot is his stirrup, and he holds a lance which is a spit impaling a chicken and the head of a piglet—and with a sausage hanging from a string attached to it. His crown is a meat pie with the feet of a chicken sticking out of it. He is attended by men in carnival costumes, one of whom is pushing the barrel, which is placed on a skid. Another holds a knife and gridiron, while a third, in a cape, plays the rummelpot, a noisy percussion instrument. On the ground are playing cards, broken eggs, and bones. In the background a woman is making pancakes, traditional Shrove Tuesday fare. The figure with whom Carnival is battling is Lent, who likewise is a caricature, seated on a wheeled platform and also holding an inappropriate weapon. In the background two farces are in progress, one *The Dirty Bride* and the other including a wildman, while in contrast a procession of penitents

---

[49] See Walter S. Gibson, *Bruegel* (New York: Oxford University Press, 1977), 79–85, figs. 47, 49–51.

emerges from the church. Indicative of the season is the fact that the religious images are covered with cloth, as was the case during the season of Lent. This scene, with its apparent satire directed at both Carnival and Lent, surely has only a tangential relevance to the Herod of these English vernacular plays or to the character of Christ, who triumphs on the cross to turn apparent defeat into a victory to be remembered over the ages—and to be imaginatively recollected on the medieval stage.

Stevens concludes that the Towneley plays are infused with Carnival "from beginning to end":

> Throughout [the carnivalesque] provides the spectator with a double vision of the Passion—the carnival and lenten perspectives in dialogic opposition. Tyrants continue to rage, and earthly political power marches forward with no restraint, but justice is now with the meek, whom we see inheriting the earth. There is clearly a significant change in emphasis after Herod the Great has made his exit. Herod climaxes the age and the celebration of misrule; the rule of law is taking shape before our eyes. As it does, we become more and more aware of the light that shines on the Lenten King and the entrance to the Cathedral, the setting in which the tympanum of every main portal proclaims the moment of the Great Judgment. We watch the carnival play from beginning to end as it deconstructs its own subversive celebration. The lunar year has come to an end.[50]

I would suggest that the emphasis here needs to be shifted from the Last Judgment[51] to Christ as victor, who in the course of the Passion was

---

[50] Stevens, "Herod as Carnival King," 61.

[51] A correction is also necessary here, since the Last Judgment is not shown on the main portal of every cathedral, at least in England. For an example, see the Last Judgment at Ely over the south portal to the angel choir; this is not a main portal, nor indeed would the people normally enter either at this door or at the main portal. At York Minster a Doom scene originally seems to have been part of the twelfth-century façade, but this was unlikely to have been part of a portal and probably was from the part of the building that was pulled down when it was replaced by the fourteenth-century nave; see Davidson and O'Connor, *York Art*, 114. The most common subject that appeared on Norman tympana seems to have been the symbolism of Christ's words "I am the way," the Agnus Dei, and the Tree of Life; see M. D. Anderson, *History and Imagery in British Churches* (London: John Murray, 1971), 83–85. On the other hand, a common placement of the Last Judgment scene was over the chancel arch of parish churches; in these cases the scene was painted on plaster, com-

understood as a sacrificial victim and healer of souls, not as a repressive and tyrannical punisher or rigid upholder of the law. Even in Last Judgment scenes such as the miniature in the so-called *Bolton Hours* (York Minster Library MS. Add. 2, fol. 208) the figure of Christ appears on a rainbow, a symbol of hope, and displays his bleeding wounds as signs of the work of redemption which at that time—i.e., at the end of history—will have been completed.[52]

The Easter sequence, *Victimae paschali*, speaks of a battle between two forces, but not in a mock conflict between Carnival and Lent: "Death and life have fought each other in a wondrous battle. The leader of the army of life, who was dead, is alive and reigns."[53] Christ, and the imperfect Church which in medieval Christianity was believed to be the mediator between him and the laity, represented not principles of death but of hope, of release from guilt, of the expectation even of life after death in bliss. In the time of mercy which involves the present cycle of the entire liturgical year, the Lenten period culminates in the exquisite joy of Easter, initiating a season that extends to Ascension, Pentecost, and Corpus Christi. Thereafter comes the liturgical half-year that Charles Phythian-Adams has designated the "secular half," which in turn culminates at the end in the preparation for the penitential season of Advent at the beginning of the next cycle.[54] In a sense the liturgical year, only part of which is organized by the lunar calendar, has no ending except in its beginning when the cycle commences once more.

---

plementing the rood with its Crucified Christ, Mary, and John. Such a wall painting appears to have been present in Wakefield's All Saints Church (now Cathedral), though the account by town historian John Walker is unreliable; see Barbara D. Palmer, *The Early Art of the West Riding of Yorkshire*, Early Drama, Art, and Music, Reference Series 6 (Kalamazoo: Medieval Institute Publications, 1990), 154–55.

[52] Davidson and O'Connor, *York Art*, 116, fig. 33.

[53] Trans. and ed. Frederick Brittain, *The Penguin Book of Latin Verse* (Baltimore: Penguin, 1962), 175; for the usual liturgical placement and musical notation, see *Liber Usualis*, 780.

[54] See Charles Phythian-Adams, "Ceremony and the Citizen: The Communal Year at Coventry, 1450–1550," in *Crisis and Order in English Towns, 1500–1700*, ed. Peter Clark and Paul Slack (Toronto: University of Toronto Press, 1972), 71. But see also the questioning of the division of the year, into a "sacred" half and a "secular" half, in Eamon Duffy, *The Stripping of the Altars: Traditional Religion in England c.1400–c.1580* (New Haven: Yale University Press, 1992), 46–47.

Part of the difficulty in applying the Carnival-Lent model to vernacular religious drama of the late Middle Ages in England is that the theoretical model determines what is seen to the exclusion of flatly contradictory evidence. It is indeed important to sort out audience reaction as much as we are able and to try to understand dialogic aspects of the religious stage. In the main it was a stage which Gail McMurray Gibson has aptly called a "theater of devotion,"[55] but of course it was also a theater of many other dimensions—that is, entertaining, festive, mirroring forth truth as it was understood by the community and the clergy, providing scenes which might serve as living devotional images, giving the people an opportunity to view the plays for the indulgences which they believed had been offered,[56] and, as Mervyn James has insisted, allowing the community to affirm its hierarchical structure and community simultaneously.[57]

On the other hand, in the popular arts such as morris dancing a more purely "carnivalesque" spirit is certainly likely to obtain, sometimes with a wicked energy that disrupted church services. There was a practical reason for prohibitions against such entertainments at the time of evensong, particularly in churchyards but also within the churches themselves. Visitation injunctions of Archbishop Grindal for the York diocese provide a list of types of entertainment which might all fit comfortably in the category of the "carnivalesque," though again none are specifically associated with Shrovetide itself:

> ITEM that the minister and churchewardens shall not suffer any lordes of misrule or somer lordes, or ladyes, or any disguised persone or others in Christmasse or at Maye games or anye minstrels morice dauncers or others at Rishebearinges or at anye other tymes to come unreverentlye into anye churche or chappell or churcheyeard and there daunce or playe anye unseemlelye partes with scoffes ieastes wanton

---

[55] See Gail McMurray Gibson, *The Theater of Devotion: East Anglian Drama and Society in the Late Middle Ages* (Chicago: University of Chicago Press, 1989), *passim*.

[56] Indulgences were also believed to have been offered at Chester; see Clopper, *REED: Chester*, 28.

[57] Mervyn James, "Ritual, Drama and Social Body in the Late Medieval English Town," *Past and Present*, 98 (1983): 3–29; for the complexity of the contemporary understanding of community, see the discussion of the term *communitas* in Maud Sellers, ed., *York Memorandum Book A/Y*, Surtees Soc., 120, 125 (Durham, 1912–15), 1:iv–v.

gestures or rybaulde talke namelye in the tyme of divine service or of anye sermon.[58]

Such prohibitions would have not been published if there had not been problems in the eyes of the Protestant hierarchy, who inherited them from the Catholic Middle Ages. Entertainments of this kind, almost entirely lost to us because they truly represented an oral tradition of music, dance, and song, pique our interest, but for that reason we must not transfer their characteristics to the vernacular civic religious plays unless there is good reason to do so.

There is more reason than ever to continue to explore the local context in which the religious plays were performed insofar as this can be done. For the York, Coventry, and Chester plays this means more careful attention not only to dramatic records but also to the entire local scene, including the evidences that we have of examples in the visual arts that will help us to establish local taste, devotional practices, and civic preoccupations as well as iconography that was visible for all to see at that time. Theory, perhaps taking into account texts but not other kinds of evidence, will not be a very good guide to the late medieval religious stage unless it is used judiciously to shake loose ideas and to help us sort through our thinking about these plays.

The late and much missed C. Clifford Flanigan, in a cautious but enthusiastic approach to the idea of Carnival as well as to Victor Turner's concept of social structure, rightly affirmed "the necessity of breaking with the formalist, aesthetic models of the past and of situating these plays in their socio-historical contexts."[59] In his discussion of the Künzel-

---

[58] *Tudor Parish Documents of the Diocese of York* (Cambridge: Cambridge University Press, 1948), 160–61; for a similar complaint by Philip Stubbes, see his *Anatomie of Abuses*, sig. M2. For one example of an actual incident, "a greate morris daunce vpon the saboath daie at eveninge praier tyme" noted in the records for Yazor, Herefordshire, see David Klausner, *Records of Early English Drama: Herefordshire, Worcestershire* (Toronto: University of Toronto Press, 1990), 183. Another example: at Stretton Grandison, Richard Perks, a minstrel, brought "his taber into the Church at divine service" where he acted unreverently (ibid., 168). Protestant clergymen were much more inclined to look at games and dancing as inappropriate or evil than their Catholic predecessors.

[59] C. Clifford Flanigan, "Liminality, Carnival, and Social Structure: The Case of Late Medieval Drama," in *Victor Turner and the Construction of Cultural Criticism*, ed. Kathleen M. Ashley (Bloomington: Indiana University Press, 1990), 47.

sau Corpus Christi play, he recognized that the drama "was thought to be enacted not merely for the town's inhabitants and tourists, but in the ritually charged presence of God and his saints." Thus the participants, plays and viewers alike, could through the play become "participants in one great drama of salvation sacramentally enacted before the eyes of the citizenry."[60] If we are to accept this analysis, we need to look to those aspects of the social structure which may help us best to understand the plays, not to take hold of aspects of theory which we can apply to the plays whether or not they are consistent with the evidence.

As an example of social analysis that is applicable to the plays we may take Mary Douglas's notion of positional symbolism.[61] Applied to the medieval religious stage, this concept may suggest how important "rightness" was in the presentation of spectacle. In this regard, it seems useful to keep in mind that a primary purpose of the play was to construct cultural memory of the events involved in salvation history. Matters of hierarchy, extending to the appropriateness of costumes and placement of the actors on stages, were of concern; parody of characters such as the Virgin Mary or a saint such as Thomas Becket would have been extremely unlikely in the context of the religious drama that was officially sponsored. Thus too characters' gestures would have been chosen with an eye to appropriateness, and indeed inappropriate gesture in some instances could have been regarded as blasphemous, a most serious offence if outside of an accepted context.[62] The indecent dropping of one's trousers to show one's backside to the saint, as in Jean Fouquet's mini-

---

[60] Ibid., 50–51.

[61] See Mary Douglas, *Purity and Danger* (1966; reprint London: Routledge and Kegan Paul, 1984); I have discussed this concept in relation to medieval drama in my "Positional Symbolism and English Medieval Drama," *Comparative Drama* 25 (1991): 66–76.

[62] An accepted context might be a festival of reversal, such as the Feast of Fools, which to be sure was not universally approved. Acts such as bringing an ass into the church to participate in the procession, censing with sausages or even shoe leather, and generally clowning during the service by the lower clergy during the Christmas season were frequently condemned. For Bishop Grosseteste's condemnation of this feast, see E. K. Chambers, *The Mediaeval Stage* (London: Oxford University Press, 1903), 1:321–22. For an example of parody at York, see the monkey funeral which parodies the funeral of the Virgin Mary in painted glass in the nave of the Minster; illustrated in David E. O'Connor and Jeremy H. Haselock, "The Stained and Painted Glass," in *A History of York Minster*, ed. G. E. Aylmer and Reginald Cant (Oxford: Oxford University Press, 1977), fig. 113.

ature showing St. Apollonia, would have been a gesture reserved to wicked characters alone.[63] If Fouquet's illumination is an actual illustration of a production of a saint play, it shows this act of insult as a possible piece of stage business.

Similarly Cain in the *Mactacio Abel* could insult his brother by telling him to "kis myne ars" (61), thus identifying his evil nature.[64] Cain is depicted as a bad-tempered farmer who not only would engage in insults against his brother and against God himself, but also would murder his brother with the jawbone of an ass. "With cheke-bon, or that I blyn, / Shal I the and thi life twyn," Cain says (326–27). This implement, which is also specified in the N-Town play[65] and the Cornish *Creacion of the World*,[66] is the one normally expected in English iconography.[67] The visual tradition was apparently sufficiently strong that such details as this would have been expected by audiences in the fifteenth and early sixteenth centuries—and missed when they were changed or not present.

So too the Ascension was pictured a certain way, concluding with Christ disappearing *upward* into a cloud—a scene which, when possible, meant the adoption of lifting technology of some sophistication and expense. The stage directions and text in the Chester Ascension play specify red garments for Christ for symbolic reasons and also verify the presence of angels, and the drama is highly embellished with appropriate liturgical music.[68] In the Harrowing of Hell, Christ takes the figure of

---

[63] *The Hours of Étienne Chevalier*, introd. Claude Schaefer (New York: George Braziller, 1971), pl. 45.

[64] Quotations are from *The Towneley Plays*, ed. Martin Stevens and A. C. Cawley, EETS, s.s. 13–14 (Oxford: Oxford University Press, 1994).

[65] In the N-Town play it is called a "chavyl bon" (3149); I quote from *The N-town Play*, ed. Stephen Spector, EETS, s.s. 11–12 (Oxford: Oxford University Press, 1991).

[66] *The Creacion of the World*, ed. and trans. Paula Neuss (New York: Garland, 1983), 94 (*s.d.* at l. 1,115): "*Abell ys stryken with a chawebone....*"

[67] See Cherrell Guilfoyle, "The Staging of the First Murder in the Mystery Plays in England," *Comparative Drama* 25 (1991): 42–51. A useful example in the visual arts is the panel showing the murder of Abel in the Great East Window of York Minster; see Davidson and O'Connor, *York Art*, 24–25, fig. 6. Though prevalent elsewhere in Northern Europe, the iconography of the jawbone as the murder weapon is not universal on the Continent.

[68] *The Chester Mystery Cycle*, ed. R. M. Lumiansky and David Mills, EETS, s.s. 3, 9 (Oxford: Oxford University Press, 1974–86), 1:373–76. On the music, see Joanna Dutka, *Music in the English Mystery Plays*, Early Drama, Art, and Music, Reference Series 2

Adam by the forearm and draws him forth from hellmouth in illustrations from Anglo-Saxon times to the Reformation.[69] Sometimes such iconography might have been flexible in details, at other times not. But there is an argument here for giving initial attention to local examples of scenes in the visual arts for their iconography as well as for what else they can teach us when we know where plays were in fact presented. This examination may extend, when such information is known, to patrons of specific examples in the visual arts since thus we are able to learn more about the spiritual and social concerns of citizens whose guilds also were deeply involved in the expenses of producing pageants in the Corpus Christi or Whitsun plays.

We see that almost any theory may be applied reductively with the resulting analysis fully as narrow and misleading as the earlier formalist literary criticism of the plays which questioned their validity as drama. The use of the idea of Carnival as a device to interpret the late medieval religious plays of England may, when misapplied, be as much of a disservice to the plays as to the spirit of the carnivalesque in May games, the King game, morris dancing, or other folk entertainments.

(Kalamazoo: Medieval Institute Publications, 1980); Richard Rastall, "Music in the Cycle," in *The Chester Mystery Cycle: Essays and Documents*, ed. R. M. Lumiansky and David Mills (Chapel Hill: University of North Carolina Press, 1983), 150–53, and Rastall's *The Heaven Singing: Music in Early English Religious Drama*, 2 vols. (Cambridge: D. S. Brewer, 1996–), 1:177–78.

[69] See the discussion of the iconography of the Harrowing in relation to the York play in my *From Creation to Doom: The York Cycle of Mystery Plays* (New York: AMS Press, 1984), 135–47.

The Medieval Stage and the Antitheatrical Prejudice

> So sithen thise miraclis pleyinge ben onely singnis, . . . they ben not onely contrarious to the worschipe of God—that is, bothe in signe and in dede—but also they ben ginnys of the devvel to cacchen men to byleve of Anticrist.—*A Tretise of Miraclis Pleyinge*[1]

Condemnation of actors and of the ludic experience as represented in the Wycliffite *Tretise of Miraclis Pleyinge* was not confined only to the radical fringe of Christianity in the late Middle Ages, but rather involved an attitude that was inherited from certain of the Church Fathers and that in the late sixteenth and early seventeenth centuries would emerge in the distaste of the theater evidenced by such Puritans as Philip Stubbes, William Perkins, and William Prynne.[2] The *Tretise* is, to be sure, an extreme example of antagonism to the stage, and it would be easy to misread its significance as a theater history document. But the *Tretise* nevertheless suggests the importance of surveying the matter of medieval hostility to actors and the stage.

It will be useful initially to call to mind the fact that a range of dramatic traditions, from dignified and stylized religious ceremony to rowdy secular entertainment, co-existed throughout the period. Some of

---

[1] *A Tretise of Miraclis Pleyinge*, ed. Clifford Davidson, Early Drama, Art, and Music Monograph Series 19 (Kalamazoo: Medieval Institute Publications, 1993), 99.

[2] Phillip Stubbes, *The Anatomie of Abuses* (London, 1583), sigs. Lv^r–Mi^v; William Prynne, *Histrio-mastix* (London, 1633), *passim*. It will, however, be important to recognize that there was considerable variation in attitude toward the stage among the Puritans; not all were entirely hostile, nor was all antagonism to the theater lodged in the Puritan camp. See Margot Heinemann, *Puritanism and Theatre: Thomas Middleton and Opposition Drama under the Early Stuarts* (Cambridge: Cambridge University Press, 1980), esp. 18–47. William Perkins, no friend of the theater, was perhaps typical in most disliking religious plays, which, like religious processions and the Roman Catholic Mass itself, are "vtterly forbidden" (*The Workes* [London, 1612], 1:17). For Prynne, plays for the stage are "the very product of Satan, and the broode of Hell" and players "*are the very dregs of men*," guilty of every offense including sodomy (*Histrio-mastix*, 16, 133, 135).

the texts that are studied by students of the drama—e.g., the *Visitatio Sepulchri* in its simplest liturgical form[3]—must be distinguished from the more representational forms, and yet in no sense should the earliest Easter dramas be seen as a step historically on the way to theatrical experiences that would raise the ire of critics from Robert Grosseteste to Prynne.

Unfortunately, popular accounts of the medieval stage continue to describe how it evolved out of the liturgy following the total demise of the theater of antiquity—a theater which is said to have been suppressed by humorless churchmen—whereupon the acceptance of drama is said to have grown gradually as new forms developed in the church and then moved out first to the church porch and eventually to the streets.[4] According to this older view, the medieval actor reclaimed his place in society through a development that took a thousand years to germinate. Unfortunately, the attitude toward the actor and the theater in the years prior to the Reformation was never so simple.

A generation ago O. B. Hardison, Jr., demonstrated that the simplistic evolutionary model fails to fit the historical facts.[5] While the theater as the ancient Romans knew it was indeed suppressed following a period of decadence, the offering of entertainments by actors, either one-person entertainers or small troupes, appears to have had a continuous history in Western Europe through the time of the High Middle Ages. Verification comes from various sources, including, most recently, the texts of the Nordic sagas and related documents which report the popularity of the *leikarar*, who were admired and who yet existed on the margins of Scandinavian society.[6] Such entertainers, though often rewarded with rich gifts

---

[3] See the text from the *Regularis Concordia*, edited by Karl Young, *The Drama of the Medieval Church*, 2 vols. (Oxford: Clarendon Press, 1933), 1:249–50.

[4] For an example (recent at the time when this article was initially published), such a description of the evolution of medieval drama appeared in an otherwise stimulating plenary address ("When Did the Middle Ages End: Perspectives of an Intellectual Historian," by Marcia Colish) at the Thirty-First International Congress on Medieval Studies, Kalamazoo, Michigan, 11 May 1996.

[5] O. B. Hardison, Jr., *Christian Rite and Christian Drama in the Middle Ages* (Baltimore: Johns Hopkins University Press, 1966), esp. chap. 1. See also David Bevington, "Discontinuity in Medieval Acting Traditions," in *The Elizabethan Theatre V*, ed. G. R. Hibbard (London: Macmillan, 1975), 1–16.

[6] See Terry Gunnell, "'The Rights of the Player': Evidence of *Mimi* and *Histriones* in Early Medieval Scandinavia," *Comparative Drama* 30 (1996): 1–31.

of clothing which they might use in their performances, were normally itinerant persons without property. Thus they were without extensive legal rights and hence were regarded as untrustworthy.[7] The indication is that there was a deep though not entirely consistent prejudice against entertainers as a class in England as well as on the Continent. This antagonism would erupt in an especially virulent fashion in England during the late sixteenth and early seventeenth centuries, and finally antitheatricalism was triumphant in 1642 when the theaters were closed and the playing companies were disbanded.

There is, however, sufficient evidence that the civic context in English municipalities such as York, Coventry, and Chester gave strong support to amateur religious drama from the end of the fourteenth century through much of the sixteenth century. While occasional complaints may be noted—e.g., a guild complaining about a particular play such as the Masons' Funeral of the Virgin pageant at York,[8] or about the excessive financial burden of supporting or contributing to a play, especially when the sponsoring organization was in decline[9]—in the main there is no reason to believe that the organizers, patrons, and players were not all united in an enthusiastic enterprise that took immense energy and demanded a substantial outlay of funds. This theatrical tradition, which was finally to be virtually suppressed by the end of the sixteenth century, was the victim to a considerable degree of Protestant hostility to the religious stage, as Father Gardiner argued a half a century ago,[10] though

---

[7] Ibid., 18–22.

[8] Alexandra F. Johnston and Margaret Rogerson, *Records of Early English Drama: York*, 2 vols. (Toronto: University of Toronto Press, 1979), 1:47–48. The Masons' complaint was that their play, in which Fergus (the attacker of the Virgin's funeral procession) was beaten, was based on an apocryphal story and caused a disturbance rather than devotion among the spectators.

[9] See, for example, R. W. Ingram, *Records of Early English Drama: Coventry* (Toronto: University of Toronto Press, 1981), 192–93, for the statement that "it is ordayned by the Authorothie . . . of the Leet that for assmuch as the companie of Tanners be not of such substance as they haue bin in tymes past to mentayne the padiant therfore To their help and profitt the Corvisers which be not chardged with the padiant therfore they shall pay yearlie vnto the said company of Tanners towards the charge of the padiant xiij s iiij d to be paid yerely from thence forth at the feast of holy Trinitye."

[10] Harold C. Gardiner, *Mysteries' End* (1946; reprint Hamden, Conn.: Archon Books, 1967). For suppression of liturgical ceremonies and dramas of Holy Week in England,

his explanation needs to be supplemented by other causes of the crisis in attitudes that would bring an end to the mysteries.[11]

The actor was naturally the central figure in an argument over the stage which never quite disappeared in the Christian West from antiquity to the closing of the theaters in 1642. Of course, the actor in liturgical drama is not overly *theatrical* as long as the play remains absorbed in ceremonial, as in the instance of the Good Friday and Easter morning *Depositio* and *Elevatio* rituals. Dunbar Ogden has commented on examples of the Easter *Visitatio Sepulchri* which are sung and acted inside Easter sepulchers so removed from the members of the congregation that the sound of the singing cannot be heard and the action cannot be seen by them.[12] But when the theatrical element appeared to any degree in the liturgical drama, the way would be open for objections, and in the sixteenth century the Council of Trent suppressed all such plays and ceremonies.[13] This suppression, like the suppression of the professional theater in England in the next century, may be seen as a triumph for the antitheatrical prejudice—a prejudice directed against the actor and his craft. The negative valuing of actors and the stage is hence quite obviously an important factor in the history of the theater prior to the modern period.

We owe the term 'antitheatrical prejudice' to Jonas Barish, whose book on the subject ranges from antiquity to contemporary critics of the stage. Barish describes how Greek philosophers in antiquity looked at the theater with suspicion, and he surveys the negative attitudes toward the

---

however, see Pamela Sheingorn, "'No Sepulchre on Good Friday': The Impact of the Reformation on the Easter Rites in England," in *Iconoclasm vs. Art and Drama*, ed. Clifford Davidson and Ann Eljenholm Nichols, Early Drama, Art, and Music, Monograph Series 11 (Kalamazoo: Medieval Institute Publications, 1989), 145–63.

[11] For a more recent account of the suppression of the mysteries, see John R. Elliott, Jr., *Playing God: Medieval Mysteries on the Modern Stage* (Toronto: University of Toronto Press, 1989), 3–14.

[12] Dunbar H. Ogden, "The *Visitatio Sepulchri*: Public Enactment and Hidden Rite," *Early Drama, Art, and Music Review* 16 (1994): 95–102.

[13] The Council of Trent's efforts were not always successful in suppressing the Easter *Visitatio Sepulchri*; see, for example, Michael L. Norton and Amelia J. Carr, "New Sources for the *Visitatio Sepulchri* at Klosterneuburg," *Early Drama, Art, and Music Review* 15 (1993): 83–90.

stage in Roman times when, in the days of the Empire, it had indeed become "thoroughly disreputable."[14] Early Christian antipathy to actors and acting has frequently been noted and is often seen as a driving force behind the demise of the Roman stage. In the mind of a Church Father such as Tertullian, the author of the harsh antitheatrical work *De Spectaculis*, the suppression of the theater could allegedly have had the effect of removing one of the prime sources of corruption in the pagan society of his time.[15]

The antipathy of the early Church toward the stage was codified in the *Apostolic Tradition* of Hippolitus. This document, written in the early third century but describing practice and ritual of the late second century, provides a listing of unacceptable trades for candidates for baptism. These include not only idol makers, astrologers, and heathen priests but also jugglers and actors: "If a man is an actor or pantomimist, he must desist or be rejected."[16] Presumably Christian burial was also to be denied to the actor who had not abandoned his craft and hence had remained unbaptized. The actor's vocation was still being condemned at the Council of Nicaea (787), and J. D. A. Ogilvy cites an episcopal edict of 789 that specified corporal punishment for *histriones* who appeared in costumes appropriate only to clergy or to monks and nuns.[17] Allardyce Nicoll quotes a canon proclaimed by the Council of Tours in 813 that ordered the clergy to flee "the obscenity of the players and the scurrilities of debased jesting."[18] In tenth-century England, the Anglo-Saxon King Edgar complained that "a house of clergy is known ... as a meeting place for actors [histrionum] ... where mimes [mimi] sing and dance,"[19] while

---

[14] Jonas Barish, *The Antitheatrical Prejudice* (Berkeley and Los Angeles: University of California Press, 1981), 38.

[15] See ibid., 44–50, for Barish's discussion.

[16] *The Apostolic Tradition of Hippolytus*, trans. Burton Scott Easton (1934; reprint Hamden, Conn.: Archon Books, 1962), 42–43.

[17] Allardyce Nicoll, *Masks, Mimes, and Miracles* (London: George G. Harrap, 1931), 146; J. D. A. Ogilvy, "*Mimi, Scurrae, Histriones*: Entertainers of the Early Middle Ages," *Speculum* 38 (1963): 608–09.

[18] Nicoll, *Masks, Mimes, and Miracles*, 147.

[19] E. K. Chambers, *The Mediaeval Stage*, 2 vols. (London: Oxford University Press, 1903), 1:32n. On the meaning of *histrio* and *mimi*, see Abigail Ann Young, "Plays and Players: The Latin Terms for Performance," *REED Newsletter* 9, no. 2 (1984): 56–62; 10, no. 1 (1985): 9–16.

The Medieval Stage and the Antitheatrical Prejudice 231

in the middle of the twelfth century Grosseteste as bishop of Lincoln would legislate not only against the Feast of Fools but also against "ludos quos vocant miracula."[20]

In 1207 Pope Innocent roundly condemned "theatrical games" associated with the Christmas season.[21] Other voices had been raised against such seasonal "games" in the previous century. For example, Richard of St. Victor had condemned the acts and "vain and foolish poetry in which sin is not wanting" that were associated with the Feast of Fools on the first day of January.[22] Curiously, one result of the hostility to such "Christmas games" seems paradoxically to have been the creation of one of the most famous of the music-dramas of the Middle Ages. At Beauvais Cathedral, the *Play of Daniel* apparently was written and produced by students who had been encouraged to do so as a way of providing an alternative to the entertainment excesses of the season.[23] It is unusual that a reform effort antitheatrical in spirit would lead to the production of a music-drama such as the *Play of Daniel*, which included the dramatization of blasphemous acts such as the misuse of sacred liturgical vessels, the clash of swords, and the presence of animal roles—i.e., the lions.[24] But ultimately of course the Beauvais *Daniel* affirms values which are

---

[20] *Records of Plays and Players in Lincolnshire, 1300–1585*, ed. Stanley Kahrl, Malone Society Collections 8 (Oxford, 1974), 99. See also the summary of such antitheatrical documents in my edition of *A Tretise of Miraclis Pleyinge*, 10–11.

[21] *Decretum Magistri Gratiani*, ed. Emil Friedberg (Graz: Akademische Druck, 1959), 2:452, as cited by Marianne Briscoe, "Some Clerical Notions of Dramatic Decorum," *Comparative Drama* 19 (1985): 1; see also Rosemary Woolf, *The English Mystery Plays* (Berkeley and Los Angeles: University of California Press, 1972), 79, 363.

[22] *Patrologia Latina*, ed. Migne, 177:1036, as quoted in translation by Margot Fassler, "The Feast of Fools and *Danielis Ludus*: Popular Tradition in a Medieval Cathedral Play," in *Plainsong in the Age of Polyphony*, ed. Thomas Forrest Kelly (Cambridge: Cambridge University Press, 1992), 73.

[23] See Fassler, "The Feast of Fools and *Danielis Ludus*," 65–99. For some recent studies on the *Daniel*, see the essays included in Dunbar H. Ogden, ed., *The Play of Daniel: Critical Essays*, Early Drama, Art, and Music, Monograph Series 24 (Kalamazoo: Medieval Institute Publications, 1996).

[24] For the complaints of Herrad of Landsberg about "priests having changed their clothes go[ing] forth as a troupe of warriors" and not only "buffoonery" but also "the clang of weapons," see Chambers, *The Mediaeval Stage*, 2:98.

consistent with liturgical correctness and the dominant culture. There is nothing in the play that allows the triumph of immoral behavior or even suggests either the indecorousness of the procession in which the *Song of the Ass* is sung or the odor of burning shoe leather and sausages substituted for that of incense emanating from the thurible.[25]

The connection of the classical stage with immorality and behavior improper for a Christian had been preserved for the Middle Ages through the writings of Isidore of Seville, who described the theater as "also a brothel, for after the shows were over, prostitutes plied their trade there."[26] As late as 1493 Johannes Trechsel's edition of Terence's comedies, printed at Lyon, contained an illustration showing mimes along with a lector presenting a drama—and also, below, the enticements of the brothel (sig. a4^v). But with the theatrical revival of the twelfth century—a time when liturgical drama flourished in such masterpieces as the plays in the *Fleury Playbook* and when other religious plays such as the Anglo-Norman *Adam* also appeared—the attitudes of the critics of the stage tend much more often than not to be mixed.

In the thirteenth century St. Thomas Aquinas would take a much more lenient view of actors who engaged in pure entertainment without obscenities or blasphemy. His defense of pleasure in instances when it serves as innocent and therapeutic recreation extends to the drama.[27] Actors, according to Aquinas, are not excluded from Christendom if their art be "moderated" and if they avoid licentious speech and "unlawful" acts intended only to amuse, but he also insists that they are not to "introduce play into undue matters and seasons."[28] It is clear that he meant blasphemy to be utterly avoided and that proper respect invariably should be given to religious topics; similarly, entertainment merely for

---

[25] *The Song of the Ass* (*Orientus partibus*) appears in British Library Egerton MS. 2615, fols. 1 and 43. This manuscript also contains the *Play of Daniel*; see Chambers, *The Mediaeval Stage*, 1:284, 294 and 2:279–82.

[26] Isidore of Seville, *Etymologiae*, ed. W. M. Lindsay, 2 vols. (Oxford, 1910), 18.42, as quoted in translation by Joseph R. Jones, "Isidore and the Theater," *Comparative Drama* 16 (1982): 33–34.

[27] Cf. Charles Reutemann, *The Thomistic Concept of Pleasure* (Washington: Catholic University of America Press, 1953), 19.

[28] *Summa Theologica* II.ii, Q. 168, Art. 2; trans. Fathers of the Dominican Province (New York: Benziger, 1947).

amusement would have been seen as inappropriate for certain holy festivals of the Church. The distinction between acceptable and unacceptable entertainment and plays has also been noted in Alexander Carpenter's *Destructorium Viciorum* (c.1425); the socially acceptable provide refreshment for the soul, as in the case of King David's harping, while disapproved for both clergy and laity are those entertainments designated as *perverse illusionis*—e.g., erotic dance or secular shows—as well as lascivious interludes.[29] The attitude here is quite different from the Wycliffite *Tretise*, which saw recreative play, even among children, as a sign of the lapsarian condition.[30]

Not untypical of the later Middle Ages, it would seem, is the treatise *Dives and Pauper*, which denounces ribaldry, lies, or "steraclis & pleyys aȝens þe feyth of holy chirche ne aȝenys þe statys of holy chirche ne aȝenys good lyuynge"; at the same time, "Steraclis, pleyys, & dauncis þat arn don principaly for deoucioun & honest merthe . . . arn leful" as long as they do not contain scurrilous material or draw people away from church services.[31] At the mention by Dives of St. Augustine's objection to plays and dances, Pauper patiently explains that "yf daunsyng and pleyȝyng now on haly-dayes steryn men and wymmen to pride, to lecchery, glotonye & slouthe, to overlonge wakyng on nyȝtys and to ydylschyp on þe werkedayes and oþer synnes, . . . þan ar þey vnleful boþe on þe halyday and on þe werke day, and aȝens alle swyche spak Sent Austyn. But aȝenys honest dauncis & honest pleyys don in dew tyme & in good maner in þe halyday spak neuer Sent Austyn."[32] This is hardly a very subtle explanation of St. Augustine's criticism of the theater,[33] but

---

[29] Alexander Carpenter, *Destructorium Viciorum* 23, as quoted by Briscoe, "Some Clerical Notions," 4–6; see also Young, "Plays and Players," *REED Newsletter* 10, no. 1 (1985): 12–13, and the discussion in Glending Olson, *Literature as Recreation in the Later Middle Ages* (Ithaca: Cornell University Press, 1982).

[30] *Tretise of Miraclis Pleyinge*, 93, 103–04, 107–08, 122.

[31] *Dives and Pauper*, ed. Priscilla Heath Barnum, EETS, o.s. 275, 280 (London: Oxford University Press, 1976), 1:293. For objections to competition with church services, see William Tydeman, "An Introduction to Medieval Theatre," in *The Cambridge Companion to Medieval Theatre*, ed. Richard Beadle (Cambridge: Cambridge University Press, 1994), 15; *REED: York*, 1:358.

[32] *Dives and Pauper*, 1:294.

[33] For Augustine's views on the theater, see Barish, *The Antitheatrical Prejudice*, 52–65.

it very probably represents the moderate view of actors and the stage in the England in which the great cycle plays were presented at York, Coventry, and Chester. But it will be noticed that this moderate view nevertheless places careful restrictions on what is permitted to actors on stage.

One may speculate whether limitations on the subject matter of players may at a later time have influenced the city government in some cases, as at York in 1595 when the Earl of Worcester's Players were given twenty shillings not to play.[34] There could, of course, have been other reasons for paying the players not to play—e.g., fear of plague or other diseases—but it is very plausible to believe that in at least some cases the troupes were considered to be a potentially bad influence in the city, perhaps stirring men and women to pride and the other Seven Deadly Sins denounced in *Dives and Pauper* and any number of other tracts and sermons of the times. Statutes of the diocese of York in the thirteenth century had decreed that the clergy should avoid "illicitis spectaculis,"[35] and in the sixteenth century similar prohibitions were being promulgated.[36]

As indicated above, the dramatic records suggest a very considerable enthusiasm for drama during the fifteenth century and through much of the sixteenth century not only in those cities where the great cycles were being presented but also elsewhere in England—an enthusiasm clearly evident also on the Continent. Because such a small percentage of the texts used in English performances are extant[37] it is not possible to gauge

---

[34] Johnston and Rogerson, *REED: York*, 1:464.

[35] *Councils and Synods with Other Documents Relating to the English Church*, ed. F. M. Powicke and C. R. Cheny (1964), 486, as cited by Ian Lancashire, *Dramatic Texts and Records of Britain: A Chronological Topography to 1558* (Toronto: University of Toronto Press, 1984), no. 1584.

[36] Lancashire, *Dramatic Texts and Records*, nos. 1587–88; *REED: York*, 1:358.

[37] See Lancashire, *Dramatic Texts and Records*, *passim*. For example, only two Middle English saint plays (*The Conversion of St. Paul* and *Mary Magdalene* in the Digby manuscript), to which may be added some fragments and a segment interpolated into the N-Town collection (see Peter Meredith, ed., *The Mary Play from the N.town Manuscript* [London: Longman, 1987]), are extant. There is, however, also the Cornish play of St. Meriasek. Most important, of course, are the great cycles of York, Chester, and Coventry as well as the Cornish *Ordinalia* and incomplete *Creacion of the World*. Unfortunately, Coventry's plays are lost except for the Shearmen and Taylors' and Weavers' pageants. Also extant are the

how carefully most plays stayed within the bounds acceptable to moralistic churchmen. Further, we cannot always tell from the texts everything we would like to know about performance practice, and actors can easily, of course, subvert the intended meaning of a text through inappropriate gesture or tone of voice. About the great cycles we can have little doubt that decorum was preserved; at York the reason for exercising quality control on the part of the Corporation seems to have been not the presence of scurrility but of actors without the ability to project or interpret the lines properly.[38] It is also unlikely that saint plays would have violated the principles of the symbolism that dictated the visual effects of the drama.[39] But even the most decorous drama could have its critics.

The Wycliffite *Tretise of Miraclis Pleyinge* is the most thoroughgoing attack on the stage at the same time that it is the most extended commentary on the aesthetics of drama in Middle English. Paul A. Johnston has demonstrated that its two parts were written by different authors who probably lived in nearby regions in Huntingdonshire (Part I) and Northamptonshire (Part II).[40] In other words, its authors would have had relatively convenient access to the great drama cycle at Coventry to which people from all over England flocked.[41] Some dramatic activity was also recorded at Northampton, and this would have been even nearer at hand.[42] In spite of the tendency among some scholars to dismiss the

---

Towneley (formerly thought to be the Wakefield Corpus Christi cycle) and N-Town collections, each approximating a cycle though neither has been positively identified with a specific civic center.

[38] Johnston and Rogerson, *REED: York*, 1:109.

[39] See my "Positional Symbolism and Medieval English Drama," *Comparative Drama* 25 (1991): 66–76.

[40] Paul A. Johnston, Jr., "The Dialect of *A Tretise of Miraclis Pleyinge*," in *A Tretise of Miraclis Pleyinge*, ed. Davidson, 53–84.

[41] William Dugdale, *The Antiquities of Warwickshire* (London, 1656), 116. For the extant plays, see *The Coventry Corpus Christi Plays*, ed. Pamela M. King and Clifford Davidson, Early Drama, Art, and Music, Monograph Series 27 (Kalamazoo: Medieval Institute Publications, 2000); see also Lancashire, *Dramatic Texts and Records*, nos. 554–78.

[42] See *Non-Cycle Plays and Fragments*, ed. Norman Davis, EETS, s.s. 1 (London: Oxford University Press, 1970), 32–42 (Abraham and Isaac play), and Lancashire, *Dramatic Texts and Records*, nos. 1213–14.

Tretise because of its association with unorthodox theology,[43] it is nevertheless in a direct line from St. Augustine with regard to a principal argument against the stage. In a passage to which Nicholas Davis has called attention, John Wyclif quoted Augustine to the effect that the actor is an example of hypocrisy because he is not in fact what he seems and hence promotes a radical separation between the sign and the thing signified.[44] This passage was apparently well known since it was included in the Lollard *Floretum*,[45] and indeed it becomes one of the driving forces behind the polemic in the *Tretise of Miraclis Pleyinge*. Needless to say, from this point of view the playing of sacred matter, especially the playing of the Passion, was to be seen as nothing short of blasphemy.[46] The *Tretise* thus insists that "these miraclis pleyinge been verrey leesing as they ben signis withoute dede and for they been verrey idilnesse, as they taken the miraclis of God in idil after theire owne lust."[47] The accusation that actors are "idil" folk is a charge that would stick to them in later times,[48] but here "idilnesse" also implies something much more serious—the thoughtless and blasphemous handling of the sacred story under the rubric of *sloth*, which is of course one of the Seven Deadly Sins.

Another argument against drama implied by the *Tretise* which deserves our attention involves its prejudice against the *visual* aspect of drama,[49] and here medieval theories of vision come into play. Augustine's view was that there were rays coming forth from the eye which, subject to the will, "would touch whatever we see."[50] To see an object or an

---

[43] The first part of the *Tretise*, however, does not espouse an unorthodox view of the Sacraments—a mark usually of a Wycliffite. See Davidson, ed., *A Tretise of Miraclis Pleyinge*, 142.

[44] Nicholas Davis, "Allusions to Medieval Drama in Britain: A Findings List (3)," *Medieval English Theatre* 5 (1983): 85.

[45] Ibid.

[46] See *A Tretise of Miraclis Pleyinge*, esp. 102.

[47] Ibid., 99.

[48] See Prynne, *Histrio-mastix*, 141, and also 501–08 for the argument that plays are a "nursery of much sloth and idlenesse."

[49] *A Tretise of Miraclis Pleyinge*, 102.

[50] Augustine, *De Trinitate* 9.3.3, as quoted in translation by Margaret Miles, "Vision: The Eye of the Body and the Eye of the Mind in Saint Augustine's *De Trinitate*," *Journal of Religion* 63 (1983): 127.

action hence meant coming into visual *contact* and engaging in *participation* with it, and for this reason inappropriate scenes in drama would be a source of pollution or contamination through the sense of sight.[51] Thus to reward players was idolatry in the view of the person who wrote a moral verse on a palace window at Downham, Cambridgeshire: "To give to Players, and to sacrifice to Deviles, is all one."[52]

But even for drama enthusiasts the playing of religious plays might not be entirely without anxiety for several reasons. R. W. Hanning has carefully examined the playing of Lucifer in the Creation and Fall of the Angels plays in the civic cycles and has pointed out how the playwrights made use of the theme of false mimesis—a theme which seems ultimately to have been a development out of Augustine's discussion of Lucifer's rebellion in the *City of God*.[53] The fall of Lucifer as presented in the plays, however, provides an example in itself of false imitation, a presentation of false sign and lack of the substance or authority that can be exercised only by the Source of all Goodness.[54] Nevertheless, the player in taking a role such as the character of God or the Devil was acting out a part with distinct problems for the actors in performance; the one involved a representation of the all-powerful deity—an action that was interpreted by some (e.g., the writers of the *Tretise of Miraclis Pleyinge*) as blasphemous—while the other meant the taking on of the role of the powers of evil which had been loosed in this world following the Fall. To impersonate the evil one, dressed in a hairy garment and emerging from the mouth of hell, very likely would have taken more confidence than many a medieval actor could easily have mustered.[55]

A further problem for the actor and audience alike was the practice

---

[51] See my article "The Antivisual Prejudice," in *Iconoclasm vs Art and Drama*, ed. Davidson and Nichols, 33–46.

[52] James Bentham, *The History and Antiquities of the Conventual and Cathedral Church of Ely*, 2nd ed. (1817), 84–85, as quoted by Lancashire, *Dramatic Texts and Records*, no. 611.

[53] R. W. Hanning, "'You have begun a parlous pleye': The Nature and Limits of Dramatic Mimesis in Four Middle English 'Fall of Lucifer' Cycle Plays," *Comparative Drama* 7 (1973): 22–50.

[54] Ibid.

[55] For evidence of anxiety with regard to playing the roles of executioners and demons in a "somer game" of the Passion, see Siegfried Wenzel, "*Somer Game* and Sermon References to a Corpus Christi Play," *Modern Philology* 86 (1989): 278–82.

of casting men in women's roles—i.e., of cross dressing. While women had a much greater role in entertainment in the late Middle Ages than previously has been suspected,[56] the transvestism involved when men put on the costumes of women and imitated their behavior would be the source of negative attitudes toward the stage as had been the case in the time of Tertullian.[57] The Wycliffite *Tretise* presumably is indicative of such practice when it denounces "veine sightis of degyse, aray of men and wymmen by yvil continaunse" and comments on the eroticism involved in playing.[58] Its authors bluntly accuse the plays of "stiring . . . to leccherie" and also argue that players are like seducers who are not sincere in their motives.[59] Concerns such as these would, of course, provide considerable fuel at a later date for the antitheatricalism that was to be advocated compendiously by Prynne in his *Histrio-mastix*. For Prynne, "the whole action of Playes is nought else but feigning, but counterfeiting, but palpable hypocrisie and dissimulation which God, which men abhorre: therefore it must needs be sinfull."[60]

The importance and force of religion in the community in the fourteenth century through at least the middle of the sixteenth century require recognition. During this period the matters discussed above were taken very seriously indeed. When their heritage as *mimi* and *histriones* is taken into account, it is not surprising that the Church should be suspicious of actors, and it was very likely a suspicion shared with the class of prominent people who controlled cities such as York, Coventry, and Chester —people who offered their own amateur drama under controlled conditions as a way of promoting the reputation of their municipalities in addition to presenting plays to the glory of God. Both professional and amateur actors would have been constantly aware of the limits imposed by the antitheatrical prejudice, which also very likely influenced their productions even when indeed it did not serve to suppress plays. In the

---

[56] James Stokes, "Women and Mimesis in Medieval and Renaissance Somerset (and Beyond)," *Comparative Drama* 27 (1993): 176–96.

[57] The topic has become a focus of very considerable interest; see especially Meg Twycross, "Transvestism in the Mystery Plays," *Medieval English Theatre* 5 (1983): 123–80.

[58] *A Tretise of Miraclis Pleyinge*, 96.

[59] Ibid., 96, 99–100.

[60] Prynne, *Histrio-mastix*, 156.

middle of Queen Elizabeth I's reign, of course, most civic plays with religious content would be suppressed.[61] The creed of political correctness in the middle and late sixteenth century also had no place for saint plays, which may at one time have been the most popular form of medieval religious drama, or for other plays with overtly Catholic content. And then eventually the conditions for the dissolution of the traditions of biblical plays prevailed as well.

One of the conditions that seems to have influenced the discontinuing of civic plays involved their expense, for the cities which staged them spent a substantial amount for these productions. The author of the second part of the Wycliffite *Tretise* had complained that "this miraclis pleyinge is verre wittnesse of mennus averice and coveytise byfore—that is, maumetrie, as seith the apostele—for that that they shulden spendyn upon the nedis of ther negheboris, they spenden upon the pleyis; and to peyen ther rente and ther dette they wolen grucche, and to spenden two or so myche upon ther play they wolen nothinge grucchen."[62] Charges such as this against religious institutions would become familiar in the sixteenth century when they were said to hold wealth that should be distributed to the poor or used for more socially useful purposes such as the putting down of vice. Indeed, this was one of the reasons put forward for the suppression of the Chester plays by an antagonist, Christopher Goodman, whose antitheatrical efforts apparently helped to put down the civic religious drama in this city.[63] Players, even amateur ones presenting religious plays, could consume wealth in ways that were felt by the antitheatrical enemies of the stage to be a negative influence on the society.

---

[61] An exception was the Corpus Christi play at Kendall; this play survived until the reign of King James. See Audrey Douglas and Peter Greenfield, *Records of Early English Drama: Cumberland, Westmorland, Gloucester* (Toronto: University of Toronto Press, 1986), 218–19.

[62] *A Tretise of Miraclis Pleyinge*, 111.

[63] Christopher Goodman, Letter to Sir John Savage, Mayor of Chester, in 1575, as cited in David Mills's unpublished paper "Sponsorship and Censorship in Tudor Chester," presented at the Eighth International Colloquium of the Société Internationale pour l'etude du Théâtre Médiéval at the University of Toronto in August 1995. Fuller commentary on Goodman is now available in Mills's *Recycling the Cycle: The City of Chester and Its Whitsun Plays* (Toronto: University of Toronto Press, 1998), 146–51; the letter, which was never sent, is summarized (150–51).

Idol and Image in Late Medieval Art and Drama

A treatise associated with the Protestant Reformation claimed that "millions of souls have been cast into eternal damnation by the occasion of images used in place of religion; and no history can record that ever any soul was won to Christ by having of images."[1] Adopting a literal interpretation of the Old Testament commandment to avoid "graven" images (Exodus 20:4)—by which, according to the Geneva Bible gloss, "all kinde of seruice & worship to idoles is forbidden"—Protestant iconomachs argued against religious images of God, Jesus, Mary, and the saints which they saw as no more valid than the Golden Calf worshipped by the Israelites.[2] In England the result would thus be total rejection of the image theology that had played such a major role in late medieval religion —an image theology that, in Hans-Georg Gadamer's words, implied "an ontological communion" between the image and the prototype.[3]

To be sure, there had been concern about idolatry prior to the Reformation. The image of the golden calf had appeared prominently in the *Biblia Pauperum*, for example, as a foreshadowing of the fall of the idols

---

[1] Nicholas Ridley, *The Works*, Parker Society (Cambridge: Cambridge University Press, 1841), 94. This treatise may not in fact be by Ridley, however; see my article "The Antivisual Prejudice," in *Iconoclasm vs. Drama and Art*, ed. Clifford Davidson and Ann Eljenholm Nichols, Early Drama, Art, and Music, Monograph Series 11 (Kalamazoo: Medieval Institute Publications, 1989), 41.

[2] On Protestant iconoclasm in England see especially Margaret Aston, *England's Iconoclasts*, I (Oxford: Clarendon Press, 1988), *passim*, but see also Eamon Duffy, *The Stripping of the Altars: Traditional Religion in England 1400–1580* (New Haven: Yale University Press, 1992); John Phillips, *The Reformation of Images* (Berkeley and Los Angeles: University of California Press, 1973); and for Continental iconoclasm, Carlos M. N. Eire, *War Against the Idols: The Reformation of Worship from Erasmus to Calvin* (Cambridge: Cambridge University Press, 1986).

[3] Hans-Georg Gadamer, *Truth and Method* (New York: Seabury, 1975), 126; the crucial passages are conveniently quoted by David Freedberg, *The Power of Images* (Chicago: University of Chicago Press, 1989), 77.

in the course of the Flight to Egypt—a fulfillment of the prophecies "Behold the Lord . . . will enter Egypt, and the idols of Egypt shall be moved at his presence" (Isaiah 19:1) and "he shall break down their idols . . ." (Hosea 10:2).[4] But idols were normally, as shown in the depictions in the fall of the Egyptian idols, distinctly different in appearance from the images of the saints or of the deity.[5] The *Biblia Pauperum* shows both the calf and the Egyptian idols atop free-standing columns rather than in the tabernacles or enclosures usually accorded to Christian saints or other holy scenes. Nor can these depictions of idols be confused with reliquary statues since, in addition to their deformed shape, there is clearly no presence of a relic to empower the statue and give it legitimacy. But in the case of the falling idols the message is even more clear: in the *Biblia Pauperum* they are grossly distorted and obviously demonic, the grotesque forms of devils who are unable to remain upright in the presence of the Holy Infant.

The central *Biblia Pauperum* illustration presents the image of power associated with truth and goodness, paradoxically in the form of Virgin and Child; at the left in the woodcut is the worship of the false image. Mary and her holy Son have only to be present in the scene to defeat the falsehood of idolatry; they are intended to evoke devotion, while, in spite of the false veneration being directed at them, the idols are to repulse and to stimulate derision. The depiction in fact is designed to define good and evil in terms of beauty and ugliness, light and darkness, power and powerlessness. At the right is another scene, the fall of Dagon reported in I Kings 5:1–5, that shows the triumph of the ark of the tabernacle over

---

[4] Avril Henry, *Biblia Pauperum* (Ithaca: Cornell University Press, 1987), 56–59. This episode, reporting the arrival of the Holy Family at Hermopolis where there was a temple containing 365 gods, appeared in the Gospel of Pseudo-Matthew; see *The Apocryphal New Testament*, trans. M. R. James (1926; reprint Oxford: Clarendon Press, 1980), 75. According to Peter Comestor's *Historia scholastica*, the Egyptians are said thereafter to have made a legitimate image of the Virgin and Child which they adored; see Adrian Wilson and Joyce Lancaster Wilson, *A Medieval Mirror: Speculum Humanae Salvationis* (Berkeley and Los Angeles: University of California Press, 1984), 162, pl. II.2b.

[5] For the iconography of the Fall of the Idols, see Gertrud Schiller, *Iconography of Christian Art*, 2 vols. (Greenwich, Conn.: New York Graphic Society, 1971), 1:117–21. Extensive examples showing depictions of idols are presented by Michael Camille, *The Gothic Idol* (Cambridge: Cambridge University Press, 1989), *passim*.

Dagon, who is depicted as a devil-shaped idol—a foreshadowing, according to the *Biblia Pauperum*, of the coming of the Virgin Mary "into Egypt with Christ her son; then the idols of Egypt fell, and aptly signify that when Christ came, images (that is, errors of the unbelieving) fell."[6]

The Flight to Egypt and the Fall of the Idols are dramatized in the Chester cycle, where they are inserted into the midst of the Goldsmiths' play of the Slaying of the Innocents (Play X). In this play, the angel who comes to warn Joseph to flee also accompanies the Holy Family and, upon arriving in Egypt, will signal the destruction of the idols:

> For mahometes both on and all,
> that men of Egipt godes can call,
> at your comminge downe shall fall
> when I beginne to synge.[7]

The stage direction which follows indicates that the angel is to sing "Ecce dominus ascendet super nubem levem, et ingrediatur Egiptum, et movebuntur simulachra Egipti a facie domini exercituum" (*Isaiah* 19:1, translated in the Douay-Rheims Bible as "Behold the Lord will ascend upon a swift cloud, and will enter into Egypt, and the idols of Egypt shall be moved at his presence, and the heart of Egypt shall melt in the midst thereof"),[8] at which point the image ("statua sive imago") is to fall *if* the players are able to carry out this effect. The sponsorship of the Goldsmiths may suggest that the idol could very well have appeared (like the Golden Calf) to be of gold, but inevitably its form must have seemed demonic and monstrous.

The veneration of legitimate images required that the worshipper should have a proper understanding of their role. One must be able to distinguish between the worship owed to God (*latria*) and the veneration appropriate to saints (*dulia*), the physical image itself and that which is

---

[6] Henry, *Biblia Pauperum*, 59.

[7] *The Chester Mystery Cycle*, ed. R. M. Lumiansky and David Mills, EETS, s.s. 3, 9 (London: Oxford University Press, 1974–86), 1:195 (ll. 285–88).

[8] This text from Isaiah has not been identified as an item in either English or Continental liturgical sources; see Richard Rastall, "Music in the Cycle," in *The Chester Mystery Cycle*, ed. R. M. Lumiansky and David Mills (Chapel Hill: University of North Carolina Press, 1983), 148.

Idol and Image in Late Medieval Art and Drama 243

represented.⁹ As Pauper explains in *Dives and Pauper*, one must "Make þin pylgrimage nought to þe ymage ne for þe ymage, for it may nought helpyn the, but to hym and for hym þat þe ymage representyȝt [to] the."¹⁰ Theologians were always quick to warn against the danger of idolatry before a legitimate image when "people do not distinguish in their prayers between the images of saints and the saints themselves."¹¹ In the case of an idol—i.e., a truly un-Christian statue or picture—however, the image could be inert, representing nothing but emptiness and imagined power, or, as suggested in Psalm 95 in the Vulgate, it could be the embodiment of a devil.¹² Jean Seznec, whose interest lay in euhemeristic explanations of the pagan gods, nevertheless pointed out that "the Church . . . had not completely expelled the antique divinities; they had been merely degraded to the rank of evil spirits."¹³ He further called attention to the story in the *Golden Legend* that recounts St. Benedict's conversion of the temple of Apollo into a chapel dedicated to St. John, whereupon the angry pagan god would return "to torment him in the form of a black monster with flaming eyes."¹⁴ Worship of an idol potentially meant an act of pollution in which one looks approvingly at an image and hence, according to the theory of vision promulgated by St. Augustine and others,¹⁵ brings oneself into direct visual contact with the monstrosity of evil. But even rejection of such an idol-devil could provide a challenge to the faithful, as the case of St. Benedict indicates.

Yet ultimately faith will prevail over idolatry. The triumph of the saints over idols is perhaps best represented in a story told of St. John in

---

⁹ See, for example, *Dives and Pauper*, ed. Priscilla Heath Barnum, EETS, 275, 280 (London: Oxford University Press, 1976), 1:1:102, 107.

¹⁰ Ibid., 1:1:85.

¹¹ William of Avergne, *De Legibus* 23, as quoted by Aston, *England's Iconoclasts*, 1:31.

¹² "For all the gods of the Gentiles are devils [daemonia]" (Psalm 95:5; Douay-Rheims). The point of view that the pagan gods were demonic creatures had an immense influence from the time of the Church Fathers.

¹³ Jean Seznec, *The Survival of the Pagan Gods*, trans. Barbara F. Sessions (1953; reprint Hew York: Harper and Row, 1961), 48.

¹⁴ Ibid., 48.

¹⁵ See Davidson, "The Antivisual Prejudice," 39.

the apocryphal *Acts of John*;[16] the *Golden Legend* provides a condensed version of the account, which narrates how on one occasion

> the idol-worshipers . . . dragged him to the temple of Diana and tried to force him to offer sacrifice to the goddess. Then the saint proposed this alternative: if by invoking Diana they overturned the church of Christ, he would offer sacrifice to the idols; but if by invoking Christ he destroyed Diana's temple, they would believe in Christ. To this proposal the greater number of people gave their consent. When all had gone out of the building, the apostle prayed, the temple collapsed to the ground, and the statue of Diana was reduced to dust.[17]

The *Acts of John* report the words of St. John's prayer, which asserted that at the name of God "every idol fleeth and every evil spirit and every unclean power. . . ." The effect of his prayer was that all the unholy things in the pagan temple fell down and its priest was killed; the altar of Artemis (Diana) broke apart, and the temple itself was half destroyed.[18] The scene is one that is shown in a miniature in the Trinity College Apocalypse: St. John is pointing, with his index finger extended in a gesture of accusation, at the idol, shown falling from a pedestal on a column. In this case she is a clothed figure of a black goddess with African features, unusually placed against a background niche like a Christian image; at the same time the roof of the temple is itself falling from the building.[19]

Though it would be hazardous to speculate about the ultimate source of the details of the destruction of the pagan temple and idol in the play of *Mary Magdalene* in Digby MS. 133, St. John's destruction of the temple and idol of Artemis-Diana may be seen as the kind of story which might well be regarded as lurking in the background.[20] In its entry for

---

[16] *The Apocryphal New Testament*, trans. James, 236–37.

[17] Jacobus de Voragine, *The Golden Legend*, trans. William Granger Ryan, 2 vols. (Princeton: Princeton University Press, 1993), 1:53.

[18] *The Apocryphal New Testament*, trans. James, 237.

[19] See Camille, *The Gothic Image*, fig. 61.

[20] For another example, see the example of St. Denis destroying idols through prayer; Camille has published an example from a *Vie de saint Denis* (Bibliothèque Nationale MS. fr. 1098, fol. 35^v) which shows five demonic-appearing nude idols crumbling and falling from three pedestals on columns in response to prayer spoken by the kneeling bishop-saint,

Mary Magdalene the *Golden Legend* recounts that upon their arrival at Marseilles she and her companions "took refuge under the portico of a [pagan] shrine belonging to the people of that area." Seeing the people of that region offering sacrifice to idols in this temple, she proclaimed the gospel to them and drew many away from their pagan worship. One of those who had previously worshipped at the temple was the local ruler, who was hoping for an heir. Following the appearance of Mary Magdalene to the ruler's wife in three visions, they welcomed the Christians among them.[21]

The Digby *Mary Magdalene* expands and dramatizes the matter of Mary's arrival in "Marcyll" and her overthrow of pagan worship. Already in an earlier scene the audience has been introduced to the King of Marcyll, whose resolution "to do a sacryfyce / Wyth multetude of myrth before ower goddys all" (1135–36) takes him to the temple attended by a fat pagan priest and his saucy clerk, Hawkyn. In this temple devotion and offerings are given to "Sentt Mahownde" (1205). While the priest is vesting, the clerk begins the lesson of Mahound ("*Leccyo mahowndys, viri fortissimi sarasensorum*"), which is made up of nonsense Latin and obscenities beginning with "*Glabriosum ad glvmandum glvmardinorum*" (1187) and ending with "*Castratum raty rybaldorum*" (1197).[22] The king then offers his confession to mighty Mahownd and gives him an offering of a gold coin, whereupon the priest calls on the clerk to begin singing "þe offyse of þis day" (1222–25). No text or musical notation is provided for this service, which is very soon broken off when the priest complains that their music has fallen into discord. The priest then calls attention to the temple's relics, including most significantly "Mahowndys own nekke bon" (1233). His speech ends with a mock blessing which names not only

---

who has his hands joined in supplication (*The Gothic Image*, fig. 70). For the Digby *Mary Magdalene*, see *The Late Medieval Religious Plays of Bodleian MSS Digby 133 and E Museo 160*, ed. Donald C. Baker, John L. Murphy, and Louis B. Hall, Jr., EETS, o.s. 283 (Oxford: Oxford University Press, 1982).

[21] *Golden Legend*, trans. Ryan, 1:376–77.

[22] According to the most recent editors of the Digby plays, the "general theme" of the mock lesson "would seem to be slippery, smooth-talking priests who fornicate with their parishioners' wives, mislead their flocks for their own gain, not caring whether their souls go 'ablackberyed', as Chaucer's Pardoner observed" (*The Late Medieval Religious Plays*, ed. Baker *et al.*, 211).

Mahownd but also "Dragon," Golias, and Belial. The "blysse ewyrlastyng" where the king and queen and others are to sing "in joy . . . / Before þat comly kyng / Þat is ower god in fere" (1245–48) is to be perceived as a place of darkness and devils rather than of true joy.

Later, when the King of Marcyll accompanies Mary Magdalene to the pagan temple, he promises the audience "a solom syth" which will reveal his "goddys myth" (1535–38). He brags about his idols: "How pleseavnttly þey stond, se þow how" (1539). No rubrics are present to describe their appearance, but we may assume a possible stage set utilizing a grouping of columns with devil-shaped idols atop them—a scene much like the one implied immediately before the Fall of the Idols during the Flight to Egypt. In the Digby play one idol stands out, and this is the image addressed by the King of Marcyll, who bows before it as he requests it to speak to Mary Magdalene. However, "he woll natt speke while Chriseten here is" (1546). The powerlessness of the pagan idol even to speak in the presence of a saint is verification of its evil nature, and it is also reflects the words of the psalmist: "The idols of the Gentiles are silver and gold, the works of the hands of men. They have mouths and speak not: they have eyes and see not" (Psalm 113.4–5; Douay-Rheims). As Michael Camille notes, Isidore of Seville claimed that "the word 'idol' is derived from 'fraud' *dolus*," but the deception involved was not to be separated from the demonic.[23]

A modern scholar, however, has defined an idol as "simply an image which has an unwarranted, irrational power over somebody; it has become an object of worship, a repository of powers which someone has projected onto it, but which in fact it does not possess."[24] Richard C. Trexler previously had identified the *image* as "a valid, participatory intelligence; the *idol* was pure object, without spirit, without efficacy."[25] But the idol which the King of Marcyll addresses seems not quite to fit these definitions, since the playwright implies that this image would have been empowered to speak through demonic forces if the saint had not been present. The stage directions identify the idol specifically as a "*mament*,"

---

[23] *Etymologiae* 8.11.5, as quoted by Camille, *The Gothic Image*, 57.

[24] W. J. T. Mitchell, *Iconology: Image, Text, Ideology* (Chicago: University of Chicago Press, 1986), 113.

[25] Richard C. Trexler, "Florentine Religious Experience: The Sacred Image," *Studies in the Renaissance* 19 (1972): 20.

Idol and Image in Late Medieval Art and Drama 247

which is said to *"tremyll and quake"* at the saint's short Latin prayer, actually adapted from the first two lines of Psalm 26 (*AV*: 27), invoking protection (1552–53). While 'mament' (or 'maumet') is another term for 'idol,' it may also may designate a statue which has oracular powers through the presence of a devil.[26] In an early sixteenth-century woodcarving by Heinrich Douvermann showing a false god falling from a column during the Flight to Egypt at the Church of St. Nicholas in Kalkar, the idol is falling over and breaking open at the waist, and a devil is coming forth from its body.[27] 'Mament,' from Old French *Mahomet*, also possibly suggests the name 'Termagent'—a name which, along with 'Mahound' and 'Apollo,' was regarded as particularly demonic.[28]

When Mary Magdalene continues her prayer in English, she asks God to "Pott don þe pryd of mamentys violatt" and "Lett natt þer pryde to þi poste pretend" (1556, 1558). The power of idols is a species of pride or, in other words, an attempt to ape the true power of the deity just as Lucifer tried to imitate the Creator before mankind was brought forth in God's image and placed in the Garden. In the Digby play, Mary Magdalene's prayer has an immediate result which in fact demonstrates the ultimate power residing in the true God of heaven: *"Here xall comme a clowd from heven, and sett þe tempyl on afyer, and þe pryst and þe cler[k] xall synke . . ."* (1561 s.d.). The idols presumably are destroyed in the conflagration—an effect which verifies their powerlessness before the power of the Christian God—while the pagan clergy descend downward in the direction of the underworld where devils reside and the wicked are punished. The "mament" or image of Mahownd is overcome by Mary Magdalene in much the same manner as the image of Artemis-Diana had been overcome by St. John in the the account in the *Golden Legend*.

That not only relics but also the images of saints could in fact possess power was frequently asserted. As John of Damascus had insisted, the falseness of idols does not invalidate the authentic image: "we have set up images of the true God, who became incarnate, and of His servants and

---

[26] *Middle English Dictionary*, s.v. 'maumet'; see also 'maumetrie.'
[27] Schiller, *Iconography of Christian Art*, 1: fig. 322.
[28] For discussion of the appearance of "Tervagant" in Jean Bodel's *Jeu de saint Nicholas*, see Camille, *The Gothic Idol*, 129–36. On Mahound see also Michael Paull, "The Figure of Mahomet in the Towneley Cycle," *Comparative Drama*, 6 (1972): 187–204.

friends, and with them we drive away the demonic hosts."²⁹ While the Western attitude toward images differed somewhat from that of the Eastern Church, the latent energy inherent in images and relics was often affirmed in popular religion if not always in official theology. The twelfth-century *Iconia Sancti Nicolai* in the *Fleury Playbook* tells of a Jew's hesitant trust in his image of St. Nicholas—trust which nevertheless does in fact seem misplaced when the image fails to protect his property from thieves. But the power of the statue is asserted after all when not the image but St. Nicholas himself intervenes for the victim, who then will of course be fully convinced of the sainthood of Nicholas.³⁰ The image has become for the Jew a source of otherwise hidden knowledge and of righteous intervention. The saint is a resident of heaven and in normal circumstances can be invoked through prayers spoken by the person venerating him through his image. Here, however, the saint responds to a threat of desecration—i.e., a promise of a beating of his image.³¹ The image is not the saint, but through the image communication is established with the saint.

Another saint play in the *Fleury Playbook* also may have implied the instrumentality of an image. In the *Son of Getron* (*Filius Getronis*), St. Nicholas comes to the aid of the parents after the boy's mother prays to him in a church dedicated to him;³² though the presence of the saint's image in the church is not mentioned, we know that such images along with relics were commonly present and were regarded as a source of spiritual and physical power. In this play the parents of the abducted child Deodatus receive their son again through the agency of St. Nicholas. The saint rescues the boy from the court of the heathen ruler, who is a

---

²⁹ *Second Apology Against Those Who Attack Divine Images*, 17, in St. John of Damascus, *On the Divine Images*, trans. David Anderson (Crestwood, N.Y.: St. Vladimir's Seminary Press, 1980), 64.

³⁰ Karl Young, *The Drama of the Medieval Church*, 2 vols. (Oxford: Clarendon Press, 1933), 2:343–51. See also the similar play by Hilarius (ibid., 2:338–41). For stained glass at Rouen Cathedral showing the Jew venerating the image of St. Nicholas, see Clyde W. Brockett, Jr., "*Persona in Cantilena*: St. Nicholas in Music in Medieval Drama," in *The Saint Play in Medieval Europe*, ed. Clifford Davidson, Early Drama, Art, and Music, Monograph Series 8 (Kalamazoo: Medieval Institute Publications, 1986), fig. 1.

³¹ For discussion of the humiliation of images found to be unsatisfactory in delivering favors, see Trexler, "Florentine Religious Experience," 27–29.

³² Young, *The Drama of the Medieval Church*, 2:351–57.

Idol and Image in Late Medieval Art and Drama

worshipper of Apollo. These two plays of St. Nicholas in any case demonstrate how the saint should be respected and venerated—and how the saint may be helpful to persons in need of assistance against evil or adversity.[33]

The saint, to be sure, fully expects his or her image to be respected and venerated. In a discussion of St. Foy at Conques, Ellert Dahl cited Bernard of Angers's report of her vengefulness "when her image is treated as an idol" by a clergyman "who makes disparaging remarks about the statue and tries to prevent the crowd from praying before it, thus 'gravely injuring the holy martyr'." The saint appears to the clergyman the next night, scolds him severely, and strikes him a death-dealing blow.[34] Bernard's account then insists "that the effigy of St. Foy deserves to be honoured, since it appears that he who reviled it, in fact blasphemed the holy martyr. . . . It is not a filthy idol."[35] In the West as in the East, there was an unambiguous distinction between the legitimate veneration of images and the worship of idols, a practice which is associated indeed with blasphemy and with devotion to evil.[36]

In a later century and after the Reformation had firmly established itself in England, an instance of the cultural memory of the veneration of images of the saints is reflected at a crucial moment in Shakespeare's *The Winter's Tale*. In the last scene of the last act of this play, Perdita responds to the statue of Hermione:

> And give me leave,
> And do not say 'tis superstition, that
> I kneel, and then implore her blessing. Lady,

---

[33] See also Freedberg, *The Power of Images, passim*, and Trexler, "Florentine Religious Experience," 7–41. For a sympathetic modern study of the role of visual images in religious experience, see Margaret R. Miles, *Image as Insight: Visual Understanding in Western Christianity and Secular Culture* (Boston: Beacon Press, 1985).

[34] Ellert Dahl, "Heavenly Images: The Statue of St. Foy of Conques and the Signification of the Medieval 'Cult-Image' in the West," *Acta ad archaeol. et artium his. pertinentia* 8 (1978): 178, citing Bernard of Angers, *Liber Miraculorum S. Fidis*, ed. A. Bouillet (Paris, 1897), 48–49.

[35] Bernard of Angers, *Liber miraculorum*, 48–49, as quoted by Dahl, "Heavenly Images," 178–79.

[36] See Gerhart B. Ladner, "The Concept of the Image in the Greek Fathers and the Byzantine Iconoclastic Controversy," *Dumbarton Oaks Papers* 7 (1953): 15.

Dear queen, that ended when I but began,
Give me that hand of yours to kiss. (5.3.42–46)[37]

Radical Protestants would indeed have said that it is superstition to kneel before an image or to kiss it, but such was the practice of many generations of people in Western Europe—people who also kept candles burning before images of saints at the altars of parish and monastic churches as a sign of their veneration. The image, perceived by the worshipper's eye, was the means by which transcendent experience might find entrance. Given the understanding of the sense of sight that we find in medieval writers—e.g., St. Thomas Aquinas[38]—such seeing was a far more effective way of apprehending the highest spiritual realities than would be the Protestant way of hearing the Word only. In late medieval popular religion, images were in practice very much more complex than mere "books for the unlearned," for an image was far more than "but a tokene and a book to þe lewyd peple."[39]

---

[37] I quote from the New Arden edition of J. H. Pafford (London: Methuen, 1963). This scene is discussed by Michael O'Connell, "The Idolatrous Eye: Iconoclasm, Anti-Theatricalism, and the Image of the Elizabethan Theater," *ELH* 52 (1985): 304–05.

[38] See Aelred Squire, "The Doctrine of the Image in the *De Veritate* of St. Thomas," *Dominican Studies* 4 (1951): 164–77.

[39] *Dives and Pauper*, 1:1:90–91. On the English Protestant rejection of the dictum that religious art serves as an essential source of knowledge—a dictum that had been promulgated by St. Gregory—see Ann Eljenholm Nichols, "Books-for-Laymen: The Demise of a Commonplace," *Church History* 56 (1987): 457–90.

Saints in Play:
English Theater and Saints' Lives

In the earliest Easter drama, in the *Regularis Concordia* of c.970, three brethren (*fratres*) vest themselves in copes and carry thuribles with incense "in imitation [ad imitationem] of . . . the women coming with spices to anoint the body of Jesus."[1] One of the women is Mary Magdalene, whose role is not yet distinguished from the roles of the other holy women who encounter the angel at the tomb of the resurrected Christ as if on the first Sunday morning following the Crucifixion. As a biblical saint whose life was regarded as a sign of the personal and spiritual renewal toward which all Christians should aspire, her function here not only hints at the surprise and wonder which accompany the recognition of the Resurrection, but also affirms for the members of the congregation that they can be touched by this event as if they were themselves living at that biblical moment.

While Christianity historically held to an understanding of saints—biblical figures, including the apostles, Mary Magdalene, and the Virgin Mary, and also martyrs and confessors of the post-biblical period—as existing both in time and in the supra-temporal realm, they had come to provide focal points in the liturgical year long before the compilation of the *Regularis Concordia*. Celebrating the date on which a saint had died, the Church's concern was to harness his or her power to achieve an experience of transcendence. It is perhaps no accident that on Easter morning at Winchester in the final years of the tenth century the scene to be dramatized in the ceremony of the Visit to the Sepulcher (*Visitatio Sepulchri*) was not the Resurrection itself but the coming of St. Mary Magdalene and two other saintly women to the empty tomb. The Resur-

---

[1] I quote from the translation by David Bevington, ed., *Medieval Drama* (Boston: Houghton Mifflin, 1975), 27; see also Karl Young, *The Drama of the Medieval Church*, 2 vols. (Oxford: Clarendon Press, 1933), 1:249–50, and Pamela Sheingorn, *The Easter Sepulchre in England*, Early Drama, Art, and Music, Reference Series 5 (Kalamazoo: Medieval Institute Publications, 1987), 20–22, which also includes a facsimile of the manuscript in figs. 3–4.

rection event was to be made visible in the drama from the perspective of the early saints who witnessed the empty tomb.

The first record of a play dramatizing the life of a post-biblical saint in England was at Dunstable, Bedfordshire, in c.1110 when the choir copes borrowed from St. Albans Abbey for the production were lost in a fire. The play (*ludus*), on the subject of St. Catherine of Alexandria and perhaps intended for a royal audience, is not extant, but was described as a "miracle" play, terminology which was noted to be the popular designation for such drama.² The medieval legend of St. Catherine is well known, especially for its spectacular scene of the broken wheels which, fitted with knives, had been intended to tear the saint apart. The wheel is therefore her emblem, though in the end she was martyred by being put to the sword and her body taken off to Mount Sinai by angels. There she was allegedly buried, in a place regarded as holy after the discovery of a body attributed to her in the eighth century. In the wake of the crusades, her fame spread widely in England—more than sixty churches are dedicated to this saint³— and other plays and quasi-dramatic tableaux, all lost but probably requiring realistic costuming rather than liturgical vestments, are noted in records from London, Hereford, and Coventry.⁴ At Coventry, the production of the drama, recorded in the City Annals in 1491, has plausibly been linked to the guild associations, since St. Catherine was one of the patrons of the important Holy Trinity Guild.⁵ Presumably the Guild's effort to make the life of one of their patron saints

---

² C. B. C. Thomas, "The Miracle Play at Dunstable," *Modern Language Notes* 32 (1917): 337–44.

³ Frances Arnold-Forster, *Studies in Church Dedications*, 3 vols. (London: Skeffington and Son, 1899), 1:117–22; 2:344–45.

⁴ See Clifford Davidson, "The Middle English Saint Play and Its Iconography," in *The Saint Play in Medieval Europe*, ed. Clifford Davidson, Early Drama, Art, and Music, Monograph Series 8 (Kalamazoo: Medieval Institute Publications, 1986), 45–52; I subsequently compiled a list of British saint plays ("Saint Plays and Pageants of Medieval Britain," *Early Drama, Art, and Music Review* 22 [1999]: 11–37) and have argued against the skeptical view of the saint play genre advanced by Lawrence Clopper; see *Early Theatre* 2 (2000): 97–113.

⁵ R. W. Ingram, *Records of Early English Drama: Coventry* (Toronto: University of Toronto Press, 1981), xx. See also Charles Phythian-Adams, *Desolation of a City: Coventry and the Urban Crisis of the Late Middle Ages* (Cambridge: Cambridge University Press, 1979), 118–22.

16. Beheading of St. Catherine. Alabaster, Hildburgh Collection. By permission of the Board of Trustees of the Victoria and Albert Museum.

seem more vivid to the people attending the play, staged in the Little Park,[6] was specifically calculated to bring the saint into the field of vision of the spectators. Because vision was held to provide the "window of the soul" and hence to place one's eyes in direct contact with an object such as a representation of the saint,[7] its goal was to achieve a participative closeness with the saint thus represented that would benefit the viewer.

Peter Brown indicates that already by the final years of the sixth century the places of burial of saints had been transformed into important centers of religious life.[8] Such holy men and women, though no longer among the living, nevertheless are dead and yet not dead; as it was said of St. Martin of Tours, his "soul is in the hand of God; but he is fully here, present, and made plain in miracles of every kind.'"[9] Much later, in 1527, the story of St. Martin may have been dramatized at Colchester,[10] and if so presumably in a manner very different from the liturgical presentation of the *Visit to the Sepulcher*. Though the records in this case are ambiguous, plays on the lives of such saints were presented in English rather than Latin and were designed, we may assume, as a source of delight, edification, and devotion among the audience who looked upon the scenes of the life of this saint. Unfortunately, like most of the saint plays from the medieval English repertoire, no text of any Colchester *St. Martin* is extant, and if one existed it presumably would have been lost among the accouterments of the "Old Religion" swept away so pre-

---

[6] Ingram, *REED: Coventry*, 74.

[7] Ellert Dahl, "Heavenly Images: The Statue of St. Foy of Conques and the Significance of the Medieval 'Cult-Image' in the West," *Acta ad archaeol. et artium hist. pertinentia* 8 (1978): 187; see also Margaret Miles, "Vision: The Eye of the Body and the Eye of the Mind in St. Augustine's *De trinitate* and *Confessions*," *Journal of Religion* 63 (1983): 127; and Sixten Ringbom, "Devotional Images and Imaginative Devotions," *Gazette-des-Beaux-Arts* 73 (1969): 159–70.

[8] Peter Brown, *The Cult of the Saints* (Chicago: University of Chicago Press, 1981), 3.

[9] E. le Blant, *Les inscriptions chrétiennes de la Gaule* (Paris, 1856), 1:240, as quoted by Brown, *Cult of the Saints*, 4.

[10] W. G. B., "'Seynt Martyns Pley' at Colchester," *Essex Review* 48 (1939): 83. This paragraph has been revised to reflect my current doubts about this event, which is listed by Ian Lancashire in his *Dramatic Texts and Records of Britain: A Chronological Topography to 1558* (Toronto: University of Toronto Press, 1984), no. 553. The term 'play' may in this context refer to *playing* in the sense of *game* rather than of drama; for a discussion of the ambiguity of this terminology, see John C. Coldewey, "Plays and 'Play' in Early English Drama," *Research Opportunities in Renaissance Drama* 28 (1985): 181–88.

Saints in Play

cipitously by the Reformation. Saints were soon to be no longer required for mediating between the time in which men lived and the eternity to which they aspired, and in Protestant England curiously they were to be seen as the objects of superstition rather than of faith, as factors alienating men from God rather than bringing them more near.

The closeness which Christians had traditionally felt with the holy dead—with the saints—was reflected in the relics which were deposited in their places of worship—relics that might on occasion be the object of their pilgrimages—and in the dedications of their churches. These phenomena are also mirrored in the desire to *see* the physical shape of the saint, who was thus frequently depicted in an image, either a painting or a three-dimensional carving. Images of saints could be deeply venerated even when no relic seems to have been present. In his will of 1458, John Dautre requested to be buried in the church of St. Michael Spurriergate in the city of York at the altar of the Holy Trinity before the image of St. John the Baptist whom he had loved above all other saints since his childhood.[11] The document is unclear about whether his devotion was to the saint or to his image, but such a distinction was clearly much less significant in the fifteenth century than in the twentieth or twenty-first. The image provides access to the saint who has been depicted; there is no clear line of demarcation between the one and the other.

In the same city of York, two other wills also from the middle of the fifteenth century refer to plays about saints, in neither case surviving. William Revetour in 1446 left a playbook of *St. James* "in six pageants" ("in sex paginis") to the St. Christopher Guild, which very likely produced the drama as part of its celebrations around the date of the Feast of St. James on 25 July.[12] The other will, prepared in 1456 by Robert Lasingby of the parish of St. Denys, gives proof of a play on the life of St. Denis, a play associated with a church that contains a contemporary

---

[11] *Testamenta Eboracensia*, ed. James Raine, 5 vols., Surtees Society (Durham, 1836–84), 2:230–31.

[12] Alexandra F. Johnston and Margaret Rogerson, *Records of Early English Drama: York*, 2 vols. (Toronto: University of Toronto Press, 1979), 1:68; see also Clifford Davidson, "The Middle English Saint Play," 32. The term *pagina* signifies both *pageant* and *page*, and hence there may be some ambiguity here, though generally it is believed that six *pageants* were implied in this record; on the term *pagina* see John Wasson, *Records of Early English Drama: Devon* (Toronto: University of Toronto Press, 1986), xxxi.

depiction of the saint in painted glass.[13] Both images and plays were popularly understood in terms of visualizing the scenes of events and persons of very great importance in sacred history. The oft-quoted Wycliffite *Tretise of Miraclis Pleyinge*, which is the most detailed piece of theatrical criticism available from the late fourteenth or early fifteenth century in spite of its hostility to the stage, nevertheless pronounces the position in defense of drama:

> Also sithen it is leveful to han the miraclis of God peintid, why is not as wel leveful to han the miraclis of God pleyed, sithen men mowen bettere reden the wille of God and his mervelous werkis in the pleyinge of hem than in the peintinge? And betere they ben holden in mennus minde and oftere rehersid by the pleyinge of hem than by the peintinge, for this is a deed bok, the tother a quick.[14]

Pictures, statues, and plays alike place the imitation of the historical events surrounding the biblical story or the life of the saint before the eyes of the people, who are thus able to *see* as if they were looking on the actual events themselves. But drama is a living art, in contrast to the static pictures of the painters and carvers.

In creating such a lively art around the lives of saints, medieval vernacular playwrights and players in England were actively responsible for theatrical displays that were designed to be deliberately popular. The evidence of the dramatic records is that the saint play genre was normal fare in England—more common, in all likelihood, than the liturgical drama or moralities, and a competitor in popularity with the folk play or biblical drama, which includes the great cycle plays which we associate with cities like Coventry, York, and Chester.[15] The popular appeal of a play of St. Francis was one of the aspects of the drama that offended the

---

[13] Johnston and Rogerson, *REED: York*, 1:88; Davidson, "The Middle English Saint Play," 33, fig. 2.

[14] *A Tretise of Miraclis Pleyinge*, ed. Clifford Davidson, Early Drama, Art, and Music, Monograph Series 19 (Kalamazoo: Medieval Institute Publications, 1993), 98.

[15] See John Wasson, "The Morality Play: Ancestor of Elizabethan Drama?" *Comparative Drama* 13 (1979): 210–21; Davidson, "Middle English Saint Play," 31; Alexandra F. Johnston, "What If No Texts Survived? External Evidence for Early English Drama," in *Contexts for Early English Drama*, ed. Marianne G. Briscoe and John C. Coldewey (Bloomington: Indiana University Press, 1989), 6–7.

author of the poem "On the Minorite Friars" in British Library, MS. Cotton Cleopatra B.ii, fol. 64^v; this anti-theatrical writer complains that Franciscans in their pride have failed to praise St. Paul and instead have staged lies about their founder. The play apparently involved some rather spectacular effects such as the appearance to St. Francis of the Seraphim in the form of a crucifix as well as the miraculous sight of the deceased saint, marked by the stigmata, to Gregory IX. The final portion of the play included as a property a "cart . . . made al of fire" with a "gray frer . . . ther-inne"—a dramatization of the appearance of St. Francis to those who were his followers at Rivo Torto.[16] Effects of this kind, which can be paralleled by those reported in connection with Continental plays, have all the marks of the popular theater, as we might expect in the case of drama allegedly sponsored and directed by members of the order. Nothing about the staging of this English saint play, however, is perhaps as sensational as the effect achieved in the Majorca *SS. Crispin and Crispinian*: "They are to be beheaded. Where they are standing, there are to be two dead bodies which are to be dummies filled with straw, and the heads are to be made with masks with calm expressions. . . ."[17]

Yet the sufferings of saints as well as oftentimes their deaths, both implying the enlisting of the empathy of members of the audience, must have appeared vividly in other dramas in the saint play repertoire in England, while in Perth, Scotland, in 1518 there is record of a play of St. Erasmus, a holy man whose symbol, the windlass, resulted in the mistaken belief that he had been martyred by having his intestines wound around such a mechanism. That such a martyrdom was included in the Scottish play is indicated by the existence of a record indicating payment of eight pence to "The cord drawer."[18] In the early sixteenth century before the suppression of his cult by Henry VIII, the show of St. Thomas

---

[16] For the text of this poem, see Davidson, ed., *A Treatise of Miraclis Pleyinge*, 22–22; for discussion, see Lawrence G. Craddock, "Franciscan Influences on Early English Drama," *Franciscan Studies* 10 (1950): 399–415. There is, however, disagreement about whether this poem refers to a play or to Franciscan iconography displayed in *tableaux vivants* or wall paintings.

[17] *The Staging of Religious Drama in Europe in the Later Middle Ages: Texts and Documents in English Translation*, ed. Peter Meredith and John E. Tailby, Early Drama, Art, and Music, Monograph Series 4 (Kalamazoo: Medieval Institute Publications, 1983), 110.

[18] Anna Jean Mill, *Mediaeval Plays in Scotland* (1924; reprint New York: Benjamin Blom, 1969), 272.

Becket[19] at Canterbury apparently utilized a false head for the saint which required frequent painting.[20] The effects required in the lost play of St. Lawrence at Lincoln in 1441–42 would, we might assume, require the gridiron for the saint's martyrdom, since this instrument of his torture inevitably appears in representations of him in the visual arts.[21]

Like most heroes of the Renaissance tragedies which were successors to the medieval saint play in England, the martyr was someone about whom the members of the audience were encouraged to care a great deal. Audience response in such a drama is, to be sure, highly complex, but consciously the saint was the focal point for sympathy and, though we cannot verify it, tears. However, we do have the witness of one of the authors of the Wycliffite *Tretise* concerning tears reportedly shed for Christ when the Passion was played; for this writer, "they ben reprovable that wepen for the pley of Cristis passioun" (they would be better off, he says, if they would weep for their own sins "and of theire children, as Crist bad the wymmen that wepten on him").[22] That tears were a characteristic of Northern piety at the end of the Middle Ages is implied by a sneering remark about Flemish painting attributed to Michelangelo by Francesco de Holanda;[23] in all likelihood weeping was considered an appropriate response to the conclusion of the life of a martyr in spite of the inevitable receipt of the saint's soul into heaven.

But all plays focusing on the lives of saints did not conclude in martyrdom, for in the fourth century a violent death at the hands of persecutors was found no longer to be essential for canonization among post-biblical saints. One such saint whose popularity extends to the present is St. Nicholas, whose life and miracles were dramatized in c.1250 at an unspecified location and possibly in c.1283 at Gloucester. Extant Latin play texts by Hilarius and in the Fleury Playbook suggest emphasis on miracles such as the resuscitation of the three clerks who had been murdered by the wicked innkeeper and his wife, or the gifts of

---

[19] Davidson, "The Middle English Saint Play," 54–55.

[20] Ibid., 55.

[21] *Records of Plays and Players in Lincolnshire, 1300–1585*, ed. Stanley Kahrl, Malone Society Collections 8 (Oxford, 1974 [for 1969]), 30.

[22] *A Treatise of Miraclis Pleyinge*, ed. Davidson, 102.

[23] Cited by Erwin Panofsky, *Early Netherlandish Painting*, 2 vols. (Cambridge: Harvard University Press, 1953), 1:2.

money which saved the three daughters of a poor man from prostitution.[24] Middle English saint plays of such saints' miracles form the only variety that is available for study today; two dramas with similarly non-violent endings have been said to comprise the entire corpus of extant texts of pre-Reformation saint plays from this language area. These are the plays of *Mary Magdalene* and *Conversion of St. Paul* in Bodleian Library MS. Digby 133.[25]

Mary Magdalene is the longer of the two plays, and it also is the more interesting in spite of the introductory section that separately introduces the Roman emperor (Tiberius), Mary's father Cyrus, Herod, and Pilate, and then shows Cyrus mortally ill on stage in the presence of his children, who also include Lazarus and Martha. Thereafter, as a result of the successful siege of her Castle of Bethany by the troops of the World, Flesh, and Devil—i.e., the Seven Deadly Sins—she falls into the sinful life as a pupil of the gallant Curiositas (Pride) and becomes the prostitute who will later be converted by Christ, whereupon the seven devils which are in fact the Seven Deadly Sins are seen literally to escape from her body in a sensational scene.

Her sinful life is briefly depicted in an episode (470–546) in the tavern—a location which, if we are to believe Mirk, is the devil's church[26]—and as she awaits her "valentynys" in an arbor (564–87); it is a life characterized by self-indulgence and waywardness, which make her thrall to the powers of evil represented by the Bad Angel and his cohorts. What has happened to her has resulted in the forging of an alliance with the powers of death and hell—an alliance ultimately implying total alienation from the powers of good. She has been "onstabyll" and

---

[24] Young, *The Drama of the Medieval Church*, 2:306–60.
[25] *The Late Medieval Religious Plays of Bodleian MSS Digby 133 and E Museo 160*, ed. Donald C. Baker, John L. Murphy, and Louis B. Hall, Jr., EETS, o.s. 283 (Oxford: Oxford University Press, 1982); quotations from the Digby *Mary Magdalene* in my text are from this edition. For commentary on the 'Single Magdalene,' a composite of three biblical women, see Davidson, "Middle English Saint Play," 73; Anselm Hufstader, "Lefèvre d'Etaples and the Magdalen," *Studies in the Renaissance* 16 (1969): 31–60; Helen Meredith Garth, *Saint Mary Magdalene in Mediaeval Literature*, Johns Hopkins University Studies in Historical and Political Science, series 67, no. 3 (1950), 19; and Marjorie Malvern, *Venus in Sackcloth: The Magdalen's Origins and Metamorphosis* (Carbondale and Edwardsville: Southern Illinois Univ. Press, 1975), *passim*.
[26] John Mirk, *Festial*, ed. Theodor Erbe, EETS, e.s. 96 (1905), 203.

"veryabyll" (588, 590), as her guardian angel tells her in a vision while she is sleeping. She is required only to "Remembyr . . . on mercy" and to "make [her] sowle clyre" (600). Such a vision of the perfect life is all that is required for her to come to a recognition of her alienated state, and she sets out to make herself close to the Second Person of the Trinity, whom she will encounter at Simon's house. When her separation from God has been overcome by Christ through his absolution of her sins, the Deadly Sins along with the Bad Angel who tempted her will *"dewoyde from þe woman, and . . . entyr into hell wyth thondyr"* (692 s.d.).

As we might expect, neither the scene of the visit to the sepulcher nor the *hortulanus* scene (in which she mistakes the risen Christ for a gardener) is omitted. Also, selected from the period prior to Christ's Passion is the important episode of the death of Lazarus, which is present as a means of stressing the connection between earthly life and the need for a power over death which the world cannot provide. The miracle inspires belief in those who stand by and, as presented in play, is intended also to affect the lives of the members of the audience—i.e., those who *look* upon the drama. But transcendental goodness and power, now identified with Magdalene herself, are much more sensationally represented in the final part of the play which dramatizes the events following Pentecost.

The remainder of the play is divided first into her missionary work with the king and queen of Marseilles and then into a final segment in which she becomes a hermit devoted entirely to contemplation. At Marseilles she successfully opposes the false rites of "Sentt Mahownde" and also his "relykys brygth," which are responsible for diabolic "miracles"— e.g., being struck with permanent blindness (1232–41). When the king and queen return from their remarkable pilgrimage to Jerusalem, she will turn entirely from the active life of a missionary to the contemplative life in the deserts of Provence where she will abide with humility. Here she foregoes earthly food, and is fed each day by angels, who bring her the communion wafers which sustain her. Her participation in this heavenly Eucharist and her separation from the values represented by the World, Flesh, and Devil reconcile her to herself, and she achieves the peace which the world cannot give. At her death, her soul is received by angels as it ascends directly into heaven. This entire segment of the play provides opportunity for spectacular staging.

After her conversion, therefore, Mary Magdalene is a model of human behavior, and in the play she is a saint whom ordinary people were invited to look upon for their spiritual benefit. She was regarded as a link between the present and the historical past and also between the audience and the miraculous power released by the Resurrection event. In his final speech in the play, the priest who had been present at the Magdalen's death speaks directly to those who are looking at the play: "Sufferens of þis processe, thus enddyth þe sentens / That we have playyd in yower syth." Then he continues: "Allemythty God, most of magnyfycens, / Mote bryng yow to hys blysse so brygth, / In presens of þat King!" (2131–35).

More central to medieval Christianity than Mary Magdalene was another biblical St. Mary, the Blessed Virgin, recognized as the Mother of God from the third century.[27] She was not only felt to be present at such shrines as Walsingham, but also her image and candles in her honor were seemingly to be found in every parish church. Her power was regarded as far greater than that of any apostle, and her intercession for the individual supplicant was often thought to be potentially crucial since the Son could not resist any reasonable request by the merciful mother. At the conclusion of the Chester banns of 1539–40, she is invoked along with Christ:

> Iesu crist that syttys on hee
> And his blessyd mother marie /
> Saue all this goodely company
> And kepe you nyght and day[28]

Often depicted standing at the right hand of Christ the Judge at the Last Judgment, she shows her kindly nature by her love, interceding for those who implore her help.

The Virgin Mary's very great popularity leads us to believe that plays about her life would have been among the most common in medieval England. Records of such dramas are not totally lost. We know, for example, that a Mary play was performed at New Romney in 1512–13.[29] A

---

[27] For convenience see *The Oxford Dictionary of the Christian Church*, 3rd ed., ed. F. L. Cross and E. A. Livingstone (Oxford: Oxford University Press, 1997), s.v. *Theotokos*.

[28] Lawrence M. Clopper, *Records of Early English Drama: Chester* (Toronto: University of Toronto Press, 1979), 39.

[29] *Records of Plays and Players in Kent, 1450–1642*, ed. Giles E. Dawson, Malone Society Collections 7 (Oxford, 1965), 130.

portion of a drama about one of her miracles has been identified in a fragment in the Durham Cathedral Library; the *Durham Prologue* dramatized a miracle of the Virgin in her role as protector of a knight who, in spite of his denial of Christ as part of an agreement to regain the riches he had lost through his profligacy, refused to relinquish worship of his Mother.[30] Another fragment, *Dux Moraud*, has also been claimed as a possible segment of a miracle of the Virgin drama, though there is considerable room for skepticism in this instance.[31] At Chester in August 1499, a play of "the Assumption of our Ladye," regularly sponsored as part of the Whitsun cycle by the wives of the city, was presented for Prince Arthur.[32] On the feast of Mary's mother, St. Anne, at Lincoln, a *visus* representing the Assumption and presumably the Coronation of the Virgin in the cathedral nave was recorded between 1458 and 1469; later, these scenes were apparently transferred to the St. Anne's Day procession.[33]

Recent study of the N-Town manuscript has shown that the Marian scenes depicting the events leading up to the birth of the Virgin and continuing through the Annunciation make up a unit that has been grafted into the main cycle.[34] Quite remarkably, therefore, we are able to see the emergence of the structure of a Marian cycle originally intended to stand alone as a dramatization of both biblical and extra-biblical material treating the early life of the Virgin Mary. Once it is separated from the

---

[30] See Stephen K. Wright, "The Durham Play of Mary and the Poor Knight: Sources and Analogues of a Lost English Miracle Play," *Comparative Drama* 17 (1983): 254–65. For the text of the fragment, see *Non-Cycle Plays and Fragments*, ed. Norman Davis, EETS, s.s. 1 (London: Oxford University Press, 1970), 118–19.

[31] Constance Hieatt, "A Case for *Duk Moraud* as a Play of the Miracles of the Virgin," *Mediaeval Studies* 32 (1970): 345–51. For the text of this fragment, see *Non-Cycle Plays and Fragments*, ed. Davis, 106–13.

[32] Clopper, *REED: Chester*, 21, 23.

[33] *Plays and Players in Lincolnshire*, ed. Kahrl, 32–62.

[34] The layers of composition in the N-Town cycle have been studied by Stephen Spector, "The Composition and Development of an Eclectic Manuscript: Cotton Vespasian D. VIII," *Leeds Studies in English*, n.s. 9 (1977): 62–83; for the conclusion that "the Marian (Contemplacio) group (plays 8–11, 13) was a separate and self-contained composite Mary play," see *The N-Town Plays: A Facsimile of British Library MS Cotton Vespasian D VIII*, ed. Peter Meredith and Stanley J. Kahrl (Leeds: University of Leeds School of English, 1977), vii. So too the *Assumption of the Virgin* in the same manuscript was undoubtedly a separate play about the life of the Virgin.

larger cycle in which it is embedded—and here the edition by Peter Meredith is very useful[35]—the Mary play may be added to the list of extant saint plays in England.

The extent of this East Anglian play's dependence on biblical sources is, to be sure, much less than its use of the New Testament apocrypha[36] as filtered through the liturgy and such works as the *Golden Legend* and the *Meditations on the Life of Christ*, the latter well known in England through Nicholas Love's translation.[37] The purpose of the play was not merely to tell an interesting story in honor of the Virgin, but rather, in Meredith's words, "to make the audience visualise and feel emotionally how the events occurred."[38] The added scene of the Parliament of Heaven presents the reconciliation of Mercy and Truth and of Justice and Peace within heaven itself as a necessary prelude to earthly reconciliation envisioned through the acts of the Son of Mary. The theology which is developed here, adapted from Psalm 84:11 (*AV:* 85:10), articulates a transcendent principle upon which subsequent earthly reconciliation may be based. The incarnation is a process that is dependent upon heaven, yet in its function of reconciliation will need to be extended to earth first of all through the miraculous birth of the Mother of Jesus whose conception will take place without the physical sexual contact of her previously barren parents. So at their meeting at the East, or Golden, Gate of Jerusalem, the parents of the Virgin exchange a "kusse of clennesse," and St. Anne remarks that "was nevyr joy sank in me so depe" (241, 243). The

---

[35] *The Mary Play from the N.town Manuscript*, ed. Peter Meredith (London: Longman, 1987); citations of this play in my text will for convenience be to this edition, but see also *The N-Town Play*, ed. Stephen Spector, EETS, s.s. 11–12 (Oxford: Oxford University Press, 1991). Additionally see Alan J. Fletcher, "Layers of Revision in the N-Town Marian Cycle," *Neophilologus* 66 (1982): 469–78.

[36] The ultimate source of the legend of the Immaculate Conception and episodes of Mary's early life is the *Protevangelium*, for which see M. R. James, trans., *The Apocryphal New Testament* (Oxford: Clarendon Press, 1924), 38–49. On the iconography, Mrs. [Anna] Jameson, *Legends of the Madonna as Represented in the Arts*, revised ed. (London: Longmans, Green, 1890), 137–95, remains useful, though the focus is not on English art. The East Anglian context has, however, been studied by Gail MacMurray Gibson in *The Theater of Devotion: East Anglian Drama and Society in the Late Middle Ages* (Chicago: University of Chicago Press, 1989).

[37] Meredith, ed., *The Mary Play*, 14–15. Meredith notes that another work, *The Charter of the Holy Ghost*, also figured as a source for the author of this play.

[38] Meredith, ed., *The Mary Play*, 14.

scene is one that received frequent illustration in the visual arts (e.g., the sculptural relief in the Lady Chapel at Ely[39]) and involved a devotional stance that was important for the medieval understanding of Mary, holy and blessed, the one who carried God within her womb and gave birth to him so that he could redeem the world.

The playwright's sources provided motivation for Mary's father's previous departure from the city. The first scene had shown the priest Ysakar during the Feast of Incense expelling Joachim from the temple (represented in the play by a separate platform) because "Þu and þi wyff arn barrany and bare" (101). Joachim's offering had been rejected. As a result, he fled to the countryside, where he was seen, temporarily alienated and ashamed, among his shepherds. But even while he was in such a state, an angel of heaven came from above as a messenger who abrogated the normal order of things to reveal to him that something remarkable will happen which will rescue humankind from its normally fallen condition.

Skipping over the birth of Mary, the playwright then focuses upon her presentation in the temple at the age of three. In the stage directions, we learn that Mary had been taken from the location of her parents' home to the scaffold representing the temple—surely the same scaffold that had been used for the rejection of Joachim's offering. The core of the scene is the sight of the three-year-old toddler unsteadily walking up the fifteen steps to the temple as she recites a paraphrase of the gradual psalms. Again, this is a scene familiar in the visual arts, and, like the illustration of the meeting at the Golden Gate, is present in the famous relief sculptures in the Lady Chapel at Ely Cathedral.[40] Mary would stay in the temple until her fourteenth year among the priests and attendant virgins, the latter ultimately adapted from the vestal virgins of antiquity who had been introduced into her story but who now are allegorized into Meditacyon, Contryssyon, Compassyon, Clennes, and Fruyssyon (481–83). Following the account in the *Golden Legend*, Mary is told by a heavenly

---

[39] See M. R. James, *The Sculptures in the Lady Chapel at Ely* (London: D. Nutt, 1895), South Side, pl. XI; *Iconoclasm vs. Art and Drama*, ed. Clifford Davidson and Ann Eljenholm Nichols, Early Drama, Art, and Music, Monograph Series 11 (Kalamazoo: Medieval Institute Publications, 1989), fig. 18. This sculpture is severely mutilated.

[40] James, *Sculptures in the Lady Chapel*, South Side, pl. XIII; *Iconoclasm vs. Art and Drama*, ed. Davidson and Nichols, fig. 19.

messenger that she will be fed heavenly food "day and nyght" by angels, who will also help her to learn more about "oure Lordys lawe" than she would otherwise be able to acquire (533–35). But the angel who comes to her with this message also declares her name to be holy and her power to extend to both heaven and hell—a strange and disturbing message to be received by a small girl.

At fourteen years of age, however, Mary will be married, and the man who is chosen through the miracle of the budding rod is Joseph, old and comic according to tradition established by the *Protevangelium*.[41] As such, he will be a guarantee of her virginity, which will be preserved even after her Child has been born. This play is intended to be a command performance throughout, with angels frequently coming down to announce words of prophecy and explanation to the human participants in the drama. Further, the play is one of the richest individual dramas in Middle English with regard to its use of music, entirely made up of appropriate liturgical items.[42]

Married and yet a virgin, Mary's famous encounter with the angel Gabriel allows the playwright to display her feelings for the audience to see and hear. After she has been saluted by Gabriel who requires her "assent to the incarnacyon" (1343), the Holy Spirit descends *"with thre bemys to Our Lady,"* followed by the Son *"with thre bemys to þe Holy Gost,"* and then the Father *"with thre bemys to þe Sone, and so entre all thre to here bosom"* (1356 s.d.). "A," Mary responds, "now I fele in my body . . . / Parfyte God and parfyte man" (1356–57). There has, she insists, been no pain; her virginity is intact—a requirement if she is to be seen as the sinless God-bearer, the "trone and tabernakyl of the hyȝ Trinité" (1549). Her pregnancy is a miracle, an abrogation of the normal laws of nature; so too seeing and hearing the story of her miraculous birth and of the conception of Jesus are expected to involve visual and aural perception that will result in an appropriate cognitive experience with supra-natural dimensions for those attending the play. Through participation in such an imaginative experience, then, viewers may have their lives touched by the imitation of an original event that lies near the center of

---

[41] *Apocryphal New Testament*, trans. James, 43.
[42] See JoAnna Dutka, *Music in the English Mystery Plays*, Early Drama, Art, and Music, Reference Series 2 (Kalamazoo: Medieval Institute Publications, 1980), 124 and *passim*.

history itself. As Mary's cousin Elizabeth says in the final scene of the Visitation,

> A, ȝe modyr of God, ȝe shewe us here how
> We xulde be meke þat wrecchis here be;
> All hefne and herthe wurcheppe ȝow mow,
> Þat are trone and tabernakyl of þe hyȝ Trinité.
> (1546–49)

Finally, Contemplation, acting as epilogue, reminds the audience that a pardon of 10,800 years[43] will be given to anyone who faithfully says "Oure Ladyes sawtere dayly for a ȝer" (1567–68). He announces that the play will end with *Ave*, the word with which the angel had hailed Mary at the Annunciation in the biblical account and the word which traditionally was regarded as the reverse of *Eva*—Eve, through whom sin had come into the world. The word is then transformed into the incipit of the antiphon *Ave regina celorum*, which in this play is directed to Mary as an act of devotion. The drama hence needs to be seen not merely as a didactic or mimetic exercise to increase knowledge or enjoyment on the part of the viewers—a pageant which basically reflects the page (*pagina*) of a book brought to life on stage,[44] a more vivid book for the unlettered—but also as a complex offering that repeats the pattern of the incarnation in bringing divinity into the womb of human experience.

Mary, even more than the other saints, was a visible presence in the parishes of medieval England, where saints' lives, legends, and miracles became adapted to the theatrical impulse which would represent them by means of living actors. Saints could even lend their names to characters in the folk drama, as in the case of St. George whose legendary battle with the dragon had become a central myth in England that survived into Protestant times.[45] But such folk expression was very different from the saint play with its mixture of the sensational, spectacular, and emotionally stimulating elements, all of them tuned to the hearts of the spectators.

---

[43] This number is a multiple of 12, on which Nordic number systems were based prior to the introduction of Roman and decimal systems.

[44] On the term *pagina* see n. 12, above.

[45] See, for example, Samantha Riches, *St. George: Hero, Martyr, and Myth* (Sutton Publishing, 2000), which has been recently published.

Signs of Doomsday in Drama and Art

The end of history was an ever-present concern during the long period when the late medieval vernacular plays were played in the cities and towns of late medieval and Tudor England. Of the extant cycles, only the Cornish *Ordinalia* failed to include a final pageant or pageants on the subject of the Last Judgment. Also, the famous but largely lost Coventry cycle, from which only the Shearmen and Taylors' and the Weavers' plays are extant, verifiably culminated in a spectacular show as part of the Drapers' Doomsday pageant.[1] Though deeply embedded in tradition, the fascination with the depiction of the end time in religious plays, in sermons, and in the visual arts must more immediately have derived, however, from the personal apprehension with which people viewed the conclusion of their own lives. Viewing scenes of the final days or moments of history on stage, in the visual arts, or in imagination was thus an existential experience for the individual, who thereby was given the opportunity to see his or her own mortality in relation to the divine order of things.

Most significantly in this regard, life was viewed as something more than that circumscribed by birth and dying. The conclusion of a man's or woman's life was not the moment of death but rather thereafter either consignment to hell or release from Purgatory. For the devout or semi-devout Christian, death meant judgment, but most often judgment to a period of purification in Purgatory, for only the saints could expect immediate elevation to the heavenly city and everlasting life among the

---

[1] For the extant Coventry plays, see *The Coventry Corpus Christi Plays*, ed. Pamela M. King and Clifford Davidson, Early Drama, Art, and Music, Monograph Series 27 (Kalamazoo: Medieval Institute Publications, 2000), esp. 44–51, for comment on the Drapers' pageant. The dramatic records of Coventry are published in R. W. Ingram, *Records of Early English Drama: Coventry* (Toronto: University of Toronto Press, 1981).

angels.[2] Not surprisingly, therefore, figure sculptures on tombs and representations on memorial brasses presented the dead in prayer, which in the late medieval period meant the hands-joined posture that had been adopted in the thirteenth century. The texts which identified men and women on brasses also conventionally requested prayers for them. The words *Orate pro anima*, or similar words to that effect, were seriously meant; prayers were believed to give needed assistance to souls in Purgatory and hence were thought to involve works of mercy often meriting indulgences for the living persons speaking them.[3] The living and the dead were both members of the Church, alike pilgrims who shared a common destination. Peter Brown has usefully defined the Church as "an artificial kin group,"[4] which contained those who existed in the past, the living, and those who were to be born.

The relationship of the living to those in Purgatory was a matter of intense interest. This place of purification, designed as a location where souls would be prepared for eventual entry into bliss, was understood to be a sort of horror chamber in the suburbs of hell. St. Birgitta, commonly known as St. Bridget of Sweden, described these horrors in her popular *Liber Celestis* as including intolerable pressure, disfigurement, broken bones, depilation, and more.[5] An altarpiece at Birgitta's own church at Vadstena in Sweden shows contrasting scenes of Purgatory and Hell which are distinguished by having those consigned to the one appearing in postures of prayer, while the others are identified only by gestures of terrifying despair.[6] Prayers are able to help souls in Purgatory, not those

---

[2] John Fisher, *Two Fruytfull Sermons* (London: William Rastell, 1532), sigs. B4^r–C4^r.

[3] Jerome Bertram, "*Orate pro anima*: Some Aspects of Medieval Devotion Illustrated on Brasses," *Transactions of the Monumental Brass Society* 13 (1983): 321–22.

[4] Peter Brown, *The Cult of the Saints* (Chicago: University of Chicago Press, 1981), 31.

[5] *The Liber Celestis of St Bridget of Sweden*, ed. Roger Ellis, EETS, o.s. 291 (Oxford: Oxford University Press, 1987), 298; cited by Eamon Duffy, *The Stripping of the Altars: Traditional Religion in England 1400–1580* (New Haven: Yale University Press, 1992), 339.

[6] Aron Andersson, *Vadstena klosterkyrka, II: Inreding*, Sveriges Kyrkor 194 (Stockholm: Almqvist & Wiksell International, 1983), figs. 34–37.

suffering eternal damnation. Bishop John Fisher (d. 1533) thus explained the need for prayers for souls in the "paynfull pryson" of Purgatory: "They be of the same fayth, hope and charyte, that we be of. They haue ben made parteners of the same sacramentes" and are our friends and kinsmen.[7] As one might approach one's death with hope and fear conjoined, so also one might grasp at a belief in the efficacy of the prayers of others who will make one's immediate ordeal easier and shorter. But it is possible that the ordeal of Purgatory might last until the final days of history—indeed, until the moment when the soul, now rejoined with the body, must stand before the Judge at the General Judgment and only then cross the final threshold.

Significantly, the burial of the body normally was either within the church where it might be designated by a monument or monumental brass, or in an unmarked grave in the churchyard without, always in proximity to the sacred space of the church with its relics of saints, its images, and its rituals, all of which were agents of transcendence. From very early in the history of the Church, burials near saints had been regarded as privileged since people felt that their own bodily resurrection at the Last Day might be more secure.[8] Later, relics and images would serve this function, as when John Dautre wished, according to his will of 1458, to be buried before the image of John the Baptist in the church of St. Michael Spurriergate in York whom he had loved from his childhood.[9] In Dautre's mind there would have been no great distinction between the actual saint and the image, the latter being an object regarded as something more than a mere help to memory.

A surprisingly common type of bequest in wills specified that money should be left to endow chantry chapels in order that they might continue "forever" or "as long as the world shall stand." The implication in the case of wills supporting these perpetual chantries was that the world had not yet run its course, but that the time would not be long. In the meantime, a priest was daily to pray for the donor's soul, the souls of his kin, and the souls of all Christians. To be sure, those who gave such bequests

---

[7] Fisher, *Two Fruytfull Sermons*, sigs. B4^v, C1^r; also quoted by Duffy, *The Stripping of the Altars*, 349.

[8] Brown, *The Cult of the Saints*, 27–34.

[9] *Testamenta Eborancensia*, ed. James Raine, 5 vols., Surtees Society (Durham: Andrews, 1836–84), 2:230.

could not know that the end would come for their endowments in a different way, at the hands of a greedy Crown that would confiscate not only the funds set aside for the purpose of prayer but also all the implements of worship; as the statute of Edward VI proclaimed, "our Sovereign Lord the King shall have and enjoy such goods, chattels, jewels, plate, ornaments, and other moveables as were to be the common goods of every such college, chantry, free chapel, or stipendiary priest. . . ."[10] Previously, people had looked forward not to a change in religion but to the continuance of the present order until shortly before the time when the Judge would return in glory in the East, the direction toward which prayers were spoken and churches were oriented. There would then be signs predicting the end.

Paradoxically, people also believed that the end—the Second Advent—might come without warning while they were yet living, for so the Bible had proclaimed. One of the sayings of Jesus had announced: "There are some standing here that shall not taste death, till they see the kingdom of God" (Luke 9:27). And 1 Thessalonians 4:14–16 also provides proof that Christ's imminent return to earth in a glorified body was expected by the first-century Church: "we who are alive, who remain unto the coming of the Lord," along with those "who have slept," will meet Christ coming down from heaven. The dead shall arise, and "[t]hen we who are alive, who are left, shall be taken up together with them in the clouds to meet Christ, into the air, and so we shall be always with the Lord." By the later Middle Ages, there was widespread skepticism concerning Christ's imminent return, but this did not remove the possibility in people's minds that he might come unexpectedly during their own lifetimes. For example, *The Pricke of Conscience* warned: "sal na man certayn be / What tyme Crist sal come til þe dome."[11] As a reminder parish churches such as St. Thomas of Canterbury at Salisbury and Holy Trinity at Coventry were typical in having wall paintings over their chancel arches that displayed the Last Judgment with Christ seated on a rainbow in the air—a scene indebted principally to the account in

---

[10] 1 Edward VI, c. 14, as quoted by G. H. Cook, *Mediaeval Chantries and Chantry Chapels* (London: Phoenix House, 1963), 77.

[11] *The Pricke of Conscience*, ed. Richard Morris (1863; reprint New York: AMS Press, 1973), 131 (ll. 4819–20); subsequent references to this work refer to line numbers and appear in my text in parentheses.

Matthew 25:31–46.[12] Bodies were rising out of tombs to face the Judge, but nowhere, contrary to the passage in the epistle to the Thessalonians cited above, were any of them rising into the air to meet the Savior, the one whose advent was announced by angel trumpeters. This was also true of the way in which the Last Judgment itself was visualized in drama, which in all the extant Middle English cycles presented a scene that brought representatives of those meriting salvation and damnation before the Judge. Thus, in the York Mercers' play, trumpets were sounded, and, according to an inventory of 1433, Christ, who appeared displaying his wounds (an effect simulated by a "Sirke Wounded"), descended from Heaven on a contraption that lowered him until he seemed to take his seat on a rainbow made of wood.[13] The scene implied in the dramatic records, together with evidence from the text of the York play, will be more or less reminiscent of the early fifteenth-century manuscript illumination on fol. 208^r of York Minster Library MS. 2, which likewise presents Christ with his wounds bleeding as he is seated on a rainbow between two angel trumpeters.[14] This illumination shows the separation of the good and wicked, presumably those who have done the Corporal Acts of Mercy and those who have not. For the latter the time of mercy is past.

---

[12] See Albert Hollaender, "The Doom-Painting of St. Thomas of Canterbury, Salisbury," *Wiltshire Archaeological and Natural History Magazine* 50 (1942): 351–70, and also conveniently illustrated in M. D. Anderson, *The Imagery of British Churches* (London: John Murray, 1955), fig. 1; George Scharf, Jr., "Observations on a Picture in Gloucester Cathedral and Some Other Representations, of the Last Judgement," *Archaeologia* 18 (1817): pl. XXXVI, fig. 1; Clifford Davidson and Jennifer Alexander, *The Early Art of Coventry, Stratford-upon-Avon, Warwick, and Lesser Sites in Warwickshire*, Early Drama, Art, and Music, Reference Series 4 (Kalamazoo: Medieval Institute Publications, 1985), 37.

[13] Alexandra F. Johnston and Margaret Rogerson, *Records of Early English Drama: York*, 2 vols. (Toronto: University of Toronto Press, 1979), 1:55. For the text of the York play, see *The York Plays*, ed. Richard Beadle (London: Edward Arnold, 1982), 406–15, and, for the related play in the Towneley manuscript, *The Towneley Plays*, ed. Martin Stevens and A. C. Cawley, EETS, s.s. 13–14 (Oxford: Oxford University Press, 1994), 1:401–25. Subsequent references to these plays are by line numbers in my text in parentheses.

[14] Clifford Davidson and David E. O'Connor, *York Art*, Early Drama, Art, and Music, Reference Series 1 (Kalamazoo: Medieval Institute Publications, 1978), 114–15, fig. 33.

The coming of the end of time according to the book of Revelation had less influence on popular English Doomsday iconography, though the Apocalypse account was the source of the depiction in the Great East Window of York Minster created in 1405–08 by John Thornton of Coventry.[15] It is hard to gauge popular enthusiasm at York or elsewhere for much of the arcane imagery which was presented in this window and which was shared with the great illuminated Apocalypse manuscripts—works designed for wealthy patrons. Spectacular as Thornton's window was, its panels of glass, each two and one-half feet square and depicting the varied events of the Last Days, were apparently unique in its urban ecclesiastical setting, though to be sure some of its subject matter was shared by the fifteenth-century German and Netherlandish block books illustrating the Apocalypse.[16] In any case, nowhere in the drama was Christ shown with seven candlesticks or with seven stars, as in Revelation 1:16.[17] While some scenes present in Thornton's glass—for example, the representation of the resurrection of the bodies of the good and of the wicked[18]—were replicated on pageant wagons in the streets of York, these did not require detailed knowledge of the Apocalypse in order to be understood. The great iconographic program of the Apocalypse, designed to appeal to the elite clergy of the Minster, found little resonance in the city's popular religious street theater. It should be remembered that the Cathedral was not embraced with the same zeal with which ordinary people supported their parish churches, for indeed many citizens viewed the Minster more or less as a foreign institution even before the Reformation.

More closely connected to the York Last Judgment play was the depiction of six of the Seven Corporal Acts of Mercy—feeding the

---

[15] See Thomas French, *York Minster: The Great East Window*, Corpus Vitrearum Medii Aevi, Summary Catalogue 2 (Oxford: Oxford University Press, 1995).

[16] The Apocalypse bosses in the cloister of Norwich Cathedral are less public in character; see C. J. P. Cave, *Roof Bosses in Medieval Churches* (Cambridge: Cambridge University Press, 1948), 201, figs. 138–41. For fifteenth-century block books, see Gertrud Bing, "The Apocalypse Block-Books and Their Manuscript Models," *Journal of the Warburg and Courtauld Institutes* 5 (1942): 143–58.

[17] French, *York Minster: The Great East Window*, fig. 11e and *passim*; Cave, *Roof Bosses*, fig. 139.

[18] French, *York Minster: The Great East Window*, fig. 2c.

hungry, giving drink to the thirsty, clothing the naked, caring for the sick, taking in the homeless, looking after prisoners (the burial of the dead is omitted)—in a window in the church of All Saints, North Street.[19] The Corporal Acts were the deciding factor in separating the saved and the damned in the account of the Last Day in Matthew 25, and so here in the glass of All Saints they are shown in detail not as devotional images but as didactic pictures that were designed to be models for behavior appropriate for persons preparing for when they shall appear before the Judge. In the York Mercers' Doomsday play, the "chosen childir" on Christ's right hand are told by him that they have performed these acts and hence are invited to come "vnto me, / With me to wonne . . ." (47.365–66), while the "cursid caytiffs of Kaymes kynne" who did "neuere [Christ] comforte in [his] care" will be destined "[i]n dole to dwelle for euermare" (47.317–18, 320). Significantly, the final words of this Doomsday play—words which are also the final words of the York cycle—are actually an admonition: "And þei þat mendid þame whils þei moght / Shall belde and bide in my blissing" (47.379–80).

Another window in All Saints, North Street, contains a representation of the Fifteen Signs of Doomsday,[20] a motif which was given authority by being attributed to St. Jerome and which appeared in various forms in art, literature, and drama. This window, painted in c.1410 and plausibly

---

[19] Eric A. Gee, "The Painted Glass of All Saints' Church, North Street, York," *Archaeologia* 102 (1969): 162–64, pls. XXV–XXVI.

[20] Ibid., 158–62, pl. XXIII. For a study of the sources of the Fifteen Signs, see William W. Heist, *The Fifteen Signs of Doomsday* (East Lansing: Michigan State University Press, 1952), who argues for the importance of the Irish *Saltair na Rann*, though many of the individual signs may be traced back to early apocryphal writings; and see also the early study by J. T. Fowler, "The Fifteen Last Days of the World in Medieval Art and Literature," *Yorkshire Archaeological Journal* 23 (1914–15): 313–37. Contrary to M. D. Anderson's claim (*The Imagery of British Churches*, 129) that the All Saints, North Street, glass contains the only English examples of this iconography, the Fifteen Signs also appear, though very incompletely, in a series of alabaster carvings (c.1440) of Yorkshire design in the British Museum (Edward S. Prior and Arthur Gardner, *An Account of Medieval Figure-Sculpture in England* [Cambridge: Cambridge University Press, 1912], 492–93, fig. 567). There are also manuscript illuminations showing the Fifteen Signs, of which the most famous are those in the *Holkham Bible Picture Book*.

17. Fifteen Signs of Doomsday. Painted glass. All Saints, North Street, York. ©Crown Copyright. National Monuments Record.

assigned to John Thornton and his workshop, remains *in situ* in the easternmost position on the north side of the original chancel.[21] Traditionally it has been called the "Prick of Conscience" Window since its iconography is recognized to have been inspired by the account in the immensely popular *Pricke of Conscience* formerly attributed to Richard Rolle.[22] More than a hundred manuscripts of this work survive. F. Harrison, who identified *The Pricke of Conscience* as the source of the inscriptions in the window, also noted quite accurately that "[t]his is a real Doom window."[23] Here are depicted the signs of the end of the world as popularly understood, complete with tracery lights showing St. Peter, who holds his symbol—a pair of keys—and admits the saved into heaven, and a monstrous devil, who forces the damned into the mouth of hell. Thus the Fifteen Signs, as preparation for the Doom, are followed by the separation of the blessed and the evil into their permanent places of residence in this final event of history.

The original inscriptions in the "Prick of Conscience" window are sometimes fragmentary and also felt the hand of nineteenth-century restorers. They were more complete in 1670 than at present, and in that year the glass was recorded by Henry Johnston (Bodleian MS. Top. Yorkshire c.14, fol. 99^r). The following discussion presents the texts, with expansions from Johnston's readings when sufficiently legible and plausible, and provides commentary on the iconography:

1. The sea rises: ". . . cubetes . . . / . . . ryse up. . . ." The text, also fragmentary in Johnston's time, may be roughly completed by reference to *The Pricke of Conscience*, which explains that the sea shall rise above "þe heght of ilka mountayne, / Fully

---

[21] John A. Knowles, *Essays in the History of the York School of Glass-Painting* (London: SPCK, 1936), 221; Gee, "The Painted Glass of All Saints' Church," 196. A thorough study is currently being made of the glass of the Fifteen Signs of Doomsday window by David O'Connor, to whom I am grateful for assistance with the captions both in the glass and in Henry Johnston's seventeenth-century transcription. My reconstruction of the texts must of necessity involve some speculation because of the condition of the glass and the inadequacy of Johnston's transcription. Johnston's handwriting is very difficult to read, and he often did not provide exact readings.

[22] Gee, "The Painted Glass of All Saints' Church," 158.

[23] F. Harrison, *The Painted Glass of York* (London: SPCK, 1927), 177–79.

fourty cubettes certayne" and stand like a hill (4759–63). The illustration in the glass, however, fails to illustrate this and instead gives three trees, plants, and grass. The sea rising up like a mountain appears elsewhere, as in Antoine Vérard's *L'Art de bien vivre et de bien mourir*, published at Paris in 1492.[24] Based indirectly on the illustration in this work is the woodcut in Wynkyn de Worde's *Arte or Crafte to Lyue Well* (1505).[25] The common interpretation of this sign as punishment for the proud, however, is not suggested by either the All Saints glass or the account in the *Pricke of Conscience*.

2. The sea subsides: "Þe second day þe se sall' be / so lawe unethe men sall it see." The account in *The Pricke of Conscience* provides a similar reading: "þe se sal be swa law / Þat unnethes men sal it knaw" (4764–65). The background in the panel is blue, and the scene is, in Gee's description, "desert-like,"[26] but there are two trees, with yellow foliage. Possibly the source of the first two signs is Nahum 1:8: "But with a flood that passeth by, he will make an utter end of the place thereof: and darkness shall pursue his enemies."

3. The waters come back to their former level: "Þe iij day yt sall be playne / And stand as yt was agayne." Compare *The Pricke of Conscience*: "þe se sal seme playn / And stand even in his cours agay[n], / Als it stode first at þe bygynnyng, / With-outen mare rysyng or fallyng" (4766–69). A tree with brown foliage appears at the right; the sea at the left has fish in it.

4. Fish and monsters of the sea roar: "Þe forth day fisches sal' make roring / hideous & hurt to mannes herign." *The Pricke of Conscience* explains that the "mast wondreful fisshes of þe se / Sal com to-gyder and mak swilk roryng / Þat it sal be hydus til

---

[24] This woodcut is reproduced by Émile Mâle, *Religious Art in France: The Late Middle Ages*, trans. Marthiel Mathews, Bollingen Series 90, pt. 3 (Princeton: Princeton University Press, 1986), fig. 246.

[25] See Edward Hodnett, *English Woodcuts 1480–1535* (1935; reprint Oxford: Oxford University Press, 1973), 19–20, who points out that the intermediary is Vérard's "Scotch" edition of 1503.

[26] Gee, "The Painted Glass of All Saints' Church," 259.

mans heryng" (4771–73), but what this means is known to God alone. In the glass panel three great fish are rising out of the sea, which also contains other fish. The fish bear no resemblance to those in Vérard's woodcut[27] but may be compared to the illumination in the *Holkham Bible Picture Book* which, however, positions them differently.[28]

5. The sea burns: "þe fift day þe se sall' bryn / And all þe waters þat may ryn." These words are borrowed with only small variation from *The Pricke of Conscience*. A flaming sea surrounding a tree in the panel of glass nevertheless contains fish. A source in the Apocalypse has unconvincingly been suggested by W. O. Hassall.[29]

6. Trees sweat blood: "Þe sex day sall herbes & trees / wyth blody dropes þat grysley bees."[30] The illustration in the glass shows the trees flaming and dropping golden fruit, which would seem to involve a misinterpretation.

7. Buildings collapse: "Þe seuent day howses mon fall / castels & towres & ilk a wall." This is again a close adaptation from *The Pricke of Conscience*. Buildings, including a church and its spire, are tumbling down in the illustration in the All Saints glass. In the version of the Fifteen Signs attributed to Lydgate, the reason for the destruction is explained as due to "Fyry floodys, ... / Brennyng as Coolys with flawmys ovir goon" and sparing nothing in the firmament.[31] In Peter Damien's account, the movement of the flood is from west to east.[32]

---

[27] See Mâle, *Religious Art in France: The Late Middle Ages*, fig. 247.
[28] W. O. Hassall, *The Holkham Bible Picture Book* (London: Dropmore Press, 1954), fol. 40^v.
[29] Ibid., 152.
[30] Gee believed that Johnston had misread "bers" for "bees" ("The Painted Glass of All Saints' Church," 160). *The Pricke of Conscience* gives little help in interpreting this caption.
[31] John Lydgate, *The Minor Poems*, pt. 1, ed. Henry Noble MacCracken, EETS, e.s. 107 (1911; reprint London: Oxford University Press, 1962), 118 (ll. 28–32).
[32] Peter Damien, *De novissimis et Antichristo*, 4; as quoted by Heist, *The Fifteen Signs*, 27–28.

8. Rocks and stones spontaneously shatter: "... þe roches & stanes / ... toged[er] all' at anes." In *The Pricke of Conscience*, the rocks and stones "strik togyder" but do not burn (4785). The stones in painted glass are yellow and appear in the foreground.

9. Earthquake; men hide: "Þe [ninth] day' erthdynis / sall be generally in ilk contrey...." This great earthquake is to be the greatest "sythen þe world bygan," according to *The Pricke of Conscience* (4793), but there is nothing there to suggest men hiding in caves, an iconographic detail probably suggested by Apocalypse 6:15. William W. Heist notes that *The Pricke of Conscience* apparently borrows "Generaly in ilka contre" from Peter Comestor's *Historia Scholastica*, while his main source remains a treatise formerly attributed to the Venerable Bede.[33] A "great earthquake, such an one as was never had been since men were upon the earth," is also predicted by Apocalypse 16:18.

10. The earth becomes one great plain: "Þe tende day for neuen / erthe sal' be playne and even." The glass shows the earth, pale buff in color; there are some plants, and the sky is red. This scene illustrates the leveling of mountains and valleys, as predicted by Isaiah 40:4; see also the Song of the Erythraean Sibyl in St. Augustine's *City of God* 18.23.

11. Men emerge from caves and holes, and move about: "... all men com owt .../ ... holes & wende a bowte." *The Pricke of Conscience* describes their moving about as like madmen: "Als wode men, þat na witt can" (4800). In the glass, one person is peeking out of a cave (at left), while three men and a woman outside are praying.

12. Dead men's bones come together and rise: "þe x ... day sal dede mens banes / Be sumen sett & ryse al at anes" (original word order, reflecting *The Pricke of Conscience*: "... sal ded men banes / Be sett to-gyder, and ryse al attanes, / And aboven

---

[33] Heist, *The Fifteen Signs*, 132.

on þair graves stand" [4804–06]). This sign is the thirteenth in *The Pricke of Conscience*, however, while in Peter Comestor's *Historia Scholastica* and in a number of manuscript illuminations it is presented as the eleventh.[34] The source of this iconography is Ezekiel 37:1–14.

13. Stars fall from heaven: "Þe thirteend day suthe sall' / Sternes from the heuen fall'." The lines are a condensation of *The Pricke of Conscience*, 4802–03. The glass painter has presented eight falling stars as bright yellow; there are yellow tracks between the four that are above and the four below. The iconography is based on Matthew 24:29–30, which predicts the darkening of the sun and moon as well as the stars falling from heaven as signs immediately prior to the appearance of "the sign of the Son of man in heaven," and also on Apocalypse 6:13: "And the stars from heaven fell upon the earth, as the fig tree casteth its green figs when it is shaken by a great wind." Damien emphasized the stars would spread tails like comets,[35] and that is apparently what is signified in the All Saints representation of this sign. John Mirk, following the *Golden Legend*, explains that the falling stars will "spred out of hom brennyng lemes."[36]

14. The death of all the living: "Þe xiiij day all' þat liues þan / sall' dy bathe childe man & woman." To this list *The Pricke of Conscience* supplies two more lines: "For þai shalle with þam rys ogayn/ Þat byfor war dede, outher til ioy or payn" (4810–11). Depicted in the All Saints glass are a man and woman, in bed; the figure of Death with a lance comes toward them from the left, while three mourners stand beside the bed. The mourner at the left, dressed in red, holds his hands clasped over his head.

15. The end of all earthly things: "þe xv day þus sal' betyde / þe werlde sall bryn on ilka syde." A passage in 2 Peter is the

---

[34] Heist, *The Fifteen Signs*, 26; see also Gee, "The Painted Glass of All Saints' Church," 202.
[35] Cited by Heist, *The Fifteen Signs*, 27–28.
[36] John Mirk, *Festial*, ed. Theodor Erbe, EETS, e.s. 96 (1905; reprint Millwood, N.Y.: Kraus, 1987), 3.

principal authority for this event: "But the day of the Lord shall come as a thief, in which the heavens shall pass away with great violence, and the elements shall be melted with heat, and the earth and the works which are in it, shall be burnt up" (3:10). *The Pricke of Conscience* and the All Saints glass are unusual in concluding with the burning of the world, which otherwise is generally placed in the fourteenth position among the signs. Peter Comestor and the *Golden Legend* conclude instead with the establishment of a new heaven and a new earth. In the *Holkham Bible Picture Book*, the burning of the world appears above on folio 42^r, and below is a depiction of Christ displaying his five wounds as he returns in the clouds and of the dead rising from their graves. The fifteenth sign in this manuscript leads directly into the Last Judgment on folio 42^v. While the All Saints glass follows *The Pricke of Conscience* in leading up to but not including such a scene among the Fifteen Signs, it does, as noted above, include Doomsday in the tracery at the head of the window.[37]

In a passage in the Towneley Judgment play spoken by 4 Malus as he rises from the dead, the coming of Christ is anticipated: "To se his woundys bledande, / This is a dulfull case" (30.75–76). These lines, not present in the York pageant which was in part incorporated into the Towneley play, were apparently added by the so-called Wakefield Master. This West Riding author, as John Robinson has demonstrated, knew a wide range of popular religious literature, including the *Meditations on the Life of Christ* and Ludolphus of Saxony's *Vita Christi*.[38] There is good reason to believe that he also was familiar with *The Pricke of Conscience*, which circulated widely in Yorkshire, or with similar descriptions of the Fifteen Signs of Doomsday and other signs of the end of history. "All this was tokyn / Domysday to drede," 1 Demon says (30.287–88).

---

[37] Jacobus de Voragine also says (*The Golden Legend*, trans. William Caxton, ed. F. S. Ellis, 7 vols. [1900; reprint London: Dent, 1922], 1:17) that "[t]he third thing that shall go before the judgment shall be the right vehement fire" which will serve as a substitute for Purgatory for those still living.

[38] J. W. Robinson, *Fifteenth-Century Stagecraft*, Early Drama, Art, and Music, Monograph Series 14 (Kalamazoo: Medieval Institute Publications, 1991), *passim*.

The passage of greatest interest here is 2 Demon's observation that "Had domysday oght tarid,/ We must haue biggid hell more . . ." (30.262–63). Recently there has been a tremendous influx of souls—a "dowbill store" (30.265)—into the place of darkness. 2 Demon comments that "Saules cam so thyk / Now late vnto hell / As euer" that the porter of hell gate has been required to be at his post early and late (30.540–45). Hell at this moment is full to capacity; no more could be accommodated. How can this be, since one might assume that among those still living there would still be many in this "warid" world who would be destined for this place of eternal pain and punishment? But, as indicated in the Fifteen Signs of Doomsday literature and as shown in the visual arts, all the living shall die previous to Christ's arrival on earth as its judge. When Doomsday comes, therefore, all those who have died will rise, and the souls in hell will all be reunited with their bodies. In the Towneley play, 1 Demon, now released from being chained, recognizes that Judgment Day has arrived since "all oure saules ar wente / And none ar in hell" (30.170–72).

The Towneley play, like the York Mercers' pageant from which it took its essential structure, provided a setting intended to resemble contemporary England and hence established a sense of place immediately relevant to potential members of the audience.[39] But this effect is much more vivid in Towneley than in York, especially on account of the devils' catalogue of social abuses as recorded in their books. The motive, of course, is to establish evidence that will serve against the perpetrators of such abuses and thus to capture these hapless humans for their punishment. Tutivillus was widely known as the recording demon, the one who wrote down idle words spoken at Mass—and he is one who is given expanded duties in the Towneley play.[40] He and his cohorts will be responsible for receiving those who have wilfully separated themselves from the community of the faithful, one linked not only to the present community in which the drama was being presented, but also to all other Christians who had lived before and to all those who were to come

---

[39] See, for example, *The Towneley Plays*, 30.185–86: "Let vs go to this dome / Vp Watlyn strete." Watling Street was the Roman road that extended from the south to the north of England, and crossed the West Riding of Yorkshire.

[40] Margaret Jennings, *Tutivillus: The Literary Career of the Recording Demon*, Studies in Philology, 74, no. 5 (Chapel Hill: University of North Carolina Press, 1977), 58–64 and *passim*.

afterward. Further, it may be useful to observe that this community in the late Middle Ages was centered on the experience of seeing the body of Christ in the consecrated Host at Mass,[41] a ritual that itself essentially served the function of binding together in amity that portion of the Church universal which was the parish.[42]

Only a genius such as the Wakefield Master could have made such subtle use of the culminating events depicted in the Fifteen Signs of Doomsday. The signs in themselves are manifestly undramatic from a theatrical point of view, as any serious consideration of the scenes in the Pricke of Conscience Window in All Saints, North Street, should demonstrate. Rosemary Woolf has commented that to represent the Fifteen Signs "upon the stage would presumably have exceeded the ingenuity of medieval producers," though she mentions one instance of a single sign at Coventry (see below) and also the prologue to a French Judgment play which promises "that the marvels of the Fifteen Signs will be performed on stage."[43] They appear, however, in the Chester plays, though here they are not actually made visible on the stage but are only described by the Expositor in one of the two plays that anticipate the Doomsday pageant. This play is *Antichrist's Prophets*, which was presented by the Clothworkers (designated in both the early and late banns as the Shearmen).[44] The signs, which follow a procession of the prophets Ezekiel, Zacharias, Daniel, and John the Baptist, are introduced by a sentence in Latin that credits them to the opinion of the doctors of the Church and, ultimately, to a source in antiquity which is here unspecified. This sentence was perhaps inserted after the Reformation in defense of

---

[41] See Ann Eljenholm Nichols, "The Bread of Heaven: Foretaste or Foresight?" in *The Iconography of Heaven*, ed. Clifford Davidson, Early Drama, Art, and Music, Monograph Series 21 (Kalamazoo: Medieval Institute Publications, 1994), 110–27.

[42] See John Bossy, "The Mass as a Social Institution 1200–1700," *Past and Present*, no. 100 (1983): 29–61.

[43] Rosemary Woolf, *The English Mystery Plays* (Berkeley and Los Angeles: University of California Press, 1972), 292–93.

[44] Lawrence M. Clopper, *Records of Early English Drama: Chester* (Toronto: University of Toronto Press, 1979), 38, 246. For the plays, see R. M. Lumiansky and David Mills, EETS, s.s. 3, 9 (London: Oxford University Press, 1974–86), 1:396–438, and, for the Peniarth text of the *Antichrist*, 1:491–516. Subsequent references to these plays appear in my text in parentheses and are to this edition.

Signs of Doomsday in Drama and Art

the inclusion in the play of the Fifteen Signs, and it was probably not spoken. Instead, as David Mills suggests, it was likely intended "as a heading" in the playbook used by the players.[45]

Though Brother Linus Urban Lucken claimed the source of the Chester version of the Fifteen Signs to be the account in Mirk's *Festial*,[46] Heist has demonstrated that they were in this case derived directly from "the most generally circulated form" of the *Golden Legend* of Jacobus de Voragine, either in Latin or in an English translation.[47] To be sure, Mirk's version of the Fifteen Signs is also based on the *Golden Legend* and includes only a few variants, but, as Heist indicates, "where Mirk mistranslates the *Legenda aurea*, the Chester Play agrees with Voragine."[48] Chester represents quite a different region of the country from York or the West Riding of Yorkshire, and there is no indication that *The Pricke of Conscience* had any influence on this West Country city's pageants concerning the end time.

Nevertheless, the concerns of the citizens of Chester who produced its plays were, in spite of stronger influence of Protestantism after the Reformation,[49] not so very different from the Northern sponsors of religious drama. The York and Chester plays alike involved the *visualizing* of sacred history on important religious festivals—Corpus Christi at York, Whitsun week at Chester in the sixteenth century. As the only fully extant play cycles that we can locate in specific urban settings, these two served secular, economic, and religious purposes—though, it must be remembered, with the religious as central. But while the York plays avoid any use of the Fifteen Signs of Doomsday so eloquently depicted in painted glass in All Saints, North Street, Chester embraced them in the

---

[45] Lumiansky and Mills, *The Chester Mystery Cycle*, 2:326.

[46] Linus Urban Lucken, *Antichrist and the Prophets of Antichrist in the Chester Cycle* (Washington, D.C.: Catholic University of America Press, 1940), 125–30.

[47] Heist, *The Fifteen Signs*, 168–69. For the Fifteen Signs as they appear in Caxton's translation, see Jacobus de Voragine, *The Golden Legend*, 1:14–15.

[48] Heist, *The Fifteen Signs*, 169.

[49] However, for evidence of continuing Catholic allegiances in plays, see Sally-Beth MacLean, "Marian Devotion in Post-Reformation Chester: Implications of the Smiths' 'Purification' play," in *The Middle Ages in the North-West*, ed. Tom Scott and Pat Starkey (Oxford: Leopard's Head Press, 1995), 237–55.

context of its play cycle, which tends to be much more homiletic in its adoption of sermon material. In pre-Reformation Chester, forty days of pardon were said to be granted to those who viewed and heard the plays "in pecible manner with gode devocion."[50] It was thus quite logical that the playwrights should look to sources such as the historical-homiletic *Golden Legend*; and in the case of the Clothmakers' play material from Jacobus on the Fifteen Signs was chosen as preparation for Antichrist and Doomsday pageants. In the *Golden Legend*, these tokens of the Doom are immediately followed by the coming and deceptions of Antichrist, and this order of events was also adopted by the Chester playwright(s).

Conventionally, and also following the account in the *Golden Legend*, the Expositor in the Chester play attributes the Fifteen Signs to St. Jerome, whose authority is further buttressed by his alleged discovery of the signs "in booke of Hebrewe" (22.263–66). Thereafter he lists each of the "tokens to come" on the days immediately "before doomesdaye" in individual stanzas or in portions of stanzas (nos. 13–14 receive only two lines each) rather mechanically (22.269–334). These are (1) the rising of the sea to a height of forty cubits, which is contrary to nature, "as a wall agaynst the wynd / above all hilles on hye"; (2) its sinking "so lowe . . . / that scarslye a man the sea shall see, / stand he never so nye"; (3) the rising out of the sea and roaring of "great fishes . . . so hideouslye / that only God shall heare"; (4) the unnatural burning of the "sea and water"; (5) bloody dew on trees and herbs, while beasts will be dazed and fowls will gather in fields "all madd and mased," not thinking to eat and drink; (6) the collapse of buildings—"church, cittie, house, and wall"—so that men try to hide in holes, and also lightning pours from the sun "to the firmament" until morning; (7) rocks breaking into parts and fighting "as fonne," and only God will hear the sound; (8) a great "yearthquake" that throws all men and beasts to the ground; (9) the leveling of hills, and stone disintegrating into sand; (10) men coming out of the caves in which they have hidden and going about "as the were madd," unable to speak; (11) throughout the day "all buryalls in the world shall be open / that dead may ryse" and stand above their graves;[51] (12) stars falling—"fyre

---

[50] Clopper, *REED: Chester*, 28.

[51] The episode of Ezekiel and the dry bones receives treatment at the beginning of the Chester *Antichrist's Prophets*. See Lumiansky and Mills, eds., *The Chester Mystery Cycle*, 2:320.

shoote[s] from them hideouslye"—while animals "shall rore and crye / and neyther eate nor drynke"; (13) the death and immediate resurrection of "all men"; (14) the burning of "all . . . , both yearth and eke heaven"; and (15) the creation of "neewe yearth, neewe heaven, through Goddes postee; / which heaven God grant us in to bee / for his names seaven." A point at which this account seems to differ from its source is in the thirteenth sign, which has the death of the living apparently followed immediately by their resurrection, while the *Golden Legend* specifically delays the rising of all the dead until in the final sign. Mirk also mistranslates: "The xiij. day all men schull be redy to aryse þat haue ben ded befor."[52] But the *Golden Legend* specifically indicates that on this day all those who are alive are to join those who have died: "The thirteenth sign, all living shall die, to the end that they should arise with the dead bodies."[53]

A third play in which the Fifteen Signs seem to have figured was the Coventry Drapers' Doomsday, which is now lost though sixteenth-century dramatic records survive that identify some of its action quite clearly. Expenditures by the Drapers provide a great deal of information about the play, which was a dramatization of the Last Day as described in Matthew 25. While there is no evidence for the inclusion of the entire series of Fifteen Signs, two of them are indicated, presumably as prelude to the appearance of Christ as Judge over humankind. One of these was the great Earthquake, the sign designated to be encountered on the eighth day according to the *Golden Legend*. In 1565 the Drapers' accounts specify payment of the amount of two shillings to the "porter for keveryng the Earth quake."[54] What it means to "cover" the Earthquake is a mystery, but its presence would seem to have been designed to assist in making an impressive beginning to the Drapers' play. The nature of the earthquake machine is revealed in an undated entry from the 1560s; this entry specifies "the baryll for the yerthe quake."[55] Again a substantial amount seems to have been paid out, but charges are lumped together with "vij skynnes for godys cott" and a pillar to be used for another effect. Nevertheless, since payments do not appear elsewhere for the earthquake,

---

[52] Mirk, *Festial*, 3.
[53] Jacobus de Voragine, *The Golden Legend*, 1:15.
[54] Ingram, *REED: Coventry*, 230.
[55] Ibid., 474.

we may assume that either it was not always used, or the machine utilized for this effect did not always need to be made anew after it had been perfected.

The other sign dramatized in the Drapers' Doomsday play was the fourteenth sign according to the *Golden Legend*. Mirk's translation explains: "The xiiij day heuen and erþe schull bren so horrybly, þat no man may tell hit."[56] This is the effect in the Coventry Last Judgment which Rosemary Woolf identifies as one of the Fifteen Signs.[57] In 1565 the Drapers paid three shillings and eightpence "for makyng of the worldes" and sixpence "for a lynke to Sette the worlds on fyre."[58] The earliest reference to the worlds in the extant Drapers' records had been in 1561, when Robert Bro (undoubtedly an error for Robert Croo) was paid three shillings and eightpence "for iij worldes."[59] Subsequent references appear in the accounts for 1562, 1563 (when Robert Croo was paid for making "the iij worlds"), 1567 (when payments "for kepyng hell mowth and settyng the worlds on fyer" began being lumped together), 1568, 1569, 1570, 1572, and 1573.[60] In addition, the undated Drapers' accounts in which the "yerthe quake" is noted also list payment to Robert Croo, but only for two shillings in contrast to the usual three shillings and eightpence, "for makyng of iij worldys"; there was likewise expenditure for a "pyllar for the wordys,"[61] presumably a support for the three worlds as they burned at the three stations at which this play was performed in the streets of Coventry. The Drapers' records list payments for rosin, a substance that was probably used also for setting the worlds on fire in addition to its use for torches.

Woolf suggests, I think correctly, that the burning of the world was "a prelude to the Last Judgment,"[62] and thus it would appear to have been in this position in the play rather than as a finale to the Doomsday play.[63]

---

[56] Mirk, *Festial*, 3.
[57] Woolf, *The English Mystery Plays*, 292.
[58] Ingram, *REED: Coventry*, 230.
[59] Ibid., 217.
[60] Ibid., 221, 224, 230, 237, 242, 246, 250, 254, 259, 264.
[61] Ibid., 474.
[62] Woolf, *The English Mystery Plays*, 292.
[63] In a previous article I had argued that the fireworks display would have been the final effect in the pageant when instead it now appears that it was instead a

Instead, it is likely, especially in the light of the appearance also of the Earthquake sign (on the eighth day), that the burning of the world was inserted, perhaps as a Marian or early Elizabethan innovation by Robert Croo, at the opening of the Doomsday play. The spectacular fireworks effect hence would not have been a throw-away at the end of the play, but rather would have been an attention-getter at the beginning of a drama that treated the ordeal believed to await all men and women at the end of time.

The noting of payments to "iij patrarckes" by the Coventry Drapers in 1561 and subsequently[64] probably does not signify anything like an Antichrist scene as prelude to their Doomsday play. Yet in the *Golden Legend* and elsewhere the account of the Fifteen Signs of Doomsday is followed by a description of the role of the Antichrist, who will be seated in God's temple as a pretender to divine power. To be sure, the temptation to speculate about the presence of such a scene is strong, for one of the authors of *A Tretise of Miraclis Pleyinge* seems to have had a real play in mind when he sneered about those who say, "Pley we a pley of Anticrist and of the Day of Dome that sum man may be convertid therby."[65] Since the authors of this treatise have been identified on linguistic grounds as coming from the nearby counties of Northamptonshire and Huntingdonshire,[66] one might guess that their condemnation was directed most immediately at the famous Coventry plays, which attracted audiences from all around the country.[67] However, if the Coventry Doomsday play in pre-Reformation times had included such a scene, there is a lack of

---

prelude to the Last Judgment, as I argue here. The presence of the Burning of the World below another sign of Doomsday, the Whore of Babylon, in a wall painting at the Guild Chapel in nearby Stratford-upon-Avon probably should be interpreted as involving events prior to Judgment Day, which appears in another painting, located over the chancel arch of this chapel. See Clifford Davidson, *The Guild Chapel Wall Paintings at Stratford-upon-Avon* (New York: AMS Press, 1988), figs. 16–17.

[64] Ingram, *Records of Early English Drama: Coventry*, 217 and *passim*.

[65] *A Tretise of Miraclis Pleyinge*, ed. Clifford Davidson, Early Drama, Art, and Music, Monograph Series 19 (Kalamazoo: Medieval Institute Publications, 1993), 101–02.

[66] Paul A. Johnston, Jr., "The Dialect," in *A Tretise of Miraclis Pleyinge*, ed. Davidson, 53–84.

[67] William Dugdale, *The Antiquities of Warwickshire* (London, 1656), 116.

solid evidence for it in the middle of the sixteenth century—that is, the time for which records of production are available.

The Chester *Coming of Antichrist* (*De Adventu Antechristi*), on the other hand, provided an unequivocal and unique staging of the Antichrist episode that, as in the *Golden Legend* and other accounts like Mirk's *Festial*, followed after the Fifteen Signs as prelude to the return of Christ in a cloud to judge humankind. In the *Golden Legend*, Jacobus says, "The second thing that shall be afore judgment, shall be the folly and malice of Antichrist";[68] thereafter, to be sure, he gives a somewhat different version of the Antichrist story than is present in the Chester play. It is a story which in its many transformations was well known in the late Middle Ages and the early modern period—well known enough to become a source of powerful anti-papal iconography in the hands of the Protestant reformers.[69] Seizing upon this iconography for propaganda purposes, John Jewel commented that "[t]here is none, neither olde nor young: neither learned nor vnlearned, but he hathe heard of Antichrist."[70] The Chester play, presented by the Dyers' guild and not without considerable potential for comedy,[71] provides the story of the demonic enemy of Christ and his Church whose appearance will be a final sign of the coming of Doomsday. Elements of the traditional story are selected to form a neatly organized dramatization that begins with Antechrist's ranting initial declamation,[72] his pretensions to messianic power, his subjugation of the kings of the earth, and his manipulation through demonic means of a

---

[68] Jacobus de Voragine, *The Golden Legend*, trans. Caxton, 1:15.

[69] The linking of the Antichrist with the Pope in the writings of Luther, John Foxe, John Jewel, and other Reformers is well known, but was an identification that had a long history; see Bernard McGinn, *Antichrist* (San Francisco: Harper, 1994), 143–99.

[70] John Jewel, *An Exposition vpon the Two Epistles of the Apostle Sainct Paule to the Thessalonians* (London, 1583), 281; also quoted by Richard K. Emmerson, "Wynkyn de Worde's *Byrthe and Lyfe of Antechryst* and Popular Eschatology on the Eve of the English Reformation," *Mediaevalia* 14 (1991 [for 1988]): 282.

[71] Leslie Howard Martin, "Comic Eschatology in the Chester *Coming of Antichrist*," *Comparative Drama* 5 (1991): 163–76.

[72] For the observation that Antichrist's rant places him "within that general dramatic tradition of the bombastic boaster," see Peter W. Travis, *Dramatic Design in the Chester Cycle* (Chicago: University of Chicago Press, 1982), 231.

"verey signe" of his godlike status—that is, his "postee" by which he appears to raise men "from death to liffe" (23.78–80). Through his power, he claims to be able to do such miracles as to turn "trees downe, the rootes upright" and to make fruit grow upon them (23.82–84), a sign reminiscent of the Fifteen Signs of Doomsday.[73] He proceeds to raise two men as if from death, and then feigns his death and his own resurrection. He even arranges a false descent of the Holy Spirit (actually the fire brought "down from heaven unto the earth in the sight of men" by the beast in Apocalypse 13:13) which parodies the Pentecost play that, according to the early banns, was positioned immediately before the Chester wives' *Assumption*.[74] After this, the kings of the earth will worship him on his throne, and he will promise "worldlye welth" to those who will "dwell with mee for aye" (23.234–36). Wynkyn de Worde's *Comyng of Antichryst* provides a woodcut which is just such a depiction of the false Antichrist, wearing an ermine cape and seated on his throne.[75]

The main conflict in the play is between the false, deceitful, and totally evil Antichrist, on the one hand, and on the other the two witnesses—the prophets Enoch and Elias—who uphold the true God, whose power can save. They prove that the apparent raising of men from the dead and other acts "were no myracles but mervelles thinges" shown

---

[73] Antichrist's claim to be able to make trees grow upside down is noted as among the "many sundrie fonde tales of the person of Antichriste" by Jewel, *An Exposition*, 282. This detail falls under the rubric of the "World-upside-down" and in this case involved the rhetorical use of impossibilities; see Ernst Robert Curtius, *European Literature and the Latin Middle Ages*, trans. Willard R. Trask (1953; reprint New York: Harper and Row, 1963), 94–98. Such false miracles, but not this particular one, had been claimed by Antichrist as early as the classic account by Adso, who wrote the most influential early history of this figure; for convenience see *Apocalyptic Spirituality*, trans. Bernard McGinn (New York: Paulist Press, 1979), 92.

[74] Ingram, *REED: Coventry*, 38. The Assumption play is not extant, and all manuscripts place the Pentecost pageant immediately prior to the *Prophets of Antichrist*. Richard K. Emmerson's point about the direct contrast between *Pentecost* and the *Coming of Antichrist* is nevertheless apt (*Antichrist in the Middle Ages* [Seattle: University of Washington Press, 1981], 183). For the iconography, a visualization of a gloss in the *Glossa Ordinaria* (McGinn, *Antichrist*, 144), see the woodcut showing flames of fire falling upon Antichrist in Wynken de Worde's *The Comyng of Antichryst* (*The Arte or Crafte to Liue Well* [London, 1505], sig. kk2^r).

[75] *The Arte or Crafte to Lyue Well*, sig. kk2^r.

"through the fyendes crafte" (23.410–13). There is an astounding moment in which Antechrist curses them (23.448–50); undoubtedly, as in the case of Titivillus in *Mankind*, he uses the sign of the left-handed "blessing."[76] The argument between the witnesses and Antechrist is clinched when Elias blesses bread in the name of the three persons of the Trinity and offers it to the men who appear to have been raised from the dead; since they are animated by demonic forces, they react hysterically to this consecrated bread. Primus Mortuus especially notices the "prynt that ys uppon hit pight," and this puts him "to great feere" (23.579–80).[77] Following his ignominious defeat and the kings' defection to worship of the true son of a Virgin (that is, opposed to Antechrist, who is the offspring of a devil and a whore, as revealed by Primus Demon: "This bodye was gotten by myne assent / in cleane whooredome" [23.667–68]),[78] Antechrist in revenge kills Enoch and Elias and all the kings that have been converted by them. But in a final segment the play asserts the ultimate triumph of good over evil when the archangel Michael slays Antechrist, whose fate is to suffer forever in "pennance and payne"; "sorrowe and care ever" will he feel throughout an eternity to be spent in hell (23.680, 697–98). In a woodcut in Wynkyn de Worde's *The Comyng of Antichryst*, angels thrust Antichrist into the gaping mouth of hell,[79] while in another woodcut, from the *Vita Antichristi*, devils pull him downward into hellmouth with a chain while stabbing him with sharp implements.[80] In the Chester play, Enoch and Elias will be revived and taken up into heaven bodily. Their fleshly bodies are "glorifyed now" (23.708).

---

[76] *Mankind*, l. 522, in *The Macro Plays*, ed. Mark Eccles, EETS, o.s. 262 (London: Oxford University Press, 1969), 171.

[77] The use of the Eucharist to defeat Antichrist seems to be an innovation by the Chester playwright; see Lucken, *Antichrist and the Prophets of Antichrist*, 63–64.

[78] See Emmerson, "Wynkyn de Worde's *Byrth and Lyfe of Antechryst*," 290–94, for discussion of the incest motif associated with the conception of Antichrist.

[79] *The Arte of Crafte to Liue Well*, sig. kk2^r.

[80] Richard K. Emmerson, "'Nowe ys common this daye': Enoch and Elias, Antichrist, and the Structure of the Chester Cycle," in *Homo, Memento Finis: The Iconography of the Just Judgment in Medieval Art and Drama*, ed. David Bevington, Early Drama, Art, and Music, Monograph Series 3 (Kalamazoo: Medieval Institute Publications, 1985), 114, fig. 12.

The conclusion of the *Coming of Antichrist* is thus a powerful assertion of the resurrection not only of the soul but also of the body. The death of the witnesses is not final, nor will the earthly demise of the faithful be the end of their lives, for they too, as the final play in the cycle shows, will see their souls and bodies rejoined in a state of glory. In contrast, those who have chosen evil in this life can look forward to a different fate, even if they have risen to the highest levels of power in Church or State. There is no reason to believe that Papa Damnatus, Imperator Damnatus, Rex Damnatus, Regina Damnatus, and the other social orders were not present in the Chester Doomsday play before the Reformation, for they form a parade of men and women arranged by degree in decreasing order of earthly authority like those arrested by Death in the popular Dance of Death series for which Lydgate provided verses.[81] Death is the great leveler, but it also presents the individual with the crisis point of his or her existence. In the deaths of Antechrist and of Enoch and Elias in the Chester *Coming of Antichrist*, the members of the audience were implicitly invited to visualize their own deaths and the two kinds of existence beyond the grave: one in glory among the saints, the other everlasting punishment among sadistic devils.

At the end of the *Coming of Antichrist*, St. Michael invites Enoch and Elias "to heaven-blysse, both blood and bone" (23.717–18) and sings *Gaudete justi in domino*, which Richard Rastall says was probably the *communio* for the common of martyrs.[82] The chant, in its Sarum form, used a verse from Psalm 32 (*AV* 33): *Gaudete justi in domino: rectos decet collaudatio* ("Rejoice in the Lord, you just ones: praise from the upright is fitting"),[83] to which is added *alleluia*. The play cycle now will move into its final drama, the Websters' Doomsday pageant (*De Judicio Extremo*), in which the Judge will return "as if in a cloud" with his angels and the instruments of the Passion and with his wound in his side bleed-

---

[81] *The Dance of Death*, ed. Florence Warren, EETS, o.s. 181 (London: Oxford University Press, 1931); Davidson, *The Guild Chapel Wall Paintings*, 50–55, figs. 19–20.

[82] Richard Rastall, *The Heaven Singing: Music in Early English Religious Drama*, 2 vols. (Woodbridge: D. S. Brewer, 1996–), 1:335.

[83] Joanna Dutka, *Music in the English Mystery Plays*, Early Drama, Art, and Music, Reference Series 2 (Kalamazoo: Medieval Institute Publications, 1980), 28, for the text, and for the music see *Graduale Sarisburiensis*, ed. Walter Howard Frere (London: Bernard Quartich, 1894), 218.

ing so that all might see.[84] If examples of popes and emperors are ultimately placed at his left side and consigned to the den of darkness, the thought of placing oneself in the context of the Last Judgment must indeed have been uncomfortable. Yet the day of vengeance—a day described by Mirk as "cruell," "ferdfull," and "horrybull"[85]—was expected also to be a day of joy for those at Christ's right side who were to enter bliss at this final moment of time—a moment indeed when time itself would be folded into eternity.

---

[84] On the significance of blood at the Passion, see my "Sacred Blood and the Medieval Stage" in the present volume, above.

[85] Mirk, *Festial*, 2.

Index

Abingdon Missal 171
Abraham and Isaac 124–48
Abraham and Sarah play 141
Actes and Monuments; *see* Foxe, John
Act of Supremacy 27, 32
Acts of John 244
Adam, Anglo-Norman play; *see Ordo Repesentationis Adae*
Adrian IV, pope 17
Adrian VI, pope, 17
Adso 289
Aelfric 110
Agrippa, Cornelius 6, 13
Alexander VI, pope 17
All Saints, North Street, York, painted glass at 121, 273–80, 282–83
All Saints, Pavement, York, painted glass at 191, 197
All Saints, Wakefield, wall painting at 220
Almondbury, Passion text at 194
Ambrose, St. 104–06, 116–17
Anderson, M. D. 273
Anne, Queen 44
Anselm, St., author of *Cur Deus homo* 117, 160, 178, 193
Anti-Catholic satire, play of 207
Anti-Christ, plays of 287–91
Antony and Cleopatra 64–94
Apocalypse, block books of 272
Apollo 249; temple of 243
Aquinas, St. Thomas 232, 250
Ariès, Philippe 132
Ariosto, Ludovico, author of *Orlando Furioso* 77

Arma Christi 197
Armin, Robert, actor 42
Artemis (Diana), altar of 244, 247
Arthur, Prince 262
Augustine, St., of Hippo 7, 21, 98, 116–17, 122, 154, 160–61, 233, 236–37, 243, 278
Austin, George, Jr. 136
Autun, sculpture at 138
Ave regina celorum, antiphon 266

Babington Plot 12
Bacon, Francis 39
Baines, Richard 8
Bakere, Jane 176
Bakhtin, Mikhail 209, 212
Barbarossa, Frederick 17, 19
Barish, Jonas 229–30
Barnes, Robert 18
Barroll, J. Leeds 68
Basilicon Doron 46, 60
Battenhouse, Roy 24
Becket, St. Thomas 19, 184, 189; show of 257–58
Bede, the Venerable 278
Belsavage Theater 4
Benedict, St. 243
Bennett, J. A. W. 193–94
Beowulf 106
Bergman, Ingmar 148
Bernard of Angers 249
Bernard of Clairvaux, St. 179, 193
Bernbrock, John E. 105
Bethell, S. L. 65
Beza, Theodore 9
Bible, Bishops' version 11, 75–76, 92–93

Bible, Geneva translation 3, 21–22, 102, 240
Biblia Pauperum 127, 150, 164, 167, 240–42
Billington, Sandra 217
Billyng, William, author of poem on five wounds 203
Bird, William, playwright 7
Birgitta, St., author of *Liber Celestis* 268; see also Brigittine iconography
Blackstone, William, author of *Commentaries on the Laws of England* 133
Blayney, Peter W. M. 51
Bloom, Harold 102
Boas, Frederick S. 17
Boccaccio, Giovanni 69
Bodley *Burial of Christ* 182–83
Bohun Psalter 106–07, 112
Bonjour, Adrien 86
Book of Common Prayer 31, 36, 61
Borromeo, St. Charles 50
Botticelli, Sandro 84, 86–87
Bradbrook, Muriel 8
Bredvold, Louis 13
Breughel, Pieter, painter of *Battle of Carnival and Lent* 218
Brigden, Susan 106
Brigittine iconography 157–59, 161
Bristol, Michael D. 214
Broadhembury, roof boss at 166
Brome Manuscript, Abraham and Isaac play in 132
Bronzino, Angelo 84
Brown, Peter 254, 268
Bruges, Holy Blood at 195–96
Bruno, Giordano 4, 13, 17
Brussels Ommegang 215
Bunny, Edmund 135
Burbage, Richard 42
Bury St. Edmunds, relics at 184
Bynum, Carolyn Walker 161

Caedmonian *Genesis* 110, 150
Cain and Abel 97–123, 211, 224
Calendar of Shepherds 36
Calvinism 3, 10–11, 37, 185–86; see also Predestination
Camille, Michael 244
Campion, Edmund, S.J. 56
Camus, Albert 25, 27
Canterbury Cathedral, painted glass at 136; relics at 184
Canterbury, plays or tableaux at 135, 189, 258
Carpenter, Alexander, author of *Destructorium Viciorum* 233
Carthusian holy card 166
Carthusian Miscellany 179, 199
Careles, John, amateur actor at Coventry 187
Castiglione, Baldassare, author of *The Book of the Courtier* 71
Catesby, Robert, Gunpowder plotter 58
Catherine of Aragon 53
Catherine, St., 252–54; alabaster of 253
Caviness, Madeline 136
Cawley, A. C. 114
Caxton, William 158
Chalgrove, wall painting at 173
Chapman, George 77–78
Charles I, King 15, 61
Charles II, King 23
Charterhouse, Coventry, wall painting at 197
Charter of the Holy Ghost 263
Chelmsford, witches of 4, 6
Chester Cathedral, seal of 176
Chester Shrovetide games 208
Chester Whitsun plays 40, 103–4, 114–15, 121–22, 137–39, 151, 154, 165, 169, 173, 175–76, 187, 189, 203–04, 210, 215–16, 218, 221–22, 224,

228, 234, 238–39, 242, 256, 261–62, 282–85, 288–92
Chichele, Archbishop Henry, tomb of 61–62
Christian IV, King of Denmark 44, 64
Christus resurgens, in *Elevatio* 193
Circe, mythological figure 77–81
Clement of Rome 97
Clement VII, pope 21
Clitheroe, Margaret, martyr 12
Cohen, Kathleen 62
Coke, Sir Edward 54, 58
Colchester, possible play at 254
Colie, Rosalie 36
comedy 105
Condell, Henry, actor 42
conjuring 6–7
Conversion of St. Paul, Digby play 234, 259
Corporal Acts of Mercy 271–73
Cottom, John, schoolmaster at Stratford 50
Coughton Court, in Warwickshire 49
Council of Nicaea 230
Council of Tours 230
Council of Trent 229
Coventry Corpus Christi plays 52, 59, 156–58, 166, 168–70, 187–88, 190, 210, 216, 218, 222, 228, 234–35, 238, 256, 267, 282, 285–88
Coventry, city of, municipal practices 99
Coventry, Holy Trinity Guild 252
Coventry, St. Catherine play at 252
Cowley, Richard, actor 42
Cowper, William 186
Cranach, Lucas, the Younger 17–18
Cranmer, Archbishop Thomas 31

Creacion of the World, Cornish 104, 109–14, 151, 224, 234
Crispin and Crispinian, SS., play at Majorca 257
Cromwell, Thomas 28
Croo, Robert 286–87
Cunningham, Dolora 90
Cunny, Joan, accused of witchcraft 4, 6
Cursor Mundi 103, 111, 125–26

Daemonology, by King James I 13, 44
Dahl, Ellert 249
Dance of Death 62–63, 291
Daniélou, Jean 126
Dautre, John, will of 255, 269
Davies, Richard 50
Davis, Nicholas 236
Day, John, printer 21
Debdale, Robert, pupil at Stratford Grammar School 56
Dee, John 4, 8, 14
Denis, St. 244–45; play of 255–56
Depositio ceremonies 229
devils 3–4, 6–7, 15–16, 22–23, 54–55, 73, 100, 102–3, 106, 112, 114, 121, 226, 237, 241, 243, 246–47, 260, 275, 281, 290
Diller, Hans-Jürgen 98
Dirty Bride, The, farce 218
discoria concors 88
Dives and Pauper 233–34, 243, 250
Doctor Faustus, by Christopher Marlowe 3–23
Dohi, Yumi 137–38
Dollimore, Jonathan 24–27, 34, 39, 41

Doomsday 43, 60, 75–76, 92–93, 101, 109–10, 113, 119–21, 138, 156, 176–78, 199, 219, 261, 267–92
Dostoyevski, Fyodor 37
Douglas, Mary 223
Douvermann, Heinrich, artist 247
Downham, Cambridgeshire, graffiti at 237
Dublin, tableaux or pageants at 135, 144
Duchess of Malfi, The, by John Webster 36–37
Dugdale, William 155
Dundee, Corpus Christi procession at 135
Dunstable, play at 252
Dürer, Albrecht 76
Durham Prologue 262
Dux Moraud 262

Eagleton, Terry 24
Earl of Worcester's players 234
Easby, wall painting at 152–53
East Harling, painted glass at 159–60
Edgar, Anglo-Saxon king 230
Edmund, St. 184
Edward the Confessor 55, 57
Edward VI, King 20, 27, 30, 270
Elevatio ceremonies 193, 229
Elizabeth I, Queen 12, 20, 27, 33, 35, 45, 49–50, 52, 54, 57, 239; Rainbow Portrait 57–58
Elliott, John R., Jr. 164
Elohim (E) 125, 128, 141
Elton, William 24, 37, 41
Ely Cathedral, sculpture at 29, 219, 264
Entombment, alabasters of 173
Epicurianism 67–68
Erasmus, St., play of 257
Erasmus, Desiderius 27, 187

Essex, Earl of 51
exorcism 6–7

Fairford, painted glass at 217
Fall, of Adam and Eve 55, 72–74, 97, 101, 126, 152–55, 178, 266
Faustbuch, of Johann Spies 3, 8–9, 11–12, 14–15, 17
Feast of Fools 223, 231
Feckenham, John, Abbot of Westminster 57
Ficino, Marsilio 14, 86
Fifteen Signs of Doomsday 273–83, 286–88
Figgis, J. N. 54
fish, as symbol 69–70
Fisher, John, St. 269
Fisher, Thomas, artist 156
Fitzroy tomb 109
Fitzwilliam Missal 158
flagellant societies 184–85
Flanagan, C. Clifford 222–23
Fletcher, Lawrence, actor 42
Fleury Playbook 124, 232, 248, 258–59
Floretum, Wycliffite 236
Florio, John 35
Formula of Concord 3, 9
Fortescue, John, author of *De Natura Legis Naturae* 133
Fortune, in public affairs 47–48, 66
Fountain of Life, iconography of 103, 202
Fouquet, Jean, painter 223–24
Foxe, John 5, 7, 14, 17–21, 30, 187, 288
Foy, St. 249
Francis, St. 256–57
Fraunce, Abraham 79–80, 84–85
Frazier, Harriet 133
Freedberg, David 179
Fulgentius 88

Index

Gadamer, Hans-Georg 240
Gardiner, Harold C. 228–29
Garnet, Henry, S.J. 43
Gash, Anthony 209–10, 212
Gatton, John Spalding 200
Gaudete justi in domino 291
Gee, Eric A. 276
George, St. 266; relic of 184
Gerard, René 105
Gibson, Gail McMurray 190–91, 221
Glossa Ordinaria 139, 289
Gloucester, play at 258
Golden Legend; *see* Jacobus de Voragine
Goodman, Christopher 239
Gospel of Nicodemus 157
Gospel of Pseudo-Matthew 163, 241
Gowrie Conspiracy 48
Grantley, Darryll 201
Gray, Douglas 158
Great Malvern Priory, painted glass at 141–43
Greg, W. W. 7, 17
Gregory the Great 33, 133–34, 181, 250
Gregory IX, pope 257
Grindal, Edmund, archbishop 221
Grosseteste, Robert 227, 231
Guilfoyle, Cherrell 111
Gunpowder Plot 22, 26, 33, 42–43, 45, 48–50, 55, 58, 64

Hailes Abbey, Blood of 196
Hamlet 33, 51–52, 61–62, 123
Hanning, R. W. 237
Hanningfield, Essex, wall painting at 108
Hardison, O. B., Jr. 227
Harrison, F. 197
Harrison, Jane 143

Harrowing of Hell 74, 154–57, 224–25; alabaster of 157
Harsnett, Samuel 10
Harvey, Gabriel 11
Hassall, W. O. 108, 277
Hatfield Broad Oak, Shrovetide play at 207
Heidegger, Martin 39
Heist, William W. 273, 283
Heminges, John, actor 42
Henderson, George 110
Henry, Avril 150
Henry II, King 19
Henry III, King 195–96
Henry IV, King 51–53
Henry VII, King 53
Henry VIII, King 18–20, 27–28, 257
Henry VIII, by William Shakespeare 53
Henslowe, Philip, Diary of 7, 14
Hercules 81
hermeticism 4
Herod 74, 131, 133, 214; in Coventry plays 52, 55–56; in N-Town plays 218; in Towneley plays 217
Herrad of Hohenbourg 41, 47
Hieroglyphics of Horapollo 173
Hilarius 248
Hippolytus, author of *Apostolic Tradition* 230
Historia Scholastica; *see* Peter Comestor
Hollanda, Francesco de 178, 258
Holkham Bible Picture Book 107–13, 115, 119, 150, 157, 163–64, 167, 170–71, 175–76, 277, 280
Holinshed, Raphael, *Chronicles* of 55, 58
Holy Trinity Church, Coventry, painted glass at 155; wall painting at 120, 177, 270

Holy Trinity, Goodramgate, York, painted glass at 195
Holy Trinity Priory, York 215
Homilies, Book of 53, 54, 73
Honigmann, E. A. J. 50
Hooker, Richard 42
Hotson, Leslie 49
human sacrifice 121, 129–30
Hunt, Simon, schoolmaster at Stratford 50
Hunterian Psalter 136
Hüsken, Wim 196

Iconia Sancti Nicolai 248
iconoclasm 29–31, 37, 62–63, 177, 185, 240
idols 240–42, 245–47
images 27, 29, 33, 37, 62–63, 119, 166, 172, 178–79, 194–95, 240–50, 254–56, 269
Improperia 184, 202
Im Christi Wunden schlaf ich ein, Lutheran chorale 187
Innocent, pope 231
Investiture Contest 19
Isaac; *see* Abraham and Isaac
Isidore of Seville 232

J; *see* Yahwist
Jacobus de Voragine 158, 169, 181, 243, 245, 247, 263–64, 279–80, 283–88
James I, King 12, 22, 26, 38, 42–46, 48–49, 52, 55. 57–58, 60–61, 64, 187
James, Mervyn 31, 40, 221
Jerome, St. 273, 284
Jewel, John 288
Jew of Malta, The, by Christopher Marlowe 23
John of Damascus 247
John of Grimstone, commonplace book of 198

John the Baptist, image of 255, 269
John the Divine, St. 76, 92
Johnston, Alexandra F. 116
Johnston, Henry 275
Johnston, Paul A., Jr. 235
Jonson, Ben 50
Josephus, Jewish historian 105, 129
Julian of Norwich 198
Junius, Francis 21

Kelly, Edward 4
Kempe, Margery 179
Kendall, Corpus Christi play at 187–88, 239
Kethe, William 208
keys, power of 20; satire on 15
Kierkegaard, Søren, author of *Fear and Trembling* 130
King, John N. 18, 20
King, Pamela M. 176, 192
King Lear 24–41, 51
King's Evil, touching for 57
King's Men, acting company 26, 42–43, 50–51
Kirkham Monument, at Paignton 169
Kirschbaum, Leo 17, 85–86, 189–90
Kolve, V. A. 126, 209
Künzelsau Corpus Christi play 222–23
Kyd, Thomas 8

Lady Godiva procession 155
Lasingby, Robert, will of 255
Lambeth Articles 10
Lawrence, St., play of 258
Laws of Henry I 99
Lay Folks Mass Book 168, 186
Lazarus, from Fleury Playbook 124
Legenda Aurea; *see* Jacobus de Voragine

Index 299

leikarar, Nordic entertainers 227–28
Leland, John 63
Leo the Great 160
Lille, pageantry and plays at 152, 215
Lincoln, plays at 258, 262; procession at 262
Lincoln Cathedral, misericord at 175; *visus* at 262
Lincoln College, Oxford, Shrovetide plays at 207
liturgy, parody of 245–46
Lollards 20, 99–100, 202, 236; *see also Tretise of Miraclis Pleyinge*
Long Melford, painted glass at 119, 172, 190
Love, Nicholas, author of *Mirror of the Blessed Life of Jesus Christ* 134, 139, 162–63, 171, 263
Lovejoy, Arthur O. 59
Lucerne Passion play 104, 108, 139, 144, 152, 162
Lucken, Linus Urban 283
Ludolphus of Saxony, author of *Vita Christi* 280
Ludus Danielis, from Beauvais 124, 231–32
Luther, Martin 3, 9, 20, 187, 288
Lutheran iconography 3, 15
Lydgate, John 63, 190–91, 277, 291
Lyff of Adam and Eue 108

Macbeth 24, 33, 42–63, 64, 72, 90, 122, 133
Machiavelli, Niccolò 36
Man of Sorrows, woodcut 196
Mankind 211–13, 290
Marcus, Leah 10
Marlowe, Christopher 3–23
Mars; *see* Venus and Mars

Martin, St., possible play of 254
Mary Magdalene, Digby play 234, 244–47, 259–61
Mary, Queen of Scots 12, 42
Mary Tudor, Queen 18, 21, 27, 32, 35, 187
Mary, St., Virgin and mother of Jesus, plays of 261–66
Massa, Michael de, author of *On the Passion of Our Lord* 183
Mass of St. Gregory 169–70, 201, 202
Mayer van den Bergh Breviary 195
Meditations on the Life of Christ 162, 171, 263, 280
Melanchthon, Philip 9
Melton, John, astrologer 16, 22
Melton, William, friar, 214–15
Meredith, Peter 263
Meriasek, Cornish saint play 234
Metz, Sacrament play at 201
Michelangelo, Buonarroti 178, 258
Mills, David 137, 239
Milton, John 75
Mirk, John 183–84, 279, 283, 285–86, 288, 292
Modane, play at 189
Molanus, Johannes 170
monasteries, dissolution of 28
Mons, play at 112, 171
Montaigne, Michel de 35
Montbéliard, Colloquy at 9
More, St. Thomas 53
Morris, Helen 76
Mountfort, William 23
Muir, Lynette 100
Mysteries, The, at National Theatre 125

Nativity, alabaster carvings of 159
New Romney Mary play 261; Passion play 170

Nicholas, St., plays of 258–59; *see also Iconia* and *Son of Getron*
Nichols, Ann Eljenholm 100, 202
Nicoll, Allardyce 230
Northampton, Abraham and Isaac play from 144–47
Northampton, pageant wagon at 144
North Cadbury, Somerset, woodcarving at 159
Northern Passion 191
Northern Rebellion (1569) 33, 54
Norwich Cathedral, roof bosses at 113, 142
Norwich, costumes for plays at 152
N-Town plays 104–5, 107, 108, 110–12, 114, 121, 140, 155–56, 161, 163, 165–66, 171, 173–74, 180, 188–89, 218, 224, 234, 262–65; *see also* Mary, St., Virgin and mother of Jesus, plays of
Notre Dame Cathedral, Paris, painted glass at 83
Nuremberg, Carnival plays at 207

O'Connell, Michael 200
O'Connor, David 275
Odyssey, of Homer 77–79
Ogden, Dunbar H. 229
Ogilvy, J. D. A. 230
"On the Minorite Friars" 257
Osbournby, Lincolnshire, woodcarving at 155
Ordinalia, Cornish 100, 104–05, 110, 112, 117, 120, 139, 175–76, 234, 267
Ordo Rachelis 124
Ordo Representationis Adae 100, 152, 232
Orphic Hymns 88
Ovid, author of *Metamorphoses* 85
Owst, G. R. 166

Oxford, play at 135
Oxhill, Warwickshire, font at 154

Palliser, D. M. 195
Palmer, Barbara D. 194, 210, 220
Palz, Johannes van 172
Paris, Matthew 196
Passe, Crispyn de 60
Passion, alabasters showing 119, 172, 191
Passion poetry 167
Patrick, William, house of 50
Paul, St. 36, 67, 147, 257
Paul, Henry 44
peace, time of universal 66, 74–75, 88–89
Peacham, Henry 47
Perkins, William 10, 226
Persons, Robert, S.J. 8, 32
Perth, play at 257
Peterborough Cathedral, wall painting at 128
Peter Comestor, author of *Historia Scholastica* 106, 108, 113, 131, 241, 278–80
Peter Damien 277, 279
Pepys, Samuel 22
Percy, Thomas, Gunpowder plotter 58
Pilgrimage of Grace 28
Pius V, pope 54
Plato, author of *Symposium* 89
Play of the Sacrament 100, 169–70, 201–02
Plough Monday 115
Plutarch 66, 68, 86
Porphyry 88
Praz, Mario 71–72
predestination, double 10–11, 23, 37
Preston, Thomas, author of *Cambyses* 189

Index

Pricke of Conscience, The 270, 275–80
Pride of Life 61
Proser, Matthew N. 84
Prosser, Eleanor 111
Protevangelium 263, 265
Prudentius, author of *Psychomachia* 83, 125–26
Prynne, William, author of *Histriomastix* 4, 11, 226–27, 238
Puddephat, Wilfrid 63
Pyrrho 13, 36

Quinones, Ricardo 112

Ralegh, Walter, circle of 8
Rastall, Richard 291
Red Bull, theater 22
Regnans in excelsis, papal bull 54, 57
Regularis Concordia 251
Resurrection, alabaster showing 175
Reynolds, William (Rossaeus) 54
Richard II 51, 66
Richard III 52, 209
Richard of St. Victor 231
Ridley, M. R. 74
Ridley, Nicholas 240
Ripa, Cesare, compiler of *Iconologia* 46–47, 69–70
Robbins, Rossell Hope 197
Robert de Lisle Psalter 163
Robert the Glazier 175
Robinson, John W. 159, 195, 280
rogation ceremonies 102
Rogers, David, of Chester, *Breviary* of 40
Rolle, Richard 166, 179, 193, 275
Rollenhagen, Gabriel 60
Romance of the Rose 83
Rome, relic at 162
Rouen Cathedral, painted glass at 248

Rowley, Samuel, playwright 7, 17
Runnalls, Graham 164, 180
Rushforth, Gordon McN. 169

St. Bavo's Cathedral, Ghent, painting at 202
St. Denys, York, painted glass at 197, 256; play at 255–56
St. Helen's Hospital, Norwich, roof boss at 159
St. James, playbook of, at York 255
St. John, Ousebridge, York, painted glass from 194
St. Mary, Collegiate Church of, Warwick, relics at 184
St. Mary-on-Hill, Chester, painted glass at 166
St. Michael Spurriergate, York, image at 255, 269
St. Neot, Cornwall, painted glass at 109, 112–13
St. Nicholas, Kalkar, woodcarving from 247
St. Peter Mancroft, Norwich, painted glass at 159
St. Saviour, York, painted glass from 191, 197
St. Thomas of Canterbury, Salisbury, wall painting at 120, 270–71
Sainte Chapelle, crown of thorns at 193
Salisbury Cathedral, sculpture at 109, 144
Salle, roof bosses at 163, 175
Saltair na Rann 273
sanctuary, law of 115
Sarum rite 127, 291
Savage, Sir John, mayor of Chester 239
Schapiro, Meyer 110
Schiller, Gertrud 198

Scot, Reginald, author of *Discoverie of Witchcraft* 3–4
Scrope, Archbishop Richard 51–52
Seaton, Ethel 75, 92
Selby Abbey, ceremonial plough at 115
Sextus Empiricus 13, 36
Seznec, Jean 83, 243
Shakespeare, John, father of playwright 32, 62
Shakespeare, William, Catholic connections 32, 49–51, 56; social background 122–23
Shaw, John 188
Sheingorn, Pamela 180
Shrovetide plays 207–9
Sir Thomas More 53
skepticism 13–14, 35–37
Sly, William, actor 42
Smith, Susan L. 167
Sonnets, by William Shakespeare 83
Son of Getron 248
Southerne, Lawrence, actor 22
Southwell, Robert, S.J., poet and martyr 12
Speculum Humanae Salvationis 109, 111, 117–18, 127, 150, 154, 158, 178
Speculum Sacerdotale 162
Spenser, Edmund, author of *The Faerie Queene* 65, 72, 79–81, 86–88; author of *Amoretti* 90
Stanzaic Life of Christ 104
Steinberg, Leo 173
Stevens, Martin 214–15, 217–19
Stimulus Amoris 149
Stoicism 65, 67
Stow, John 63
Stratford-upon-Avon, Guild Chapel at 29–30, 32, 62, 156, 177, 287
Stubbes, Philip 208, 226

Tamburlaine, by Christopher Marlowe 12
Tasso, Torquato, author of *Jerusalem Delivered* 65, 78–79, 91
Tempest, The 82
Tennyson, Alfred, Lord 38
Terence 232
Tertullian, author of *De Spectaculis* 200, 230, 238
Thierry of Alsace 195
Thomas, Keith 6
Thomson, Peter 44
Thomson, J. A. F. 195
Thornton, John, of Coventry 152, 272, 275
Through a Glass Darkly; see Bergman, Ingmar
Till Eulenspiegel 14
Topcliff, Richard, pursuivant 12
Towneley plays 100, 103–5, 107, 109–12, 114–19, 121, 128–29, 140, 164–66, 174, 191, 193–94, 210–11, 214, 217–19, 224, 235, 280–82
transi tomb 61–62
Travis, Peter 103, 137, 169, 189, 204
Trechsel, Johannes, printer 232
Tretise of Miraclis Pleyinge, A 133–34, 142, 178, 180, 200, 204, 226, 233, 235–39, 256, 258, 287
Trexler, Richard C. 170, 246
Trinity, alabaster of 195
Trinity College Apocalypse 244
Trithemius, Abbot 14
Troilus and Cressida 25, 59
Trotton, wall painting at 177
Turner, Victor 222
Twycross, Meg 175
Tydeman, William 152

Index

Urban IV, indulgences of 215

Vadstena, altarpiece at 268
Valenciennes, twenty-day play at 111
Venus and Mars 82–90
Vérard, Antoine 276–77
Vernon Psalter 154
Victimae paschali, Easter sequence 220
Victor IV, anti-pope 17
Vincent of Beauvais 132
Visitation Articles, of Elizabethan Church 6, 62, 221
Visitatio Sepulchri (*Visit to the Sepulcher*) 227, 251–52, 254
Vita Antichristi 290

Wakefield Master 103–5, 114, 116, 210–11, 214, 282
Walker, John, patron of Corpus Christi Guild at York 195
Walker, John, Wakefield historian 220
Walker, Roy 53
Walsingham, Francis 8
Walsingham, shrine at 261
Wars of the Roses 122
Weever, John, author of *Ancient Funerall Monuments* 187–88
Wergeld 99
West Kingsdown, Kent, wall painting at 112
Westminster Abbey, Holy Blood at 196; shrine of Edward the Confessor in 57
Whetstone, George 70
Whitney, Geffrey 78
Whore of Babylon 76–77, 92–93
Wienhausen, woodcarving from 197–98
Wigtoft, Lincolnshire, benchend at 159

Williams, Arnold 130
Wimpfeling, Jacob 172, 179
Winchester Cathedral, roof boss at 119
Winter's Tale, The 249–50
witchcraft 4, 6, 24, 44–45, 65, 72, 77
Wither, George 60–61, 68
"Wofully araide," poem of the Passion 198
Woolf, Rosemary 97, 139, 193, 282, 286
Worcester Cathedral, misercords at 128, 142–43, 163
Worde, Wynkyn de, author of *Arte or Crafte to Lyue Well* 276; of *Comyng of Antichryst* 289–90
Wressle, Shrovetide play at 207
Wyclif, John 100, 236

Yahwist (J) 101–02, 125, 128, 141
Yates, Francis 14, 21
Yeats, William Butler 27
Ymagines secundum diversos doctores 83
York Corpus Christi plays 99, 103, 109, 111, 118, 120–21, 140, 131, 157, 161, 165, 168–69, 173, 175, 179, 184, 191–95, 199, 209–10, 214–17, 222, 225, 228, 234–35, 238, 256, 271, 280–81, 283
York, Corpus Christi Guild 195
York, Corpus Christi procession at 122, 168–69, 214, 216
York Creed play 209
York diocese, statutes of 234; visitation articles of 221
York Hours: York Minster, *MS. Add. 2* 158, 176, 192, 220, 271, and *MS. XVI.K.6* 175–76, 197; printed hours, diocese of York, 158

York Minster 216, 219; painted
glass at 51–52, 97, 111, 113,
117, 120, 137, 152, 161–62,
169, 175–76, 192, 194–95,
199, 217, 223–24, 272–73;
relic at 190; roof bosses at
161, 175
York, mock siege at 208
York Pater Noster play 209
York, St. Christopher Guild 255